BRITISH ELECTIONS & PARTIES REVIEW

VOLUME 13

EDITORS

Colin Rallings • Roger Scully
Jonathan Tonge • Paul Webb

FRANK CASS

LONDON • PORTLAND, OR

First published in 2003 in Great Britain by
FRANK CASS PUBLISHERS
Crown House, 47 Chase Side, Southgate, London N14 5BP

and in the United States of America by
FRANK CASS PUBLISHERS
c/o ISBS, 920 N.E. 58th Avenue, Suite 300
Portland, Oregon 97213-3786

Website www.frankcass.com

British Library Cataloguing in Publication Data

British elections & parties review
Vol.13
1. Elections – Great Britain 2. Political parties – Great
Britain 3. Great Britain – Politics and government – 1997–
I. Rallings, Colin
324.9'41'086

ISBN 0 7146 5526 0 (cloth)
ISBN 0 7146 8419 8 (paper)
ISSN 1368 9886

Printed in Great Britain by
MPG Books Ltd, Bodmin, Cornwall

CONTENTS

PREFACE

This is the thirteenth annual volume published under the auspices of the Elections, Public Opinion and Parties (EPOP) specialist group of the Political Studies Association of the United Kingdom. EPOP continues to thrive as a PSA specialist group and the success of these volumes reflects its vigour.

The articles in this volume were originally presented at EPOP's annual conference hosted by the University of Salford in September 2002. A total of nearly 40 papers were offered, reflecting the diversity and high quality of the research being done in the fields of political science covered by EPOP's remit. As in all previous volumes of the *Review*, the articles included here have been independently refereed and extensively revised before publication. We are grateful to all the authors for the timely way in which they responded to referee comments and produced revised versions of their papers.

A highlight of the 2002 conference was the presence of an unprecedentedly large number of overseas guests. Several of their contributions are included in this *Review*. They were able to attend thanks to generous financial support for the conference from the Economic and Social Research Council; the ESRC Research Programmes on Democracy and Participation (Director, Paul Whiteley), Devolution and Constitutional Reform (Director, Charlie Jeffery), and Future Governance (Director, Ed Page); the Arthur McDougall Trust; and the PSA.

We are grateful to the University of Salford and to the local organiser, Jon Tonge, for ensuring that the conference ran so smoothly. Once again it is also a pleasure to thank Cathy Jennings of Frank Cass for the interest she takes in the *Review* and for the constructive guidance she provides to the editors.

For more information on EPOP membership and our annual conferences, please visit our website at www.psa.ac.uk/spgrp/epop/epop.htm.

Colin Rallings   Roger Scully   Jon Tonge   Paul Webb

NOTES ON CONTRIBUTORS

Robert Andersen is Assistant Professor in the Department of Sociology at the University of Western Ontario and Research Fellow at the Centre for Research into Elections and Social Trends, and he teaches in the ICPSR Summer Program in Quantitative Methods at the University of Michigan. His research interests are broadly in social statistics and political sociology.

Susan A. Banducci is a Senior Research Fellow in the Department of Political Science at the University of Twente, the Netherlands. She is currently engaged on a project on political gender gaps in Europe funded by the Dutch Science Foundation.

Stephen E. Bennett is Research Professor of Political Communication at Appalachian State University. His research focuses on patterns of political communication, public opinion, and political behaviour in the U.S. and Western Europe.

Lynn Bennie is Lecturer in Politics in the Department of Politics and International Relations at the University of Aberdeen. Research interests cover elections, political parties and environmental politics. Recent works include publications on small parties, candidate selection for the Scottish Parliament and Welsh Assembly, and the British General Election of 2001.

Shaun Bowler is Professor of Political Science at the University of California, Riverside. He is author (with Todd Donovan) of *Demanding Choices: Opinion, Voting, and Direct Democracy* (University of Michigan Press, 2000).

Catherine Bromley is a Senior Researcher at the National Centre for Social Research, Scotland, and is Co-Director of the *Scottish Social Attitudes* and *British Social Attitudes* surveys.

Alistair Clark is a research student in the Department of Politics and International Relations, University of Aberdeen. Interests include comparative political parties and party systems. His doctoral research, which is supported by the ESRC, is examining local party organization in Scotland.

John Curtice is Head of Research at the National Centre for Social Research, Scotland, Deputy Director of the Centre for Research into Elections and Social Trends, and Professor of Politics and Director of the Social Statistics Laboratory at Strathclyde University.

David Denver is Professor of Politics at Lancaster University. With Gordon Hands he pioneered the use of nation-wide surveys to investigate the nature and impact of constituency campaigning in general elections and co-authored *Modern Constituency Electioneering* (Frank Cass, 1997). His latest book is *Elections and Voters in Britain* (Palgrave Macmillan, 2003).

Geoffrey Evans is Professor of the Sociology of Politics at Nuffield College, Oxford. He is Joint Editor of *Electoral Studies*, and has published widely in the fields of electoral change in both western and eastern Europe, class and political behaviour, and Irish politics.

Richard S. Flickinger is Professor of Political Science at Wittenberg University, Springfield, Ohio. He has published widely on aspects of British politics, including political parties, political behaviour and public policy. Much of his recent work studies comparatively the connections between media consumption and political attitudes and behaviour in the U.S. and Europe.

Gérard Grunberg is Director of Research at Le Centre d'Étude de la Vie Politique Française (CEVIPOF) within the Fondation Nationale des Sciences Politiques (FNSP), Paris. He was Director of the 2002 French Election Study. His recent publications include *Europe at the Polls: The European Elections of 1999* (Palgrave, 2002), edited with Pascal Perrineau and Collette Ysmal, and *La démocratie à l'épreuve. Une nouvelle approche de l'opinion des Français* (Presses de Sciences-Po, 2002), edited with Nonna Mayer and Paul Sniderman.

Gordon Hands is Senior Lecturer and Head of the Department of Politics and International Relations at Lancaster University. He is co-author, with David Denver, of *Modern Constituency Electioneering* (Frank Cass, 1997) and has published widely in the electoral studies field.

Anthony Heath is Professor of Sociology at the University of Oxford and Co-Director of the ESRC Centre for Research into Elections and Social Trends (CREST). He has co-authored several books based on the British Election Surveys, most recently *The Rise of New Labour* (OUP 2001).

Joop J.M. Van Holsteyn is Associate Professor of Political Science, Leiden University, the Netherlands. His most recent book is *Democratie in verval? [Democracy in Decay?]* (Boom, 2002), co-edited with Cas E. Mudde. He has published extensively on right-wing extremism, and elections and voting behaviour in the Netherlands.

Robert Ingram is a PhD student in the Department of Government at the University of Strathclyde. He is currently working on an Economic and Social Research Council funded study into the theory of second-order elections and whether this model can be applied to the first elections to the Scottish Parliament and Welsh Assembly of 1999.

Galen A. Irwin is Professor of Political Science, Leiden University, the Netherlands. He has published extensively on political participation, and elections and voting behaviour in the Netherlands, and is co-author of *Governance and Politics of the Netherlands* (Palgrave, 2002) with Rudy B. Andeweg.

Lindsey Jarvis is a Research Director at the National Centre for Social Research and Co-Director of the *British Social Attitudes* series.

Ron Johnston is Professor in the School of Geographical Sciences at the University of Bristol, and has been researching the impact of local campaigns at British elections since the 1970s. His recent books include *From Votes to Seats* (Manchester University Press, 2001), with Charles Pattie, Danny Dorling and David Rossiter, and *The Boundary Commissions* (Manchester, 1999), with Rossiter and Pattie.

Richard Wyn Jones is Senior Lecturer in the Department of International Politics at University of Wales, Aberystwyth, and Director of the Institute of Welsh Politics. He is co-Director of the Welsh Electoral Surveys 2001 and 2003, a project funded under the ESRC's Devolution and Constitutional Change programme.

Jeffrey A. Karp is a Senior Research Fellow in the Department of Political Science at the University of Twente, the Netherlands. He has published research on elections, electoral systems, and political attitudes across three continents.

Iain MacAllister is a Researcher in the Scottish Executive. He was formerly Research Associate at Lancaster University, working with David Denver and Gordon Hands on constituency campaigning in the 2001 general election.

Michael Marsh is an Associate Professor of Political Science at Trinity College Dublin. He is also a principal investigator for the 2002 Irish election study. His recent work includes a co-authored book with Michael Gallagher on members of the Fine Gael Party, *Days of Blue Loyalty* (PSAI

Press, 2002), and he edited *The Sunday Tribune Guide to Irish Politics* (The Sunday Tribune, 2002) and, with Michael Gallagher and Paul Mitchell, *How Ireland Voted 2002* (Palgrave, 2003).

Charles Pattie is Professor of Geography at the University of Sheffield. He has recently completed a book on the ESRC's Citizens' Audit, *Atomised Citizens: Democracy and Participation in Contemporary Britain*, with Patrick Seyd and Paul Whiteley, and is now working with Ron Johnston on *Putting Voters in Their Place*, an introduction to the electoral geography of the United Kingdom.

Colin Rallings is Professor of Politics and co-Director of the Local Government Chronicle Elections Centre at the University of Plymouth. He recently published (with Michael Thrasher and James Downe) *One Vote, One Value* (Ashgate, 2002), a study of electoral redistricting in English local government.

Catherine Rothon is a Research Officer for CREST at the University of Oxford.

Roger Scully is Lecturer in European Politics in the Department of International Politics at University of Wales, Aberystwyth. He has recently completed an ESRC-funded study of the representative role of British Members of the European Parliament.

Donley T. Studlar is Eberly Family Distinguished Professor of Political Science at West Virginia University and Executive Secretary of the British Politics Group. He has written extensively on many aspects of British politics, including *Great Britain: Decline or Renewal?* (Westview, 1999). He has been a Visiting Fellow at the Universities of Strathclyde and Warwick.

Jonathan Tonge is Professor of Politics and Director of the Centre for Irish Studies at the University of Salford. His recent research has been on political parties in Northern Ireland, and his publications include *Northern Ireland: Conflict and Change* (2nd edition, Pearson, 2002) and *Peace or War? Understanding the Peace Process in Northern Ireland*, edited with Chris Gilligan (Ashgate, 1997).

Martin P. Wattenberg is Professor of Political Science at the University of California, Irvine. His most recent book is *Where Have All the Voters Gone?* (Harvard University Press, 2002), and he has co-edited *Parties Without*

Partisans (OUP, 20000, and *Mixed Member Electoral Systems: The Best of Both Worlds?* (OUP, 2001).

Paul Webb is Professor of Politics at the University of Sussex. His research interests focus on representative democracy, particularly party and electoral politics, and his recent books include *The Modern British Party System* (Sage, 2000) and *Political Parties in Advanced Industrial Democracies* (OUP, 2002).

ABSTRACTS

The 2002 French Elections: The Re-establishment of the Primacy of the President
Gérard Grunberg
The results of the first round of the 2002 French presidential election astounded everyone in France and abroad. However, the 2002 elections as a whole were not characterized by a break with the past or by realignment. They signalled neither a decisive advance of the extreme right, nor any irreversible drop in electoral participation, nor any overturning of the French party system. Instead they marked a return to the Gaullist functioning of Fifth Republic institutions, a serious defeat and a possible lasting weakening of the left, and a growing crisis of popular confidence with respect to the leadership elites.

The Irish General Election of 2002: A New Hegemony for Fianna Fail?
Michael Marsh
The result of the Irish general election of 2002 saw the Fianna Fáil-Progressive Democrat coalition government returned to office, the first time that an incumbent government had been re-established since 1969. The established opposition, and in particular Fine Gael, did very poorly, and there were significant seat gains for Sinn Féin, Greens and independents as well as for the government parties. Given that the government had presided over economic growth at an unprecedented rate, its re-election was unsurprising, although the scale of the old opposition parties' rejection came as a shock. There were issues on which the government was vulnerable, but dissatisfied voters tended to opt for niche parties and independents – perhaps because no real alternative government seemed viable. The new Dáil is more fragmented than for half a century and Fianna Fáil's position at the centre of Irish politics stronger than ever.

A New Kid on the Block: Pim Fortuyn and the Dutch Parliamentary Election of May 2002
Galen A. Irwin and Joop J.M. Van Holsteyn
The election of May 2002 was one of the most, if not *the* most spectacular election in the history of the Netherlands. The government coalition parties suffered record losses, while a new party, the List Pim Fortuyn, entered parliament with a record 26 seats. This article concentrates on explanation of the extraordinary success of this new party. A prominent explanation of this success was that the electorate had shifted to the right. A comparison of

the views of respondents from the 1994, 1998 and 2002 Dutch Parliamentary Election Studies on left–right self-placement and a set of issues rejects this argument. Very little change is found in the viewpoints held by the electorate. Instead, Pim Fortuyn provided the electorate with a choice that it had not previously had. He rallied voters who had negative sentiments towards immigration and immigrants, who were cynical about politics, who were dissatisfied with the performance of previous government coalition. It was not a shift in the views of the electorate that brought electoral change, but an addition to the selection of political parties from which it could choose.

Government for the English Regions? An Examination of the Basis of Support for Constitutional Change
Anthony Heath, Catherine Rothon and Lindsey Jarvis
This article analyses variation in support for regional assemblies in England. An examination of the 'core–periphery' dimension forms the central part of the article. The findings suggest that this distinction provides some part of the explanation for divergence in support for regional devolution. However, differences between core and peripheral regions are relatively small. Following this, analyses of the variation of opinion between 'locals', those who have never lived outside England, and those who display various levels of 'cosmopolitanism' are presented. The data support this division to a greater extent. It is suggested that tendencies towards Europeanization and globalization will mean that this divide will become even more significant.

The Lost Voters of Scotland: Devolution Disillusioned or Westminster Weary?
Catherine Bromley and John Curtice
This article examines the reasons behind the low turnout in Scotland in the 2001 UK general election. While turnout was uniformly low across Britain a number of Scottish-specific factors could potentially explain what happened north of the border. We start by investigating the extent to which Westminster is still thought to matter in Scotland. This is followed by a discussion of attitudes towards devolution itself. The final part looks at whether devolution has failed to stem a growing voter disinterest in elections that is to be found both north and south of the border. The importance of Westminster has by no means diminished with the advent of devolution, and while there is considerable unease about the parliament's performance this is not found to have an impact on turnout. Therefore we conclude that devolution has not acted as a buffer to the Britain-wide malaise that existed at the 2001 general election and that Scottish politics is still very much affected by UK-wide influences.

A 'Settling Will'? Public Attitudes to Devolution in Wales

Richard Wyn Jones and Roger Scully

This article explores the development of public attitudes to devolution in Wales since the September 1997 referendum that narrowly approved the creation of the National Assembly. After reviewing the history behind Welsh devolution, we examine survey evidence on public attitudes, demonstrating that though perceptions of the Assembly failing to improve many areas of life are widespread, opposition to devolution has fallen substantially since the referendum. These findings are reinforced by evidence from focus group research. Although such data indicate only limited public engagement with devolution, the principle appears widely accepted, with much support existing for giving the National Assembly greater powers. The final section of the article constructs a multivariate model to explain variation in support for devolution. Attitudes to the *principle* of devolution appear well-defined (primarily by national identity, party attachments and generational differences), but differences in the level of devolution desired are much less readily predictable.

First or Second Order? Will the Scottish and Welsh Elections Deliver Devolution?

Robert Ingram

Analysis of European and local elections has given rise to the concept of second-order elections. This article examines one of the characteristics of the second-order model, low turnout, in relation to the 1999 devolved elections in Scotland and Wales. Using mostly logistic regression analysis, we build up models to test whether the behaviour of voters in both countries demonstrates that, on low turnout at least, the theory of second-order elections can equally be applied to these devolved polls. Furthermore, what does this behaviour tell us about the impact of the devolution process in both countries?

Towards Moderate Pluralism: Scotland's Post-Devolution Party System, 1999–2002

Lynn Bennie and Alistair Clark

The creation of a new Scottish Parliament in 1999 raised a number of questions concerning the development of Scotland's political parties and party system. Crucially, the adoption of a more proportional electoral system suggested that Scottish parties would have to cooperate to a greater extent than under Westminster rules. This article is concerned with assessing the dynamics of party competition during the first four years of the Scottish Parliament, and relating this to broader party system debates. The analysis identifies a move towards a model of moderate pluralism, as described by Sartori, while highlighting the need for parties to adopt what Dahl terms cooperative-competitive strategies. Moderate pluralism in Scotland during this period displayed tri-polar characteristics. While Labour and the Liberal Democrats cooperated to form a coalition government, ideological differences ensured that the Conservatives and SNP continued to view each other with suspicion.

Electoral Turnout: The New Generation Gap
Martin P. Wattenberg
The phenomenon of relatively low turnout among young people is reviewed for a number of established democracies, with special focus given to the case of the United States. It is shown that the problem of getting young people to the polls is fairly common. It is demonstrated that a tremendous gap has opened up between the young and the elderly on measures of political interest, media consumption of politics, political knowledge and turnout. Thirty years ago scholars might rightly have concluded that the pattern of young people voting less than older people in the USA was simply due to registration problems, as the young evidenced interest in politics and knowledge about it. Now, however, young Americans can be classified as a 'know-nothing' generation when it comes to politics. An important explanatory factor is the development of 'narrowcasting' by television companies.

Constituency Marginality and Turnout in Britain Revisited
David Denver, Gordon Hands and Iain MacAllister
It is generally agreed that there is a positive relationship between constituency marginality and turnout in general elections and this is confirmed when data covering all elections from 1951 are analysed. The strength of the relationship varies, however, depending upon which party is in government. This arises because of complex relationships between the socio-economic character of constituencies, marginality and turnout. Similarly, it is difficult to decide whether the relationship between marginality and turnout is a function of more effective mobilization of voters in marginal seats by the parties, since marginality and campaign intensity are themselves closely related. In order to make progress in understanding and explaining the relationship between marginality and turnout, researchers need to look beyond multivariate regression analysis and find ways of disentangling the impact on turnout of socio-economic variables, marginality and campaign intensity. In this article, the potential for Structural Equation Modelling to provide a way forward is explored.

Turnout in European Parliament Elections: Towards a European-Centred Model

Donley Studlar, Richard S. Flickinger and Stephen Bennett

This article addresses the puzzle of declining turnout in European Parliament elections. After reviewing the influential 'second order elections' explanation emphasizing domestic influences on turnout, especially Mark Franklin's recent study stressing the importance of electoral salience factors, we develop a revised model to incorporate EU as well as domestic variables. Our model indicates that EU influences, at least on the aggregate level, may have more effect on EP elections than previously reported. Tests of our model for the first five EP elections, 1979 through 1999, find that it provides an alternative explanation of turnout similar in power to Franklin's model. Because of changes in membership of the EU, our alternative model may be preferable for explaining future turnout variation in EU elections.

Electoral Systems, Party Mobilization and Turnout: Evidence from the European Parliamentary Elections 1999

Jeffrey A. Karp, Shaun Bowler and Susan A. Banducci

Much of the comparative literature on turnout suggests that party mobilization efforts can explain the turnout advantage among electoral systems that use proportional representation (PR). We examine this question in the context of the 1999 European Parliamentary elections. Using survey data from a range for European countries, we show that party campaign activity is not the mechanism that produces the higher levels of turnout found in PR systems. If anything, citizens are more likely to be mobilized under candidate-based systems rather than closed-list PR. There are, moreover, predictable differences in campaign activity across different electoral systems.

Who Blairs Wins? Leadership and Voting in the 2001 General Election

Robert Andersen and Geoffrey Evans

Do leaders matter for votes? Journalistic wisdom says unreservedly 'yes', whereas academic analyses have been more sceptical. The goal of this article is to examine the effects of the electorate's evaluations of the main party leaders – Blair, Hague and Kennedy – on voting in the 2001 British election using the 1997–2001 British Election Panel Study. For this purpose we specify a model of influences on voting decisions that includes enduring values, election-specific issues and assessments of the government's record, social background variables, and both current (party image) and long-standing indicators (1997 vote) of party preferences. We find that appraisals of Blair, Hague and Kennedy were significantly and strongly related to vote in 2001. These results persist even after controlling for many other relevant factors. We conclude, however, by signalling caution with respect to the causal interpretation of such estimates of leadership effects.

Do Canvassing and Campaigning Work? Evidence from the 2001 General Election in England

Ron Johnston and Charles Pattie

Over the last two decades an increasing volume of research has demonstrated the efficacy of constituency campaigns at British general elections, using a range of indicators. In general, the more intense a party's campaign in a constituency, relative to its opponents', the better its performance there. These conclusions have been reached using aggregate-level data, and are confirmed again here in respect of English constituencies at the 2001 election. In addition, however, the novel before-and-after design of the 2001 BES allows us to test for the impact of constituency campaigning at the level of the individual voter. Analyses of these data provide strong supporting evidence to the aggregate-level analyses: people who intended to vote for a party when the campaign started were more likely to do so if it contacted them during the campaign.

ELECTIONS IN EUROPE IN 2002

The 2002 French Elections:
The Re-establishment of the Primacy
of the President

Gérard Grunberg

The results of the first round of the 2002 French presidential election astounded everyone in France and abroad. The elimination of the Socialist candidate, incumbent Prime Minister Lionel Jospin, and the qualification of the *Front National* candidate Jean-Marie Le Pen, for the second round, did indeed cause a minor earthquake in the French political landscape. Analysts mainly emphasized the rise of the extreme right, the high abstention rate and the crisis affecting the French party system.

Our interpretation of the results of the 2002 elections (presidential and legislative) is considerably different. We will first show that these elections did not signal a decisive advance of the extreme right, or any irreversible drop in electoral participation, or any overturning of the French party system. However, these elections are significant for other reasons: they marked a return to the Gaullist functioning of Fifth Republic institutions, a serious defeat and a possible lasting weakening of the left, and lastly a growing crisis of confidence, especially among the working classes, with respect to the leadership elites.

Varying Electoral Participation and the Rejection of the Extreme Right

As shown in Table 1, voter turnout in the first round of the 2002 presidential election was the lowest since the beginning of the Fifth Republic (72%). But, in the second round of the election, turnout increased by eight points compared to the first round, equalling 1995 levels even though the absence of a candidate from the left in the second round could have had the opposite effect, as in 1969. How does one explain this relatively significant abstention in the first round and relatively high level of participation in the second?

All of the recent studies on voter turnout in France demonstrate that the tendency toward lower turnout is not due to an increase in regular abstentionism, but rather to an increase in intermittent abstentionism. Thus,

TABLE 1
% TURNOUT AT PRESIDENTIAL AND PARLIAMENTARY ELECTIONS, 1958–2002

Year	Presidential Elections First round	Presidential Elections Second round	Parliamentary Elections First round
1958			77
1962			69
1965	85	85	
1967			81
1968			80
1969	77	69	
1973			79
1974	85	88	
1978			83
1981	81	86	71
1986			78
1988	81	84	66
1993			69
1995	78	80	
1997			68
2002	72	80	64

only 13% of voters participated in neither round of the 2002 presidential and parliamentary elections, but only 19% voted in all four voting rounds. French voters today go to the polls only when convinced of the importance of the issues at stake. How else to explain the low turnout in the first round of the presidential election? (Muxel, 2003)

Several explanations may be offered. First, the polls forecast a second round between the incumbent president Jacques Chirac and the then prime minister Lionel Jospin, and a number of voters therefore thought that there was no need to vote in the first round. The two main candidates, especially Lionel Jospin, did not involve themselves greatly in the first round campaign battle, as they also were awaiting the second round. Finally and above all, the left–right cleavage, which continues to be the dominant political cleavage – i.e. around which politics and the party system are organized – has ceased to constitute the dominant ideological divide (Schweisguth, 2002). More than half of voters questioned on the eve of the election held the view that there was no difference between the agendas of the two main candidates and it is known that there is a link between the perception of differences in the political agendas and voter turnout (Jaffré, 2003). In the 1970s and beginning of the 1980s, the two cleavages (political and ideological) overlapped. The conflict between the left and the right was the organizing principle of both the functioning of the political system and ideological confrontations. Political passions were expressed through this conflict. Today, even if the left–right cleavage retains an ideological dimension, the principal ideological conflict is organized around the confrontation between the far right and the other political parties, in particular the parties on the left. This is true in particular with respect to younger generations, who are precisely those who vote the least today. Indeed, as shown in Table 2, it was among young people that the increase in turnout between the first and second rounds of the presidential election was greatest.

TABLE 2
% TURNOUT BY AGE IN THE TWO ROUNDS OF THE PRESIDENTIAL ELECTION
2002 AND IN THE FIRST ROUND OF THE PARLIAMENTARY ELECTIONS OF 2002

	Turnout first round of the Presidential Election	Turnout second round of the Presidential Election	Difference	Turnout first round of the Parliamentary Elections
18–39 years old	72	84	+12	54
40 years and more	83	90	+7	79

Source: CEVIPOF-CIDSP survey May 2002

Young people are both the group most likely to classify themselves as neither left nor right (Table 3) and the group most hostile to xenophobia, a theme associated with the extreme right. For many of them, the first round did not appear to have much ideological importance, since the election seemed headed towards a duel between Jospin and Chirac; in contrast, the second round did.

TABLE 3
POLITICAL AND IDEOLOGICAL POSITIONING OF FRENCH VOTERS
BY AGE

	Neither left nor right	Anti-xenophobic
18–39 years old	30	51
40 and older	16	35

Source: CEVIPOF-CIDSP survey May 2002

In the second round, young people were as likely as their elders to vote for Jacques Chirac in order to bring about the defeat of Le Pen (Table 4). In contrast, in the parliamentary elections, while 64% of voters generally went to the polls, the proportion doing so was barely one-half among the young, thus demonstrating that in these elections, once the threat of the far right had been eliminated, nothing crucial was at stake.

TABLE 4
VOTE FOR CHIRAC AND LE PEN IN THE TWO ROUNDS OF THE PRESIDENTIAL
ELECTION OF 2002 BY AGE (% OF ELECTORS REGISTERED)

	Chirac (first round)	Chirac (second round)	Difference	Le Pen (first round)	Le Pen (second round)	Difference
18–39 years old	9	64	+55	11	12	+1
40 and older	18	65	+47	15	15	0

Source: CEVIPOF-CIDSP survey May 2002

The second round of the presidential election had thus been transformed into an anti-Le Pen referendum mobilizing 80% of the electorate, 82% of whom voted in favor of Jacques Chirac. Consequently, there is no irreversible lowering of voter turnout. But the incentive must be significant to prompt voters, especially young voters, to go to the polls.

The Far Right's Performance

Since 1984, the far right has always exceeded 9% of the vote in national, European and regional elections (Table 5). It is true that the score obtained in the first round of the 2002 presidential election, 19.2% including 17% for the *Front National* (FN), is the highest ever obtained in France by this political movement. It should be noted, however, that the far right did not make progress between the two rounds, even losing ground in relation to ballots cast. The mobilization against the far right was extremely strong, and the 82% obtained by Jacques Chirac shows the extent of the rejection of the FN by the French. In the parliamentary elections, the movement obtained only 12.4% of votes cast. This result is far from negligible and confirms that the far right does indeed constitute a significant and lasting electoral force. But this score did not enable it either to hamper the right, which obtained an absolute majority in the National Assembly, or to obtain a single seat. Politically, this constitutes a serious failure for the FN, which is paying the price for its isolation. It is unable either to seriously disturb the functioning of the French political system or to diminish the political importance of the left–right cleavage. Rejection of the far right is quite broad as evidenced by an analysis of vote transfers between the first and second rounds of the presidential election (Table 6).

Stability of the Party System

The results of the first round of the presidential election were characterized not only by the progression of the far right and the elimination of Lionel Jospin. They were also, and above all, characterized by the weak showings

TABLE 5
VOTES FOR THE FAR RIGHT, 1984–2002

Elections		Far right votes	% registered	% cast
1984	European	2,227,837	6.0	11.0
1986	Legislative	2,727,870	7.3	9.7
1986	Regional	2,682,654	7.2	9.6
1988	Presidential (1st round)	4,375,894	11.5	14.4
1988	Legislative(1st round)	2,391,973	6.3	9.8
1989	European	2,154,005	5.7	11.9
1992	Regional	3,423,176	9.0	13.8
1993	Legislative (1st round)	3,229,462	8.3	12.7
1994	European	2,050,086	5.2	10.5
1995	Presidential (1st round)	4,656,107	11.6	15.3
1997	Legislative (1st round)	3,827,544	9.7	15.0
1998	Regional	3,297,209	8.4	15.1
1999	European	1,568,315	3.9	9.0
2002	Presidential (1st round)	5,471,739	13.3	19.2
2002	Presidential (1st round)	5,525,032	13.4	17.8
2002	Legislative (1st round)	3,215,554	7.8	12.4

Note: These results include all far right candidates (Poujadists, *Alliance Républicaine*, and after 1972, *Front National* and other small groupings: PFN, FON, POE, MNR, etc.).

TABLE 6
VOTE TRANSFERS BETWEEN THE TWO ROUNDS OF
THE PRESIDENTIAL ELECTION (%)

	Abstention, blank ballot, invalid	Chirac	Le Pen
Laguiller	33	63	4
Besancenot	18	77	5
Hue	14	79	7
Jospin	21	76	3
Mamère	10	86	4
Chevènement	27	70	3
Bayrou	10	88	2
Chirac	4	94	2
Madelin	2	94	4
Saint Josse	7	77	16
Le Pen	8	16	76
Abstention, blank and invalid	48	46	6
Overall	23	63	14

Source: CEVIPOF-CIDSP survey May 2002.

of the two main contenders and the high percentage of votes cast for extremist parties and candidates who, like Chevènement and Saint Josse, defined themselves as neither left nor right. These results can be explained in several ways. First, since the likelihood of a second round between Jospin and Chirac was considered a virtual certainty, on both the moderate left as well as the moderate right, all of the parties wanted to run in the contest, as shown in Table 7. And, for the same reasons, a large number of voters in both camps voted for candidates other than the two main contenders, taking advantage of the first round to express their dissatisfaction with the two main protagonists of the 'cohabitation' arrangement. Chirac and Jospin thus obtained together just 35.3% of the ballots cast whereas the Jospin/Chirac total in the first round of the 1995 presidential election reached 43.7% and the Mitterrand/Chirac total in the first round of the 1988 presidential election reached 53.7%.

Only the 'pro-sovereignty' movement on the right did not wish or was unable to field a candidate in the 2002 election, and this helped Jacques Chirac. It might be supposed that if the polls had not been mistaken, always showing Chirac and Jospin leading, Lionel Jospin would have outpolled Le Pen, as indicated in Table 8. Jospin could have attained 20–22% of the ballots cast if all voters had not 'wasted' their vote in the first round.

A comparison of the vote structure in the 1995–97 presidential and parliamentary elections shows that the 1997 and 2002 parliamentary elections have the same structure. The far right is very weak, as are the

TABLE 7
PARTY SYSTEM, PRESIDENTIAL CANDIDACIES AND RESULTS OF
THE FIRST ROUND 2002

Party system	Party	Candidates	Votes
Extreme Left	LO	Laguiller	5.7
	LCR	Besancenot	4.3
	PT	Gluckstein	0.5
Moderate Left	PS	Jospin	16.2
	PC	Hue	3.4
	Green	Mamère	5.3
	Radical	Taubira	2.3
Former Moderate Left (pro-sovereignty)	Citizens Movement	Chevènement	5.3
Moderate Right	RPR	Chirac	19.9
	UDF	Bayrou	6.8
	DL	Madelin	3.9
		Lepage	1.9
		Boutin	1.2
Former Moderate Right (pro-sovereignty)	MPF		–
	RPF		–
Anti-European regionalist	CPNT	Saint-Josse	4.1
Extreme Right	FN	Le Pen	16.9
	MEN	Mégret	2.3

TABLE 8
REACTIONS OF ELECTORS VOTING FOR LEFTIST CANDIDATES TOWARD
RESULTS OF FIRST ROUND OF 2002 PRESIDENTIAL ELECTION (%)

Voted for	Dissatisfied by elimination of Lionel Jospin	If had to do it over, would vote differently	Would vote for Jospin among those who would vote differently
Laguiller (LO)	67	40	67
Besancenot (LCR)	70	32	90
Hue (PC)	87	24	91
Jospin (PS)	98	1	0
Taubira (Radical)	78	52	87
Mamère (Greens)	58	35	96
Chevènement (Pôle Républicain)	79	34	65

Source: CEVIPOF-CIDSP survey May 2002

'neither left nor right' groups. The FN is between 12.6% and 15%, and the two major groupings on the moderate left and moderate right, who together garnered 60.9% of the ballots cast in the 2002 presidential election, obtained 80.6% in the parliamentary elections the same year, i.e. approximately the same level as in the 1997 parliamentary elections. The only notable difference is the left–right flip-flop: the right, defeated by the left in 1997, comes out ahead in 2002 (Table 9).

TABLE 9
RESULTS OF THE PRESIDENTIAL AND THE PARLIAMENTARY ELECTIONS
1995–2002 (%)

	Presidential Election 1995 First round	Parliamentary Elections 1997 First round	Presidential Election 2002 First round	Parliamentary Elections 2002 First round
Extreme Left	5.3	2.1	10.4	2.8
Moderate Left	35.2	41.5	27.2	37.1
Moderate Right	39.4	36.5	33.7	43.5
Extreme Right	15.3	15.1	19.2	12.6
Neither Left nor Right and Pro-Sovereignty	4.7	4.8	9.5	5.2
Moderate Left + Moderate Right	74.6	78.0	60.9	80.6
PS	23.3	23.5	16.2	24.1
PC	8.6	9.9	3.4	4.8
Green	3.3	3.6	5.3	4.5
RPR (UMP Parliamentary Elections 2002)	20.5	15.7	19.9	33.3
UDF	18.5	14.2	6.8	4.9

On the eve of the 2002 elections, we had characterized the French party system, stabilized since the 1980s, as an alternating bipolarized multiparty system with two dominant parties: the Socialist Party and the Gaullist Party, the RPR. The 2002 elections have not significantly changed this system, as shown in Tables 9, 10 and 11.

TABLE 10
COMPETITION ON THE SECOND BALLOT OF THE PARLIAMENTARY ELECTIONS
IN THE 577 CONSTITUENCIES

	Parliamentary Elections		
	1993	*1997*	*2002*
Elected First round	94	29	58
One candidate	17	12	3
Two candidates	451	457	506
Left/Right	334	399	469
Left/FN	5	25	8
Right/FN	81	31	20
Right/Right	30	2	7
Left/Left	1	0	2
Three candidates	15	79	10
Left/Right/FN	12	76	10
Right/Right/FN	2	0	0
Left/Right/Right	1	3	0
Total	577	577	577

TABLE 11
DEPUTIES ELECTED IN 1993, 1997 AND 2002

	Parliamentary Elections		
	1993	*1997*	*2002*
Extreme Left	0	0	0
PC	24	37	21
PS	56	246	141
Radical	5	13	7
Other Left	10	9	6
Green	0	8	3
Citizens Movement	4	7	0
UDF	206	109	22
RPR	258	139	369
Other Right	13	8	8
CPNT			0
Extreme Right	0	1	0
Left	99	320	178
Right	478	257	399
Total	577	577	577

Although there was a change of party in power in 2002, the two major political groups are even more dominant at the polls than before the elections. On the left, the communists collapsed and the Greens remained relatively weak; on the right, the UDF (*Union pour la Démocratie Française*) collapsed with the UMP (*Union pour la Majorité Présidentielle*) now clearly dominating. In contrast to 1997, the FN made it to the second round of the parliamentary elections in only a small number of constituencies and was unable to handicap the moderate right, which secured a big majority of seats in the National Assembly. The UMP and the PS combined obtained 410 seats out of 577 as compared to 385 in 1997 and 314 in 1993. The extreme parties and the 'neither left nor right' movements did not win a single seat. The left–right cleavage and the opposition between moderate left and moderate right shaped the political contest. The party system paradoxically comes out strengthened following the 2002 elections.

The True Changes Brought About by the 2002 Elections

The foregoing analysis does not however signify that the 2002 elections have brought about no change whatsoever in the French institutional and political landscape. Three elements of change can be seen: the end of the cohabitation and the return to the 'normal' functioning of institutions; the crisis on the left, in particular within the Socialist Party; and the crisis of confidence by a portion of the voters, especially within the working classes, with respect to the political elites and political representation.

Return to the Normal Functioning of the Fifth Republic

In 1997, with the victory of the left in the parliamentary elections and the continuation in office of President Chirac elected for seven years in 1995, commenced the third period of cohabitation. The two preceding cohabitations (1986–88 and 1993–95) had each lasted two years. The third lasted for the entire term of the legislature – i.e. five years. This long cohabitation had two opposite effects. On the one hand, because of its length, it almost institutionalized this form of government, not intended by the founder of the Fifth Republic. There was a division between a governing administration supported by a parliamentary majority holding the bulk of power, and a President of the Republic, head of the opposition, to whom the constitution and political practice reserved a real political influence, especially in foreign policy and defence matters, but also in the appointment of the highest officials in government. On the other hand, although the strength of political institutions demonstrated that this form of government was possible, the length of the third period of cohabitation caused the political class as well as a growing segment of the population to come to the realization that such an arrangement had serious disadvantages. The President was led, somewhat unwillingly, to carry out a constitutional reform that instituted a shortening of the presidential term to five years, a reform supported by the Socialist Party and certain centrists. The reform was conceived as a means of limiting the risks of cohabitation and harmonizing the duration of the presidential and parliamentary terms of office. By chance, the electoral calendar was such that this constitutional reform, adopted by referendum in 2001, made it so that the legislative and presidential elections would both take place in 2002. Lionel Jospin, convinced that his party and he himself had a better chance of winning the presidential election than the legislative elections, had his parliamentary majority adopt an inversion of the electoral calendar so that the presidential election would take place before the parliamentary elections. Thus, as a result of a political paradox, the socialists themselves ended up making possible the return to a functioning of governing institutions consistent with the Gaullist tradition. The presidential election again became the major election within the French political system, with the legislative elections having as their main purpose to give the new president a parliamentary majority. The political primacy of the presidency thus stood a good chance of being fully re-established. Everything happened as the socialists had foreseen from an institutional standpoint, but not as had been hoped for in terms of the political result. Once Jacques Chirac had been re-elected, the parliamentary elections held in the wake of his success resulted in an absolute majority for the 'president's party'. He could then name the Prime Minister of his choosing. The socialists tried to convince the French, between the two elections, of the resulting danger to the French political system if all power was given to a single man and to a single party. But their argument did not go very far as they themselves had defended the opposite reasoning when they hoped to win the presidential election. This time the voters, while having voted against the president in power in the course of the 1997 parliamentary elections, adhered to the original logic of the institutions of the Fifth Republic. Twenty per cent of those voting on the left in 1997 cast their vote for the right in the first round of the 2002 parliamentary elections. Among such voters more than a third felt that cohabitation was a bad thing for France.

The return to the original logic of governing institutions may have significant consequences for the future to the extent that the restoration of the primacy of the presidential election will have an impact on the party system. Indeed, save in the case of an unforeseen event, henceforth each five-year election cycle will open with the presidential election. The parties must therefore adapt to this situation in order to win the decisive contest, especially given the dangerous proliferation of candidacies in the first round of the 2002 presidential campaign. In this respect, the right seems to have gained a significant advantage over the left in 2002, an advantage that might endure.

The Overwhelming Defeat of the Left and the Difficulties of the Socialist Party

The governing left came out of the 2002 elections extremely weakened. It finds itself again at the very low levels at which it stood in the 1993 parliamentary elections, with 37% of the vote, whereas the moderate right has similarly risen to its quite high 1993 levels, with 44% of the ballots cast. Now, it is important to remember that, in 1997, the left obtained victory even though it had a minority of the votes (left plus far left), thanks in part to the FN and, above all, because the elections, organized following the dissolution of parliament by President Jacques Chirac, presented an opportunity to voice a vote in protest against the Juppé government. However, this time around, the circumstances are much more difficult for the left than they were during that period.

There are a number of reasons. First, beginning in 1994, the creation of the *Gauche plurielle* ('pluralist left') made it possible to bring together a communist party anxious to come back into power, a Green party, which had decided to align itself with the left and try out its first experiment in government, and the followers of Jean-Pierre Chevènement within the Citizens Movement, around a socialist party that finally had succeeded in finding an appropriate leader, Lionel Jospin. Today, after five years in power and a rout at the polls, the communists, considerably weakened, and the Greens, disappointed with their showing, are highly divided, lacking any true leadership, and in doubt as to the wisdom of any potential participation in a future government. The Socialist Party no longer has a leader capable of uniting, and it is extremely divided on the strategic approach and proposals to adopt. The pluralist left is moribund and Chevènement's own movement, the *Pôle Républicain*, was still-born.

The left's problems, however, also stem indirectly from the changes that have occurred on the right. Indeed, the moderate right has been weakened since the mid-1970s by its division into two political families – the Gaullist family and the centrist-liberal family – and, since the mid-1980s, by the electoral advance of the extreme right. However, both of these weakening factors, while still present, were substantially reduced in the wake of the 2002 elections. Within the moderate right, supporters in the Chirac camp, who, in advance of the elections, had begun preparations to create a large inclusive party of the right, took advantage of Jacques Chirac's clear victory in the presidential election and the poor showings by centrist (Bayrou) and liberal (Madelin) candidates in the first round of the election to carry out their plans. On April 23, the UMP (*Union pour la majorité présidentielle*) was established. On May 11, in anticipation of the parliamentary elections, the UMP published an initial list of candidates which included 52% from the RPR, 20% from the UDF and 16% from DL (Haegel, 2002). The latter party eventually disappeared when it definitively merged with the RPR into the UMP. On November 17, the UMP was founded as a party bringing together substantially all three of the moderate right groups. The UDF did not disappear, but can no longer vie for the leadership of the moderate right against the RPR, which constitutes the major component of the new party. If the UMP is able to come together and field one candidate for the next presidential election, it will hold a considerable advantage over the left since it will have less trouble qualifying its candidate for the second round. On the other hand, the left has no procedure for designating a joint candidate for the next presidential election.

The FN, which initially threatened the right in the past, is now above all a danger to the left, as witnessed during the first round of the 2002 presidential election. Indeed, the danger that the extreme right represents to the right is diminishing for two reasons. In contrast to what occurred in 1997, the FN was unable to pose a threat to the UMP in the 2002 parliamentary elections. With the basic rule requiring a score of 12.5% of registered voters to qualify for the second round of the elections, few FN candidates were able to advance. The end of cohabitation and the UMP's further shift to the right on the issue of law and order may contribute to reducing the influence of the FN.

Moreover, the right's victory will enable the new government to adopt an electoral law for the upcoming regional elections that will considerably weaken the political influence of the FN and the UDF as well as their representation in regional assemblies. This law will further strengthen the current bipolarized party system around the UMP and the PS. Lastly, the right has succeeded in winning the battle against the socialists for credibility on the issue of crime, an issue of major concern for the French. The left has acquired a handicap that is likely to be lasting on this issue and will not be able to counterbalance it through strong credibility on the issue of fighting unemployment after three legislatures with a socialist government.

The Crisis of Confidence

In addition to these political considerations, it should be added that the governing left has lost its support among the social classes that it claims to represent first and foremost: the working classes. This has been increasingly the case for the past several years. The question of the representation of the popular classes by the moderate left and, more generally, by the governing parties, right and left, has henceforth been clarified: nearly 40% of working class votes were cast for extremist parties in the first round of the presidential election (in contrast to 30% for the electorate as a whole). Thirty-one per cent voted for the moderate right and 30 per cent for the moderate left. In other words, the majority of workers voted on the right, with the working class constituting the largest segment of the extreme right electorate in the first round of the presidential election.

TABLE 12
OCCUPATION AND VOTE IN FIRST ROUND OF 2002 PRESIDENTIAL ELECTION

Occupation of person surveyed	Far left	Moderate left	Moderate right	Far right
Farmer	4	14	60	22
Shopkeeper, craftsmen	2	20	70	29
Senior Manager/ professionals.	5	35	44	17
Teacher	12	53	32	3
Intermediate professions	11	35	38	16
Salaried employee	13	26	37	24
Blue collar	13	30	31	26
Student	14	46	32	9

Source: CEVIPOF-CIDSP survey May 2002.

This poses a serious problem for the left, which is tempted by a certain radicalization but runs the risk, through such a radicalization, of losing ground with the middle classes, except with teachers, who always tend to vote left. The popular classes have entered a period of distrust and rejection of governing elites. The socialist party, after 15 years in government since 1981, might experience a new cycle characterized by defeat at the polls. For all of these reasons, the right has gained a decisive advantage over the left in these elections. The PS remains the only governmental party on the left. But it will be difficult for it to manage to rebuild a party-based alliance capable of winning the next elections. On its own, it can garner barely a fourth of the ballots cast and it cannot therefore go it alone without allies. But which allies?

Conclusions

In conclusion, the 2002 French elections were indeed important elections. However, they were not elections characterized by a break with the past or by realignment. They were not critical elections. The political system withstood the electoral surges of the extreme parties. The Gaullists and the socialists remain the major political forces. Once again, a change in the party in power occurred and the second round of the presidential election has shown that the electorate was willing to come out in large numbers to voice its rejection of the FN. The FN remains powerful but cannot, in view of its isolation, destabilize the system. Its progression is not irreversible. The 2002 elections were important for other reasons. First, they signaled the return to the 'normal' functioning of the institutions of the Fifth Republic. The period of power-sharing was brought to an end, and, this time, probably for a long period. Henceforth, ordinarily each election cycle will begin with the presidential election and this will have major implications for the political process.

In this respect, the victory of the right and its organizational changes may turn out to be decisive for a relatively long period. It is true that the left can take comfort from the fact that, since 1981, every incumbent government has without exception lost the parliamentary elections. Bearing this in mind, the left may quietly wait for the next elections, which will take place in 2007. This is not likely. First, the rightist government, by trouncing the FN in the second round of the presidential election and then forming a new party, the UMP, has acquired the means to better deal in the future with the two dangers that have weakened it over the last 20 years, internal division and the threat from the far right. In addition, whereas the right is organized around the Gaullist party, the left, extremely weakened at the polls, is politically divided. The PS, lacking strong leadership or any strategy, looks no longer able to organize an alliance around itself capable of winning the next elections. Its former allies are themselves weakened and divided. The left has no procedures enabling it to select, in a unified manner, a candidate for the next presidential election. The FN is therefore, as demonstrated by the 2002 elections, a greater danger to the left than to the right. Furthermore, the left is experiencing the full brunt of the crisis of confidence of the working classes with respect to the traditional governmental parties. Blue collar workers are now voting more for the right – and especially for the far right – than for the left. The domination of the UMP right could turn out to be more enduring than anticipated by the left.

REFERENCES

Haegel, Florence (2002) 'Faire l'Union: la refondation des partis de droite après les élections de 2002', *Revue Française de Science Politique*, Oct.–Dec. 2002 : 561–76.
Jaffré, Jérôme (2003) 'Comprendre l'élimination de Lionel Jospin' in Pascal Perrineau and Colette Ysmal (eds.) *Le vote de tous les refus*. Paris: Presses de Sciences-Po.
Muxel, Anne (2003) 'La participation électorale', in Pascal Perrineau and Colette Ysmal (eds.) *Le vote de tous les refus*, Paris: Presses de Sciences-Po.
Schweisguth, Etienne (2002) 'La dépolitisation en questions', in Gérard Grunberg, Nonna Mayer and Paul Sniderman (eds.) *La démocratie à l'épreuve. Une nouvelle approche de l'opinion des Français*. Paris: Presses de Sciences-Po.

The Irish General Election of 2002: A New Hegemony for Fianna Fáil?

Michael Marsh

The general election of 2002 was a long time coming. When Fianna Fáil and the Progressive Democrats (PDs) agreed to form a government in 1997 with the support of four independents, few commentators expected that it would last the full term. Either the independents would break ranks, or the PDs would make a demand that could not be met. Fianna Fáil's record as a coalition partner was not good; the first coalition with the PDs, in 1989, lasted only two years and the Fianna Fáil–Labour coalition formed in 1992 did little better. The independents too seemed a motley crew. Add to that the fallout from the McCracken Inquiry into links between a supermarket millionaire and the former Fianna Fáil Taoiseach, Charles Haughey, and it appeared that the coalition would be subjected to stresses that it would not be tough enough to endure.

Certainly there were strains, starting with Ray Burke, who eventually resigned both his position as Minister for Foreign Affairs and his seat in the Dáil only a few months into the life of the government, following new allegations that he had received corrupt payments from builders. Many other current and past members of Fianna Fáil also found their names linked with real or alleged misdeeds as the various investigative committees and tribunals of inquiry steadily uncovered what appeared to be evidence of widespread corruption, and several members of the Fianna Fáil parliamentary party were forced to resign the whip.

There were other problems, most notably the O'Flaherty affair, concerning the appointment of a former judge to a plum European job only months after he had been forced to step down from the High Court when news broke that he had behaved improperly when investigating, on behalf of a friend, the progress of a criminal case. Public dissatisfaction on this issue manifested itself in a particularly bad by-election result, although the government actually failed to win any of the five by-elections of this parliament.

But there were also triumphs. The achievement of the Belfast Agreement on Good Friday 1998 was the highlight, but the continued health of the economy was even more important. Growth was rapid, unemployment fell to unprecedented low levels and taxes were cut in accordance with the promises made by the government parties during the 1997 election. This all helped to maintain the government. In particular, it made it much easier to keep the independents onside. Given the sort of access to government that Fianna Fáil backbenchers could only envy, the 'gang of four' were able to see all sorts of pet projects implemented, and were informed enough to be able to claim the credit for whatever goodies were being handed out to their constituents. Although they had to wait until 2002 for it, they even got a referendum on abortion that sought yet again to roll back the judgement of the Supreme Court in the 'X' case.[1]

Of course there was a downside to the government's record. While growth was substantial, the fruits of that growth were not distributed equally. Personal income inequalities had grown, and perceptions of inequalities between different regions were significant. Expectations were also rising and it was clear that the public services were falling well short of what should characterize a rich first world country. The health services, with long waiting lists for those not in private schemes and moves towards the centralization of many facilities, provoked much anger. Inadequate transport infrastructures and woeful public transport services also seemed out of place now Ireland was an economic star. John Bruton, the Fine Gael leader, launched an ill-fated 'Celtic snail' campaign in 2000 in preparation for a 2001 election. This was intended to highlight how the government had mismanaged the boom, but the mirth provoked by the campaign was one of the final straws that eventually broke Bruton's long tenure as party leader early in 2001.

Going into the election the government was in good shape. Polls in March indicated that satisfaction with the government was extremely high, showing a surplus of 24% of those satisfied over those dissatisfied. The Taoiseach was even more popular, and the Tánaiste more popular than any opposition politician. Fianna Fáil was also riding high in the polls, Irish Marketing Surveys (IMS) putting the party at around 50% in all its recent polls – although Market Research Bureau of Ireland's (MRBI) new adjusted estimate for the Fianna Fáil vote was much lower, at around 41–42%.[2] Moreover, the main pillars of any alternative government were shaky. Fine Gael's vote had been in the low 20s at best for some time. The popularity of its new leader, Michael Noonan, was lower even than that of his predecessor, John Bruton, who had been replaced because he was seen to be unpopular with the electorate. Labour had amalgamated with Democratic Left to create a stronger left, and while this improved Labour's front bench, in electoral terms the whole was less than the sum of its parts, little more than 10% in recent polls. Moreover Labour had rejected Fine Gael's proposed 'Rainbow Coalition' alternative, which would have included Fine

Gael, Labour and the Greens, keeping all of its options open in the event of the PDs proving inadequate to the task of sustaining a Fianna Fáil administration – even if Fine Gael was Labour's preferred option.

Fianna Fáil dominated the campaign. The party accepted the fact that there were problems in areas like the health services and transport, but nonetheless claimed that its record was a good one. It took responsibility for the strong economy over the last few years and promised to continue its work to improve the public services: 'A lot done. More to do' was the slogan. Then the leader was sent on a tour of the country, pressing flesh rather than speaking to reporters, while the Fianna Fáil media centre coordinated a highly professional operation, modelled on New Labour's in the UK, which provided space-filling food for the ever greedy media and 'pre-butted' adverse messages. Fine Gael and Labour chose to contest the election on Fianna Fáil's ground, highlighting what needed to be done, but doing little to refute Fianna Fáil's claims to effective economic management. Most voters saw Fianna Fáil as simply more capable. Fine Gael also made the mistake of promising something to everyone, a tactic that may have worked for Fianna Fáil in the past, but sat uneasily with Fine Gael's reputation for honesty and financial probity and probably served to weaken the party's already strained credibility with the voters. Despite the fact that there was ample evidence that the boom was now over, and that the government's estimates of income and expenditure in 2002 were dangerously inaccurate, and there was significant media attention given to this situation, the opposition parties seemed to collude with the government to ignore the problem. No party was willing to miss out on the opportunity to promise more of something to someone.

The initial polls then removed whatever relevance Fine Gael might have had for the outcome, all of them putting Fianna Fáil within touching distance of an overall majority, and IMS in particular giving grounds for thinking, in the words of the *Irish Independent's* headline, that it was 'All over–bar the voting'. The only question to be answered was who, if anyone, would form the next government with Fianna Fáil? 'One-Party Government? NO Thanks' said the Progressive Democrat Michael McDowell, energizing his party's campaign, warning of the dangers of one-party rule and, in typically colourful language, attacking the integrity of the very people his party had been in government with since 1997. Even so, from a near impossibility before the campaign started, a one-party government became the strongest probability with the bookies as poll followed poll and Fianna Fáil's vote showed no signs of falling.

The introduction of electronic voting machines in three constituencies ensured that some results would be known, if not before midnight on election day, at least soon after, providing a hint as to the possible outcome many hours before the usual harbinger, the 'early tallies'. When the results for Meath, Dublin North and Dublin West were declared, the possibility of an overall majority remained open: Fianna Fáil's vote was up, but not hugely.[3] What was certain was that the count would be a long, bad day for Fine Gael and so it turned out. This now appears as it if will be the last of the hand-counted elections, but 2002 gave us much to remember with several counts going on past the weekend and the final result in two constituencies delayed for several days.

Fianna Fáil eventually finished just short of an overall majority, but Fine Gael collapsed to its worst seat total for half a century and Labour stood still, while Greens, Sinn Fein and independents, as well as the PDs, all saw their stock rise handsomely. The government was reconstructed, this time with an overall majority, ending a run of government-changing elections dating back to 1973. As the Finance Minister Charlie McCreevy pointed out, the novelty of this election was that it was the opposition that had been voted out of office. Fine Gael and Labour between them held 75 seats going in to the election, but emerged with only 52.

Fianna Fáil won 41.5% of the vote and 81 seats (see Table 1). This was an increase of only just over 2% on 1997 and also similarly up on its 1990s average vote, but it brought rich rewards. The vote was actually up in 28 of the 41 constituencies. More votes sometimes won more seats, but the party also won where its vote did not increase to any significant extent. The last three elections have given the party its three lowest votes since 1932 and this probably indicates that the days of Fianna Fáil winning the 45%+ it has averaged since the foundation of the state are now over. However, the fact that it is able to come so close to an overall majority with such a relatively small vote indicates that the judgement of those who decided that the party could never again win an overall majority was premature. The party won 81 seats in February 1982 and did the same again in 1987, although with a significantly larger vote. 44% this time would have given the party a landslide win.

Fine Gael dropped 5% of the vote, down 3.8% on its recent average; if not quite the electoral 'meltdown' implied in some polls, was a disaster in terms of seats. It lost 24 seats, winning only 31. It was the Fine Gael's worst performance since 1948 by any measure, and this time there was not the compensation of winning office. Still, in ten constituencies the party's vote did go up, if only marginally in most cases. Mostly it was down, in 22 constituencies by more than 5%. It was there that the seats tended to be lost. Nowhere did its vote go up enough to win a seat. The collapse was particularly marked in Dublin. Its highest vote share there in any constituency was 20%; outside Dublin it topped 40% in only two constituencies and 30% in three others. Labour is now the second largest

TABLE 1
VOTES AND SEATS IN THE IRISH ELECTION 2002

	Votes	%	Cands	Seats	%	Vote seat difference	% vote change from 1990s average
FF	770,748	41.5	106	81	48.8	7.3	+2.2
FG	417,619	22.5	85	31	18.7	-3.8	-3.8
Labour	200,130	10.8	46	21	12.7	1.9	-6.8
PDs	73,628	4.0	20	8	4.8	0.8	-0.7
Greens	71,470	3.8	31	6	3.6	-0.2	+1.7
SF	121,020	6.5	37	5	3.0	-3.5	+4.4
Others	203,287	10.9	138	14	8.4	-2.5	+2.6
Total	1,857,902	100		463	166	100	

party in terms of votes in Dublin; when it comes to seats Fine Gael lags behind all of the other parties apart from Sinn Fein.

Labour's result was a deeply disappointing one. It hoped the merger with Democratic Left would provide the basis for a move back to the heights of the 30+ seats won in 1992 but its campaign never took off and the eventual total of 21 seats was no better than that won by Labour and Democratic Left separately in 1997. Overall, its vote was down 2% on the combined total of Labour and Democratic Left in 1997 and almost 7% below the recent average. While its vote was up in 13 constituencies, it was up by 5% in only one and it fell by more than 5% in eight. Moreover, its extra seats all came at the expense of Fine Gael, its most likely coalition partner, while it lost some of its own seats to Sinn Fein and left-wing independents.

The PDs had a triumphant election that brought the party double the number of seats held at dissolution. All the gains came from Fine Gael. A concentrated campaign, that saw the party focussing on seats rather than votes, helped to do the trick. The party ran only 20 candidates in 18 constituencies, compared to 26 in 26 last time, so the fact that its vote was down by 0.6% may be discounted. Where it had no TD but won significantly more votes it generally picked up a seat and where it held a seat the vote stayed firm, or rose. Only in one constituency did it fall, and there the seat was retained anyway.

For the *Greens* and *Sinn Fein* this was the election in which they each crossed a threshold, if not to formal parliamentary group status (which requires eight deputies) then at least to a state where a meeting of their parliamentary party is not a joke. The Green Party increased its vote by 1.7% above its recent average. Fielding five more candidates than in 1997, it gained four seats, all at the expense of Fine Gael. In only nine constituencies did its vote fall; in 25 it rose, by between 1% and 5%. But only in three constituencies did the party top 10% (the PDs did so in eight) so its hold on this new status is precarious, and its chance of significant increase would require a lot more votes.

Sinn Fein appears stronger than the Greens in most respects, despite winning one fewer seat. Up almost 5% on its vote average in the previous decade, its vote rose almost everywhere and exceeded 10% in ten constituencies. It ran 37 candidates as against 15 in 1997, a tactic that boosted the overall vote and increased the spending allowed to the party nationally. Its gains generally came from Labour, not from Fianna Fáil as has been the traditional expectation.

Independent and minor party candidates also proved more popular this time, winning a few more votes and seven more seats, all but one of them from Fine Gael. This group of independents is the largest since 1951. The substitution of the traditional deposit by a requirement of 30 signatures did not lead to a plethora of candidates this time: there were only 138, which was 21 less than in 1997. Their share of the vote rose in 21 constituencies and fell in 20 so there was no clear trend. It shows perhaps that the electorate almost everywhere is receptive where there is a good candidate. Independents were very diverse of course. Several independents were disaffected Fianna Fáil members who had been denied a nomination at some point. There are also independent left candidates. Discontent with the health services underlay some of these campaigns, and formed the major plank in the campaigns of others with no strong party pedigree. The ability of independents to win concessions from the outgoing government obviously made a vote for such a candidate a more credible option in 2002, particularly given the absence of any alternative to a Fianna Fáil led government. It will be interesting to see whether this changes before the next election.

Many observers were taken aback by the extent of seat changes. How could Fianna Fáil come so close to an overall majority with such a relatively small share of the vote, and Fine Gael lose so many seats with just a 5% drop in its vote? How could independents could do so much better with virtually the same vote as in 1997. Fianna Fáil's 'bonus' of 12 seats equalled its haul in 1997 and exceeded the 9 seats in won in 1969 and 1977; Fine Gael's shortfall of 6 was its worst ever.

Two features of the electoral system make this possible: the small size of the multimember constituencies means the strict proportional allocation of seat shares to first-preference votes is problematic, and the importance of second, third and minor preferences under the system of the single transferable vote means that, to some degree, the comparison of seats with first preference votes is inappropriate. Even so, these features are not new, but they do make possible the sort of results we have seen in 2002.

Fine Gael lost so many seats because the margin by which it had won many seats last time was so small. It won seats in 1997 with a lot less than a full quota in a particular constituency.[3] The fall in votes, which was generally more than 5% where seats were lost, left the party well below totals where it had any chance of winning a seat. Transfers also explain differences between seats won and first preferences obtained. Obviously a party that does well out of lower preferences effectively tops up its first preference votes and wins more seats. The Greens did much better in terms of later votes than Sinn Fein, which is how Greens were able to win more seats with fewer first-preference votes. Independents also did very well out of transfer votes in some places, but the persistent shortfall in seats for such candidates is because independents do not transfer consistently to one another. The category is a convenience for the analyst rather than the voter. Transfers also explain some of Fianna Fáil's seat bonus. In the past the party neither sought nor obtained transfers from other parties. Now that it has decided to look for lower preferences it reaps the benefit that we would expect to accrue to a large party simply because it has the candidates in the frame to get transfers. In fact it received more transfer votes than any other party, though nowhere near the 41.5% share of first preferences. Add to that the weakness of the Fine Gael–Labour link in 2002 and Fianna Fáil's seat return is less surprising. Over 50% of terminal transfers from Fine Gael and Labour went to one another in 1997; in 2002 it was only a little over 30%. Previous failures by Fine Gael to win 'bonus' seats typically also coincided with weak transfers from Labour, and it was in those years that Fianna Fail's bonus was greatest. Fianna Fáil, and Fine Gael, were once able to keep the vast majority of their vote within the family. Intra-party transfer rates have now declined, with less than two-thirds of votes staying within the fold when that is possible. However, the effectiveness of Fianna Fáil in picking up votes from elsewhere more than compensates.

But what accounts for the voters' choices in 2002? A full answer must wait for the analysis of the data from the first ever Irish Election Study,[4] but there is extensive opinion poll evidence from the election. The basic stability of Irish politics – most votes are won by Fianna Fáil, Fine Gael and Labour, and in that order – stems from long-term predispositions, best seen as partisanship, although this is waning (Marsh et al., 2001). Leaders and candidates change – and small parties in particular may owe much to the quality of local candidates – but the main factors which alter from election to election are the issues of the day: what concerns voters, and how the government has performed. On this count, the incumbent government did well. Economic growth undoubtedly produced a feel-good factor that concerns about public services could not dispel.

Health, economic management and honesty were (along with crime, which had almost no impact) the major motivations reported by voters in an exit poll. Voters were also asked whether their standard of living had improved over the last five years. The poll reported a clear majority of voters as saying their standard of living and quality of life had got better since 1997. Figure 1 shows the impact of these issues on the vote for individual parties, as measured by the difference between the actual distribution of the vote and the distribution of the vote amongst those for whom, for example, health was not an issue, or who did not see any improvement in living standards.

FIGURE 1
IMPACT OF ISSUES ON THE VOTE FOR INDIVIDUAL PARTIES

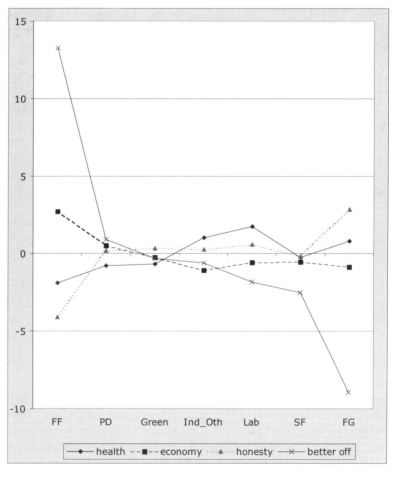

Source: calculated from RTE/Lansdowne Exit Poll 2002

By far the biggest effect is of living standards, although the base line here, of no improvement, is implausible. The bonus from this accrued to Fianna Fail rather than the PDs; the loss was born by Fine Gael and Labour. The other factors all had discernable effects, with honesty and health concerns hurting Fianna Fáil and concerns about economic management benefiting that party. The health issue did not help Fine Gael much, but seems to have benefited Labour and independents, who tapped more effectively into local discontent with the availability of service,

The failure of Fine Gael and Labour to do better lay in a loss of confidence in the established opposition. This opened a gap, and the independents, Greens and Sinn Fein moved into the space. The fact that the election seemed 'all over – bar the voting' helped the smaller parties by removing the major government alternative from the equation. As in a European Parliament election voters could perhaps express themselves rather than concern themselves with who would govern.

Figure 2 shows the link between each voter's preference for government and Taoiseach and their vote.

FIGURE 2
IMPACT OF PREFERENCE FOR A FIANNA FÁIL GOVERNMENT AND TAOISEACH
ON THE VOTE FOR INDIVIDUAL PARTIES

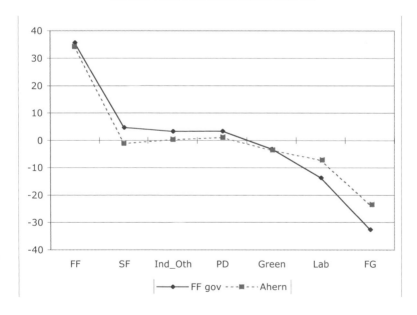

Source: calculated from RTE/Lansdowne Exit Poll 2002

A desire for a Fianna Fáil government of some kind, and Ahern as Taoiseach, helped Fianna Fáil, and hurt the Greens, Labour and Fine Gael – the alternative opposition that never got beyond a gleam in Fine Gael's eye. While many voters still claim to concern themselves primarily with the local candidate they do vote as if they care about the Taoiseach and the government.

Irish politics are traditionally seen as lacking the social structural cleavages typically of politics elsewhere in Europe. This remains true although, as Figure 3 demonstrates, there are still differences in voting behaviour according to age, class, sex, church attendance and urbanization.

FIGURE 3
IMPACT OF SOCIAL STRUCTURE ON VOTE FOR INDIVIDUAL PARTIES

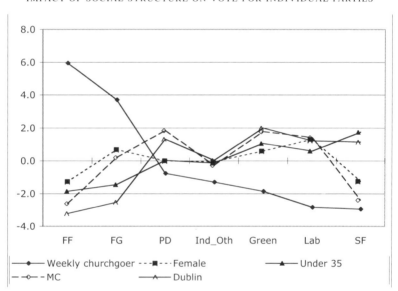

Source: calculated from RTE/Lansdowne Exit Poll 2002.

To some degree the smaller parties are (relatively) more attractive to urban, younger, more secular voters, and the most nationalist parties, Fianna Fáil and Sinn Féin to male voters. More surprisingly, class differences are very muted. Fianna Fáil once had cross-class appeal while Labour and Fine Gael stood for working class and middle-class opposition respectively. Now the latter two are almost classless, particularly by comparison with the middle-class Greens and PDs and working-class Sinn Féin. It perhaps indicates how the traditional appeals of the established parties have become blurred.

The new Dáil promises some interesting politics over the next few years with competition within the opposition as fierce as that between the opposition and the government. The declining economy and the tribunals promise rich pickings for opposition scavengers. However, since 1989, when Fianna Fáil abandoned its so-called 'core value' of rejecting coalition, that party has been well placed to cope with whatever any opponents might throw at it. Barring a massive increase in the strength of Fine Gael it remains hard to see any alternative to a Fianna Fáil led coalition, and barring a similar improvement in Labour's fortunes it is also hard to see how a government led by even a resurgent Fine Gael could form. Like Italy's Christian Democrats for so many years, and Sweden's Social Democrats, Fianna Fáil's strength, allied to its centrist position and a fragmented opposition, make it indispensable. Of course the graveyards of politics are full of those who were indispensable, as the Italian Christian Democrats found out when the party system was completely reformed in the wake of scandals that make our own look like children's mischief. Barring such a catastrophe, however, the outlook is good for Ireland's largest party.

NOTES

1. In this 1992 case, which concerned a minor who had been raped and was pregnant, the 1992 Supreme Court held that the possibility that she might commit suicide was an acceptable ground for an abortion under the constitution as amended in 1983. This judgement appalled those who had fought for the amendment so as to prevent courts from introducing a more liberal abortion regime, as had occurred in the US and since 1992 they had been seeking another amendment.
2. The adjustment is based on estimates made by MRBI in 1997 of differential turnout across parties.
3. The quota is defined as one more than the valid vote divided by one more than the number of contested seats in a constituency.
4. See www.tcd.ie/Political _Science/ElectionStudy

REFERENCES

Donnelly, Sean (2002) *Elections 2002*, Dublin: Sean Donnelly.
Gallagher, Michael (2003) 'Stability and turmoil: analysis of the results', in Michael Gallagher, Michael Marsh and Paul Mitchell (eds) *How Ireland Voted 2002*. London: Palgrave.
Garry, John, Fiachra Kennedy, Michael Marsh and Richard Sinnott (2003) 'What decided the election?' in Michael Gallagher, Michael Marsh and Paul Mitchell (eds) *How Ireland Voted 2002*. London: Palgrave.
Kennedy, Geraldine (2002). *Nealon's Guide to the 29th Dail*. Dublin: Irish Times.
McElroy, Gail and Michael Marsh (2003) 'Why the opinion polls got in wrong in 2002', in Michael Gallagher, Michael Marsh and Paul Mitchell (eds.) *How Ireland Voted 2002*. London: Palgrave

Marsh, Michael, Richard Sinnott, John Garry and Fiachra Kennedy (2001) 'The Irish election study: puzzles and priorities', *Irish Political Studies* 16: 161–78.

Marsh, Michael (ed.) (2002) *The Sunday Tribune Guide to Irish Politics*. Dublin: Sunday Tribune.

Mullen, John and Noel Whelan (2002) *The Tallyman's Guide to Election 2002*. Dublin..

A New Kid on the Block:
Pim Fortuyn and the Dutch
Parliamentary Election of May 2002

Galen A. Irwin and Joop J.M. Van Holsteyn

No one really saw it coming, at least not until it was too late. As the 2000–2001 parliamentary year ended, some ten months before the general election in May 2002, the biggest question in Dutch electoral politics was whether the popular Prime Minister, Wim Kok of the Labour Party (*Partij van de Arbeid*, PvdA), would retire or return to lead his party during the upcoming campaign.[1] His likely successor, Ad Melkert, was seen as a competent but not as a popular politician. Moreover, he was involved in a discussion concerning the appropriation of European funds while he was minister of social affairs in one of the preceding coalition governments. The emphasis at that time in the polls and in the media was on electoral stability. At the end of August 2001, the polls were showing that the affair over European funds was not costing the Labour Party votes. Labour was expected to lose two seats and remain the largest party in Parliament, while its major coalition partner, the Liberal Party (*Volkspartij voor Vrijheid en Democratie*, VVD), was expected to win one seat. The major opposition party, the Christian Democratic Appeal (*Christen Democratisch Appel*, CDA) stood at 28 seats, a loss of one seat (*De Telegraaf*, 21.8.2001).

On 20 August, Pim Fortuyn, a former university professor of sociology and political columnist, an outspoken homosexual with a flamboyant lifestyle – Ferrari, Bentley with chauffeur, butler, two lap dogs, portraits of John F. Kennedy in his lavishly decorated home which he referred to as 'Pallazo di Pietro', and a second home Rocca Jacoba in Italy – announced during an interview on television his intention to run for parliament and his ambition to become prime minister. At that moment it was not clear on which party list he might stand: Livable Netherlands (*Leefbaar Nederland*, LN), the CDA, or his own list. The announcement warranted only small notices in most newspapers.

After returning from his summer holiday, Kok announced his decision to retire and on 29 August anointed as his successor Melkert, who had more or less been cleared of any wrongdoing in the European funds affair. The media reported that this change of leadership would cost Labour three seats (e.g. *De Telegraaf*, 4.9.2001).

In September the focus turned to the Christian Democratic Appeal. In a struggle between the party leader, Jaap de Hoop Scheffer, and the party chairman, Marnix van Rij, both resigned. The parliamentary caucus chose the relatively unknown Jan Peter Balkenende as their chairman. The party quickly followed and named him the leader for the upcoming campaign. The leadership crisis so soon before the elections had a negative impact on electoral support: the first polls showed a loss of between 3 and 5 seats for the party (e.g. *De Telegraaf*, 18.10.2001). One of Balkenende's first moves was to announce that his party would follow a harder line with respect to asylum seekers and the immigration of ethnic minorities.

Livable Netherlands was the national extension of a movement that had begun in a number of municipalities at previous local elections. In 2002 it hoped to make a strong entry into Parliament. In October the party leadership advised the party congress to choose Pim Fortuyn as the party leader. Polls at the beginning of November indicated that LN might expect to receive 6 to 8 seats at the upcoming elections. By the end of the month, LN had increased to 10 seats, while the Labour and Liberal parties were in a tight race over which would be the largest party: Labour was at 41 seats while the Liberal Party was at 40. On November 25 Fortuyn was chosen as leader of Livable Netherlands and on this occasion he introduced his slogan, 'At your service', at the end of his acceptance speech.

Only in December 2001 did the first signs appear of what was to come – and even then they were not taken too seriously. In December, polls showed a loss of seats first for the Liberals and then for Labour. In January LN and its leader Fortuyn had climbed to 16 seats. In the same month it was announced that Fortuyn would also be on the list of candidates in Rotterdam for the local party Livable Rotterdam. (It should be noted that the various local 'livable' parties were independent of the national party Livable Netherlands and were not branches of or otherwise formally bound to this national party.)

As the election year 2002 began, the established parties were becoming nervous. The issue of foreigners, immigration politics and asylum seekers, often combined with the crime issue, was to become top of the political agenda, not least as a result of speeches and interviews made by Pim Fortuyn. The other political parties were reacting and on the defensive. At the party congress at which Hans Dijkstal was chosen as leader of the Liberal Party, for example, there were calls for tougher talk from the leader and the party. Most newspapers noted the surge to the right by the Liberal Party in reaction to the rise of Pim Fortuyn. In the CDA, Balkenende made statements that although immigration enriched Dutch culture, communal norms and values were important. By February the polls were suggesting that Livable Netherlands might win more than 20 seats; at the same time the 'purple' governmental coalition of Labour Party, Liberal Party and the social-liberal Democrats 66 (*Democraten '66*, D66) looked in danger of losing its majority.

Because of his colourful appearance and statements and the apparently unstoppable rise in the polls, Fortuyn received extensive coverage in the media. However, on Saturday February 9, an interview was published which for a time appeared to mark the sudden and definite end of his march to power. In *de Volkskrant* he stated that Islam was a backward culture, that no new asylum seekers would be allowed, and that if necessary to protect freedom of speech the first article of the Constitution should be repealed. These remarks were contrary to the official party platform and also contrary to what had been agreed upon between Fortuyn and the campaign staff of Livable Netherlands. This bombshell led the leadership of Livable Netherlands to dismiss him one day later as the leader for the elections. Fortuyn himself, however, claimed in a television interview: 'I have a mission, I have a job to do. I will continue.' Some of his supporters immediately took the initiative to found a new political party, which was to become the List Pim Fortuyn (*Lijst Pim Fortuyn*, LPF). To the surprise of many observers, who had always held the opinion that Dutch voters voted for a party and not for a candidate, polls showed that even before he had a (new) party and a list of candidates or official party manifesto, support for Livable Netherlands was transferring to Fortuyn.

In municipal elections on March 6 Livable Rotterdam, on which party list Fortuyn was still number one, became the largest party in the local council with the support of more than one third of the total vote in the city. At the first television meeting between Fortuyn and the other national party leaders, in the late night of election day, the former beamed with his success, while in particular Melkert but also Dijkstal sat slouched in their chairs with long faces. During the remainder of the campaign, neither was fully able to shake these images of 'losers' from the memories of the voters. In a reaction to the municipal elections, *de Volkskrant* (7.3.2002) spoke of a 'surge to the right' in which voters were sensitive to the 'simplistic' solutions that were being offered by Fortuyn in areas such as healthcare waiting lists, asylum seekers, and education.

After the municipal elections, the campaign centred as much on Fortuyn as on the issues. In debates, only Paul Rosenmöller of GreenLeft (*GroenLinks*, GL) seemed able to respond to him, while Balkenende generally stayed out of the firing line. The List Pim Fortuyn reached a peak of 29 seats in the polls, but also showed the first signs of slippage. On 12 April *De Telegraaf*, by far the largest newspaper in the Netherlands, published a selection of answers from its readers concerning what was wrong with governmental policy. 'Hundreds of readers indicate that they are not dissatisfied with Purple in terms of financial policy, but because in their eyes the Cabinet has failed in other areas, particularly asylum seekers, crime, health care and education. There is also general disgust with indecent, improper behavior and the slippage of values.'

Two days later, on 14 April, Prime Minister Kok rather surprisingly announced that he had submitted the resignation of the Cabinet to the Queen. Collectively they took responsibility for the events in Sebrenica (Bosnia) in the early 1990s. His resignation came in reaction to the publication of a scientific report on the events. Somewhat surprisingly there was almost no reaction to this resignation by voters, as measured by the election polls.

But there were even more dramatic events to come. As early as February it had been reported in the media that Fortuyn did not dare appear in public because he had been threatened. In March he was the victim of an attack by pie-throwing activists at the launch of his new book 'The Mess of Eight Years Purple' (*De puinhopen van acht jaar Paars*). Despite such incidents, the authorities never felt there was enough reason to provide extra protection for Fortuyn and he himself never formally requested it. Nevertheless on Monday May 6, a week before the elections, the country was appalled to learn on the early evening news that Pim Fortuyn had been murdered. He had been shot at close range outside a radio studio. The campaign was stopped at once and began again only half-heartedly after the funeral. Some even suggested that the elections should be postponed. Pieter Langendam, one of the founders of the LPF, stated that the 'left' was guilty of the murder of Fortuyn and fingers were pointed in particular at Melkert and Rosenmöller. This even further poisoned the electoral atmosphere.

On the evening of May 15, when the dust had settled and the votes were counted the results differed from the final published polls. The losses by the Labour and Liberal parties were the largest ever suffered: Labour fell from 45 seats in 1998 to 23 seats, the Liberal party from 38 to 24. The CDA, which had been in disarray in September of the previous year, emerged as the largest party (43 seats, compared to 29 in 1998) and Balkenende became the prime candidate for prime minister. The LPF – not yet a proper political party, and with its leader and only well-known candidate killed one week before the elections – received 17% of the vote and 26 seats in Parliament. This was a record number of seats for a new party; the largest number that a new party had previously achieved at its first national election was 7 (D66, in 1967).

Analysis

There are many questions surrounding this election that will occupy researchers for some time, including what contributed to the disastrous results for the governmental parties and what accounted for the strong revival of the Christian Democrats – their second unexpected revival, the first having been the electoral success in the mid-1980s under the political leadership of Ruud Lubbers. Nevertheless one question stands out above all others. How did a party that was not a political party in any proper sense, whose list of candidates had only just met – if they had – and whose leader was deceased, achieve the most spectacular results ever by a first-time list and become the second largest party in the country? This question and the attempt to find an answer to it will be the focus of this article. Who were the LPF voters and what led them to cast their votes for this party?

The analysis will be based on the results of the 2002 Dutch Parliamentary Election Study (DPES). One difficulty with the 2002 DPES that emerged immediately was a fairly severe under representation of the LPF vote. Whereas the LPF received 17% of the vote, only 10.6% of the DPES sample reported casting such a vote. What accounts for this under representation and what effect it has (if any) on the relationships investigated here is not and maybe will never be known. Because of this under-representation, in examining the results presented, it will be necessary to concentrate on the strength of relationships more than on the precise levels of LPF support.

Demographics

The search for an answer to the central question of this article can begin by examining the social or demographic characteristics of LPF voters. The percentages voting for the LPF broken down by age, sex, social class, income, education, religion and church attendance are presented in Table 1. This table shows that support for the LPF did not come from any specific social group or part of the electorate. There are relationships between these social characteristics and the vote, but some are not statistically significant (age, subjective social class, income) and the strength of the significant relationships is rather moderate. Gender gaps have not often been found among Dutch voters, but there is one in this case. Table 1 shows a gap of six percentage points between men and women, with men more likely to vote for the LPF. Thus, whereas one could have imagined that the flamboyant, homosexual life style of Pim Fortuyn might have turned off male voters, maybe his aggressive manner and the message he conveyed had a special appeal to them.

TABLE 1
DEMOGRAPHIC CHARACTERISTICS AND THE VOTE FOR THE LPF, 2002 (%)

	Vote for the LPF	N=
Age		
18-25 years	14	84
26-45 years	10	496
46-65 years	10	617
66 years and older	12	317
Total	11 [not significant]	1514
Sex		
male	14	732
female	8	782
Total	11 [sig. < .01]	1514
Subjective social class		
upper class	7	54
upper middle class	7	340
regular middle class	12	840
upper working class	10	69
regular working class	13	172
Total	11 [not significant]	1514
Income		
high	7	357
middle	11	591
low	12	389
will not say	13	177
Total	11 [not significant]	1514
Education		
high	5	517
middle	13	701
low	13	293
Total	11 [sig. < .01]	1511
Religious preference		
Roman Catholic	11	381
Dutch reformed	7	190
Gereformeerd	4	141
other	9	69
none	13	728
Total	11 [sig. < .01]	1509
Church attendance		
weekly	3	206
2-3 time per month	9	94
monthly	3	79
a few times a year	9	302
(almost) never	14	832
Total	11 [sig. < .01]	1513

Three variables that are related to the social class or social position of voters also indicate very modest relationships. In general, the percentages voting for the LPF are lower among those with higher levels of education, higher levels of income, and those who consider themselves upper middle class or higher class. However, there are LPF voters in these groups and the percentages voting LPF are only a few percentage points lower than in middle or lower groups. The relationship with class and income is not statistically significant. Finally, the appeal of the LPF to Protestant voters was less than among Catholics and those with no religious preference. Fortuyn was himself Catholic and the mass held at his funeral was broadcast nationally. It is hard to know whether this had a direct impact on voters. Regular church attendance seems to have acted as a barrier to voting for the LPF; we know that voters who go to church regularly are very loyal supporters of the confessional parties.

Change in the Electorate

With such major changes in the electoral outcome, it is understandable that many early comments on the results concentrated on presumed major shifts of opinion in the electorate. A 'surge to the right', as one major newspaper called it, indicated not only that the results brought success for this new party that was seen as a party of the right, but that the electorate had shifted to the right in its views (*NRC Handelsblad*, 16.05.2002). It is therefore rather surprising to see in the results from the 2002 DPES that this was *not* the case. In Table 2, the distribution of self-placement on a left–right scale, a straightforward indicator of any possible shift to the right, is compared for the election years 1994, 1998 and 2002.

The results from the last three election studies reveal almost complete stability in the distribution of the electorate along the left–right scale. The results from the 1994 10-point scale are almost identical with those from 1998, whereas the results for the 11-point scale of 1998 differ only a little with those in 2002. And the slight differences in percentages are to a degree accounted for by the lower percentage in 2002 who were unable or unwilling to place themselves on the scale.

No surge to the right is found in terms of how voters perceived themselves along the left–right scale. There is nevertheless the possibility that shifts had occurred with respect to specific political issues and that the electorate had moved to the right along these issues. After some of the early statements by Fortuyn and in particular after the notorious interview in *de Volkskrant* that led to his break with Livable Netherlands, he was strongly associated with restrictive viewpoints on allowing asylum seekers into the country and demanding that immigrants adhere to Dutch values. If the surge

TABLE 2
DISTRIBUTION OF LEFT–RIGHT SELF-PLACEMENT, 1994–2002

	10-point scale		11-point scale	
	1994	1998	1998	2002
	%	%	%	%
Left				
1	4	2	1	1
2	4	4	3	3
3	11	12	6	8
4	11	14	13	13
5	14	15	12	13
6	14	16	21	19
7	13	16	11	11
8	12	11	14	16
9	2	2	8	11
10	4	1	2	3
11			2	2
Right				
Do not know/ no answer	11	7	8	2
N=	1812	1814	2101	1574

to the right can be found, then surely it would be found on such issues. The Dutch national election studies have asked respondents to place themselves with respect to a number of political issues. There is a core set of issues that is asked in each survey. Additional questions may be posed depending upon the political context of the particular election. Table 3 presents placements on various issue scales, where possible for the past three elections. The two classic issue dimensions, secular versus religious and the socio-economic left–right, are represented by the issues of euthanasia (see Table 3a) and income differences (3b). In both cases the shift in opinion is quite limited. There seems to have been a slight shift away from the most liberal position on euthanasia, which might be the result of the new law passed in 2001 and the debate surrounding its passage. But the change is within the most liberal positions and hardly qualifies as a surge to the right. In the case of whether governmental policy should be oriented towards making the differences in incomes larger or smaller, the shift in the period 1994–2002 is again minimal. And to the extent that any shift can be observed on this socio-economic issue, it is in the direction of a swing to the left and not to the right.

Some scholars have, following Ronald Inglehart, referred to a new issue dimension, often called the post-materialist dimension. The issue in the Dutch election studies that would seem to come closest to representing this

TABLE 3
ATTITUDES TOWARDS POLITICAL ISSUES, 1994–2002 (%)

(a) Attitudes towards euthanasia

	Forbid euthanasia					Allow if patient desires			
	1	2	3	4	5	6	7	dk/na	N
1994	8	4	4	9	13	25	34	3	1812
1998	8	5	5	10	17	26	28	1	2101
2002	9	6	4	12	17	28	24	1	1906

(b) Attitudes towards income differences

	Should be larger					Should be smaller			
	1	2	3	4	5	6	7		
1994	7	8	11	24	14	14	18	4	1812
1998	3	5	8	23	19	20	20	2	2101
2002	2	4	9	28	21	20	14	1	1906

(c) Attitudes towards nuclear power plants

	Should build more					Never build			
	1	2	3	4	5	6	7		
1994	5	7	7	14	10	15	36	6	1812
1998	2	4	8	15	12	18	34	7	1814
2002	7	8	8	14	9	14	38	2	1574

(d) Attitudes towards treatment of criminals

	1994: Tough enough 2002: Is too tough					Should be tougher			
	1	2	3	4	5	6	7		
1994	7	5	6	10	12	21	39	2	1812
2002	1	2	3	10	21	30	33	1	1906

(e) Attitudes towards asylum seekers

	Should allow more					Should send back			
	1	2	3	4	5	6	7		
1998	4	10	12	31	18	13	11	2	2101
2002	2	7	11	29	21	16	12	1	1906

(f) Attitudes towards immigrants and integration

	May preserve customs					Should assimilate			
	1	2	3	4	5	6	7		
1994	5	7	9	19	15	17	26	2	1812
1998	3	8	11	21	21	18	16	1	2101
2002	2	5	9	16	19	26	23	1	1574

dimension is attitudes towards building nuclear power plants. After the accident in Chernobyl in 1986 attitudes towards nuclear energy shifted dramatically. Since then the Dutch electorate has steadfastly opposed building new nuclear plants. Table 3c shows that these attitudes have not changed over the past three elections. In 2002 the electorate was as opposed as ever.

A popular theme on the right has been the question of how tough the government has been and should be on criminals. There were indications that personal safety was an issue of concern in the 2002 election. The political commentator of *De Telegraaf* saw law and order and the fighting of crime as the issue of the election (16.5.2002). One out of five respondents in the DPES 2002 mentioned this as the most important national problem facing the Netherlands. Table 3d indeed shows a trend away from the feeling that the government is too tough in its treatment of prisoners. Whereas in 1994 18% of the sample placed themselves on this side of the scale (based on a slightly different wording of the question, however), in 2002 this had been reduced to only 6%. The shift, however, is not to the most extreme position for which the percentage has actually dropped from 39% to 33%, but in the two positions just right of centre. Although it might be concluded that there was a shift to the right, it was hardly a surge.

Finally, results are presented for two questions that were posed with respect to the influx and integration of foreigners in the country (3e and 3f). One referred to whether the government should be more lenient and allow more asylum seekers to enter the country versus sending as many as possible back, whereas the second referred to whether immigrants and ethnic minorities should be allowed to preserve their own customs or fully assimilate into Dutch society and culture. Opinions among the electorate were indeed more anti-immigrant in 2002 than at the two preceding elections of 1994 and 1998, with more being of the opinion that immigrants should assimilate into Dutch society. The percentage taking the tougher positions (points 5, 6 and 7) was 10 percentage points higher than in 1994 and 13 higher than in 1998. In light of the events of 11 September 2001 this shift is perhaps important but hardly sufficient to have caused the major shakeup at the election. The question that seems more directly related to possible support for the LPF, whether to allow more asylum-seekers or send as many as possible back, shows an even smaller rise from 42% to 49% on the more anti-immigrant side of the scale.

So, in none of the issues included in the DPES can there be said to be a clear surge to the right. Granted, the shifts that have occurred are possibly strongest in terms of personal safety and anti-immigrant issues, but they are not so great as to indicate that it was a major change in the electoral market that accounted for the dramatic election results of 15 May 2002. One of the appeals of Fortuyn seems to have been the fact that he was an outsider in politics. He offended and ridiculed the bureaucrats and 'established' politicians in The Hague – the location of the Second Chamber and the government. Thus, rather than an appeal based upon issue or ideological position, it is possible that there had been a shift in attitude by an electorate that had become more cynical and detached from politics and politicians.

TABLE 4A

LEVELS OF POLITICAL CYNICISM, 1994–2002 (%)

	High			Low	N
1994	18	31	44	7	1527
1998	18	27	44	11	1814
2002	22	32	39	7	1574

Note: The political cynicism score is based on the responses to the following statements:
  Although they know better, politicians promise more than they can deliver.
  Ministers and state secretaries are primarily concerned about their personal interests.
  One is more likely to become a member of parliament because of one's political friends than because of one's abilities.

TABLE 4B

LEVELS OF POLITICAL EFFICACY, 1994–2002 (%)

	Low				High	N
1994	5	22	19	22	31	1527
1998	6	19	18	22	36	1814
2002	5	24	21	21	29	1574

Note: The political efficacy score is based on the responses to the following statements:
  Members of parliament do not care about the opinions of people like me.
  Political parties are only interested in my vote and not in my opinion.
  People like me have absolutely no influence in governmental policy.
  So many people vote in elections that my vote does not matter.

To examine this, possible changes in cynicism and political efficacy between 1994 and 2002 are examined in Tables 4A and 4B. The top two points on the cynicism scale are 9 percentage points higher in 2002 than in 1998 and 5 points higher than in 1994. The measure of efficacy declined by 8 points at the highest levels between 1998 and 2002 and was 3 points lower than in 1994. These are both in the direction that is predicted by this explanation of Fortuyn and LPF support – but do not amount to a shift of the magnitude that would explain the dramatic election results and a gain of 26 seats.

The governing parties (Labour, Liberal Party and D66) intended to base their campaign in 2002 on their economic achievements, sometimes referred to as the 'Dutch Miracle'. Such a strategy had been successful in

1998, at least for two of the cooperating parties, and had led to gains in seats for both the Labour and Liberal parties. The same strategy failed miserably in 2002 as both parties suffered dramatic losses and received fewer seats in Parliament than either the Christian Democrats or the LPF. Table 5(a–c) shows, however, that these losses did not occur because of a major shift in attitudes towards governmental performance in the economy. Dutch voters had been quite negative concerning governmental performance in 1994, feeling that the government had had an unfavourable impact on the economy, on employment, and on their personal finances. These attitudes turned around dramatically in 1998, when solid majorities of the electorate did indeed feel that the government had had a favourable impact on reducing unemployment and on the economy in general. More voters also felt the impact on their own personal finances had been positive. If anything, attitudes towards the governmental economic policy seem to have been even more positive in 2002 than in 1998. Thus for this election at least the Clinton campaign slogan of 1992 must be altered to read, 'It's *not* the economy, stupid'. The governing parties had every reason to expect that they would again be rewarded by the voters. But in 2002 voters apparently had become accustomed to these achievements. The parties had already received their rewards in 1998. In 2002 voters seemed more interested in issues other than the economy.

TABLE 5
EVALUATION OF GOVERNMENTAL ECONOMIC PERFORMANCE, 1994–2002 (%)

(a) *Effects of governmental performance on general economy*

	Favourable	Unfavourable	Neither	Dk/na	N
1994	14	32	42	11	1812
1998	58	8	31	4	2101
2002	52	11	35	2	1907

(b) *Effects of governmental performance on employment*

	Favourable	Unfavourable	Neither	Dk/na	N
1994	8	54	32	6	1812
1998	62	12	24	3	2101
2002	66	10	22	2	1907

(c) *Effects of governmental performance on personal finances*

	Favourable	Unfavourable	Neither	Dk/na	N
1994	13	37	46	4	1812
1998	26	23	49	2	2101
2002	35	18	45	2	1907

TABLE 6
GENERAL SATISFACTION WITH GOVERNMENTAL PERFORMANCE, 1994–2202 (%)

	Very satisfied	Satisfied	Not (un)satisfied	Unsatisfied	Very unsatisfied	Dk/na	N
1994	0	18	49	27	4	2	1812
1998	1	43	41	11	1	2	2101
2002	1	33	43	19	3	1	1907

However, these results should not be taken to indicate that the electorate was fully satisfied with governmental performance. Table 6 shows that general satisfaction with the government had dropped by 10 percentage points between 1998 and 2002. This is still considerably higher than the level of satisfaction in 1994, in which year the parties in government (Labour, CDA) lost heavily at the elections, but it does indicate that something was beginning to bother the electorate.

Issues and the Vote

Based upon the above analyses we must reject any explanation of the 2002 election results that centres upon a major surge to the right among the Dutch electorate.[2] In terms of left–right self-placement and on the stands taken on various important political issues, shifts in opinion are moderate, if there are any significant shifts at all. The electorate had not become hugely more cynical or less efficacious. Nor did the voters view governmental performance in the area of the economy unfavourably, although there was some rise in general dissatisfaction with the government.

However, the fact that the election results cannot be accounted for on the basis of shifts in attitudes and opinions of the electorate by no means implies that there is no relationship between these opinions and the vote cast. In almost all cases there is in fact a statistically significant relationship between an issue attitude and voting for the LPF. For example, the LPF clearly had a stronger appeal to voters who saw themselves to the right of the left–right scale, with Table 7 showing a difference of 17 percentage points between the left and right in propensity to vote LPF. Given this, we would also expect LPF voters to be found to the 'right' on the various issues. Table 8, which reports the percentage voting LPF for each position along the issue scale, shows that this is in general the case.

The relationship between issue positions and the LPF vote is weakest for euthanasia and nuclear power plants. The highest percentage on the euthanasia scale is actually for the more liberal, rather than the more conservative position, and on the nuclear power plants issue the differences

TABLE 7
LEFT–RIGHT SELF-PLACEMENT AND VOTE FOR THE LPF, 2002

	Left (positions 1–4)	Centre (positions 5–5)	Right (positions 8–11)	Total
%LPF	2	9	19	11
N=	355	656	482	1493

TABLE 8
ISSUES AND THE LPF VOTE, 2002 (%)

Issues	Forbid euthanasia	Income differences greater	Send refugees back	Govt harder on criminals	Build more nuclear energy plants	Foreigners must assimilate	European integration gone too far
1.	3	29	37	21	17	24	19
2.	5	24	20	9	17	12	18
3.	13	13	8	3	13	6	9
4.	7	10	4	2	11	4	10
5.	9	9	1	7	10	2	6
6.	9	9	1	4	7	3	7
7.	20	10	0	13	9	4	10
	Allow if patient desires	Income differences smaller	Allow more refugees	Govt too hard on criminals	No new plants	Foreigners retain customs	Further European integration

between the percentages are fairly modest. Although it was not discussed above, the question of European integration is included here. On this scale the differences between percentages for the LPF do not differ greatly, certainly as compared to the differences on the other issues. Even on the traditional left–right issue of income differences, the percentage voting for the LPF is 19 or 20 points higher for the most extreme right position as compared to the leftist positions. Those who take the toughest position on the treatment of criminals scale are also considerably more likely to vote for the LPF than those with other opinions.

However, it is on issues with respect to immigrants that the votes differ the most. Those on the side of allowing immigrants to retain their own cultural customs or who feel the government should be more tolerant in allowing asylum seekers into the country hardly ever cast a vote for the LPF. By contrast, those taking the two most restrictive opinions on these issues were far more inclined to vote for the party. The highest percentage casting a vote for the LPF – 37%! – is found among those who feel as many as possible asylum seekers should be sent back to their country of origin. Clearly issues involving immigrants, but also more traditional opinions concerning differences in incomes and treatment of criminals, were important factors in leading people to cast a vote for the LPF. The following tables indicate that these opinions often were combined with a low level of political efficacy and high level of cynicism about whether they were being heard in The Hague. Table 9A indicates that as political cynicism increases, the vote for the LPF rises substantially, whereas Table 9B reveals that fully 42% of the LPF voters in the 2002 sample had the highest level of cynicism, as compared to only 18% among voters for other parties. The same pattern is found for political efficacy (Tables 10A and 10B). Those with the lowest level of efficacy cast votes for the LPF at far higher percentages than did

TABLE 9A
CYNICISM AND LPF VOTE, 2002 (%)

	High			Low	Total
% LPF	22	10	6	4	11
N=	312	480	607	115	1514

TABLE 9B
CYNICISM OF LPF VOTERS, 2002 (%)

	LPF voters	Other voters	Total
High cynicism	42	18	21
	31	32	32
	24	42	40
Low cynicism	3	8	8
N=	162	1352	1514

TABLE 10A
POLITICAL EFFICACY AND LPF VOTE, 2002 (%)

	Low				High	Total
% LPF	30	17	11	7	6	11
N=	66	364	308	324	427	1514

TABLE 10B
EFFICACY OF LPF VOTERS, 2002 (%)

Efficacy	LPF voters	Other voters	Total
Low	12	3	4
	37	23	24
	20	20	20
	15	22	21
High	15	32	30
N=	162	1352	1514

those with a high level of efficacy. Almost half of the LPF voters are found within the two lowest levels of political efficacy, as compared to only just over one quarter of those with the highest levels.

Although majorities of the electorate felt that government performance had had a favourable effect on the economy and employment, there were those who felt the effect had been unfavourable. These persons were more likely to vote for the LPF, as were those who thought that government performance had had an unfavourable impact on their personal finances. These results are seen in Table 11 (a–c). However, the differences are modest, again indicating that government economic performance was not uppermost in the minds of the voters in 2002. General satisfaction with the government does, though, appear to have a strong relationship with the LPF vote (see Table 12). Of those who were 'very satisfied' with government performance over the previous four years, none (of the 15 respondents) voted for the LPF and the percentage among those who were satisfied was quite low. On the other hand, among those who were dissatisfied with government performance, substantial numbers cast a vote for the LPF.

TABLE 11

EVALUATION OF GOVERNMENTAL ECONOMIC PERFORMANCE AND LPF VOTE,
2002 (%)

(a) Evaluation of effect on general economy

	Favourable	Unfavourable	Neither	Dk/na	total
%LPF	7	18	14	7	11
N=	789	166	521	28	1513

(b) Evaluation of effect on employment

	Favourable	Unfavourable	Neither	Dk/na	total
%LPF	8	20	14	11	11
N=	1017	147	322	28	1514

(c) Evaluation of effect on personal finances

	Favourable	Unfavourable	Neither	Dk/na	total
%LPF	7	16	11	10	11
N=	527	283	681	20	1511

TABLE 12

GENERAL SATISFACTION WITH GOVERNMENT PERFORMANCE AND LPF VOTE
(%)

	Very satisfied	Satisfied	Not (un)satisfied	Unsatisfied	Very unsatisfied	Dk/na	Total
%LPF	0	5	8	24	30	13	11
N=	15	510	647	287	47	8	1514

Conclusion

Although further research is certainly in order, the picture that emerges from this analysis of the support for the new kid in town, Fortuyn and his List Pim Fortuyn, is becoming quite clear. There was no great surge to the right among the Dutch electorate in 2002. Voters had pretty much the same opinions that they had held over the previous two elections. If one tries to think in Downsian terms, there is little change in the distribution of opinions among the electorate. Shifts in opinions do not account for the change in electoral outcome. The difference is not on the demand side, i.e. the opinions the electorate wishes to see implemented, but on the supply side, i.e. the parties from which they may choose.

For many elections the traditional parties of the Netherlands operated almost as a cartel, with a stranglehold on the party space. A protest party on the left, the Socialist Party, was able to mobilize some of the frustration of the electorate, but did not appeal to those who held the most rightist positions on issues such as treatment of criminals and immigrants. During the period 1994–98, the Liberal leader Frits Bolkestein used his position in the parliament to make just enough strong statements, particularly on the latter issue, to keep voters behind his party. However, between 1998 and 2002, the new leader, Hans Dijkstal, was quiet on this issue. His silence, and the party's eight-year cooperation with the Labour Party and D66, opened up space on the right for a new party. Pim Fortuyn was the appropriate catalyst to mobilize all those voters with rightist positions who were frustrated that their voice was not being heard in The Hague. Indeed when asked why they voted for the LPF, one-third mentioned the party programme and ideas, and one-third mentioned a desire to shake the country up, get rid of the Cabinet or similar, related responses.

Epilogue

After the unique success of the List Pim Fortuyn at the election of May 2002, the question arose whether the party should be included in a new government coalition. Both because of this spectacular success and because it controlled approximately one-sixth of the seats in the Second Chamber of Parliament, it would have been difficult *not* to have included it in the new government. Having again become the largest party, the CDA assumed a leading role in the Cabinet formation process and eventually supplied the new Prime Minister, Jan Peter Balkenende. The Liberal party had lost heavily and briefly indicated that it did not wish to be included in the negotiations. However, this opposition quickly evaporated and the party joined the new coalition of Christian Democrats, Liberals, and List Pim Fortuyn.

The members of the parliamentary caucus of the List Pim Fortuyn had hardly known each other before the election and certainly had never functioned as a political party. To supply Cabinet ministers they had to rely upon individuals who until their appointment (and in at least one case even afterwards) had been members of other political parties. With their leader having been assassinated, the party suffered seriously from a lack of leadership. The leader who had conducted the Cabinet formation negotiations was replaced, but later returned after his successor was dismissed. Two members of the caucus were expelled and formed their own group in parliament, as did the dismissed party leader. The internal difficulties suffered by the party became daily news and the party became a laughing stock.

The internal problems eventually reached the Cabinet, where Minister of Health Bomhoff and Minister of Economics Heinsbroek clashed openly. They were forced to resign on 16 October 2002, but this was not enough to convince the other partners in the coalition to continue. Liberal leader Zalm was most open in his lack of confidence in the coalition and 'pulled the plug', forcing the Cabinet to submit its resignation to the Queen on October 17. It had served only 87 days. At that time, public opinion polls indicated that support for the List Pim Fortuyn had fallen to less than 5 seats and that the CDA and Liberal parties could win a small overall majority. New elections were called for 22 January 2003. The Labour Party staged a dramatic resurgence and recovered 19 of the 22 seats that had been lost in May. The CDA won a single extra seat and the Liberal Party won four more seats, but these were not enough to control a majority of the Parliament. Although the LPF lost substantially, it did somewhat better than had been anticipated and maintained 8 of its 26 seats. The flames of protest had been rapidly dampened, but not entirely distinguished.

NOTES

1. This contribution is solely based on newspaper reports and the Dutch Parliamentary Elections Study 2002. For this reason no references to the literature on voting and electoral behaviour in the Netherlands in general, or the general elections of 2002 in particular, are made. For a later and more general account of the parliamentary elections of May 2002 and the support for the List Pim Fortuyn, see Joop J.M. Van Holsteyn and Galen A. Irwin, 'Never a Dull Moment', *West European Politics* 26 (2003).

2. All relationships presented in this section are statistically significant at .01, with the exception of the relation between the attitude towards nuclear plants and the LPF vote, which is significant at .05.

DEVOLUTION

Government for the English Regions? An Examination of the Basis of Support for Constitutional Changes

Anthony Heath, Catherine Rothon and Lindsey Jarvis

Centre and Periphery

With the rise of Scottish and Welsh nationalism in the 1970s, and the subsequent debates over devolution, it has become conventional to think of Britain (strictly the UK) as a multinational state, and a great deal of research has focused on differences between England, Wales and Scotland (see, for example, Taylor and Thomson, 1999). However, as Steed (1986, S92) has cogently argued, 'There is much evidence that this trichotomous organization of the data and of research has simplified reality in a misleading way.' In place of this trichotomous view, he has suggested an analysis based on the notions of core and periphery, with a more graduated set of distinctions within both core and periphery. Thus he distinguishes an inner core of London and the South East, an outer core of the Midlands, East Anglia and Wessex, an inner periphery of the North of England, Wales and the Southwest peninsula, and an outer periphery of Scotland, which 'correspond reasonably well with arcs drawn around London at 80, 200 and 300 miles' (Steed, 1986, S99). He suggests that there is a gradation in political attitudes and behaviour as we move from the inner core to the outer periphery, rather than a sharp contrast between England on the one hand and Scotland and Wales on the other. The aim of this article is to investigate these differences within England and to test how useful the concepts of core and periphery are in understanding regional variation in England.

The theoretical ideas lying behind the core–periphery dimension are not always clearly articulated. (For a good overview see Wellhofer, 1989). We can distinguish several different versions but common to them all is the claim that cores are advantaged and peripheries economically disadvantaged. The periphery is thought of as being less developed, involving primary economies, with low technology and labour-intensive activities (Rokkan and Urwin, 1982, 1983).

Unequal political power is a second key element and one that is often, as by Hechter (1975), used to explain the economic inequalities. Thus the core is seen to be the locus of political power, and the implication is that the interests of the periphery therefore receive less recognition than those of the core. An extreme case of this would be one where the core has expanded its power from its original territorial base and colonized the peripheral regions, and this is the essence of Hechter's concept of 'internal colonialism'. However, while this extreme case might be applicable to the relations between England and the other territories of the UK, it is not self-evidently applicable to relations within England.

Thirdly, there are expected to be cultural differences between core and periphery. The core is seen to be the cultural centre and to be culturally dominant. The peripheral regions are seen to have local cultures that are fragmented from each other and linked through the core rather than directly to each other. Following Merton's ([1949] 1957) distinction between locals and cosmopolitans, we might expect peripheral regions to have a greater proportion of people with primarily local attachments while cosmopolitans, oriented towards national or international concerns, would be more common at the centre.

These three aspects of core–periphery inequalities imply that members of the periphery are likely to accord the core lower support and legitimacy and to be less satisfied with existing economic and political arrangements. They may show less support for national symbols since these will tend to be identified with the core. This kind of reasoning has been used to explain support for separatist movements in peripheral territories such as Scotland and Wales, although most theories would emphasize the importance of having a distinct ethnic or national group in the peripheral region to form the focus of the separatist movement. In the case of peripheral regions within England, therefore, we would not expect to find anything like the pressures for political change or devolution that have been seen in Scotland or Wales. However, where there are distinct regional cultural identities we may find some pressure for political reform. In short, then, we expect the same kinds of relationships that occur between England and the other three territories of the UK to be apparent, albeit in a weakened form, in the relationships between the core region of England (which we take to be London and the South East) and the more peripheral regions.

Our expectations, then, following from these accounts of centre/periphery relations, are that the peripheral regions in England will tend to be economically disadvantaged; they will show lower levels of support for central, core political institutions; and, where there are distinct regional cultures, they will also show higher levels of support for regional devolution.

These analytical concerns have added interest in the context of current debates about regional government for England. The proposal for regional assemblies appears to be based on an analogy with the new Scottish and

Welsh institutions and to assume that there are distinct interests and/or identities in the English regions analogous to the distinct claims made by the Welsh and Scots. The arguments in favour of regional assemblies seem to involve both economic and political aspects. Economically, it is implied that regions may have distinct local interests (perhaps for inward investment or for economic regeneration) that diverge to some degree from those of the country as a whole. Politically, it is suggested that regional assemblies would provide greater local accountability for regional institutions that are currently answerable only to Westminster. The new White Paper (Office of the Deputy Prime Minister 2002) emphasizes the way in which the proposed assemblies can cater for regional diversity. If on the other hand England is indeed homogeneous, both economically and culturally, it is less clear what useful role there is for regional assemblies and one suspects that there will be less demand for them.

To explore these issues we use data from a module fielded in the British Social Attitudes Survey 2001 as part of the ESRC's Devolution and Constitutional Change Programme. The module was administered only to respondents resident in England and our sample therefore consists solely of residents in England, not the full BSA sample. Full technical details of the sample and questionnaire are available in the report on the BSA 2001 (Park et al., 2002, Appendix I).

We begin by examining the differences between the English regions with respect to their economic situation, cultural differences and support for central and local political institutions. The analysis here utilizes the Government Office Regions classification. This corresponds exactly with the areas covered by the main current institutions, namely Regional Development Agencies (RDAs) and Regional Chambers, which are likely to be the basis of any future regional assemblies. Regional Development Agencies were launched in eight English regions in 1999. The ninth, in London, was established in 2000 following the formation of the Greater London Authority (GLA). Their aim is to coordinate regional economic development and regeneration, enable the English regions to improve their relative competitiveness, and reduce the imbalances that exist within and between regions.

Regional Chambers were set up shortly after the creation of RDAs. There is a Regional Chamber for each of the RDAs outside London. They comprise voluntary groupings of councillors from local authorities in the region and representatives of sectors with a stake in the region's economic, social and environmental well-being. They generally include representatives from business; education and training; the voluntary, cultural and environmental protection sectors; and the trade unions. Each RDA consults its Chamber on strategy and other key documents such as the annual report and the corporate plan. In addition, the RDA is expected to supply its Chamber with information and to give an account of itself to the Chamber. Government Offices (GOs) continue to be the arm of Government in the regions and have a number of responsibilities, including housing, planning and transport. They are encouraged to work closely with the RDAs.

Economic Differences

We start by looking at official measures of regional economic differences. The first column of Table 1 shows gross disposable household income for the English regions, grouped under Steed's headings of inner core, outer core and inner periphery. We see that the regions broadly fit into Steed's model. London and the South East certainly belong to the inner core with per capita income well above the English average. However, the East region would appear better placed in the inner core rather than in the outer core where Steed located it. This may be because the data shown in the table are for a region covering not only the more peripheral areas of East Anglia (which is what Steed had in mind) but also the London-oriented southern parts, such as Hertfordshire, Bedfordshire and Essex. The distinction between outer core and inner periphery does not work particularly well on this economic criterion: there is little difference between the two other regions of the outer core – the East and West Midlands – and the regions of the inner periphery. It is only really the North East that is clearly less advantaged economically.

There are, then, a number of anomalies that do not fit well into Steed's overall categorization, loosely based on distance from London. To be sure London and its environs stand out as the inner core, but the distinctions between outer core and inner periphery do not look quite so convincing. On the other hand Steed is right to reject a simple trichotomous model of England, Wales and Scotland. There are clearly major regional variations within England, and in economic terms they are greater than the variations between England, Wales, Scotland and Northern Ireland. Thus within the UK per capital household income varies from a high of £10,237 in England to a low of £8659 in Northern Ireland, a range of around £1500, but within England it varies from a high of £12036 in London to a low of £8353 in the North East, a range of over £3500.

These official economic measures are reflected in the reports provided by our survey respondents. Respondents were asked to select their gross household income from a set of banded options. Column 2 of Table 1 shows the percentages who reported that they had household incomes of less than £8,000. These self-report figures of low income in fact follow Steed's

TABLE 1
ECONOMIC ASPECTS OF THE CORE AND PERIPHERY

	Gross disposable household income per capita £	% with income <£8,000p.a.	% finding it difficult on current income	Base N (columns 2 and 3)
Inner core				
London	12,036	12	21	299
South East	11,249	10	10	394
Outer core				
East	11,255	14	11	292
East Midlands	9,346	13	13	217
West Midlands	9,195	14	17	254
Inner periphery				
North East	8,353	21	10	169
North West	9,375	16	14	301
Yorkshire and Humber	9,305	18	13	281
South West	9,825	14	15	243
England	10,237	15	14	2450

Sources: Column 1, National Statistics (2001); columns 2 and 3, BSA Survey 2001.

distinctions between inner core, outer core and periphery rather better than do the official figures of average household income. London and the South East have the lowest proportions; the inner periphery (with the exception of the South West) has the highest proportion with incomes below £8,000, and the outer core lies in between.

However, our third measure in Table 1 tells a very different story. Respondents were asked to choose a phrase to describe how they were currently managing on their household's income. In Column 3 we report the percentages who reported that they were 'finding it difficult' or 'finding it very difficult on their present income'. There is no clear-cut regional variation. Indeed London has the highest proportion who reported that they were finding it difficult or very difficult to manage on their current income while the North East has the lowest proportion. This may well be because of regional differences in the cost of living, especially the cost of housing. This pattern is completely at odds with the centre/periphery concept. While theorists such as Hechter do not make it explicit, we might expect subjective feelings of economic difficulty to be rather more important than income per se in generating political dissatisfaction and demands for constitutional change. Given this evidence of lack of economic dissatisfaction in the more peripheral regions, we might begin to doubt whether there will be much political dissatisfaction in those regions.

Socio-Cultural Differences

Cultural differences are a crucial feature of many accounts of minority nationalism, and we might expect to find that they would also be important in generating demands for regional devolution too. As with economic differences, we have both objective and subjective measures. First we have behavioural measures of whether our respondents could be classified as locals or cosmopolitans. Respondents were asked whether they had ever lived anywhere other than England for more than a year. Those that had done so were also asked whether they had lived elsewhere inside or outside the UK. We define cosmopolitans as those who had lived outside the UK. Respondents were also asked how long they had lived in their present area of the country. (It was left to the respondent to determine what they meant by 'area'.) We define locals as people who had lived for more than 20 years in the same area.

An alternative approach to the measurement of locals and cosmopolitans would have been to use a battery of attitude questions to construct a Likert scale of cosmopolitan orientations – compare Heath et al.'s (1999) measure of British national sentiment. While such a measure might be very useful, and would indeed be much closer to some (but not all) of the theoretical definitions of locals and cosmopolitans, it would not be entirely appropriate in the present context. Firstly, there is a danger of circularity with the use of attitude measures: there is a risk that an attitudinal measure of localism would be hard to distinguish from our dependent variable measuring orientation to the region. We might achieve high associations but at the risk of tautology. A behavioural measure, such as the one we adopt here, has the great advantage that it is clearly distinct from our attitudinal dependent variable. It is also comparable in nature with our other predictors – region, income and so on. This makes for a much tougher test of the theory of locals and cosmopolitans. We do recognize however that a measure of cosmopolitan orientations would be valuable as a way of validating our behavioural measure.

Table 2 shows that there are clear differences between the English regions in the proportions of locals and cosmopolitans. The inner core of London and the South East clearly has the highest proportion of cosmopolitans while the three northern regions (and somewhat surprisingly the West Midlands) have the highest proportions of locals. The regions of the outer core lie in between (with the South West once again coming closer to the pattern of the outer core than of the inner periphery).

These results are paralleled by our subjective measure. Respondents were asked how much pride they had in being someone who lives in their region (with the name of their Government Office Region substituted in) or

TABLE 2
LOCATION OF LOCALS AND COSMOPOLITANS IN THE CORE AND PERIPHERY

	% who have lived outside UK	% who have lived in the area that they live in now for more than 20 years	Base N
Inner core			
London	32	44	343
South East	28	34	444
Outer core			
East	21	50	316
East Midlands	21	50	255
West Midlands	16	64	289
Inner periphery			
North East	10	55	184
North West	12	53	338
Yorkshire and Humber	12	59	302
South West	22	46	268
England	24	44	2739

Source: BSA 2001.

TABLE 3
REGIONAL PRIDE IN THE CORE AND PERIPHERY

	Very proud	Somewhat proud	Not very/ not at all proud	Don't think in that way	Base N
Inner core					
London	19	31	7	43	343
South East	8	17	3	72	447
Outer core					
East	11	13	3	73	318
East Midlands	12	21	4	62	255
West Midlands	17	20	6	58	293
Inner periphery					
North East	44	26	3	27	185
North West	34	29	3	34	342
Yorkshire and Humber	46	24	3	27	305
South West	21	21	2	56	269
England	22	22	4	52	2757

Source: BSA 2001.

whether they did not think of themselves in that way at all. The results are shown in Table 3.

Here we see a very clear pattern with much higher levels of regional pride in the three northern regions than elsewhere, while lower levels are generally found in the inner and outer core areas. Rather than a gradation from inner core to periphery, however, there does seem to be a North/South divide on this particular measure of cultural identity, with a clear break between the three northern regions and all the others, rather than a gradual pattern of increasing pride as distance increases from London.

The pattern does not accord very well with Steed's model, with the South West in particular showing a lower level of regional pride than might have been expected from its notional position in the periphery. However, the Government Office regions may not correspond particularly well with the actual geographical distribution of cultural identities. Within the South West, for example, many people may feel a strong regional identity with being 'Cornish' but may not respond to the Government Office Region descriptions used in the question, that is 'the South West of England'. The problem may be not so much in Steed's theory as in the mismatch between local identities and Government Office Regions. With the three northern regions there may well be a much better fit.

Political Responses

We turn now to the political responses of our respondents in the inner core, outer core and inner periphery. Our expectation is that respondents in the peripheral regions will show lower levels of support for central, national political institutions than will the members of the inner core. We have two sorts of measure of support for national institutions. The first is an affective measure, respondents being shown the Union Jack and Cross of St George and being asked whether the flag made them 'feel proud, hostile or not feel much either way'. Following Steed, one would expect more attachment to national symbols in the core regions as these symbols are typically identified with the core. One might also have expected that higher levels of regional pride (as we have just found in the three northern regions) might be associated with reduced levels of pride in national symbols. However, Table 4 shows that in the three northern regions levels of pride in the national flag are virtually the same as or higher than the national average for the whole of England. So there is little evidence that regional loyalties conflict with British loyalties.

TABLE 4
ATTACHMENT TO THE UNION JACK AND CROSS OF ST GEORGE
IN THE CORE AND PERIPHERY

	Proud of the Union Jack	Proud of the Cross of St George	Base N
Inner core			
London	51	35	341
South East	66	42	448
Outer core			
East	57	42	318
East Midlands	57	42	254
West Midlands	61	44	293
Inner periphery			
North East		61	42
185			
North West	58	43	342
Yorkshire and Humber	65	42	304
South West	52	31	268
England	59	40	2753

Source: BSA 2001.

Our second measure is a more conventional attitude question in which we asked respondents for their opinion on the 'present system of governing Britain'. We would again expect from Steed's viewpoint that the inner core would show more support for the existing political system and that the further we move away from London, the more people would feel remote, attitudinally as well as geographically, from the concerns of the Westminster parliament. Table 5, however, shows that there is remarkably little variation and the slight differences found would indicate that the opposite of the hypothesis holds true. Those in the peripheral Northern regions, in particular Yorkshire and Humber, were slightly *less* likely to criticize the present system of governing Britain. Other areas showed similar levels of support for change as each other, apart from the greatest concentration of discontent in the East Midlands.

However, while support for national institutions does not vary across the English regions, we do find evidence for regional variations in demands for regional assemblies. To investigate views on how England should be governed, we asked the following question:

TABLE 5
OPINIONS ABOUT THE PRESENT SYSTEM OF GOVERNING BRITAIN
IN THE CORE AND PERIPHERY

	Needs a great deal/ quite a lot of Improvement	Could be improved in small ways	Works extremely well	Base N
Inner core				
London	56	40	2	338
South East	52	45	2	443
Outer core				
East	52	45	2	314
East Midlands	61	38	0	253
West Midlands	56	41	2	291
Inner periphery				
North East	50	45	5	183
North West	49	47	2	338
Yorkshire and Humber	44	52	2	299
South West	54	42	2	264
England	52	44	2	2721

Source: BSA 2001.

'*With all the changes going on in the way the different parts of Great Britain are run, which of the following do you think would be best for England? For England to be governed as it is now, with laws made by the UK parliament*

For each region of England to have its own assembly that runs services like health

Or for England as a whole to have its own new parliament with law-making powers?'

The differences between regions are relatively small, but as Table 6 shows those who live in the periphery show greater support for regional assemblies. In all four of the inner periphery regions we find that support for regional assemblies is higher than the national average for the whole of England. This support for regional assemblies tends to come at the expense of support for an English parliament. In the South East, for example, respondents are split more or less 50:50 between these two options. In the three northern regions, in contrast, the balance is 2 to 1 in favour of regional assemblies rather than an English parliament.

TABLE 6
ATTITUDES TOWARDS CONSTITUTIONAL CHANGE IN ENGLAND
IN THE CORE AND PERIPHERY

	England to be governed as it is now	Each region of England to have its own assembly	England as a whole to have its own parliament	None, don't know	Base N
Inner core					
London	59	21	13	7	345
South East	58	19	20	3	448
Outer core					
East	60	18	19	3	318
East Midlands	49	22	20	8	256
West Midlands	60	22	13	5	293
Inner periphery					
North East	59	29	10	4	185
North West	54	28	13	5	342
Yorkshire and Humber	58	25	12	5	305
South West	54	25	19	2	269
England	57	23	16	5	2761

Source: BSA 2001.

The main conclusions we have identified so far in examining regional differences are that

• Objective economic indicators are reasonably close to Steed's core–periphery model with substantial regional variation within England. However our measure of subjective economic dissatisfaction, which is arguably more relevant to the theory, does not fit nearly so well with the core–periphery model.

• Objective measures of cosmopolitans and locals are also reasonably close to Steed's core–periphery model with much higher proportions of cosmopolitans in the inner core and higher proportions of locals in the peripheral regions. Subjective measures also exhibit regional variation with regional pride being much stronger in the three northern regions than elsewhere.

• There is no systematic core–periphery variation in a sense of attachment to national symbols or in support for the present system of British democracy and, if anything, the northern regions were more positive than others.

• There is somewhat more support for regional assemblies in the three northern regions although differences tend to be small.

Multivariate Analysis of Regional Pride and Support for Regional Assemblies

So far we have undertaken aggregate-level analyses comparing regions with respect to their economic situation, regional culture, political attitudes and support for regional assemblies. This aggregate-level analysis has suggested that the distribution of support for regional assemblies is more similar to the distribution of regional pride rather than to the distributions of the economic and political indicators. There are however well-known dangers in inspecting aggregate data. In this section, therefore, we carry out a multivariate, individual-level analysis of support for regional assemblies. Our interest is, firstly, which variables are associated with support for assemblies at the individual level and secondly which ones can account for the regional differences in the level of support for assemblies. To answer the first question we need to check whether the individual explanatory variables have significant net associations with support for assemblies. To answer the second we need to see whether the inclusion of these explanatory variables in the model accounts for the regional differences by reducing the parameter estimates for the size of the regional differences.

Before turning to support for regional assemblies we investigate the determinants of regional pride. We carry out a logistic regression distinguishing respondents who felt very proud from those who gave the other possible responses. (Strictly speaking our measure of regional pride is an ordinal one and we should use ordinal logistic regression. However, for ease of comparison with the following table, which looks at support for regional assemblies, we have preferred binary logistic regression.)

In the first model we simply include region as a predictor. This is in effect repeating the information in the original cross-tabulation but puts this into a standard form that enables us to compare it with the full multivariate model. As in the cross-tabulation, we find that all the four regions in the inner periphery – the North East, North West, Yorkshire and the Humber, and the South West – exhibit significantly higher levels of regional pride than does the South East (the reference category). The West Midlands and London also stand out from the South East, although not as markedly.

In the second model we introduce our individual-level explanatory variables. We find a significant improvement in fit. However, it is noticeable that neither social class nor income has a significant relationship with regional pride. On the other hand, age, education and length of residence in the area (our measure of localism) and residence outside England (our measure of cosmopolitanism) are all fairly strongly linked with pride; the more educated, cosmopolitan or the younger someone is, the less likely they are to exhibit pride in their region. Conversely, the longer

TABLE 7
BINARY LOGISTIC REGRESSION OF REGIONAL PRIDE

	Model 1	Model 2
South East (ref)	0	0
London	0.90 (.26)***	0.86 (.26)***
East	0.47 (.28)*	0.29 (.28)
East Midlands	0.35 (.31)	0.18 (.32)
West Midlands	0.93 (.27)***	0.67 (.28)**
South West	1.33 (.26)***	1.25 (.26)***
Yorks & Humber	2.37 (.23)***	2.23 (.24)***
North West	1.95 (.23)***	1.84 (.24)**
North East	2.27 (.26)***	2.12 (.27)***
Income		0.00 (.00)
Class VII (ref)		0
Classes I/II		0.02 (.20)
Class III		−0.26 (.22)
Class IV		0.11 (.24)
Classes V/VI		−0.09 (.17)
No qualification (ref)		0
Higher education		−0.68 (.19)***
Alevel		−0.55 (.21)***
Other qualification		−0.43 (.16)**
Age		0.05 (.00)***
Length of time in area		0.01 (.00)***
Never outside England (ref)		0
Elsewhere in UK		−0.20 (.26)
Outside UK		0.08 (.16)
Elsewhere in UK and outside		−0.69 (.38)*
Constant	−2.59 (.20)	−2.67 (.35)
Model improvement	249.1 (8 df)	338.0 (21 df)
N	2394	2394

Source: BSA 2001. Numbers in parentheses are standard errors.

* $p < 0.10$; ** $p < 0.05$; *** $p < 0.01$.

they have lived in their local area, the more likely they are to be proud of their region. This makes good theoretical sense. We might expect older people to have had more time to build up local attachments while on the other hand higher education might be expected to lead to a more cosmopolitan orientation and to a weaker attachment to the local area.

While these explanatory variables explain some of the individual variation in whether people feel pride in their region, they have relatively little impact on the regional variation in levels of pride (as measured by the region parameters, which all remain very large and highly significant). In other words, the differences between the northern regions and the south east cannot be explained by the individual-level characteristics that we have included in the model, and we doubt if there are other individual characteristics that we have omitted that would make much inroad into the size of the regional parameters. While this kind of analysis cannot be conclusive, it is consistent with the idea that there are distinctly different regional identities and loyalties that are a product of local cultures rather than of individual characteristics.

Finally, we turn to the analysis of support for regional assemblies and follow the same procedure as with the analysis of regional pride. In the first model we simply include region as a predictor, in effect repeating the information in the original cross-tabulation. In the second model we include the same individual-level explanatory variables that we used in Table 7. Finally, we add a third model in which we introduce the subjective measures of economic dissatisfaction and of regional pride.

Table 8 shows the results for the multivariate analysis of regional devolution. In the first model, as in the crosstabulation, we find that the regions of the inner periphery - the North East, North West, Yorkshire and the Humber, and the South West – all have significantly higher support for regional devolution than does the reference category of the South East. But the parameter estimates are much smaller than those for regional pride.

In the second model we see that our most cosmopolitan group – those who had lived both elsewhere in the UK and abroad – were significantly less likely to support regional devolution than the 'locals' who have never lived outside England. Among the other individual-level variables, class and income have no impact but more surprisingly length of residence in the neighbourhood has no significant association either and the pattern with education is not nearly as clear as it was with regional pride. There is however a significant negative association between age and support for regional devolution. That is to say, older people are less likely to favour change in the constitutional arrangements. This is the exact opposite of what we found with regional pride, where older people were more likely to feel pride in their region. However, the pattern in Table 8 is similar to the ones found in Wales and Scotland where it tends to be younger people who favour Scottish and Welsh devolution. The explanation is likely to be that older people, who have lived for many years with existing constitutional arrangements, have become accustomed to them and see no great reason for change. Younger generations, on the other hand, as has been shown often in other contexts, are more receptive to new arrangements since they have had less time to become socialized into existing practices.

TABLE 8
BINARY LOGISTIC REGRESSION OF SUPPORT FOR REGIONAL ASSEMBLIES

	Model 1	Model 2	Model 3
South East (ref)	0	0	0
London	0.24 (.19)	0.20 (.19)	0.19 (.20)
East	−0.09 (.20)	−0.16 (.21)	−0.15 (.21)
East Midlands	0.12 (.21)	0.07 (.22)	0.09 (.22)
West Midlands	0.20 (.20)	0.10 (.21)	0.11 (.21)
South West	0.42 (.20)**	0.36 (.20)*	0.36 (.20)*
Yorks & Humber (.20)	0.33 (.19)*		0.22 (.20) 0.20
North West	0.54 (.18)***	0.42 (.19)**	0.41 (.19)**
North East	0.62 (.22) ***	0.52 (.22)**	0.51 (.23)**
Income		0.01 (.00)	−0.00 (.00)
Class VII (ref)		0	0
Classes I/II		0.07 (.19)	0.06 (.19)
Class III		0.17 (.20)	0.17 (.20)
Class IV		0.19 (.23)	0.18 (.23)
Classes V/VI		0.14 (.16)	0.14 (.16)
No qualification (ref)		0	0
Higher education		−0.05 (.18)	−0.03 (.18)
A level		−0.61 (.20)***	−0.59 (.20)***
Other qualification		−0.27 (.15)*	−0.26 (.15)*
Age		−0.02 (.00)***	−0.02 (.00)***
Length of time in area		0.00 (.00)	0.00 (.00)
Never outside England (ref)		0	0
Elsewhere in UK		−0.20 (.23)	−0.19 (.23)
Outside UK		−0.22 (.15)	−0.22 (.15)
Elsewhere in UK and outside −0.62 (.31)**			−0.61 (.31)**
Living comfortably (ref)			0
Coping			0.00 (.12)
Finding it difficult/v difficult			0.16 (.17)
Doesn't think that way (ref)			0
Proud			0.09 (.11)
Not proud			−0.19 (29)
Constant	−1.43 (.13)***	−0.27 (.29)	−0.38 (.)
N	2394	2394	2394
Model improvement	20.6 (8df)	.63.6 (21df)	65.7 (25df)

Source: BSA 2001.

Numbers in parentheses are standard errors
* p< 0.10; ** p< 0.05; *** p< 0.01.

In the final model we introduce the subjective measures of economic dissatisfaction and regional pride. Neither has a significant relationship at the individual level with support for regional devolution, and not surprisingly they fail to explain the regional differences.

Conclusions

The multivariate analysis, therefore, highlights that there are some strong relationships between our variables and regional pride but much weaker ones with support for regional devolution. Both the parameter estimates and the model improvement are considerably smaller in the case of regional devolution than regional pride. Almost certainly this is because demands, or perhaps we should say sympathies, for regional assemblies are not yet well developed and this is not an issue on which people are likely to have thought a great deal. The debate in England is years behind that in Scotland and Wales and has not been politicized to any great extent. It would be surprising therefore if the associations were as strong as those found in comparable analyses of Scotland and Wales. Indeed, it is rather striking that for such a low-profile issue we have been able to find any structure at all in the pattern of attitudes. Regional pride on the other hand seems to be well entrenched and thus offers a potential for support for regional assemblies to grow in the regions concerned.

Our analyses have also given considerable, albeit qualified, support for Steed's argument that it is as big a mistake to treat England as a homogeneous whole as it was to treat Britain as a homogeneous unit. While the details of the theory of centre/periphery relations does not appear to fit all that well with the English case, there are certainly some major differences between the core of London and the South East on the one hand and the inner periphery of the North East, North West, Yorkshire and Humber, and the South West. However, while there are major regional differences within England, it is not clear that the notions of core and periphery provide the basis for a satisfactory explanatory theory. Members of peripheral regions do not appear to experience greater subjective dissatisfaction either with their economic circumstances or with the political system than do people living in the core. Nor do subjective feelings of dissatisfaction engender support for regional devolution.

Our analyses have given more, although qualified, support to Merton's theory of locals and cosmopolitans. The distinction cannot be reduced to the usual sociological heavyweights of class, age and education but adds something new to our analysis. We suspect that in the modern world with its tendencies towards globalization on the one hand and fragmentation on the other these differences may become even more significant. Cosmopolitans may tend towards identification with supra-national bodies such as Europe while locals may identify with subnational and local cultures.

Finally, our results suggest that distinct regional cultures, especially those in the north, may have considerable potential both for social explanation and for the emergence of viable regional institutions. It is too simple to relate these cultures to the economic and political distinctions implied by the theory of core and periphery. Rather, they seem to play a role analogous to that of the minority nationalisms of Wales and Scotland, albeit in a much weaker guise. They are based, we suspect, on a sense of local community that is absent from much of southern England.

REFERENCES

Heath, Anthony F., Bridget Taylor, Lindsay Brook and Alison Park (1999) 'British National Sentiment', *British Journal of Political Science* 29: 155–75.
Hechter, Michael (1975) *Internal Colonialism*. London: Routledge and Kegan Paul.
Merton, Robert K ([1949] 1957). *Social Theory and Structure*. New York: Free Press.
National Statistics (2001) *Regional Gross Domestic Product*. www.statistics.gov.uk/themes/economy/articles/regional accounts.asp.
National Statistics (2001) *Regional Household Sector Income and Consumption Expenditure*, www.statistics.gov.uk/themes/economy/articles/regional accounts.asp.
Office of the Deputy Prime Minister (2002) *Your Region, Your Choice: Revitalising the English Regions*, www.regions.odpm.gov.uk/ governance/whitepaper.
Park, Alison, John Curtice, Katarina Thomson, Lindsey Jarvis and Catherine Bromley (eds.) (2002) *British Social Attitudes: The 19th Report, Appendix I*. London: Sage.
Rokkan, Stein and Dale Urwin (1982) *The Politics of Territorial Identity: Studies in European Regionalism*. Beverly Hills: Sage.
Rokkan, Stein and Dale Urwin (1983) *Economy, Territory, Identity: Politics of European Peripheries*. Beverly Hills: Sage.
Steed, Michael (1986) 'The Core-periphery Dimension of British Politics', *Political Geography Quarterly*, supplement to vol 5: S91–S103.
Taylor, Bridget and Katarina Thomson (eds) (1999) *Scotland and Wales: Nations Again?* Cardiff: University of Wales Press.
Wellhofer, E. (1989) 'Core and Periphery: Territorial Dimensions in Politics', *Urban Studies* 26: 340–55.

The Lost Voters of Scotland: Devolution Disillusioned or Westminster Weary?

Catherine Bromley and John Curtice

One of the aims of devolution was to increase Scots' sense of trust and confidence in their system of government (Dewar, 1998). Yet far from strengthening the bonds between voters and politicians, the immediate advent of devolution has seen voters stay away from the ballot box in record numbers. In the first election to the Scottish Parliament in 1999, the turnout was just 58.2%, down no less than 13 points on the already relatively low figure recorded in the 1997 UK general election. And then in the 2001 UK general election, the experience was repeated with just 58.1% going to the polls. Such voter disinterest was hardly the outcome devolution was meant to deliver.

So it appears that perhaps devolution should be put in the dock. Rather than strengthening the bonds between voters and politicians, perhaps devolution has weakened them. There would appear two alternative explanations why this might be so. The first is that the decline in voter turnout is an unintended consequence of the success of devolution. If the Scottish Parliament has come to be regarded as the political crucible of the nation, then perhaps Westminster, and thus a Westminster election, is no longer regarded as relevant. True, turnout was no higher in the first Scottish Parliament election in 1999 than it was in the 2001 Westminster election. But perhaps the relative importance of the Scottish Parliament has only become apparent to voters since it has been up and running. Or perhaps some voters think that Westminster matters, others the Scottish Parliament, and as a result little more than half the country think it is worth turning up for either kind of election?

The alternative explanation runs along almost the opposite lines. Perhaps devolution has come to be seen as a failure in the eyes of the Scottish electorate, the perceived reality falling far short of the high expectations they had when they voted for it in the 1997 referendum (Surridge and McCrone, 1999)? If so, then whatever trust and confidence they had in politics and the political system before the advent of devolution may have been completely eroded. Disillusioned and cynical about politics, many Scottish voters may have simply decided it is not worth turning out to vote for any kind of election at all.

But perhaps these charges against devolution are misplaced. After all the low turnout in 2001 varied little across Britain (at 59.1% the turnout in England was almost as low as it was north of the border, and the fall in turnout since 1997 was almost as great as well). So if devolution has not achieved the aspirations of its advocates, then perhaps this is because it has not made much impact one way or the other. As a result, far from devolution bringing about a radical and distinctive change to the Scottish political landscape, perhaps it has left voters in Scotland subject to much the same influences on their propensity to vote as their counterparts south of the border? If so, then the challenge is to find what those influences might have been.

The aim of this article is to establish what clues the low turnout in the 2001 UK general election gives us about the impact of devolution on the mind of the ordinary Scottish voter. We start by investigating the extent to which Westminster is still thought to matter in Scotland. This is followed by a discussion of attitudes towards devolution itself. The final part then looks at whether devolution has simply failed to stem a growing voter disinterest in elections that is to be found both north and south of the border.

Data

Our evidence about voter attitudes north of the border at the time of the June 2001 UK general election comes from the 2001 Scottish Social Attitudes (SSA) survey. Conducted by the National Centre for Social Research Scotland, this survey interviewed a random sample of 1,605 adults aged 18+ in the period between June and October 2001. Funding from the ESRC Devolution and Constitutional Change research programme enabled the survey to carry a wide range of questions on attitudes towards devolution and voting behaviour.

Of course, we cannot examine whether devolution has lived up to expectations or why turnout was lower in 2001 than in 1997 simply by looking at voter attitudes in 2001. Many of our key questions had, however, previously been asked on the 1997 Scottish Election Study (SES) (Brown et al., 1999), the 1997 Scottish Referendum Study (Taylor and Thomson, 1999), the 1999 Scottish Parliamentary Election Study/Scottish Social Attitudes survey (Paterson et al., 2000), and the 2000 Scottish Social Attitudes survey (Curtice et al., 2001). We thus make extensive use of these surveys in our analysis as well. In addition we also take advantage of the fact that a number of our key questions were also asked on the 2001 British

Social Attitudes survey (Park et al., 2002), as a result of which we are able to discern how far the patterns we find in Scotland are different from those in England.

One problem faced by all surveys is that typically they find a higher proportion of people saying they voted than is recorded in the official turnout statistics. Indeed, 70% of the respondents to our 2001 survey said they voted in the general election. This does not, however, simply mean that respondents lie about whether they have voted (Swaddle and Heath, 1989). Indeed, the 'official' turnout figure is an underestimate of the proportion of the electorate that votes because of redundancy on the electoral register. But it does mean that surveys tend to be more successful at obtaining interviews with those who did vote than they are with those who did not. However, what is important for our ability to explain why turnout was so low in 2001 is that the trend in turnout across our surveys should mirror the official figures. This it largely does. The 1997 Scottish Election Study recorded an 81% turnout, so the difference between our 1997 and 2001 surveys of 11 points is close to the 13-point drop in the election result. Meanwhile, the turnout in our 1999 survey is, at 72%, largely in accordance with our expectation that it should be the same as in 2001.

Westminster No Longer Matters

We begin by examining whether Westminster has been rendered irrelevant in the eyes of people in Scotland. The 1999 Scottish Social Attitudes survey asked the following questions:

*When the new parliament starts work, which of the following do you think **will** have most influence over the way Scotland is run ...*

*And which do you think **ought** to have most influence over the way Scotland is run ...*

... the Scottish parliament,
the UK government at Westminster,
local councils in Scotland,
or, the European Union?

These questions were asked again in the 2000 and 2001 surveys, but with the wording updated of the first question changed to ask which institution **does** have most influence. The table below reveals the existence of a significant mismatch between expectations of which body would have the most influence and perceptions of what has proven to be the case. In 1999, four in ten thought that the Scottish Parliament would be the main 'show in town', whereas in 2000 and 2001 less than one in six thought this was actually the position. In fact, as many (if not slightly more) have come to think that the EU or local councils have most influence as think the parliament does.

Saying that you think the new parliament *will* have most influence does not of course necessarily imply that you think it *ought* to. So, it could be that back in 1999 more people actually said it would have most influence than wanted it to. However, the table suggests that quite the opposite is true. In 1999, almost twice as many people said that the parliament *ought* to have the most say than said they thought it would have, and the proportion who think this – around three-quarters – has remained static ever since. So, perceptions of which body has the most influence in Scotland are significantly lower than the expectations people held in 1999, and are far short of what people currently think ought to be the case.

TABLE 1
ATTITUDES TOWARDS POLITICAL INSTITUTIONS IN SCOTLAND, 1999–2001

	Which will have most influence?	Which does have most influence?	
	1999	2000	2001
Scottish Parliament	41	13	15
UK Government	39	66	66
Local councils	8	10	9
European Union	4	4	7

	Which ought to have most influence?		
	1999	2000	2001
Scottish Parliament	74	72	74
UK Government	13	13	14
Local councils	8	10	8
European Union	1	1	1
N	1482	1663	1605

Source: SSA 1999–2001.

We have, then, two contradictory pieces of information. Scots would prefer the Scottish Parliament to be the most influential body in Scotland, but Westminster is still seen to be pre-eminent in practice. But perhaps we can paint a clearer picture if we look at people's perceptions of whether the outcome of Westminster and Scottish Parliament elections matters. Perhaps the former are no longer regarded as important despite Westminster's perceived pre-eminence? We can examine this by looking at the answers to the following questions:

Some people say that it makes no difference which party wins in elections, things go on much the same... how much of a difference do you think it makes who wins in elections to the Scottish parliament?

And how much of a difference do you think it makes who wins in general elections to the UK House of Commons?

A great deal
Quite a lot
Some
Not very much
None at all

If Westminster has become secondary to Holyrood in the public's mind then we might expect people in Scotland to think that the outcome of general elections to the UK House of Commons makes less of a difference than do people in England. Moreover, they could be expected to think that the outcome of Westminster elections is less important than that of Holyrood elections. But, as the next table highlights, this is not the case. Rather, three points stand out. Firstly, the proportion of people in Scotland who in 2001 thought that who wins elections makes a difference was practically the same for Westminster elections (45%) as it was for Holyrood contests (43%). Secondly, the proportion of people in Scotland who said that the results of elections make a difference declined (by similar amounts) in respect of both Westminster (9 points) and Holyrood (13 points) contests. Lastly, the outcome of Westminster elections is thought to be just as important by people in Scotland as it is by people in England (44%). In short, although Holyrood is very much the people's choice when it comes to who should decide policy within Scotland, there is nothing to suggest that the perceived importance of Westminster in practice has been relegated as a result.

But do people's stated views on the question of how much difference it makes who wins elections affect whether they vote or not? Could it be that although views on this matter are identical north and south of the border, those who think that the outcome of Westminster elections does not matter are less likely to vote in post-devolution Scotland than are voters in England? Table 3 examines the relationship in Scotland and in England between turnout in the 2001 general election and attitudes towards the outcome of Westminster elections. It shows that the pattern of association between turnout and perceptions of the importance of election outcomes

TABLE 2
HOW MUCH DIFFERENCE IT MAKES WHO WINS ELECTIONS,
SCOTLAND AND ENGLAND, 1999–2001

% who think it makes a
great deal / quite a lot of
difference who wins

| | *Scotland* | | *England* |
	1999	*2001*	*2001*
Westminster elections	54	45	44
Holyrood elections	56	43	na
N 1482	1605	2761	

Source: SSA 1999, 2001; BSA 2001.

TABLE 3
HOW MUCH DIFFERENCE IT MAKES WHO WINS ELECTIONS, BY TURNOUT
IN ENGLAND AND SCOTLAND, 2001

How much difference it makes
who wins Westminster elections ...

| | | *% who voted in 2001 GE* | | |
	Scotland	*N*	*England*	*N*
Great deal / quite a lot	78	713	79	1203
Not very much / none at all	55	562	52	936

Source: SSA, BSA 2001

was largely the same on both sides of the border. In both countries eight in ten of those who said that the outcome of Westminster elections makes a great deal or quite a lot of difference voted in 2001 compared with around half of those who said that the results make very little difference. It is, then, little wonder that the turnout in both countries was so similar.

Devolution Disillusion?

Westminster, then, is still very much in the minds of voters in Scotland, or at least to the same extent that it is south of the border. But could the low turnout in 2001 in Scotland be – in part at least – a reflection of disillusion with devolution? During the Clause 28 debate in the summer of 2000, one Scottish Labour MP voiced concern that voters would use the record of Labour's MSPs in Holyrood to pass judgement on Westminster MPs at the next general election (Hassan, 2002). And we have a number of measures to test whether assessments of devolution in Scotland were in any way connected to participation at the 2001 general election. We begin by looking at expectations of the Scottish Parliament.

Expectations versus Reality

The 1997 Scottish Referendum Survey carried a number of questions designed to tap people's expectations of the proposed Scottish Parliament. Some of these have subsequently been repeated on a number of occasions with very little alteration to the wording. Two examples of these questions are:

> *As a result of having a Scottish parliament, will **Scotland's economy** become better, worse or will it make no difference?*

> *And as a result of having a Scottish parliament, will the **standard of the health service** in Scotland become better, worse or will it make no difference?*

At the same time we can also examine the answers to another set of questions where, at the time of the 1997 referendum, people were asked what impact they thought having a Scottish Parliament would have, but subsequently were asked about what impact they thought it had actually had.[1] In 2001 these questions read:

> *From what you have seen and heard so far, do you think that having a Scottish parliament is giving Scotland a stronger voice in the United Kingdom, a weaker voice in the United Kingdom, or, is it making no difference?*

> *[D]o you think that having a Scottish parliament is giving ordinary people more say in how Scotland is governed, less say, or, is it making no difference?*

> *[D]o you think that having a Scottish parliament is increasing the standard of education in Scotland, reducing the standard of education in Scotland, or, is it making no difference?*

The following table shows the answers these questions elicited between 1997 and 2001. In 1997, expectations were very high. Between two-thirds and eight in ten expected devolution to deliver a positive outcome across the range of subjects covered. Thereafter, expectations have fallen while perceptions of actual outcomes do not match the expectations held in 1997. By 2001, less than half of people in Scotland thought that having a Scottish

Parliament would mean that Scotland's economy or its health service would become better. And while slightly more than half felt that devolution had given Scotland a stronger voice in the UK, little more than a quarter felt that it had brought about an improvement in education standards. In short, disillusion with the Scottish Parliament appears to have been widespread by the time of the 2001 election, at least as compared with the expectations held by many people in Scotland just four years previously.

Evaluations, Trust and Turnout

TABLE 4
EXPECTATIONS AND PERCEPTIONS OF THE IMPACT OF THE
SCOTTISH PARLIAMENT, 1997–2001

Expectation/Perception	*1997 referendum*	*1999*	*2000*	*2001*
Scotland's economy become better	64	43	36	43
Standard of NHS become better	65	49	na	45
Scotland have a stronger voice in the UK	70	70	52	52
Ordinary people have more say in how Scotland is governed	79	64	44	38
Education standards in Scotland increase	71	56	43	27
N	676	1482	1663	1605

na=not asked

Source: 1997: SRS, 1999–2001: SSA

But what wider impact has this disillusion had? Has it reduced levels of political trust and efficacy? Does it in any way, either directly or indirectly through its impact on levels of trust and efficacy, account for the low turnout in the 2001 election, thereby providing a distinctly Scottish account of why so few people voted? As a first step in assessing this proposition we have constructed a political trust scale from respondents' answers to the following three questions:[2]

> *How much do you trust British governments of any party to place the needs of the nation above the interests of their own political party?*

> *How much do you trust the UK government to work in Scotland's best long-term interest?*

> *[H]ow much do you trust the Scottish parliament to work in Scotland's best interests?*

Table 5 shows the relationship between three measures of perceptions of the Scottish Parliament's performance to date and levels of trust as measured by our scale. It quite clearly demonstrates that those who think that the Scottish Parliament is performing well have higher levels of trust than those who think it is making no difference. For example, nearly half (47%) of those who think the parliament is giving ordinary people more say in how Scotland is governed have a high level of trust, compared with just over a quarter (27%) of those who think it is making no difference. A similar analysis of the relationship between levels of political efficacy and evaluations of devolution (not presented here) reveals the same pattern: those with positive evaluations have high levels of efficacy while those with negative views have lower levels (see Curtice, 2001 for previous examples of this kind of analysis).

But if disillusion engenders distrust, does it also encourage abstention?

TABLE 5

PERCEPTIONS OF THE SCOTTISH PARLIAMENT, BY LEVEL OF TRUST, 2001

Scottish parliament is:

		High	*Level of trust* *Medium*	*Low*
Giving Scotland stronger voice in UK	%	41	56	4
No difference	%	24	64	12
Giving Scots more say in govt	%	47	51	4
No difference	%	27	64	9
Increasing education standards	%	46	51	3
No difference	%	29	62	9
N		507	907	116

Source: SSA 2001

Table 6 explores this possibility by looking at the relationship between turnout and both perceptions of the Scottish Parliament and levels of political trust. While the differences in the table appear relatively small, they are nevertheless in a consistent direction and are statistically significant: people who said that the parliament was not making a difference were less likely to vote in the 2001 UK general election than those who said it was making an impact. And those with low levels of trust were much less likely to have voted.

TABLE 6
PERCEPTIONS OF THE SCOTTISH PARLIAMENT AND LEVEL OF TRUST,
BY TURNOUT IN 2001 (%)

Scottish parliament is:

	Voted in 2001	N
Giving Scotland stronger voice in UK	70	*836*
No difference	65	*643*
Giving Scots more say in govt	73	*604*
No difference	66	*899*
Increasing education standards	75	*436*
No difference	67	*932*
Level of trust		
High	75	*507*
Low	58	*116*

Source: SSA 2001.

Evaluations of the political system: England and Scotland

But to demonstrate that disillusion with devolution provides a distinctly Scottish account of turnout in the 2001 election we need to show two things. Firstly, we need to demonstrate that political trust and efficacy have fallen more in Scotland than in England. And secondly, we need to show that evaluations of devolution are still significant once other factors associated with turnout are taken into account. Table 7 looks at trends in England and Scotland in three key measures of political trust and system efficacy. The first row shows the trend over time in the proportion of people who say they trust governments to place the needs of the nation above the interests of their own political party 'just about always' or 'most of the time'. The next two rows look at the proportions who strongly agree with the following statements:

Parties are only interested in people's votes, not in their opinions.

Generally speaking those we elect as MPs lose touch with people pretty quickly.

In order to provide a longer time series, readings for the mid 1980s and 1990s were calculated by combining the Scottish samples within the British Social Attitudes surveys in 1986 and 1987, and 1994 and 1996 (the overall responses in these years were very similar).

Two key trends stand out. Firstly, both countries have experienced a similar decline in political trust and increase in cynicism. Despite the advent

TABLE 7
TRUST IN GOVERNMENT AND POLITICAL EFFICACY, 1980s–2001

	Mid-1980s	Mid-1990s	1997	2000	2001	Mid-1980s–2001 change
% trust Government always / most of the time						
Scotland	37	29	29	13	27	–10
England	38	23	34	17	29	–9
% strongly agree that parties are only interested in votes						
Scotland	11	29	16	24	21	+10
England	18	26	16	26	26	+8
% strongly agree that MPs lose touch pretty quickly						
Scotland	11	26	na	24	22	+11
England	17	25	na	23	24	+7
N Scotland	276	216	882	1663	1605	
England	2511	1972	3150	2887	2761	

Source: Mid 1980s: BSA 1986 and 1987. Mid 1990s: BSA. 1994 and 1996: BES/SES. 2000 and 2001: SSA.

of the Scottish Parliament, political trust fell as sharply in England as it did in Scotland between 1997 and 2000. Meanwhile, so far as system efficacy is concerned, Scotland and England were even more similar in their views in 2001 than had been the case in the mid-1980s.

So it seems that so far as political trust and efficacy are concerned, disillusion with devolution has not made any difference. Although disillusion with devolution may be associated with political trust and efficacy, the fact remains that levels of trust in Scotland and England are almost identical, so devolution per se cannot be held responsible for any of the trends in the table above.

But what of our finding that disillusion with devolution appeared to have an impact on turnout in 2001? What happens if we put this finding into an appropriate multivariate analysis that also takes into account the impact of perceptions of the importance of the outcome of elections? In the following logistic regression we examine the relationship between turnout and: trust; efficacy; perceptions of how much difference Holyrood and Westminster election results have; and three evaluations of devolution.[3] As Table 8 demonstrates, efficacy and the perceived impact of election results were significantly associated with turnout in 2001. In contrast our measures of the performance of the Scottish Parliament that had appeared to be

TABLE 8
MODEL OF SCOTTISH TURNOUT AT UK 2001 GENERAL ELECTION

	Coefficient	Standard Error
Difference who wins Westminster elections		
Great deal / quite a lot	0.295	0.093**
Some	0.009	0.101
Not very much / none at all	–0.304	0.095**
Difference who wins Holyrood elections		
Great deal / quite a lot	0.293	0.092**
Some	–0.109	0.096
Not very much / none at all	–0.184	0.096
Level of efficacy		
Very low	–0.450	0.136**
Low	–0.067	0.098
High	0.073	0.110
Very high	0.444	0.180*
Scottish parliament is:		
Giving Scotland stronger voice in UK	–0.162	0.172
Weaker voice	0.398	0.266
No difference	–0.089	0.173
Giving ordinary people more say in how Scotland is run	–0.361	2.166
Less say	–0.401	2.179
No difference	–0.460	2.166
Increasing education standards	0.136	0.127
Reducing education standards	–0.039	0.203
No difference	–0.004	0.106
Level of trust		
High	0.057	0.111
Medium	–0.005	0.093
Low	–0.052	0.154
Constant	1.312	2.167
Pseudo R2	0.073	

Source: SSA 2001

**=Significant at 5% level
*=Significant at 1% level
N=1482

significant in the earlier bivariate analysis no longer feature. However, this model explains very little of the overall variance (note the low R^2), and in any case recent changes in levels of efficacy, or indeed in any of the other measures we have examined so far, have not been large enough to alone account for the low turnout in 2001. We evidently need to look elsewhere to understand why so few people voted in 2001.

Westminster Weary?

So far, then, we have found little evidence that the low level of turnout in the 2001 UK general election in Scotland can be blamed on the advent of devolution. It is certainly not the case that the Scots no longer care what happens at Westminster: two-thirds of Scots believe that Westminster still has most influence on what happens in Scotland anyway, while Scots in general were no less likely than people in England to think that the outcome of the election mattered. True, Scots' expectations of their parliament have not been met and they were slightly more cynical about the political system in 2001 than they were four years previously. But it appears that there is no particular connection between the Scottish Parliament's failure to meet expectations and the decline in Westminster voting, at least not once other factors that influence turnout are taken into account. As for the increase in cynicism about the political process in general, this has affected England as much as Scotland.

In short, it is beginning to appear that, in practice, devolution made little difference to the propensity of Scots to turn out and vote in the 2001 UK general election. Indeed, as Table 9 shows, this appears to be true even of the relative willingness of supporters of the different parties to turn out and vote. It might have been thought that SNP voters would be particularly likely to see less reason to vote in a UK general election now that the Scottish Parliament is in place. Not only could they be expected to find voting in a Scottish election a more congenial experience, but they are likely to be aware that their party's prospects of winning seats are much lower in a UK general election. And, indeed, we can see that, compared with other parties' identifiers, SNP supporters were relatively less likely to vote in 2001, while this had not been the case in the 1999 Scottish Parliament election. However, we can also see that SNP identifiers were already less likely to vote in the 1997 UK general election, held before the Scottish Parliament was in place.

So why was turnout so low in 2001 by the standards of previous UK general elections? What made Scots imitate the behaviour of people south of the border? Can we identify one or more apparently Britain-wide influences that might have been responsible and to which devolution did not make Scotland immune? There would appear to be two possibilities. The first is that, perhaps because of social changes they have experienced in common, voters have changed on both sides of the border. We have already seen that they have become more disillusioned even if we have also seen

TABLE 9
TURNOUT IN SCOTLAND BY PARTY IDENTIFICATION, 1997–2001

	1997	N	% Voting 1999	N	2001	N
Conservative	86	140	76	231	75	164
Labour	83	406	71	625	75	735
Liberal Democrat	90	104	81	166	83	154
SNP	78	151	79	290	70	253

Source: 1997: SES, 1999 and 2001: SSA

that this does not appear to be an adequate explanation of the low turnout in 2001. But perhaps voters on both sides of the border have become disengaged from the political process?

The second possibility is that, while the propensity of voters to turn out and vote has not particularly changed, what was different in 2001, and perhaps in 1999 too, was that voters in England and in Scotland simply did not receive sufficient stimulus or encouragement to vote. In particular, they may have decided there was little difference between the parties, and thus it did not matter who won. In addition, they may have formed the impression from the opinion polls that the outcome of the election was already a foregone conclusion. In other words, both Scottish and English voters might well have been as engaged or disengaged in the political process as they ever were, but they lacked sufficient political stimulus to persuade them that it was worth going to the polling station.

There is in fact no consistent evidence, as indeed there is not for Britain as a whole (Bromley and Curtice, 2002), that the Scottish electorate was significantly less engaged in 2001 than it had been in 1997. Table 10 shows what people said when they were asked after the last two UK elections and the last Scottish election:

> *How much interest do you generally have in what is going on in politics ...*
> *... a great deal,*
> *quite a lot,*
> *some,*
> *not very much,*
> *or, none at all?*

On each occasion around a quarter said that they had a 'great deal' or 'quite a lot' of interest.[4] It thus seems unlikely that disengagement accounts for the low turnout in 2001.

TABLE 10
TRENDS IN POLITICAL INTEREST 1997–2001

	1997	1999	2001
Great Deal	9	6	7
Quite a lot	18	17	19
Some	35	36	33
Not Very Much	30	31	27
None	7	9	13
N	882	1482	1605

Source: 1997: SES, 1999 and 2001: SSA.

What then of the stimulus that voters received? Did they form the impression, as content analysis of the British party manifestos suggests they might reasonably have done (Bara and Budge, 2001), that there was little difference between the parties? Or should we bear in mind that Scotland now has a different party system than England, that the main contest is between Labour and the SNP, and whatever narrowing of the difference may have happened to Labour and the Conservatives across Britain as a whole, Scotland's two main protagonists are still seen as fundamentally divided because of their differing stances on the issue of independence?

TABLE 11
PERCEIVED DIFFERENCE BETWEEN THE PARTIES, SCOTLAND,
1992–2001

	1992	1997	1999	2001
Conservative and Labour				
Great	53	32	30	21
Some	28	44	35	39
Not Much	17	20	32	38
SNP and Labour				
Great	na	na	41	33
Some	na	na	40	42
Not Much	na	na	15	19
N 957	882	1482	1605	

Source: 1992, 1997: SES.

Table 11 indicates that voters in Scotland were certainly less likely to think there was much of a difference between the parties than they had done at any other recent election, including the 1999 Scottish election. Just one in five thought that there was a great difference between them, whereas over half took that view as recently as 1992. Moreover, this drop is almost exactly in line with the trend across Britain as a whole, as shown in the next table. Any expectation that the Conservatives' opposition to devolution up to the 1997 referendum would have made Scottish voters more likely to think there was a big difference between them and Labour proves erroneous. Instead, as was the case across Britain as a whole (Bromley and Curtice, 2002), the perception that there is much of a difference between Britain's two main governing parties reached an all time low.

Moreover, it is far from clear that the perceived difference between Labour and the SNP gave Scottish voters an alternative reason to go to the polls that their English counterparts lacked. True, appreciably more Scots, one in three, felt that there was a great difference between the SNP and Labour, than felt the same about Labour and the Conservatives. But this figure is not only down on what it was at the time of the first Scottish Parliament election, but is much lower than the 53% recorded for the perceived difference between Labour and the Conservatives in 1992. Even the SNP/Labour battle has come to be seen as less consequential.

TABLE 12
PERCEIVED DIFFERENCE BETWEEN CONSERVATIVE AND LABOUR, BRITAIN,
1992–2001

	1992 %	1997 %	2001 %
Great difference	56	33	17
Some	32	43	39
Not Much	12	24	44

N   1794   2836   1076

Source: 1992, 1997: BES; 2001: BSA.

That feeling there is not much difference between the parties does actually influence the probability that someone will vote is shown by the next table. Indeed, such a perception seems to have been particularly important in 2001. Still it might be thought that even the 17-point difference between those who thought there was a great difference and those who did not recorded in 2001 is not particularly large.

One reason why this is so, is because not seeing much of a difference between the parties really only makes a difference to whether someone votes if they do not have strong prior predisposition to go to vote. In other words, a voter needs more stimulus and encouragement to go to the polls the less they are politically engaged. We can see this in Table 14, which shows that amongst those with a great deal or quite a lot of interest in politics, those who did not see much of a difference between the parties were almost

TABLE 13
TURNOUT BY PERCEIVED DIFFERENCE BETWEEN CONSERVATIVE AND
LABOUR, 1997–2001

			% voted				
1997	*N*	*1999*	*N*	*2001*	*N*	*Change*	
						1997–2001	
Difference between Con and Lab							
Great	88	286	79	452	78	*356*	−10
Some	78	383	73	497	70	588	−8
Not Much	78	177	68	482	61	626	−17

Source: 1997: SES, 1999–2001: SSA.

as likely to go to the polls as were those who thought there was a great difference. In contrast amongst those with little or no interest in politics, not seeing much of difference between the parties reduced the likelihood of someone voting by around 20%.

TABLE 14
TURNOUT BY PERCEIVED DIFFERENCE AND INTEREST IN POLITICS, 2001
(% WHO VOTED)

Perceived Difference between:

	Con and Lab				SNP and Lab			
Political Interest	*Great*	*N*	*Not Much*	*N*	*Great*	*N*	*Not Much*	*N*
Great Deal/Quite a lot	79	*115*	79	*138*	83	*195*	78	*53*
Not Very Much/None	69	*125*	50	*308*	67	*149*	48	*190*

Source: SSA 2001.

This result can be generalized more widely. If indeed, voters in Scotland, like their counterparts in England, failed to go to the polls in 2001 because they did not think enough was at stake – or indeed that the polls were saying that the result was a foregone conclusion – then we should expect to find that turnout should have fallen most amongst those who are least engaged. And the next table lends some support to this argument. Turnout fell by 15 points between 1997 and 2001 amongst those who have no interest in politics, but by only ten points amongst those who have a great deal or quite a lot of interest. True, this pattern was even more apparent at the time of the Scottish Parliament election, when turnout was down on 1997 by only two points amongst the politically interested, but by 13 amongst those with no interest in politics at all. Equally, the pattern is not as strong as it was across Britain as a whole in 2001 where there was only a six-point drop in turnout amongst the politically interested and no less than a 28-point drop amongst those with no interest at all. But even so it appears that lack of stimulus did play a role in depressing turnout in Scotland much as it did in the rest of Great Britain.[5]

TABLE 15
TURNOUT AND POLITICAL INTEREST, 1997–2001

Political interest	1997	N	% who voted 1999	N	2001	N	Change 1997–2001
Great Deal/Quite a lot	90	240	88	350	80	413	−10
Some	85	309	75	527	75	525	−10
Not Very Much	75	268	67	467	63	439	−12
None	54	64	41	138	39	226	−15

Source: 1997: SES; 1999–2001: SSA.

Thus, neither Scotland's different party system nor the advent of devolution was able to insulate the country from the impact of a perception that grew throughout Britain that there was too little at stake for it to be worth voting. To this perception may well have been added – though we cannot test it directly from our survey evidence – that the result was a foregone conclusion. The final British polls gave Labour on average no less than a 14-point lead over the Conservatives, while those taken north of the border only reinforced the message by putting Labour as much as 20 points ahead. True, voters had received much the same message from the polls as in 1997, but this time around it had the added disadvantage of signalling that little or nothing was going to change. Little wonder perhaps that, despite devolution, politics seemed so dull.

Conclusion

Our analysis fails to uphold the most serious of the possible charges against devolution. It may not have lived up to expectations, but the failure of voters to go to the polls in the 2001 UK general election cannot be blamed on their disillusion with devolution. Those who now think the Scottish Parliament is not achieving very much were only slightly less likely to vote in the general election than were those think it is – and once other factors are controlled for, this relationship disappears. Despite the fears of the critics of devolution, it does not appear to have done any damage to the bond between Scotland and Westminster.

On the other hand, devolution does not appear to have done much good either. It has evidently failed to insulate Scottish voters from adverse trends that were taking place in the rest of Britain. Scottish voters were less likely trust their government or feel efficacious about their political system in 2001 than they had been in 1997, and in this they were similar to the voters in England. Meanwhile, despite the potential drawing power of an alternative battle between Labour and the SNP, Scottish voters, just like English voters, were less likely to think that there was much difference between the parties, and this appears to have been one reason at least why those voters who needed some encouragement to go to the polls were particularly likely to stay at home. Thus it appears that Britain-wide politics is alive and kicking in the post-devolution world (see also Curtice, 2002).

ACKNOWLEDGEMENTS

Much of the data reported in this article was collected in surveys funded via the ESRC Devolution and Constitutional Change Programme (grant numbers L219 25 2033, L219 25 2018) for which we are grateful.

REFERENCES

Bromley, C. and J. Curtice (2002), 'Where Have All the Voters Gone?', in A. Park, J. Curtice, K. Thomson L. Jarvis and C. Bromley (eds.) *British Social Attitudes: The 19th Report*. London: Sage

Brown, A., D. McCrone, L. Paterson and P. Surridge (1999), *The Scottish Electorate*. London: Macmillan

Curtice, J. (2002), 'Devolution and Democracy: Old Trust or New Cynicism?', in J. Curtice, D. McCrone, A. Park, and L. Paterson (eds.), *New Scotland, New Society*. Edinburgh: Polygon.

Curtice, J., D. McCrone, A. Park and L. Paterson (eds.) (2002) *New Scotland, New Society*. Edinburgh: Polygon.

Dewar, D. (1998), 'The Scottish Parliament', *Scottish Affairs: Special Issue on Understanding Political Change*, pp.4–12.

Park, A., J. Curtice, K. Thomson, L. Jarvis and C. Bromley (eds.), *British Social Attitudes: The 19th Report*. London: Sage.

Paterson, L., A. Brown, J. Curtice, K. Hinds, D. McCrone, A. Park, K. Sproston, and P. Surridge (2001) *New Scotland, New Politics?* Edinburgh: Polygon.

Surridge, P. and D. McCrone (1999), 'The 1997 Scottish Referendum Vote' in B. Taylor and K. Thomson (eds.), *Scotland and Wales: Nations Again?* Cardiff: University of Wales Press.

Taylor, B. and K. Thomson (eds.) (1999), *Scotland and Wales: Nations Again?* Cardiff: University of Wales Press.

NOTES

1. Taking the example of education standards, the wording has altered as follows: 1997: 'Would a Scottish Parliament improve the standard of education in Scotland, reduce the standard of education, or would it make no difference?'

   1999: 'Will a Scottish Parliament increase the standard of education in Scotland, reduce the standard of education, or will it make no difference?'

2000: 'From what you have seen and heard so far, do you think that having a Scottish Parliament is going to increase the standard of education in Scotland, reduce the standard of education in Scotland, or will it make no difference?'

2001: 'From what you have seen and heard so far, do you think that having a Scottish parliament is increasing the standard of education in Scotland, reducing the standard of education in Scotland, or, is it making no difference?'

2. The scale was constructed by adding the respondent's scores for each item (ranging from 1 = just about always to 4 = almost never) and dividing by the total number of items. These results were then rounded to the nearest integer. As just two people had the highest score those with scores of 1 and 2 were combined. The reliability of this scale as measured by Cronbach's alpha was 0.72.

3. The three items were: standards of education; ordinary people having more say in how Scotland is run; Scotland having a stronger voice in the UK.

4. Another potential indicator of engagement is strength of party identification, which it has long been recognized is in long-term decline (Crewe and Thomson, 19999). Although the same question about strength of party identification was asked on the 1997 Scottish Election Study, and the 1999 and 2001 Scottish Social Attitudes surveys, in 2001 it came after a different question about the direction of a respondent's identification than it did in 1997 or 1999. This same difference also exists in the British Election and British Social Attitudes surveys, and the evidence of those surveys suggests that the sequence of questions used on the 2001 survey regularly reports a lower incidence of strong party identification than that used on the 1997 and 1999 surveys (Bromley and Curtice, 2002). As a result we do not attempt to report a trend for strength of party identification. We can however look at the figures obtained by the Scottish booster to the 2001 British Election Study which did use exactly the same sequence of questions as the 1997 and 1999 surveys. This suggests that between 1997 and 2001 there was no more than a gradual continuation of the long-term decline that has occurred in strength of party identification. 52% reported a very or fairly strong identification, down five points on 1997 but up one on 1999.

5. For example, turnout fell by no less than 33 points compared with 1997 amongst those with no party identification, but by only seven points amongst those with a very or fairly strong party id, a not dissimilar pattern to that across Britain as a whole (Bromley and Curtice, 2002).

A 'Settling Will'?
Public Attitudes to Devolution in Wales

Richard Wyn Jones and Roger Scully

A mere 6,721 votes was the margin by which the voters of Wales approved the establishment of a devolved National Assembly for Wales (NAW) in September 1997. Since the night of the cliff-hanging referendum count, politics in Wales has continued to offer 'interesting times' for all political actors in Wales (Trystan et al., 2002; Wyn Jones, 2001; Chaney et al., 2001). The un-preparedness of virtually all involved for the realities of devolution has been conspicuous;[1] the new National Assembly for Wales (NAW) saw major political upheavals in its first year of existence;[2] and the operation of devolution in Wales has been subject to persistent and often scathing criticism, particularly in the news media.

With (at time of writing) the completion of the first, four-year term of the NAW, and the second set of Assembly elections approaching, and as the Richard Commission continues deliberations over the future powers and functioning of the Assembly, it is an appropriate juncture at which to assess public reactions to devolution in Wales. Do public attitudes remain as they did in 1997 – with many voters apathetic and the remainder split more-or-less down the middle? Or has public opinion moved in a more definite direction – either for or against devolution? If the latter is the case, why, and what underpins support for devolution in Wales? This article explores these questions.

The Coming of Devolution to Wales

Securing some measure of self-government has been a recurrent theme in Welsh political life since the 1880s when franchise reform led to the election of a group of young, radical Liberal representatives who spoke as the self-conscious representatives of the Welsh *gwerin*.[3] It was one of their number, Meirionnydd MP T.E. Ellis, who tabled the first parliamentary motion aimed at establishing a 'Welsh National Council', with his amendment to the 1888 Local Government Bill. That attempt was followed by numerous other, equally unsuccessful attempts to put a measure of Welsh

'Home Rule' – or more latterly, the rather more anodyne 'devolution' – onto the statute book. Providing an account of all these various attempts is beyond scope of this article (for discussion of a number of them see Jones 1987, 1988, 1989a, 1989b, 1990, 1992; Morgan 1981 provides the best overall discussion of Welsh politics in the contemporary era). A number of general features characterizing devolutionary politics in Wales during this period may, however, be identified – characteristics which, as will become clear, retain their relevance even today.

First, it is important to underline that presence should not be confused with salience. That is, although devolution was a regular feature of the political agenda, this does not mean that securing self-government was a particular priority for a substantial section of the population. The opposite was clearly the case. Occasional episodes such as the brief, dramatic, efflorescence of the *Cymru Fydd* movement in the late nineteenth century, under the inspirational leadership of Ellis and the then-nationalist firebrand Lloyd George, or the securing a quarter of a million signatures on the Parliament for Wales petition in the early 1950s, signalled the existence of at least some latent support for devolution among the electorate (Williams, 1986; Jones, 1992). But this support did not translate into deep and sustained public engagement with the issue. So while in the Welsh context it is almost certainly a mistake to regard support for the main nationalist party, Plaid Cymru, as a proxy for levels of public support for devolution (given that all other parties in Wales have had proponents of home rule within their ranks – including even the occasional Conservative!) the fact remains that electoral support for the only party for which increased self-government represents its *sine qua non* remained at derisory levels until the late 1960s. Devolution – like much of the constitutional reform agenda in Britain as a whole – remained the passion and preserve of a relatively narrow, largely intellectual stratum in Welsh society.

A second, and surely related, characteristic of devolutionary politics in Wales was that engagement with the issue remained as shallow as it was narrow. That is, over the past century and more during which self-government has been touted by some as at least part of the solution to the nation's ills, discussion of the issue has tended to remain at the level of general principle. There was very little by the way of sophisticated debate about the particular concrete, constitutional forms that a future devolved body might take. A number of reasons may be adduced for this striking lacuna at the very heart of the devolutionary cause. In part it simply reflects the absence of clear public support for the basic principle itself – in such circumstances, enhancing support for the principle may have been a higher priority than 'academic' discussions over form. Other contributory factors may well also include, *inter alia*:

- The 'culturalist' bent of Plaid Cymru, which has meant that the party has been notably less concerned with constitutional details than is usually the case with nationalist parties (on the evolution of Plaid Cymru's constitutional thinking see Wyn Jones, 1999); and,
- The dismissive attitude of the Labourist tradition – the dominant political formation in Wales during most of the twentieth century – to constitutional questions (the *locus classicus* of the analysis of Labourism is Nairn 1964a, 1964b); and,
- The absence of a distinctive Welsh legal system and, hence, a general lack of constitutional expertise in Wales (in stark contrast to the situation in Scotland).

But whatever the precise causes of its absence, the lack of sustained engagement with the constitutional architecture of a devolved body has rendered such debates as have taken place in Wales rather unsophisticated and largely derivative of the discussions in the other Celtic countries, most notably Scotland.

While the result of the 1997 referendum provided a less than convincing mandate for the establishment of the National Assembly, when compared to the only previous attempt to formally gauge public support for devolution – the 1979 referendum on the implementation of the 1978 Wales Act – it nevertheless revealed a very significant shift in public attitudes to devolution. In the final days of the Callaghan administration, and by an overwhelming four to one majority, the Welsh electorate delivered the *coup de grace* to a plan to establish a Welsh Assembly that had already been subjected to a prolonged parliamentary mauling at the hands of a group of determined Labour rebels (Foulkes et al., 1983). In the aftermath, the celebrated Welsh historian Gwyn A. Williams wrote in apocalyptic terms of the implications: 'the Welsh electorate in 1979 wrote *finis* to nearly two hundred years of Welsh history. They declared bankrupt the political creeds which the modern Welsh had embraced. They may in the process have warranted the death of Wales itself' (Williams, 1985: 295). In contrast, however, the contemporary judgement of the equally distinguished K. O. Morgan was more measured. 'The idea of Welsh devolution,' he claimed, 'did not disappear from history in March 1979' (Morgan in the Foreword to Foulkes et al., 1983: x). And while it is almost certainly the case that Williams's verdict most accurately captured the despair felt by most devolutionists in the early 1980s, it is Morgan's judgement that was (eventually) vindicated.

Given the trauma of the 1979 referendum it is perhaps unsurprising that the main impetus to re-engage with the issue of devolution came from outside Wales. In 1982, John Prescott, then Labour Spokesman on Regional

Policy and Devolution, developed plans for regional bodies in England to complement the established commitment to a Scottish Assembly (Prescott and Pendry, 1982). But even under pressure to support Welsh devolution as part of the development of this broader, Britain-wide strategy, the Wales Labour Party remained extremely cautious. When proposals for an Assembly were finally put before the party conference in 1986, it was in the context of local government reform *and* plans for English regional assemblies (Labour Party 1986). The key point to note in terms of this process is that neither then, nor at any other point during their subsequent evolution up until 1997, were Labour's devolution proposals subject to broad public debate in Wales. Indeed, reviewing the evolution of Labour's proposals during its time in opposition, it is clear that one of the primary concerns of the leadership of the Labour Party in Wales was precisely to avoid such discussion (Wyn Jones and Lewis 1998; Morgan and Mungham 2000). For example, when plans were mooted at the 1992 Wales TUC Conference for a Welsh Constitutional Convention closely modelled on the Scottish convention, they were swiftly rejected by the Wales Labour Party Executive (Wyn Jones and Lewis 1998). Rather than participate in a forum that the party might be unable to control, it established a Policy Commission that embarked on a 'consultation process', including six public consultation meetings around Wales. Although the party claimed that this was intended 'to produce a blueprint for the type of Assembly that will command the broadest range of support in Wales at the next General Election', it is difficult to see the consultation process as being anything more than a cosmetic exercise (Wales Labour Party 1995; Wyn Jones and Lewis 1998). The reality is that the documents outlining the structure and powers of the Welsh Assembly presented at the 1995 and 1996 Wales Labour Party Conferences were the products of internal, largely closed discussions within the party itself (Wales Labour Party 1995, 1996). Moreover, these discussions, such as they were, concentrated on the general principle of devolution rather than the constitutional architecture of a devolved body. In fact, the structure suggested was essentially the same 'executive devolution' model that had been rejected so emphatically by the electorate in 1979 (for details see Rawlings, forthcoming). There was no real development in constitutional thinking in Wales between 1979 and 1997 and no attempt to address the manifest and manifold weaknesses of the 1978 Wales Act.

What is striking is that even after Tony Blair's surprise announcement on 27 June 1996 that the party's proposals for devolution for Wales and Scotland would be subject to referendums, in Wales at least this did not provoke any substantial discussion of those proposals. Devolution hardly registered as an issue in the run-up to the 1997 UK general election in Wales; Labour's promise of a subsequent referendum effectively deferred the issue until a later date. During the referendum campaign it was, yet again, the general principle of devolution that was the point at issue rather than the substance of the proposals. For their own reasons, both the 'Yes' and the 'No' campaigns focused on generalities (see the contributions to Barry Jones and Balsom, 2000). On the part of the 'Yes' campaign this was at least in part a reflection of the fact that many of its most active supporters were supporters of legislative devolution along the lines of the proposed Scottish Parliament, rather than the executive devolution being offered to Wales. To focus on specifics would therefore be to invite divisions. For 'No' campaigners the issue at stake was the principle: no form of directly elected devolved body would be acceptable to them. So again the focus remained on the general rather than the particulars of the package being put to the Welsh electorate. The fact that the 1997 referendum was pre-legislative – in contrast to the post-legislative 1979 poll – served (quite deliberately) to concentrate attention on the principle rather than the substance.

   Given this history it is plausible to argue that politically if not constitutionally-speaking, the 1997 referendum is best regarded as delivering a verdict on the general principle of devolution rather than the specific form that self-government should take in Wales. In fact, there was almost no discussion between 1979 and 1997 of the merits and demerits of the various possible models of devolved government, and very little public debate about or even interest in devolution per se. What people could be expected to make of devolution once it actually happened was, therefore, very much unexplored territory.

Devolution and the Welsh Public

Public Attitudes to Devolution

How have the people of Wales responded to devolution since 1997? The immediate signs were not good: voter turnout in the 1999 NAW election was a mere 48%, substantially lower than in the simultaneous Scottish Parliament elections, and particularly unimpressive given that Wales has long sustained slightly higher levels of voter participation at Westminster polls than either England or Scotland. Widespread abstention suggested continuing voter apathy, if not actual hostility, towards devolution. But a more definite and detailed picture on the evolution of public preferences can be gleaned from survey evidence: specifically, the three major surveys of the Welsh electorate conducted between 1997 and 2001.[4]

   The first, and perhaps most important question to consider is whether the views of the Welsh people on the *principle* of devolution have changed since 1997. The most straightforward means of examining this issue is to consider voters' preferred constitutional structure for the government of Wales. Table 1 reports evidence from a question giving respondents four options over the government of Wales, ranging from independence, through an elected parliament with primary legislative and tax-varying powers, an assembly with limited powers as exists now, and the *status quo ante* of no devolved body.

TABLE 1
CONSTITUTIONAL PREFERENCES IN WALES, 1997, 1999 and 2001 (%)

Constitutional Preference	1997	1999	2001
Independence	14.1	9.6	12.3
Parliament	19.6	29.9	38.8
Assembly	26.8	35.3	25.5
No Elected Body	39.5	25.3	24.0
Weighted N	641	1173	1044

Sources: 1997 Welsh Referendum Survey (WRS), 1999 Welsh Assembly Election Survey (WAES), 2001 Wales Life and Times Study (WELT).

A number of salient points emerge from this table. This first is that the current constitutional position, of an elected assembly with quite limited powers, has never been favoured by a majority of the electorate. While this was the most popular single option in the immediate aftermath of the first NAW election, even at that point only slightly more than a third of the electorate thought this to be the best way to govern Wales. By 2001, after two years experience of devolution, this proportion was down to one-quarter.

However, this failure of the Assembly option to gain support does not mean that most voters wish to return to how Wales was governed until 1999. The proportion wishing to see a return to the pre-devolutionary position has dwindled significantly. From being the preference of two-fifths of voters, a clear plurality among the four constitution options, at the time of the referendum, this stance is now adopted by less than one in four of Welsh voters. At the same time, public support for the other 'extreme' option, independence for Wales outside the United Kingdom, shows no significant increase across the three surveys. Rather, while few voters are currently tempted by the independence option, a clear plurality now support the devolved chamber becoming a more powerful institution: in other words, a Welsh Parliament with tax-varying and law-making powers. In 1997 this was the favourite option for fewer than one in five of the electorate; by 2001, support for a Welsh Parliament had more than doubled, and this was, by some distance, the most favoured constitutional position among Welsh voters.

Explaining Changing Public Attitudes: Two Hypotheses

The figures reported above indicate that support for devolution in Wales has grown substantially since 1997, but that a significant number of Welsh voters wish the principle of devolution to be taken further. Why might the change in public attitudes observable since 1997 have occurred? Two rather contrasting hypotheses suggest themselves.

The first, more 'positive' interpretation is that opposition to devolution has fallen, and support for a more powerful devolved institution has grown, because the National Assembly has been widely seen as a success. The 1997 government White Paper, *A Voice for Wales*, claimed that the creation of the NAW would bring government closer to the people and thus make it more effective. It may be that, despite criticism of the NAW from the news-media, the public have responded to what they see as a more effective system of government perceived to be delivering tangible benefits, and so wish to empower the Assembly further.

An alternative, more negative hypothesis, is that while devolution may not have produced results quite as bad as suggested by the more cataclysmic predictions made prior to the 1997 referendum, support for an extension of the powers of the National Assembly might arise from a widespread belief among Welsh voters that the current, limited devolution settlement does not permit the NAW to make a substantial improvement to their lives and that in order for it to do so it requires more far-reaching constitutional prerogatives. In this sense, support for extending devolution may be inspired more by a perception of failure than by one of success. The following section draws on both qualitative and quantitative data to explore these two hypotheses.

Explaining Change in Public Attitudes: Survey Evidence

Several sets of questions in recent surveys allow us insight into public reactions to devolution in Wales. To probe general views on the NAW and its overall effects on governance, our 2001 survey asked respondents whether they thought the National Assembly had improved the way Britain is governed. The most striking feature of responses to this question (see Table 2) is the extent of indifference relating to the Assembly. Relatively few respondents believed that the Assembly had made things worse; but, on the other hand, barely more than one in five thought that devolution had improved the way Britain is governed. A very substantial majority of respondents felt that the Assembly has made no difference to the way that Britain is governed. In terms of governance, therefore, the electorate believe that the Assembly has made little impact.

TABLE 2
IMPACT OF NAW ON 'HOW BRITAIN IS GOVERNED' (%)

Improved it a lot	2.1
Improved it a little	20.8
Made no difference	62.3
Made it a little worse	7.5
Made it a lot worse	3.6
It is too early to tell	3.7
Weighted N	1024

Source: WELT.

A number of items permit us to probe further into both expectations of the Assembly prior to devolution and whether those expectations have been met. As Table 3 shows, findings relating to the 'Voice' that the Assembly would give Wales within the UK, and whether the Assembly would give ordinary people more say in government show a significant disjuncture between expectations and judgements on the early performance of the Assembly. By 2001, the proportion thinking the Assembly had made no difference in terms of giving Wales a stronger voice in the United Kingdom had increased from a third in 1997 and 1999 to almost one half of the electorate. Similarly, while a majority of respondents in 1997 and 1999 thought that the Assembly would give ordinary people more say in government, by 2001 three-fifths of respondents said that the Assembly had not made any difference in this respect.

Another way of examining expectations and perceived performance of the Assembly is in relation to specific policy areas. However we find here, for the most part, a very similar pattern to that observed above: few people believing that devolution has made things worse, but a majority thinking that it has made little positive difference either. As Table 4 shows, in relation to 'standard of living', 31 per cent of the electorate in 1997 thought the Assembly would make a positive difference, and by 2001 a slightly greater proportion thought that the Assembly had made such a difference. In education however, fully one half of respondents in 1997 thought the NAW would help improve standards in education. But by 2001 some 70 per cent of electors thought the Assembly had made no difference, while only a quarter of voters believed it had improved things. A question about the health service in 2001 elicited responses similar to those on education.

TABLE 3A
NAW WILL GIVE/HAS GIVEN 'WALES A STRONGER VOICE IN THE UK' (%)

Response	1997	1999	2001
Stronger	53.6	63.0	50.5
No Difference	34.7	32.1	46.1
Weaker	11.7	4.9	3.4
Weighted N	649	1236	1062

TABLE 3B
NAW WILL GIVE/HAS GIVEN 'ORDINARY PEOPLE MORE SAY IN GOVERNMENT'
(%)

Response	1997	1999	2001
More	57.3	57.7	35.1
No Difference	38.0	39.7	61.5
Less	4.6	2.5	3.4
Weighted N	647	1224	1055

Sources: WRS, WAES and WELT.

TABLE 4A
IMPACT OF NAW ON STANDARD OF LIVING (%)

Response	1997	1999	2001
Improve	31.0	28.3	34.7
No Difference	56.3	66.2	57.4
Reduce	12.7	5.5	7.9
Weighted N	630	1185	1028

TABLE 4B
IMPACT OF NAW ON EDUCATION STANDARDS (%)

Response	1997	1999	2001
Improve	54.9	45.4	25.0
No Difference	39.7	51.2	71.4
Reduce	5.4	3.4	3.5
Weighted N	627	1175	964

TABLE 4C
IMPACT OF NAW ON HEALTH SERVICE (%)

Response	2001
Improve	31.0
No Difference	63.6
Reduce	5.4
Weighted N	1042

Sources: As Table 3.

However, the picture is not one of uniform disappointment with the National Assembly. We also asked in our 2001 survey how far respondents 'trusted the UK Government / the National Assembly to act in Wales' best interests'. The figures reported in Table 5 reinforce the fact that contemporary levels of distrust in politicians and government are considerable. However, not all politicians and levels of government are distrusted equally: over 60 per cent of respondents trusted the Assembly to act in Wales' best interests at least most of the time, compared to less than 25 per cent (!) for the UK government. These figures do suggest that the Assembly is seen by many Welsh voters as something of a 'champion of Wales' – albeit a rather ineffectual one at present.

TABLE 5
TRUST IN UK GOVERNMENT/NAW TO 'ACT IN WALES' BEST INTERESTS' (%)

Response	UK Government	National Assembly
Just about always	0.9	12.1
Most of the time	22.4	49.2
Only some of the time	58.7	31.9
Almost never	17.0	6.7
Weighted N	1058	1047

Source: WELT.

The findings in Table 5 plausibly help explain the paradox in our data – that while most people see the NAW as a disappointment, most also believe that it should have greater influence over the government of Wales. Indeed, other ways of asking about the powers and influence of the National Assembly suggest that the constitutional question-format reported in Table 1 may actually understate the degree of public support for extending devolution further. As Table 6 shows, though few people currently believe the Assembly to be the dominant force in the government of Wales, a large

proportion of the Welsh electorate favour further devolution to a point
where the NAW would become the most influential institution.

TABLE 6
MOST INFLUENCE OVER 'THE WAY WALES IS RUN' (%)

Response	Does Influence	Ought to Influence
National Assembly	17.0	56.2
UK Government	64.4	26.3
Local Councils	15.5	16.5
European Union	3.2	1.0
Weighted N	1033	1047

Source: WELT.

Probing Further: Evidence from Focus Groups

While the survey evidence presented above tells us much about public
attitudes to devolution in Wales, closed-ended, large-N surveys also have
certain, well-known, limitations. These are, arguably, of particular
relevance when one is concerned with a new institution like the NAW about
which public knowledge may be very limited. Fortunately, we have a
second source of data on which to call – the findings of a series of
qualitative focus groups conducted throughout Wales during 2002. While
the construction of the groups was somewhat skewed towards those
unlikely to vote in the 2003 NAW election, they nonetheless provide us with
a rich source of data that complements well our survey findings.[5]

Unsurprisingly, our focus groups reported a considerable lack of interest
in, and cynicism towards, conventional party politics. Lack of interest
appears to stem from a number of sources, including the feeling that
differences between the major parties have become blurred and that there
are fewer divisive figures on the political scene than previously. But
alienation from the political process induced by such feelings is exacerbated
by cynicism about the motives of politicians. As one voter opined,

> The bigger the politician, the bigger the ego he's got. It's not about the
> policies he makes, it's about how long he can stay in power and how
> much more powerful he can get (Swansea group participant).

Devolution, and members of the NAW are by no means excepted from such
attitudes: 'The people on the Assembly, they've all got other jobs. They are
all connected' (Merthyr Tydfil group participant).

Knowledge of the National Assembly was shown to be very limited.
Some younger focus group participants professed to being unaware of the

existence of the body, while others appeared unaware that it was an elected institution! As one observed, 'I don't know what the Assembly is … I don't have a clue about it' (Swansea group participant). Even among most other voters, understanding of the powers of the Assembly is very limited – mainly consisting of an awareness that, as distinct from the arrangement for Scotland, Wales does not have a parliament. Quite what that means, however, is hazy: 'It's not the same as Scotland, that's more independent' (Caernarfon group participant); 'I know it has some powers but I don't know what they are' (Swansea group participant); 'The Scottish Parliament has got a lot more power than the Welsh Assembly. A lot more money to be able to control things and influence certain big issues' (Wrexham group participant). Many voters assume that the Assembly requires approval from Westminster for any actions:

> *The Welsh Assembly is in the arms of the Central Government…it's just an arm of Central Government and the decisions are made down there* (Wrexham group participant).

> *You don't really get the impression that they are in control* (Wrexham group participant).

> *It's all talking that's being done. They have no direct control over Wales* (Swansea group participant).

Our focus groups revealed strikingly little evidence of actual hostility towards devolution and the idea of having a National Assembly. Despite the general cynicism towards politicians that is prevalent, many voters do expect the National Assembly to be more likely to act in the best interest of Wales than the UK government, by virtue of its Welshness, and respond well to this:

> *I really like the idea. I'm very much for the Welsh standing on their own* (Wrexham group participant).

> *I think it's good for Wales to say… 'we are doing what we think, not necessarily what England is doing'* (Cardiff group participant).

However, while it was uncommon to encounter actual hostility to the concept of an Assembly for Wales, more widespread was the notion that the Assembly has been set up in order to 'placate' Wales, in the absence of a body which has genuine powers to make changes in Wales:

> *It's a false sign of independence…All major decisions are made by*

people in London. It's just to fob us off: give them something to shut them up (Swansea group participant).

It's a bit patronising as well the way that they said 'oh all right then, you can have your own separate little government' but not actually have the power to do anything (Swansea group participant).

Nonetheless, such opinions reveal that while few seem strongly opposed to the *concept* of devolved government in Wales, the accomplishments of devolution thus far are judged to be few and far between:

Nothing else has changed – the hospitals and so on. No better facilities or more jobs (Caernarfon group participant).

You're not seeing any benefits from it. There could be, but we don't know that they've done anything (Wrexham group participant).

I was really looking forward [to Wales having an Assembly]. We were getting a new voice, a new beginning. It's been a big disappointment. We feel we're being forgotten (Caernarfon group participant).

And among some voters at least, this sense of limited accomplishment by the Assembly appears to be one of the factors driving support for enhanced powers:

It's a good idea, but it doesn't have enough powers to make it work (Cardiff group participant).

I think it needs to develop, because we are a nation in our own right. We should have the same sort of set-up as Scotland has (Wrexham group participant).

To summarize, our qualitative findings generally support, and thus reinforce, those produced by our examination of quantitative survey data. In doing so, they offer little support for our first hypothesis regarding the increased support for devolution in Wales since 1997, and generally appear far more in line with our second hypothesis. That is, we find little to suggest that the people of Wales have come to be more favourable to devolution – and even, increasingly, to support empowering the National Assembly further – because they have responded to the manifest successes produced by devolution so far. Rather, there seems to be increasing support for the *principle* of devolution alongside disappointment with what limited self-government has hitherto achieved. Relatively few voters in Wales now wish to return to the pre-devolution settlement, and many seek to give the National Assembly more powers as a means to deliver more definite 'results' from self-government.

Modelling Attitudes to Constitutional Choice

While we have examined the factors that help explain the change since 1997 in attitudes towards devolution in Wales, we have not thus far gone very far in explaining cross-sectional variation in public attitudes. That is, while public opinion was more pro-devolution in 2001 than four years previously, the figures in Table 1 still reveal a considerable spread of support across the four major constitutional options. In this section, therefore, we construct a multivariate model that attempts to examine the relative importance of major factors that might be expected to underpin individuals' degree of enthusiasm towards devolution.

Our analysis draws on our most recent (i.e. 2001) survey data. The dependent variable in our initial analysis is taken from the constitutional preferences reported in Table 1. This gives respondents four broad options – independence for Wales, enhanced devolution, the current devolution settlement, and no devolution. As these four categories could not seriously be argued to form an interval-level scale, a linear regression model would be inappropriate; we therefore specify a multi-nomial logit model.

Several independent variables are included in the model. First, we include a standard battery of control variables for social class (based on the standard 'objective' measure of social class, with dummy variables specified for each class category from 'A', through 'B', 'C1', 'C2', 'D' and 'E'),[6] age (grouped in categories, with those over 65 the omitted 'reference' group), and gender (coded '1' for female, '0' for male). Second, we include a set of dummy variables for identifiers with each of the four major political parties in Wales; the clear expectation here being that Plaid Cymru identifiers should be strongly inclined to favour greater self-government for Wales than those of other parties, particularly the Conservatives. Third, we include a measure of national identity that captures the differing degrees of 'Welsh' and 'British' identity that prevail across much of the population of Wales.[7] We also include a variable gauging competence in the Welsh language (a dummy coded '1' for Welsh speakers and '0' otherwise). For both the language and national identity measures, the most plausible hypothesis is that greater 'Welshness' is likely to correlate positively with support for greater self-government for Wales. Finally, however, we specify variables that gauge how assessments of the performance of the NAW so far condition broader attitudes towards devolution. Some authors have suggested that voters in Scotland supported devolution in 1997 less as an expression of nationalist sentiment and more because of 'sociotropic' expectations of the benefits that would follow the creation of the Scottish Parliament (Brown et al., 1999, ch.6).[8] Although our analysis thus far indicates that support for devolution has not grown in response to positive evaluations of the NAW's performance, the relationship of such evaluations to current devolution attitudes remains to be specified more precisely. We therefore include two variables directly related with evaluations of the performance of the Assembly: one is based on responses to a question concerned with the 'voice' given to Wales in the UK by devolution;[9] the second examines the impact of assessments of the Assembly's policy outputs by constructing an additive scale based on the three policy items (health, education and standard of living) reported in Table 4.[10]

Multinomial logit results are presented in Table 7. The three main columns in the table present coefficients relating to the contrast between support for varying degrees of self-government for Wales (an Assembly with limited powers, a more powerful parliament, or independence for Wales) on the one hand, and no devolution on the other. The model overall produces a reasonable 'fit', and several interesting findings emerge. The gender variable is consistently insignificant, while those for social class have only a modest impact at most. Nor is competence in the Welsh language (net of other factors) related to attitudes to self-government for the nation. The age variables, however, are of importance: in comparison to the oldest cohort, younger voters in Wales are generally supportive of political autonomy for Wales. The youngest (18–24 year olds) are particularly inclined to support independence, while slightly older cohorts lean more towards more limited forms of self-government. This finding reinforces other work that tends to find British national identity and attachment to pre-devolution constitutional structures is greatest in Scotland and Wales among elder citizens. Partisan identity is also related to attitudes to self-government, and in expected directions. Identifiers with all parties except for Plaid Cymru are relatively hostile to independence for Wales; Conservatives and (though to a lesser extent) Labour identifiers tend to oppose enhancing devolution by turning the assembly into a parliament.

The most consistent, and strongest, markers of support for self-government for Wales identified in our model, however, are national identity and evaluations of the performance of the National Assembly. Those who feel more definitely 'Welsh' are more inclined to favour political autonomy for Wales; so too are those who put positive evaluations on the experience of devolution so far. While not particularly surprising in themselves, these findings do partially contradict those for Scotland of Brown et al. (1999) in suggesting that support for self-government can be *both* an expression of national(ist) sentiment *and* shaped by evaluations (whether prospective or retrospective) of the policy benefits associated with political autonomy.

TABLE 7
MULTINOMIAL LOGIT ESTIMATES (STANDARD ERRORS) FOR SUPPORT FOR
SELF-GOVERNMENT FOR WALES

Variable	Assembly	Parliament	Independence
Welsh National Identity	.19 (.09)*	.38 (.09)**	.56 (.13)**
Welsh Language	−.28 (.28)	.07 (.26)	.06 (.34)
Female	−.05 (.23)	.25 (.22)	−.03 (.30)
Age 18–24	1.03 (.52)*	.98 (.50)	1.80 (.59)**
Age 25–34	.50 (.38)	.97 (.35)**	1.33 (.46)**
Age 35–44	.96 (.34)**	.95 (.33)**	1.16 (.44)**
Age 45–54	.12 (.32)	−.48 (.32)	−.07 (.45)
Age 55–64	.18 (.34)	.25 (.32)	−.49 (.53)
Soc. Class Category 'A'	.35 (.67)	.47 (.68)	−1.14 (1.29)
Soc. Class Category 'B'	.28 (.34)	.55 (.33)	.31 (.42)
Soc. Class Category 'C1'	.46 (.33)	.56 (.33)	−.81 (.52)
Soc. Class Category 'C2'	−.05 (.36)	.56 (.34)	−.07 (.44)
Soc. Class Category 'D'	.33 (.35)	.57 (.34)	.50 (.43)
Soc. Class Category 'E'	−.25 (.57)	−.36 (.57)	1.00 (.61)
Conservative Identifier	−.52 (.39)	−1.32 (.38)**	−1.78 (.53)**
Labour Identifier	−.21 (.35)	−.61 (.32)	−1.25 (.40)**
Lib-Dem Identifier	−.14 (.47)	−.00 (.43)	−1.59 (.68)*
Plaid Identifier	.33 (.57)	.32 (.53)	.63 (.58)
NAW 'Voice for Wales'	1.03 (.22)**	1.11 (.21)**	1.11 (.28)**
Policy Impact of NAW	.46 (.11)**	.65 (.11)**	.58 (.14)**
(Intercept)	−1.24 (.50)	−1.77 (.48)	−2.90 (.66)

Initial −2 log likelihood = 2243.57
Model Improvement = 352.26
Nagelkerke Psudo R^2 = .36
Weighted N = 867
* = p < .05; ** = p < .01

The most notable and striking finding to emerge from the analysis, however, is the sheer consistency of the empirical results. That is, in comparison to a position of no devolution, the *same* factors generally predict support for quite different degrees of home rule in Wales. How can we interpret this finding? The most plausible interpretation, and one consistent with our qualitative data discussed earlier, is probably one that starts from an appreciation that thinking about self-government in Wales amongst the bulk of the population is relatively unsophisticated. Many (though not all) people will have some view on whether Wales should have some degree of political autonomy, but their views on quite how far this should go are probably very vague. There may well be, in the aggregate, declining opposition to the principle of devolution, and a general sense abroad that the assembly's perceived lack of impact might be tackled in part by making it a more powerful institution. Nonetheless, the distinction between an 'assembly' and a 'parliament' (and perhaps even between a 'parliament' and 'independence) is likely to be opaque to many. Thus, multivariate models will find it hard to identify factors that underpin a constituency of support for a parliament, as distinct from an assembly, largely because such clearly defined constituencies of support do not exist. Testing the plausibility of this interpretation directly is difficult. Panel data would provide one possibility,[11] but unfortunately none is currently available for Wales. Another approach, however, is to conduct a series of logistic regression analyses in which the dependent variable is coded as '1' for expressed support for any one of the four main constitutional positions, '0' for all other answers. To the extent that a clear and identifiable constituency of support for a particular constitutional option is present, the fit of a well-specified multivariate model should be good; if it is absent, the model fit should be poor. In Table 8, therefore, we report results for the same model used previously, but applied via logistic regression to support for Independence, a parliament for Wales, an assembly, and no devolved body.

TABLE 8
LOGIT ESTIMATES (STANDARD ERRORS) FOR SUPPORT FOR FOUR
CONSTITUTIONAL OPTIONS

Variable	No Devolution	Assembly	Parliament	Independence
Welsh National Identity	− .32 (.08)**	− .11 (.07)	.14 (.07)*	.30 (.11)**
Welsh Language	.09 (.24)	− .30 (.21)	.19 (.18)	.10 (.27)
Female	− .12 (.20)	− .23 (.17)	.23 (.16)	− .21 (.24)
Age 18–24	−1.11 (.47)*	.13 (.33)	− .07 (.29)	.92 (.41)*
Age 25–34	− .83 (.31)**	− .21 (.29)	.44 (.24)	.67 (.37)
Age 35–44	− .96 (.30)**	.28 (.25)	.23 (.23)	.37 (.37)
Age 45–54	.18 (.27)	.43 (.26)	− .44 (.25)	.17 (.39)
Age 55–64	− .13 (.28)	.17 (.28)	.31 (.25)	− .62 (.48)
Soc. Class Category 'A'	− .26 (.60)	.07 (.52)	.29 (.52)	−1.59 (1.42)
Soc. Class Category 'B'	− .40 (.29)	− .03 (.26)	.40 (.24)	− .03 (.34)
Soc. Class Category 'C1'	− .34 (.30)	.33 (.25)	.58 (.24)*	−1.16 (.45)*
Soc. Class Category 'C2'	− .18 (.31)	− .27 (.28)	.66 (.25)**	− .34 (.35)
Soc. Class Category 'D'	− .42 (.30)	.02 (.27)	.32 (.24)	.12 (.34)
Soc. Class Category 'E'	.03 (.47)	− .37 (.46)	− .67 (.44)	1.15 (.46)*
Conservative Identifier	1.19 (.32)**	.46 (.31)	− .54 (.29)	− .96 (.46)*
Labour Identifier	.64 (.29)*	.38 (.26)	− .05 (.23)	− .80 (.30)**
Lib-Dem Identifier	.38 (.39)	.19 (.35)	.61 (.31)*	−1.44 (.59)*
Plaid Identifier	− .30 (.49)	− .02 (.38)	− .04 (.31)	.41 (.37)
NAW 'Voice for Wales'	−1.07 (.19)**	.30 (.17)	.38 (.15)*	.26 (.23)
Policy Impact of NAW	− .57 (.10)**	− .02 (.08)	.26 (.07)**	.09 (.10)
(Constant)	.49 (.42)	−1.15 (.39)	−1.92 (.36)	−2.84 (.56)
−2 log likelihood	738.06	947.14	1085.45	564.85
% cases correctly predicted	79.5	76.1	66.3	87.4
Nagelkerke Psuedo R^2	.34	.05	.14	.21
Weighted N	891	890	891	891

* = p < .05; ** = p < .01

Our expectations are largely supported by the findings reported in Table 8. Our model has little success in explaining preferences for an assembly versus all other constitutional options, while the model fit for 'parliament' is also quite modest. Regarding the latter, a preference for a parliament is predicted to some degree by stronger Welsh national identity and positive perceptions of the performance of the NAW, as well as by some of our class dummies and by being a Liberal Democrat identifier. The fit of our model improves further for the Independence option. As was shown in Table 1, relatively few people endorse this position, but we can predict those who do so moderately well through a few variables – stronger 'Welsh' identifiers, the young and the lower working classes are disproportionately inclined towards this position, Conservative, Labour and Liberal Democrat identifiers are all likely to be opposed, while evaluations of the performance of the Assembly so far are unrelated towards attitudes to independence. The table shows, however, that our model has greatest success in predicting attitudes towards opposition to devolution. Reinforcing our earlier findings, the results show a strong negative relationship between opposition to devolution and both stronger Welsh national identity and more positive endorsements of the performance of the National Assembly. Younger age cohorts also tend to support the principle of devolution to a greater extent. On the other hand, opposition to devolution is positively associated with Tory and (though to a lesser extent) Labour Party identity. In sum, the findings support the interpretation of our previous analysis. Attitudes to the *principle* of devolution are reasonably clear amongst much of the Welsh public, and they are associated with identifiable and explicable factors such as national and partisan identity and evaluations of how the devolved institution has performed hitherto. Attitudes towards independence are also somewhat predictable. However, this is much less true of attitudes towards differing degrees of devolution – whether Wales should have an assembly, as now, or a more powerful Parliament.

Conclusion

According to Andrew Rawnsley, the prevailing view at the heart of government is that Wales is Scotland's smaller, uglier sister (Rawnsley, 2000: 238). Despite this patronizing attitude – indeed, in some ways, precisely because of it – in analytical terms, the Welsh experience of devolution is at least as interesting as that of the undoubtedly larger and allegedly fairer sister. That Wales should have a form of devolved government is increasingly the 'settled will' in Wales, as it was in Scotland in 1997. Support for some form of home rule has strengthened considerably over the last five years. What remains at issue, however, is the form that home rule should take. Support for the present settlement has now been outstripped by support for a parliament with primary legislative and, indeed, tax-varying powers. Moreover, there is a clear public expectation that the powers of the National Assembly will be enhanced in coming years. Given the inauspicious beginnings of a less than convincing referendum mandate followed by successive political crises, this finding is rather surprising. It is, nonetheless, supported by other pieces of evidence now available, such as the focus groups work we have also discussed here. It is important not to claim too much: there is no evidence that the Welsh electorate have become passionately engaged with the devolution project. Indeed, both our qualitative evidence and our modelling efforts suggest that the distinction between a parliament and an assembly may be a rather ill-defined one for most of the people of Wales. Nonetheless, more than five years on from the referendum that only narrowly approved the creation of the assembly, a clear majority of the Welsh electorate appear to have accepted devolution; and many of them have begun, however tentatively, to develop a taste for more.

NOTES

1. This statement is true of even those groups and organizations who might have been expected to find devolution most conducive. So, for example, the Welsh language pressure group, *Cymdeithas yr Iaith Gymraeg* (The Welsh Language Society) has found it extremely difficult to adapt its methods or goals to the new context and, for the first time in its 40-year history, has found its pre-eminent position as the main campaigning group for equal status for the language challenged by *Cymuned* (Community), an organization only founded in 2001 (Wyn Jones 2002).
2. In February 2000, Alun Michael was forced to resign as First Minister in the face of a looming 'no-confidence' motion being passed against him; in the autumn of that year, Michael's successor, Rhodri Morgan, concluded a controversial coalition deal with the Liberal Democrats to give his administration a secure majority in the assembly.
3. This term is overlain with such a deep set of historical and cultural allusions that the literal English translation – people – does not begin to capture its resonance in Welsh political discourse (see, *inter alia*, Harvie, 1992; Llywelyn-Williams, 1960: 41–161; Morgan, 1986). The Welsh historian Gwyn A. Williams attempted to conjure up the self-image attached to it as follows:

> The *gwerin* was a cultivated, educated, often self-educated, responsible, self-disciplined, respectable but on the whole genially poor or perhaps small-propertied people, straddling groups perceived as classes in other, less fortunate societies. Welsh-speaking, Nonconformist, imbued with the more social virtues of Dissent, bred on the Bible and good practice, it was open to the more spiritual forms of wider culture and was dedicated to spiritual self-improvement. It cherished many of the 'traditional' habits of Welsh culture, derived ultimately from the poets' guild, nurtured country poets, skilled in verse and wordplay; it was learned in a somewhat antiquarian manner, interested in letters and cultivated a deep pacifist patriotism, controlled by religion … This *gwerin* was the heart and soul of the Welsh nation. (Williams, 1985: 237–8)

Although the era of the *gwerin* was brought to a close on the killing fields of First World War France, it is striking that the trope still surfaces in contemporary Welsh politics. So, for example, in his speech in a conference held in March 2000 to mark the centenary of the Labour party, the then Welsh Secretary Paul Murphy proclaimed Welsh Labour as the party of 'Gwerin Cymru' (Cymru being Welsh for Wales) (*The Welsh Mirror*, 24.3.2000). The term, it seems, may yet retain some residual hold on the Welsh political imagination.

4. These surveys are the 1997 Welsh Referendum Survey, the 1999 Welsh Assembly Election Study, and the 2001 Wales Life and Times Study. All three surveys were funded by the Economic and Social Research Council of the UK (Grant Numbers M543285001;R000 23 8070; and L219252042 respectively), and co-directed by Anthony Heath and Richard Wyn Jones, with fieldwork conducted by the National Centre for Survey Research. Prior to 1997, only one major election study of Wales had ever been conducted (in 1979). While Welsh respondents have featured in British Elections Studies, the number of Welsh cases was generally very small (no Welsh booster sample was included in the BES until 2001), and few questions dealt with matters of specific concern to students of Welsh politics.

5. Ten focus groups were conducted, at several locations throughout Wales, as part of a research project exploring public attitudes towards voting and devolution in Wales. The project was commissioned by the Electoral Commission, and carried out jointly by the Institute of Welsh Politics at Aberystwyth and NOP. Further details are available in Electoral Commission (2002).

6. The comparison group for the class variable are those respondents not assigned to a class category.

7. This measure is based on the now-standard so-called 'Moreno' measure; the five response categories are 'Welsh not British', 'More Welsh than British', 'Equally Welsh and British', 'More British than Welsh', and 'British not Welsh'. This variable is specified as a quasi-interval level measure, coded from 1 ('British not Welsh') through to 5 ('Welsh not British').

8. Some analyses of voting in the Scottish referendum give greater weight to national identity than Brown et al. – see, for instance, Denver et al., 2000, ch.7. National identity differences were also found to be important in explaining voting patterns in the Welsh Assembly referendum – see Wyn Jones and Trystan (1999).

9. The question asks, 'Do you think that having a Welsh National Assembly is giving Wales…', with potential responses being 'A stronger voice in the United Kingdom' (coded '1' for the empirical analysis), 'A weaker voice in the United Kingdom' (coded '–1'), 'or is it making no difference?' (coded '0'). The distribution of responses were as listed in Table 3A.

10. The additive scale on Assembly policy impact is constructed by summing assessments in the three areas of education, health, and 'standard of living'. Positive assessments on each individual item were coded '1', negative assessments coded '–1', and 'no difference' assessments coded '0'. The scale thus potentially runs from –3 to 3.

11. Panel data might, for instance, permit examination of the degree to which respondents interviewed at different time periods offered consistent answers to the question on constitutional preference. The more clearly defined that positions are, the less one would expect to see 'cycling' between support for different constitutional options across different waves of a panel survey.

REFERENCES

Davies, R. (1999) *Devolution: A Process Not an Event*. Cardiff: Institute of Welsh Affairs.

Electoral Commission (2002) *Wales Votes? Public Attitudes Towards Assembly Elections*, accessed at www.electoralcommission.org.uk/about-us/walesvotes.cfm.

Harvie, C. (1992), 'The Folk and the *Gwerin*: The Myth and the Reality of Popular Culture in 19th-Century Scotland and Wales', in *Proceedings of the British Academy*, Vol.80, pp.19–48.

Foulkes, D., J. Barry Jones and R.A. Wilford (eds.) (1983), *The Welsh Veto: The Wales Act 1978 and The Referendum*. Cardiff: University of Wales Press.

Jones, I.W. (2001) *O Gynulliad I Sennedd*. Aberystwyth: Institute of Welsh Politics.

Jones, J. Barry and D. Balsom (eds.) (1999), *The Road to the National Assembly for Wales*. Cardiff: University of Wales Press.

Jones, J.G. (1987), 'E.T. John and Welsh Home Rule', *Welsh History Review*, 13: 453–67.

Jones, J.G. (1988), 'Early Campaigns to Secure a Secretary of State for Wales, 1890–1939', *Transactions of the Honourable Society of Cymmrodorion*, pp.153–75.

Jones, J.G. (1989a), 'E.T. John, Devolution and Democracy, 1917–24', *Welsh History Review* 14 (3): 439–69.

Jones, J.G. (1989b), 'Socialism, Devolution and a Secretary of State for Wales', in *Transactions of the Honourable Society of Cymmrodorion*, pp.135–59.

Jones, J.G. (1990), 'Alfred Thomas's National Institutions (Wales) Bills 1891–92', *Welsh History Review* 15 (2): 218–39.

Jones, J.G. (1992), 'The Parliament for Wales Campaign, 1950–56', *Welsh History Review* 16 (2): 207–36.

Llywelyn Williams, A. (1983), *Y Niwl, Y Nos a'r Ynys: Agweddau ar y profiad rhamantaidd yng Nghymru 1890–1914*, Caerdydd : Gwasg Prifysgol Cymru.

Morgan, K. and G. Mungham (2000), *Redesigning Democracy: The Making of the Welsh Assembly*. Bridgend: Seren.

Morgan, K.O. (1981), *Rebirth of a Nation: Wales 1880–1980*. Oxford: Oxford University Press and University of Wales Press.

Morgan, P. (1986) 'The *Gwerin* of Wales – Myth and Reality', in I. Hume and W.T.R. Pryce (eds.), *The Welsh and their Country: Selected Readings in the Social Sciences*. Llandysul: Gomer, pp.134–52.

Nairn, T. (1964a), 'The Nature of the Labour Party (Part I)', *New Left Review* 27: 38–65.

Nairn, T. (1964b), 'The Nature of the Labour Party (Part II)', *New Left Review* 28: 38–62.

Patterson, L. and R. Wyn Jones (1999) 'Does Civil Society Drive Constitutional Change? The Cases of Scotland and Wales' in B. Taylor and K. Thomson (eds.), *Scotland and Wales: Nations Again?* Cardiff: University of Wales Press, pp.169–97.

Prescott, J. and T. Pendry (1982), *Alternative Regional Strategy*.

Rawlings, R. (2003), *Delineating Wales*. Cardiff: University of Wales Press.

Rawnsley, A. (2000) *Servants of the People: The Inside Story of New Labour*. London: Hamish Hamilton.

Wales Labour Party. (1995), *Shaping the Vision – A Report on the Powers and Structure of the Welsh Assembly*. Cardiff: Wales Labour Party.

Wales Labour Party (1996), *Preparing for a New Wales – A Report on the Structure and Workings of the Welsh Assembly*. Cardiff: Wales Labour Party.

Williams, E.W. (1986) 'The Politics of Welsh Home Rule 1886–1929: A Sociological Analysis', unpublished PhD thesis, University of Aberystwyth.

Williams, Gwyn A. (1985), *When Was Wales? A History of the Welsh*. London: Penguin.

Wyn Jones, R. (1999), 'Saunders Lewis a'r Blaid Genedlaethol' [Saunders Lewis and the Welsh Nationalist Party], in Geraint Jenkins (ed.), *Cof Cenedl Vol. XV*. Llandysul: Gomer, pp.163–92.

Wyn Jones, R. (2001) 'On Process, Events and Unintended Consequences: National Identity and the Politics of Welsh Devolution,' *Scottish Affairs* 37: 34–57.

Wyn Jones, R. and B. Lewis (1998), 'The Wales Labour Party and Welsh Civil Society: Aspects of the Constitutional Debate in Wales'. Paper presented to PSA Annual Conference, University of Keele.

Wyn Jones, R. and D. Trystan (1999) 'The Welsh Referendum Vote', in B. Taylor and K. Thomson (eds.) *Scotland and Wales: Nations Again?* Cardiff: University of Wales Press.

First or Second-order?
Will the Scottish and Welsh Elections
Deliver Devolution?

Robert Ingram

One of the key aims of the advocates of the establishment of the Scottish Parliament and Welsh Assembly was that the conduct of public policy should be more sensitive to public opinion in those countries. Whilst both countries already enjoyed a substantial measure of administrative devolution (more so in Scotland than in Wales), who ran the Scottish and Welsh Offices was determined by who won power across the United Kingdom as a whole and not by the balance of opinion within each country. Thus it was argued that the two countries required new institutions that were elected by the people of Scotland and Wales.

Whether or not elections to the new institutions secure their advocates' aims depends on how people vote in the elections. If their aims are to be achieved it will need to be the case that voters vote in the elections on the merits as they see them of the parties' promises and performance within Scotland and Wales. If they do so, those elected to the parliament and assembly will be able to claim a distinctive mandate, separate from that accorded to the Westminster Parliament. In contrast, if voters vote in these elections according to their views on the respective merits of the parties at Westminster, then it will not be clear that members of the Scottish Parliament or the Welsh Assembly will have a distinctive mandate. As a result, they are likely to be regarded as clearly inferior in status and power to the UK Parliament.

This is not an unfamiliar story. Elections have long been held to local councils in order to ensure that those who administer local services are accountable to the people that they serve. More recently, over the last 20 years, direct elections to the European Parliament have been held. In both cases it appears that many voters vote not on the basis of the issues relevant to those institutions but on the basis of their views about the incumbent national government (Miller, 1988; Reif, 1985). Far from giving democratic legitimacy, these elections appear to demonstrate the unimportance, if not indeed the irrelevance, of local government and the European Parliament in the minds of most voters.

Analysis of the first European parliamentary elections of 1979 has given rise to the theory of first- and second-order elections. According to Reif and Schmitt (1980), first-order elections are the national parliamentary or presidential elections. Elections to the European Parliament are classified as second order as are other contests such as by-elections and local elections.

There are three important characteristics that distinguish these contests from those held in the first-order arena. Firstly, turnout is relatively low. Secondly, the incumbent administration and the principal opposition party lose support in these polls. The former usually does badly in these elections because voters (including those who identify with the governing party) use this type of poll as an opportunity to pass an adverse mid-term judgement on the current performance of the government at the national level. Both features stem from the fact that the institutions are unimportant in the minds of the voters. As van der Eijk et al. stipulate:

> Voting in these second-order elections can be thought of as a way in which voters communicate to the national government (and to the other political parties) their views on its current performance and electoral prospects (cited in Heath et al., 1997: 2).

In other words, *those that do vote do so on the basis of what is happening in an arena other than the institution being voted for.* Thirdly, as a by-product of the above, smaller, less established parties do better in second-order elections.

It has been acknowledged that the second-order election model developed by Reif and Schmitt remains a very influential framework when looking at the study of voting behaviour (Norris: 1997). Indeed, analysis of the four subsequent European elections gives strong support to the propositions of the second-order model.

Whether or not the Scottish and Welsh elections prove to be first or second order will be crucial both to the likely future role of the Scottish Parliament and the Welsh Assembly and the impact they have on the United Kingdom as a whole. Fears that they will lead to conflict are likely not to be realized if the elections prove to be second-order ones. Hopes that they will increase the accountability of public policy may be fulfilled if they are first order.

The principal task of this article is to test one of the characteristics of the second-order election model, that of turnout, on the first devolved elections in Scotland and Wales.

Brief Overview of the Actual Results

On 6 May 1999 voters in Scotland and Wales went to the polls to elect members to their newly devolved institutions, the Scottish Parliament and

Welsh Assembly respectively. These elections followed on from the 1997 Scottish and Welsh referendums, promised in the summer of 1996 by the then Labour opposition, when the electorate in both countries had the opportunity to vote on whether such institutions should be established. The results in both referendums paved the way for the 1999 elections to be held.

The events of 6 May 1999 were unprecedented in British electoral politics for two reasons. Firstly, these elections were the first of their type to be held in mainland Britain and secondly, the voting system used to elect members to both institutions meant the electorate had two votes in each poll. As well as comprising the traditional 'first-past-the-post' method, the voting procedure also included an additional 'top-up' proportional system – the Additional Member System – for the first time. The purpose of the electorate having two votes was to ensure that the elections would produce a more proportional result than what would probably occur if only the first-past-the-post system was adopted.

In Scotland, from a total of 129 Members of the Scottish Parliament (MSPs), 73 were elected from individual constituencies (the same number of seats that make up Scotland's representation at Westminster) with an additional 56 members being elected from closed party lists (7 MSPs from each of Scotland's eight regions). These regions were the same as the current European parliamentary constituencies. From a total of 60 Members of the Welsh Assembly (MWAs), 40 members representing individual constituencies were elected under the first-past-the-post system, with an additional 20 members selected from the party lists (4 MWAs each from the five Welsh regions).

The results brought mixed news for the UK government. As the votes were counted, it became clear that the Labour Party would be the largest single party in the two institutions, but due for the most part to the proportional representation element to the voting procedure, they would fall short of majorities in both countries. In Scotland, on a turnout of nearly 59%, Labour won 56 seats in the parliament. The great majority of their members – 53 – were elected from the first-past-the-post component of the vote. The remainder were made up from the 'top-up' lists through the proportionality system. Overall, the party was 9 seats short of the 65 required for an absolute majority in the parliament. In Wales, on a turnout of 46%, Labour won 28 of the 60 seats in the Welsh election, all but one of these gained from the constituency vote in the principality. The party was three seats short of an absolute majority in the assembly.

Turnout in Scotland and Wales: How Much Was at Stake?

We might anticipate that elections to the Scottish Parliament and Welsh Assembly would be regarded as less important than elections to the

Westminster Parliament. As these first elections to the devolved institutions do not affect government formation at Westminster then it could be viewed that these elections are less relevant. As a result, fewer voters will exercise their right to vote. In other words, if Reif and Schmitt were right about lower turnout in second-order elections then we would expect to find fewer voters turning out in these polls. To what extent therefore, can the turnout in Scotland and Wales be explained by how much was thought to be at stake?

Furthermore, the issue of how much was at stake will not necessarily have impacted to the same degree in each country. What makes our analysis of the second-order election model more interesting is the fact that there was a significant difference in turnout between Scotland and Wales. Clearly, some factor(s) must have influenced more voters in Scotland to turn out than those in the principality. This would appear to demonstrate that on turnout at least, the election in Scotland was less second order than the contest in Wales. We will now attempt to unravel what indeed influenced voters and determine if there was something unique to Scotland (or Wales) that could help explain the turnout differential. This can only be satisfactorily determined by proper modelling of individual level data.

The Alleged Benefits of Devolution

One possible answer that could shed some light on how much was thought to be at stake and whether this issue motivated the public to vote in these elections would be assessing how the public perceive the alleged benefits of devolution. One of the arguments put forward by proponents of devolution is that a decentralized form of governance will improve the electorates' sense of engagement with the political process. They have long argued that the new institutions in both countries will give Scotland and Wales a stronger voice within the United Kingdom and that the new parliament and assembly will give the people of Scotland and Wales more say in self-government. If these specific arguments hold true then our expectation would be that the public would be more likely to vote in the devolved elections.

Our first set of tables will give us some clues as to the public's expectations of self-government. These will not only demonstrate to what extent individual voters thought that devolved government mattered but also whether these expectations differed between Scotland and Wales.

Table 1 provides support to the argument put forward by pro-devolutionists that people believed the institutions would give Scotland and Wales a stronger voice in the United Kingdom. If anything Scots had slightly higher expectations of their parliament giving Scotland a stronger

TABLE 1
WHETHER PEOPLE THOUGHT THE PARLIAMENT/ASSEMBLY WOULD GIVE
SCOTLAND/WALES A STRONGER VOICE IN THE UK (%)

	Scotland	Wales
Weaker voice in the UK	7	5
No difference	21	32
Stronger voice in the UK	72	63
N	1453	1236

Note: Excludes 'don't knows' and 'not answered'.

Source: Scottish Parliamentary and Welsh Assembly Election Survey 1999.

voice within the United Kingdom than voters did in Wales. Nearly three quarters of Scots believed the Scottish Parliament would give the country a stronger voice within the United Kingdom while two-thirds of voters in Wales believed this of their assembly. However, not an insignificant number in both countries (especially in Wales) believed that the institutions in the post-devolution era would have a neutral effect in their relationship with the United Kingdom.

But what is also clear is the very small number in both countries who held the view that the parliament/assembly would give Scotland and Wales a weaker voice in the United Kingdom. Therefore, those who have argued that having the parliament and assembly set up would strengthen the voice of Scotland and Wales within the UK appears to be endorsed by the electors of both countries.

TABLE 2
WHETHER PEOPLE THOUGHT THE PARLIAMENT/ASSEMBLY WOULD GIVE
THEM MORE SAY IN SELF-GOVERNMENT (%)

	Scotland	Wales
Less say	2	2
No difference	32	40
More say	66	58
N	1453	1224

Note: Excludes 'don't knows' and 'not answered'.

Source: Scottish Parliamentary and Welsh Assembly Election Survey 1999.

Table 2 shows that voters in both countries also had high expectations that the setting up of the institutions would give them more say in the running of devolved government. As was also suggested from the evidence in Table 1, these expectations were slightly greater amongst people in Scotland than in Wales. Nearly seven out of ten Scots expected their new parliament to give them more say in self-government while in Wales nearly six out of ten voters expressed this view. Overall, a clear majority of voters appear to hold the view that devolution would improve their sense of engagement with the political process. Only a very few people in both countries believed that the parliament and assembly would give them less say in the workings of decentralized government. So far at least, we can conclude that the positive attributes of devolution continue to be borne out by these findings.

But the general impact of devolution on the lives of the public may also play in the minds of the electorate when deciding to vote or not. Whether the result of the Scottish and Welsh elections will make any significant *difference* to the lives of the people of Scotland and Wales could influence their decision. Of course advocates of devolved government would argue that the result of these elections are important. Those elected to the parliament/assembly will be able to claim a distinctive mandate, working for the people of Scotland and Wales, which was separate to that accorded to the Westminster parliament.

However, second-order elections do not matter, it is argued, because it does not make a difference which party wins these contests. In contrast, outcomes in the first-order arena should make more of a difference as more is thought to be at stake. Therefore we should anticipate that fewer people in Scotland and Wales believe the devolved elections will make a difference as compared to a general election. The following two tables show if this was true. In Table 3A we show for each country the extent that voters believed the result in Scotland and Wales would make a difference. Table 3B shows the expectation of a general election outcome.

The first point to note is the remarkable similarity between voters' expectations of the outcomes in the two types of contests, particularly in Scotland. The main difference one can deduce is that slightly more voters in Wales believed the outcome of a general election was more important. Over seven out of ten Scots believed it would make at least some difference who won the Scottish election and the general election. In Wales, while nearly seven out of ten people thought the result of the devolved election would make at least some difference, over seven out of ten said the same about a general election. However, we should not ignore a significant number of people in both countries who supported the view that the outcome would not matter much. About a quarter of Scots believed that it would not make very

TABLE 3A
WHETHER PEOPLE THOUGHT IT WOULD MAKE A DIFFERENCE
WHO WON IN SCOTLAND AND WALES (%)

	Scotland	Wales
None at all	5	10
Not very much	19	23
Some	19	20
Quite a lot	29	23
A great deal	28	25
N	1447	1200

Note: Excludes 'don't knows'.

Source: Scottish Parliamentary and Welsh Assembly Election Survey 1999.

TABLE 3B
WHETHER PEOPLE THOUGHT IT WOULD MAKE A DIFFERENCE
WHO WON IN THE UNITED KINGDOM (%)

	Scotland	Wales
None at all	5	7
Not very much	22	20
Some	18	16
Quite a lot	28	28
A great deal	27	29
N	1456	1240

Note: Excludes 'don't knows'.

Source: Scottish Parliamentary and Welsh Assembly Election Survey 1999.

much difference which party won the Scotland election or the UK poll. A third of voters in Wales also held this view of the outcome in the principality while just over a quarter believed the general election result would not make much difference.

Two main points are clear from the above evidence. Firstly, not only does the result of a general election appear important to many voters in Scotland and Wales but they also have a similar opinion of the devolved elections at least in terms of what the outcome would mean. Most people were optimistic that the results of both contests would make a difference to their lives. This gives support to the assertion espoused by the advocates of devolution that these elections do matter. Furthermore, it also casts a cloud over one of the propositions of the second-order model that many voters conclude that it does not matter who wins these lower level contests because the outcome does not make a difference. But secondly, a small but not insignificant number (more so in Wales) had doubts on what impact the results of the new elections would have in both countries. In short, whilst most voters appeared to care about the outcome some voters were sceptical.

But are the above assertions sufficient for us to assume these elections were important? Not quite. The significance of voters believing the result will make a difference will be questioned if the people of Scotland and Wales have misgivings on what they see as the roles of the two institutions. The proponents of devolution in both countries would be somewhat disheartened to find out that whilst people in Scotland and Wales believed the results mattered they were also wary on how much influence the Scottish Parliament and Welsh Assembly would have in their respective countries. If these results were to matter, the public should also have some faith in the institutions being the linchpin of devolved government and not other bodies exerting influence on such matters.

Therefore we now consider how the public perceived the level of influence that the institutions would have in both Scotland and Wales. While people in Scotland and to a slightly less degree in Wales may have taken the view that the outcome would make a difference to their lives did they also expect that the devolved bodies would exert the most influence on the way Scotland and Wales is run? Table 4 demonstrates if this was indeed the case.

TABLE 4
WHAT WILL INFLUENCE THE WAY THE SCOTLAND/WALES IS RUN? (%)

	Scotland	Wales
Scottish Parliament/Welsh Assembly	41	30
UK government at Westminster	39	44
Local councils in Scotland/Wales	8	12
European Union	4	7
Don't know	8	7
N	1480	1255

Note: Excludes 'not answered'.

Source: Scottish Parliamentary and Welsh Assembly Election Survey 1999.

It is clear from this evidence that people in Scotland and Wales have reservations about the ability of their new institutions to be the most influential playmakers in the post-devolution settlement. Two points are worth noting. Not only is there much pessimism in both countries as to the influence that the parliament and assembly would have in running the affairs of Scotland and Wales, but this pessimism is more striking in Wales than in Scotland. In Wales, while nearly a third of people expected the assembly to be influential, over four in ten people believed that the UK government at Westminster would exert more influence. Of course we can speculate why this may be so. Was it because of the more lukewarm attitude to devolution in Wales? (clearly demonstrated in the devolution referendum of 1997). Was it because of the limited powers that the Welsh Assembly has? But even in Scotland, arguably more receptive to the concept of devolution and with a parliament that has more substantial legislative powers than the assembly does in Wales, many voters were also sceptical. Roughly the same number of people believed that the Scottish Parliament would influence the way Scotland is run as those who expected Westminster to play a leading part.

A further point worth noting is the relatively high number of 'don't know' responses to this question. Since this survey was taken just after the elections in May 1999 then perhaps some voters have not yet formed an opinion on the new institutions. Maybe they are waiting to see if the institutions 'find their feet' and what kind of relationship develops between the new bodies and Westminster.

These tables give us a relatively simple indication of how people perceived the consequences of devolution, and by and large they see these effects as positive attributes but not overwhelmingly. Our first three tables give some support to some of the claims of the pro-devolution camp, with more support in Scotland than in Wales. However, a significant number of people in Scotland and even more so in Wales succumbed to the view that the first-order arena would play a pivotal role in devolved issues. When assessing Reif and Schmitt's assertions on how voters *perceive* lower level elections then at this stage we can conclude that their propositions are only partially validated.

Multivariate Analysis of the Probability of Voting

Of course the above analysis provides only half the picture. While these tables give us some indication on whether voters thought the *institutions* mattered, they tell us little about whether the *elections* mattered. What we now have to demonstrate in a multivariate analysis is to what extent these perceptions made any difference to the probability of voting in these elections. For Reif and Schmitt to be correct, voters' evaluations of the devolved institutions not only have to be low but also have to have an impact. We have addressed the first of these questions in the above tables; now we go on and look at the second.

When modelling individual level data we not only test variables that we might think will prove or disprove a particular theory, we also should consider to what extent these variables exert influence independently from other characteristics that are often thought to be an influence at any election. Previous research has shown that a number of socio-demographic factors such as age, marital status and housing tenure influence turnout in elections (Crewe et al., 1977). The purpose of these 'control' variables is to demonstrate to what extent our main variables are strong, independent influences when controlling for these other factors.

We keep two things in mind when building multivariate statistical models: we always start with the simplest model and, as far as possible, have reasonably parsimonious models throughout the modelling process. The model in Table 5 is a simple logistic model where our dependent variable is whether individuals voted or not in the Scottish and Welsh elections and all the independent variables are our control variables.[1] As well as age, marital status and housing tenure we have also included two other controls: whether respondents have a degree or not, and whether they thought it would make a difference who won the UK general election. We include this latter variable to test the proposition that respondents who thought voting in a first-order election would make no difference were also more likely not to vote in the first Scottish and Welsh elections.

TABLE 5
LOGISTIC MODEL OF TURNOUT IN SCOTTISH AND WELSH ELECTIONS
(CONTROL MODEL)

	Voted versus	Not Voted
	B	SE
Age (60+)		
Age (18–34)	–1.44	(0.13)***
Age (35–59)	–0.62	(0.13)***
Married	0.26	(0.10)**
Tenure (Other rented)		
Tenure (Owner occupied)	0.53	(0.15)***
Tenure (LA rented)	0.59	(0.17)***
Educational Qualification	0.56	(0.13)***
Diff who wins UK election	0.27	(0.04)***
Constant	–0.25	(0.21)
Cox & Snell R Square	10%	
N	2639	

*** significant at 0.1%; ** significant at 1%

Source: Scottish Parliamentary and Welsh Assembly Election Survey 1999.

Table 5 suggests that all our control measures have highly significant parameter estimates, especially the 'general election' variable – the coefficient of which is nearly seven times its standard error. The proposition that this variable tests is given robust support in our model.

We can therefore conclude that the model confirms the importance of socio-demographic factors on turnout. As previous research has confirmed, younger people are less likely to vote in elections. Those who are owner-occupiers are more likely to vote as are people with a higher educational qualification.

While it is useful to reassert the relative importance of these factors as determinants of turnout, they do not shed any light on the subject that this article attempts to address. What about the indicators that could test whether the propositions of the second-order election model also hold in the first elections in Scotland and Wales?

Table 6 expands the model from Table 5 where the dependent and control variables are the same as before. However, we also include the variables shown in Tables 1, 2, 3A and 4 to test the theory of second-order elections.[2] Are some of the propositions put forward by Reif and Schmitt, revealed in the patterns of association rather than the marginals, supported in these elections?

TABLE 6
EXPANDED LOGISTIC MODEL OF TURNOUT IN
SCOTTISH AND WELSH ELECTIONS

	Voted versus	Not Voted
	B	SE
Age (60+)		
Age (18–34)	–1.51	(0.14)***
Age (35–59)	–0.71	(0.14)***
Married	0.29	(0.10)**
Tenure (Other rented)		
Tenure (Owner occupied)	0.64	(0.15)***
Tenure (LA rented)	0.74	(0.18)***
Education Qualification	0.45	(0.14)**
Difference who wins UK Election	0.00	(0.04)
Expectations		
Difference who wins in Scot/Wales	0.48	(0.05)***
Parl/Assem give S/W stronger voice in UK	–0.03	(0.09)
Parl/Assem give more say in self-gov	0.30	(0.10)***
What will influence way Parl/Assem run	0.36	(0.10)***
Constant	–1.50	(0.27)***
Cox & Snell R Square	*16%*	
N	2477	

*** significant at 0.1%; ** significant at 1%

Source: Scottish Parliamentary and Welsh Assembly Election Survey 1999

TABLE 6
LOGISTIC MODEL OF TURNOUT IN SCOTTISH
AND WELSH ELECTIONS (NEW REDUCED MODEL)

	Voted versus	*Not Voted*
	B	SE
Age (60+)		
Age (18–34)	–1.52	(0.14)***
Age (35–59)	–0.73	(0.14)***
Married	0.29	(0.10)**
Tenure (Owner occupied)	0.64	(0.15)***
Tenure (LA rented)	0.75	(0.18)***
Education Qualification	0.49	(0.14)**
Expectations		
Difference who wins in Scot/Wales	0.48	(0.04)***
Parl/Assem more say self-gov	0.28	(0.09)***
Influence way Parliament/Assembly run	0.33	(0.10)***
Constant	–1.48	(0.24)***
Cox & Snell R Square	*16%*	
N	2522	

*** significant at 0.1%; ** significant at 1%

Source: Scottish Parliamentary and Welsh Assembly Election Survey 1999.

The first model in Table 6 shows that most of the control variables continue to exert influence on turnout but crucially, our new items that we have added to the model appear to have an independent influence on turnout. At first glance, the model appears to validate some of Reif and Schmitt's assertions but we should be cautious in interpreting this as evidence that the elections resembled those of a second-order contest.

True, the model shows, for the most part, that individuals who did not believe the new institutions mattered were less likely to vote. Those in Scotland and Wales who thought that both institutions would give people less say in the running of self-government were less likely to turn out. Furthermore, those who thought it would make no difference whoever wins the election in Scotland and Wales were clearly less likely to vote in the first devolved elections than those who thought the opposite. Indeed, as we commented on Table 3A the spread on this variable suggested a fair number of people were pessimistic about the outcome of the devolved elections.

What we should also note is that the variable expressing whether people believe it makes a difference who wins the UK election becomes insignificant, mostly 'swallowed up' by the impact of the similar variable on the Scottish and Welsh elections. Those voters who believe that voting in the UK election would not make a difference were also less likely to vote in the elections in Scotland and Wales.

The one variable that gives robust support to the second-order model is what institutions will influence the way Scotland and Wales are run. Those who thought it would be an institution other than the devolved bodies (Table 4 shows there were many) were less likely to vote in the elections. This suggests that it is the variables that had lower evaluations of the devolved institutions that are most strongly correlated with turnout.

However, the impact of whether people thought the parliament or assembly would give both countries a strong voice in the UK is somewhat muted. The variable does not appear to validate Reif and Schmitt's argument and it is statistically insignificant. It may be the case that the variable is an anomaly. It is not implausible to suggest that there would be a biased response to this question from many respondents of a nationalist persuasion who would probably argue that devolution should first and foremost serve the interests of Scotland and Wales and not be associated with government at the UK level.

The second model in Table 6 shows our new reduced model after omitting the two variables that were clearly insignificant in the first. The remaining items in this model have a similar impact to those in the previous table.

So far then, evidence of second-order characteristics in the Scottish and Welsh elections is patchy. Three out of the four variables we have included in our logistic regression analysis lend support to Reif and Schmitt's hypothesis. However, two of the four frequency distribution tables showed that only a few people in Scotland and Wales felt that devolution would reduce their sense of engagement with the political process.

How therefore might we investigate further the potential second-orderedness of the Scottish and Welsh elections? An obvious question to consider is to what extent people in Scotland and Wales perceived the importance of these elections in comparison to that of a general election. Were people in Scotland and Wales more inclined to vote in a general election than the first elections to the parliament and assembly? And is there much difference between the two countries in their perception of the relative importance of the two types of electoral contests?

The following tables compare the levels of reported turnout in the Scottish and Welsh elections to that of a general election. To determine whether voters were more likely to turn out in a general election than the devolved elections the survey asked respondents a hypothetical question: how they would have voted on 6 May 1999 if a general election had been held on that day.[3] Table 7A compares the level of turnout in Scotland and 7B for Wales.

A COMPARISON OF THE LEVELS OF REPORTED TURNOUT IN THE SCOTTISH
AND WELSH ELECTIONS TO THAT OF A GENERAL ELECTION (%)

| | TABLE 7A | | | TABLE 7B |
| | *Scotland* | | | *Wales* |
	General Elec	*Scottish Elec*	*General Elec*	*Welsh Elec*
Yes	84	72	80	57
No	16	28	20	43
N	1482	1482	1256	1254

Source: Scottish Parliamentary and Welsh Assembly Election Survey 1999.

Two points are striking. At first glance, most people in Scotland and Wales appear more motivated to vote if a general election had taken place. In fact, it appears that there would not have been much difference in the level of turnout in the two countries in a general election. Eight out of ten respondents in both countries indicated that they would have voted in a general election. Secondly, the difference between turnout in a general election as compared to the devolved elections is more striking in Wales. While over seven out of ten Scots in our survey indicated they voted in the Scottish election, only about six out of ten people in Wales did so.

On the one hand this appears to validate one of the assumptions of the second-order election model, that of higher turnout in a first-order arena. The model correctly suggested that, since less is believed to be at stake in lower level elections, voters would be less likely to turn out and vote in the Scottish and Welsh elections. On the other hand however, the turnout differential raises more questions. Why did fewer people vote in the devolved elections than said they would have done in a general election? Furthermore, why was turnout in the devolved elections not similar in Scotland and Wales? Can the difference be explained away simply by the fact that even less was at stake in Wales? Or are there other factors that the second-order theory does not address which may explain the difference in turnout? Our next set of logistic models will attempt to explain more about the turnout differential and whether we can explain the difference in turnout between Scotland and Wales.

To address the question of why fewer voters in Scotland and Wales voted in the devolved elections when they indicated they would have done so in a general election we expand the logistic model further by including the general election variable from Tables 7A and B. This is shown in Table 8.

TABLE 8
EXPANDED MODEL OF TURNOUT IN SCOTTISH AND WELSH ELECTIONS

	Voted versus Not Voted	
	B	SE
Age (60+)		
Age (18–34)	–1.33	(0.15)***
Age (35–59)	–0.69	(0.14)***
Married	0.24	(0.11)*
Tenure (Other rented)		
Tenure (Owner occupied)	0.59	(0.16)***
Tenure (LA rented)	0.66	(0.19)***
Education Qualification	0.38	(0.15)**
Expectations		
Difference who wins in Scot/Wales	0.39	(0.04)***
Par/Assem give people more say self-gov	0.30	(0.09)***
What will influence way Parl/Assembly are run	0.35	(0.10)***
Vote if general election on 6th May 1999	1.49	(0.13)***
Constant	–2.41	(0.27)***
Cox & Snell R Square	21%	
N	2522	

*** significant at 0.1%; ** significant at 1%; * significant at 5%

Source: Scottish Parliamentary and Welsh Assembly Election Survey 1999.

Adding this variable has now changed the meaning of the model. Clearly, those voters who suggested they would vote in a general election were more likely also to vote in the Scottish and Welsh elections. In other words, we have now learnt that voters who turned out in 1999 were also more likely to turn out at any election. The parameter estimate of this variable is very highly significant – more than ten times the value of its standard error. Importantly, the effects of all the other variables, in particular those that we have included to test the assumptions of Reif and Schmitt, remain independently significant. So we can now see that these variables help explain why few voters in Scotland and Wales voted in the devolved elections than would have been the case in a general election.

What about Wales?

However, what does the logistic model inform us of the difference between Scotland and Wales in terms of turnout? Our interpretation so far of these models takes in the Scottish and Welsh dimension collectively. We have stated that another of our objectives is to try and explain the turnout differential between Scotland and Wales and ultimately to test whether the Welsh election was clearly more second-order than the Scottish election. To further examine this possibility, we need to add another variable to our model. This variable is whether or not the respondent lived in Wales; it is scored 1 for those who live in Wales while those who reside in Scotland are scored 0. This variable measures whether the probability of voting in the Welsh elections is greater or less than in Scotland. Table 9 shows what impact this additional variable has to our model.

TABLE 9
EXPANDED MODEL OF TURNOUT IN SCOTTISH AND WELSH ELECTIONS

	Voted versus B	Not Voted SE
Age (60+)		
Age (18–34)	–1.37	(0.15)***
Age (35–59)	–0.71	(0.14)***
Married	0.21	(0.11)*
Tenure (Other rented)		
Tenure (Owner occupied)	0.62	(0.16)***
Tenure (LA rented)	0.55	(0.19)**
Education Qualification	0.41	(0.15)**
Expectations		
Difference who wins in Scot/Wales	0.37	(0.04)***
Parl/Assem give people more say in self-gov	0.29	(0.09)**
What will influence way Parl/Assem are run	0.28	(0.11)**
Vote if general election on 6th May 1999	1.52	(0.13)***
Wales	–0.66	(0.10)***
Constant	–2.00	(0.28)***
Cox & Snell R Square	22%	
N	2522	

*** significant at 0.1%; ** significant at 1%; * significant at 5%

Source: Scottish Parliamentary and Welsh Assembly Election Survey 1999.

TABLE 10
EXPANDED MODEL OF TURNOUT IN SCOTTISH AND WELSH ELECTIONS (+
FOUR INTERACTIONS)

	Voted versus B	Not Voted SE
Age (60+)		
Age (18–34)	−1.38	(0.15)***
Age (35–59)	−0.72	(0.14)***
Married	0.22	(0.11)*
Tenure (Owner occupied)	0.62	(0.16)***
Tenure (LA rented)	0.55	(0.19)**
Education Qualification	0.40	(0.15)**
Expectations		
Difference who wins in Scot/Wales	0.35	(0.06)***
Parl/Assem give people more say self-gov	0.33	(0.13)*
What will influence way Parl/Assem run	0.28	(0.15)*
Vote if general election on 6th May 1999	1.51	(0.13)***
Wales	−0.70	(0.37)*
Interact (Will influence x Wales)	−0.00	(0.21)
Interact (Diff who wins in S/W x Wales)	0.04	(0.08)
Interact (Stronger UK voice x Wales)	0.06	(0.14)
Interact (More say in self-govt x Wales)	−0.11	(0.19)
Constant	−1.99	(0.33)***
Cox & Snell R Square	22%	
N	2511	

*** significant at 0.1%; ** significant at 1%; *significant at 5%

Source: Scottish Parliamentary and Welsh Assembly Election Survey 1999.

Two points are evident from Table 9. Firstly not only is the probability of voting in Wales lower than in Scotland but appears to be so even after considering all the other variables in the model. True, two of the items included to test the theory of second-order elections have marginally less impact than was demonstrated in Table 8, but all the variables remain statistically significant and still lend support to some of the propositions of the second-order model. However, they do not answer the question of turnout differential between both countries. This raises a second crucial point. The model assumes that the processes of the likelihood of voting are similar in Scotland *and* Wales but they are *not* a sufficient explanation to help understand why turnout is lower in Wales than in Scotland.

How then can we try and explain this difference between Scotland and Wales? Our next logical step would be to include some interaction terms in the model. These terms have a two-fold purpose. Firstly, they will show if there is a significant difference in their effect between Scotland and Wales and whether this accounts for the difference in turnout between the two countries. Secondly, they will also check the robustness of our assumption that what Reif and Schmitt claim should have equal validity in both countries.

Table 10 is expanded to include four interaction terms that test the above.

The model shows that explanations of the turnout differential still remain elusive. While the standard error of the 'Wales' coefficient increases from that found in the previous table, the variable just remains significant at the 5% level; therefore the probability of voting in Wales continues to be lower in Wales than in Scotland. Furthermore, the four interaction terms are highly insignificant. Characteristics of the second-order model do not have more of an impact in Wales than in Scotland.

The addition of these interaction terms also inflates the standard errors of some of the variables which results in them having reduced significance from that shown in Table 9. This will be addressed in future models when these interaction terms are omitted.

The Element of Protest

As we noted earlier, another characteristic of the second-order model concerns the behaviour of those who identify with the party of government at the time these types of elections are held. Lower level elections are an ideal occasion for supporters of governing parties to give an assessment of the performance of the government to date. This judgement is more often a negative one as governments in the mid-term period of office usually suffer from an increase in unpopularity due to their supporters becoming increasingly disgruntled at the administration's record to date. Identifiers of governing parties voice their disapproval in two ways: either they will switch their allegiance to another party or alternatively they just do not vote (Reif, 1984). Our task for now is to consider whether Labour identifiers were less likely to turn out in the devolved elections than voters of other parties.

If Labour voters were unhappy with the performance of the government at a UK level then we would anticipate that they would be less likely to vote in the lower level elections to the Scottish Parliament and Welsh Assembly than identifiers of other parties.

To test if this indeed was the case we now add another variable to our logistic model. This variable is whether or not voters identified closely with the Labour Party and is scored 1 for those that identify with Labour and 0 for identifiers of other parties.[4] Table 11 shows what impact this additional variable has to our model.

TABLE 11
EXPANDED MODEL OF TURNOUT IN SCOTTISH AND WELSH ELECTIONS
(+ LABOUR IDENTIFIERS)

	Voted *versus* B	Not Voted SE
Age (60+)		
Age (18–34)	–1.28	(0.15)***
Age (35–59)	–0.67	(0.14)***
Married	0.21	(0.11)
Tenure (Owner occupied)	0.61	(0.16)***
Tenure (LA rented)	0.63	(0.19)***
Education Qualification	0.37	(0.15)*
Expectations		
Difference who wins in Scot/Wales	0.38	(0.04)***
Parl/Assem give people more say self-gov	0.33	(0.09)***
What will influence way Parl/Assem run	0.29	(0.11)**
Vote if general election on 6th May 1999	1.76	(0.14)***
Wales	–0.61	(0.10)***
Party-id		
Labour identifiers	–0.57	(0.10)***
Constant	–2.15	(0.29)***
Cox & Snell R Square	23%	
N	2483	

*** significant at 0.1%; ** significant at 1%; *significant at 5%

Source: Scottish Parliamentary and Welsh Assembly Election Survey 1999.

The impact of this variable is highly significant. It does appear to lend support to the argument that those who identify with the party of government are less likely to vote in mid-term elections and therefore upholds one of the claims of the second-order election model. One outlet for Labour identifiers to demonstrate their unhappiness about the performance of their party was to protest and stay at home. Turnout in Scotland and Wales appears to have been affected by the number of Labour identifiers in both countries deciding not to vote.

The model also shows how the interaction terms included in the previous model affected the robustness of the other variables. Most of these items become more significant again. The one variable that has been generally weak throughout the multivariate analysis and now becomes insignificant is the married variable. This will be omitted in the next model.

The next step is to consider again the lower turnout in Wales. Were Labour identifiers in Wales less likely to vote than their counterparts in Scotland and if so does this go some way to account for the difference in turnout between the two countries?

We now fit a new interaction term that includes Labour identifiers to see if this was the case. This is shown in Table 12.

TABLE 12
EXPANDED MODEL OF TURNOUT IN SCOTTISH AND WELSH ELECTIONS
(+ LABOUR INTERACTION TERM)

	Voted versus B	Not Voted SE
Age (60+)		
Age (18–34)	–1.28	(0.15)***
Age (35–59)	–0.62	(0.14)***
Tenure (Owner occupied)	0.66	(0.16)***
Tenure (LA rented)	0.62	(0.19)***
Education Qualification	0.37	(0.15)*
Expectations		
Difference who wins in Scot/Wales	0.38	(0.04)***
Parl/Assem give people more say self-gov	0.33	(0.09)***
What will influence way Parl/Assem run	0.28	(0.11)**
Vote if general election on 6th May 1999	1.77	(0.14)***
Wales	–0.47	(0.14)***
Party-id		
Labour identifiers	–0.41	(0.14)**
Interact (Lab identifiers x Wales)	–0.30	(0.20)
Constant	–2.13	(0.29)***
Cox & Snell R Square	23%	
N	2486	

*** significant at 0.1%; ** significant at 1%; *significant at 5%

Source: Scottish Parliamentary and Welsh Assembly Election Survey 1999.

The interaction term is not significant and will now be omitted from the model. Labour identifiers in Wales were no more likely to stay at home than those who support the party in Scotland. This suggests that the claim that those who identify with the governing party would protest by staying at home is of equal validity in Scotland and Wales. We can further test the impact of party identification when considering identifiers of other parties. In this instance the next logical step will be to test whether those of a nationalist persuasion were more or less likely to vote than identifiers of other parties. Therefore we now include another variable to our model, that of whether or not voters identified closely with the two nationalist parties and is scored 1. Those who identify with other parties or are non-party identifiers are scored 0. Table 13 shows the effect of adding this variable.

TABLE 13
EXPANDED MODEL OF TURNOUT IN SCOTTISH AND WELSH ELECTIONS
(+ NATIONALIST IDENTIFIERS)

	Voted versus B	Not Voted SE
Age (60+)		
Age (18–34)	–1.37	(0.15)***
Age (35–59)	–0.67	(0.14)***
Tenure (Owner occupied)	0.69	(0.16)***
Tenure (LA rented)	0.60	(0.19)**
Education Qualification	0.41	(0.15)**
Expectations		
Difference who wins in Scot/Wales	0.36	(0.04)***
Parl/Assem give people more say self-gov	0.29	(0.10)**
What will influence way Parl/Assem run	0.28	(0.11)**
Vote if general election on 6th May 1999	1.73	(0.14)***
Wales	–0.62	(0.14)***
Party-id		
Labour identifiers	–0.36	(0.11)**
Nationalist identifiers	0.60	(0.15)***
Constant	–2.07	(0.29)***
Cox & Snell R Square	24%	
N	2486	

*** significant at 0.1%; ** significant at 1%;

Source: Scottish Parliamentary and Welsh Assembly Election Survey 1999.

Clearly, identifiers with the nationalist parties were more likely to vote than supporters of other parties. However, the difficulty at this stage of our analysis is to give a clear interpretation of the behaviour of these identifiers. We can offer two plausible explanations. Firstly, what does the behaviour tell us about the characteristics of the second-order model? If we presume that both nationalist parties were the main opposition parties going into these elections then clearly the impact of this variable in the model does not lend support to Reif and Schmitt. The theory claims that governing parties and principal opposition parties in combination lose support because those who identify with those parties either stay at home or vote for a smaller party. With respect to the former claim, the impact of the nationalist variable casts doubt on that assertion.

But of course these elections cannot be dismissed as just a typical mid-term election, and perhaps explanations of turnout within the framework of the second-order model are insufficient. Not only were these elections held for the first time, but they were also held in two of the countries that are part of the United Kingdom. Constitutional change and the impact in general these elections would have on the multi-national state that is the United Kingdom were high on the political agenda.

The second-order election model does not consider the above issues. What may have motivated supporters of nationalist parties to turn out was the fact that these elections first and foremost signified some form of constitutional change within the United Kingdom. As was the case with the referendums of 1997, those voters who were strongly attached to the Scottish National Party and Plaid Cymru were more likely to view these elections as a stepping stone towards independence and turn out to vote.

But was there a difference between the behaviour of nationalist supporters in Wales and those in Scotland? Were Plaid Cymru supporters less likely to vote in Wales than supporters of the Scottish National Party were in Scotland, and if so does this go some way to account for the difference in turnout between the two countries? We now fit a new interaction term that includes nationalist identifiers to see if this was the case.

From the evidence shown in Table 14 it would appear that being a nationalist supporter makes more difference in Wales than in Scotland to the probability of voting in the elections. On the one hand this suggests that nationalist supporters in Wales were more likely to vote than those supporters in Scotland, but we should be cautious at this stage about stating the importance of this finding, as it does not appear statistically significant.

TABLE 14
EXPANDED MODEL OF TURNOUT IN SCOTTISH AND WELSH ELECTIONS
(+ NATIONALIST INTERACTION TERM)

	Voted versus B	Not Voted SE
Age (60+)		
Age (18–34)	–1.37	(0.15)***
Age (35–59)	–0.67	(0.14)***
Tenure (Owner occupied)	0.69	(0.16)***
Tenure (LA rented)	0.61	(0.20)**
Education Qualification	0.40	(0.15)**
Expectations		
Difference who wins in Scot/Wales	0.36	(0.04)***
Parl/Assem give people more say self-gov	0.30	(0.09)***
What will influence way Parl/Assem run	0.27	(0.11)*
Vote if general election on 6th May 1999	1.73	(0.14)***
Wales	–0.69	(0.11)***
Party-id		
Labour identifiers	–0.35	(0.11)**
Nationalist identifiers	0.37	(0.19)*
Interact (Nat identifiers X Wales)	0.52	(0.28)
Constant	–2.04	(0.29)***
Cox & Snell R Square	24%	

N   2486

*** significant at 0.1%; ** significant at 1%; *significant at 5%

Source: Scottish Parliamentary and Welsh Assembly Election Survey 1999.

Conclusion

This article has tested one of the most important characteristics of Reif and Schmitts's second-order election model – low turnout in lower-level elections. By studying the behaviour of voters in Scotland and Wales we have attempted to answer (a) why turnout was low and whether such findings confirmed the second-orderedness of these elections and (b) why turnout was lower in Wales than in Scotland.

In answer to the first part we can conclude that there was some evidence of second-orderedness in the elections but it is clear that Reif and Schmitts's hypothesis on turnout is not wholly validated. With respect to lower turnout in Wales, we are not further forward in providing a robust explanation for the difference in turnout with Scotland. What we appeared to find, though more statistical analysis requires to be undertaken, was that nationalist identifiers in Wales were more likely to vote than those in Scotland.

Testing Reif and Schmitt

We first considered what the people of Scotland and Wales thought about the possible consequences of devolution and whether these showed that the expectations of what devolution would deliver were high in both countries. In doing so, we addressed Reif and Schmitt's claim that lower-level elections were inferior in status to those held at the first-order level. On the whole, voters in both countries agreed with the proponents of devolution who argue that devolved government has many benefits for the electors it represents. People expected to have more say in self-government and that both institutions would give Scotland and Wales a stronger voice within the United Kingdom. They also adhered to the view that the results in Scotland and Wales would make a difference.

The one possible consequence of devolution where voters (especially in Wales) had some misgivings was whether the newly devolved bodies would exert the greatest influence in each country. Many voters held the view that the Westminster Parliament would be more influential. Overall, however, the number of respondents who felt positive about the consequences and benefits of devolution were higher than those than those who had doubts about the implications of the process of devolution. Therefore in terms of the *perceptions* of the importance of these particular lower-level elections, our evidence casts some doubt on the assertions of those who devised the second-order election model.

But as we acknowledged, the perceptions of devolution are a limited yardstick to test the theoretical rationale of the second-order model. The likelihood of people voting in these elections is what we really need to test. By building logistic regression models we showed how these perceptions impacted on the probability of the people of Scotland and Wales voting in their respective elections. Again however, the evidence from these models suggests that Reif and Schmitt's hypothesis on turnout does not neatly fit into these polls. While most of the variables gave support to their claims we also noted that the number of voters who did not think the elections mattered was very small. Only the question relating to the influence of the devolved bodies gave robust support to the second-order model. This was the key question that demonstrated that many voters believed the first-order arena to be more important. Overall however, our success in testing these variables was limited.

What we also began to consider was the possible differences between the behaviour of voters in Scotland to those in Wales. We found that the likelihood of voting in Wales was indeed lower than was the case in Scotland but further analysis suggested that characteristics of the second-order model did not have more of an impact in Wales than in Scotland. This adds credence to the assumption that Reif and Schmitt's arguments should be of equal validity in both countries, but explanations as to why turnout was lower in Wales than in Scotland remained elusive.

We then turned to other indicators that may have had an influence on the probability of voting in both countries. We considered whether party identification was influential in persuading people to vote. This appeared highly significant. The model argues that identifiers of the incumbent administration will either vote for another party or stay at home. With regard to the latter assertion, our evidence suggests that indeed Labour supporters were less likely to vote. Turnout in Scotland and Wales appears to have been affected by the number of Labour supporters in each country deciding not to vote. However, we also found that Labour identifiers in Wales were no more likely to stay at home than those who support the party in Scotland.

We also considered the behaviour of nationalist identifiers and whether they were more or less inclined to vote in these 'Scottish' and 'Welsh' elections. We found that they were more likely to vote than those who identified with other parties (and indeed there appears to be some difference between Scotland and Wales) but we touched on how this evidence relates to the theory of second-order elections. The four-party system that is now more evident in Scotland and Wales, coupled with the first-past-the-post electoral system, has resulted in our not being able to clearly distinguish who were the principal opposition in each country at the time the devolved elections were held. In the 1997 general election, the nationalists in Scotland attained more votes but fewer seats than the Liberal Democrats. In Wales, Plaid Cymru received fewer votes but more seats than the Conservatives.

As we stated, since the theory claims that governing parties and principal opposition parties in combination lose support, then explanations, within the framework of the original crude model, as to why nationalist identifiers were more motivated to vote are limited. This appears to highlight one of the weaknesses of the original second-order model and more research requires to be carried out that takes on board these kinds of issues. Furthermore, this raises an important point about how well the model stands up as an important framework for the study of electoral behaviour in these devolved elections. Admittedly, a more rigorous evaluation of the theory of second-order elections can really only be undertaken once other characteristics of the model – governing parties losing support and success for smaller parties – are tested.

Finally, what is the larger conclusion we can make on the deliverance of devolution in Scotland and Wales? Again, due to the narrow scope of this article we can only offer tentative conclusions at this stage. Based on turnout alone, there is some evidence that some voters in Scotland and Wales did treat these devolved polls as typical mid-term by-elections. But the reasons why other voters decided to vote were because of what these elections were *for*. This, at least, should give some reassurance to those in the pro-devolution camp in the run-up to the elections in May 2003.

It would be appropriate to end this article by substantiating that last point. We should acknowledge that we have had only one round of devolved elections in Scotland and Wales to study the behaviour of this particular electorate. In that respect, perhaps the evidence we provided in Table 4 should not be viewed in a pessimistic light as was first suggested. Analysis of the elections in May 2003 may well provide more insight not only into the relative merits of the second-order model but the issue of devolution itself. In many ways, those respondents in the 1999 survey were giving answers based on their *expectations* of what the institutions might or might not achieve in future years. In May 2003 voters will vote (or perhaps not) on the basis of *evaluating* what the institutions have done in the last four years. In years to come, 1 May 2003 may be looked back on as the symbolic date when the people of Scotland and Wales decided how important their new institutions were.

ACKNOWLEDGEMENTS

The data for this analysis is drawn from the Scottish Parliamentary and Welsh Assembly Election Survey 1999. The Economic and Social Research Council funded the study. The survey was designed to yield a representative sample of adults aged 18 or over in Scotland and Wales. The Scottish element of the study involved a face-to-face interview with 1482 respondents. The Welsh study was a combination of telephone and face-to-face interviewing. Overall, 1256 respondents were interviewed in Wales. Copies of the questionnaires are available from the National Centre for Social Research.

I would like to thank Professor John Curtice for his invaluable advice in assisting me with this paper. I would also like to thank Professor Jon Tonge for his comments and suggestions on the re-draft of the paper, after the EPOP conference presentation at the University of Salford.

NOTES

1. The dependent variable is scored 1 for voted and 0 for not voted. The age variable is categorical. Because we have three age categories (scored 1 for youngest through to 3 for oldest grouping) it is described by two dummy variables. The first compares the youngest with oldest and the next the middle age grouping with oldest. Married is scored 1 for married and living as married and 0 otherwise. Tenure is also categorical (three categories; scored 1 for owner, 2 local authority rented and 3 for other rented). Educational qualification is scored 1 for degree, 0 otherwise. The 'Difference who wins UK election' is an interval variable; scored 1 for none at all through to 5 for a great deal of difference.

2. The 'Difference who wins in Scotland and Wales' is a similar interval variable to the UK election variable and is scored 1 for none at all through to 5 for a great deal of difference. The 'stronger voice' variable is scored 0 for weaker UK voice, 1 for no difference and 2 for stronger UK voice. The 'give more say' variable is scored 0 for less say, 1 for no difference and 2 for more say. We have made the 'influence' variable into a dummy one. It is scored 1 for Scottish Parliament/Welsh Assembly and 0 for all other possible answers. This will give us a clearer indication of the impact of the new institutions against all others together.
3. The actual question in the survey asked respondents which political party did they think they would have voted for if a general election were held on 6 May 1999 or would they not have voted. At this stage of our analysis we are not concerned with what particular party people would have voted for, rather if they had voted in the first instance. Therefore the figures displayed for a general election in Tables 7A and B group all those who stated a party under the 'Yes' response. Those that indicated they would not have voted are in the 'No' response. This re-coding is also used in the subsequent logistic regression models.
4. The '0' category also includes voters who did not identify with any party.

REFERENCES

Crewe, I., Tony Fox, and J.E. Alt (1977) 'Non-voting in British General Elections, 1966–October 1974' in Colin Crouch (ed.), *The British Political Sociology Yearbook,* Vol.3. London: Croom Helm.

Heath, A., I. McLean and B. Taylor (1997) *How Much Is at Stake? Electoral Behaviour in Second-order Elections,* CREST Working paper No.59, September.

Miller, W.L. (1988) *Irrelevant Elections? The Quality of Local Democracy in Britain.* Oxford: Clarendon Press.

Norris, P. (1997) 'Second-order Elections Revisited', *European Journal of Political Research* 31 (1–2): 109–14.

Reif, K. (1984) 'National Electoral Cycles and European Elections 1979 and 1984', *Electoral Studies* 3 (3): 244–55.

Reif, K. (1985) 'Ten Second-Order National Elections', in K. Reif (ed.) *Ten European Elections.* London: Gower.

Reif, K. and H. Schmitt (1980) 'Nine Second-Order National Elections: A Conceptual Framework for the Analysis of European Election Results', *European Journal of Political Research* 8 (1): 3–44.

Towards Moderate Pluralism: Scotland's Post-Devolution Party System, 1999–2002

Lynn Bennie and Alistair Clark

In this article, we examine the development of Scotland's party system since the creation of the Scottish Parliament in 1999. The establishing of a new political institution is a rare event and provides us with a new case with which to test existing ideas. In particular, institutional reform can be an important source of party and party system change. Importantly, the study of party systems involves more than just the study of individual political parties. Instead, what is key to party systems analysis is the pattern of interactions that results from party competition. In the context of Scottish politics, the interaction of parties has been a neglected subject, both prior to and following devolution. This analysis of Scotland's post-devolution party system proceeds in three parts. We begin with a discussion of the classification of party systems. There follows an assessment of the electoral strength of the parties in Scotland, their ideological character and policies, and the patterns of interaction between the parties. Thirdly, we attempt to characterize the emerging key aspects of Scotland's post-devolution party system, bearing in mind that it is ultimately relations between the parties that determine the nature of the party system.

Understanding Party Systems

Many traditional approaches in the study of party systems use numerical criteria to assess the number of parties and their relative strength (Duverger, 1964; Blondel, 1968). Blondel's (1968) classification, for example, involved two-party systems, two-and-a-half-party systems, and multi-party systems. The problem with these approaches, however, is that they lack an emphasis on inter-party relationships. Sartori (1966, 1976) bases his typology on numerical criteria but provides some innovation by introducing the concept of ideological distance, or left–right polarization, into his classification. Thus, he distinguishes between two-party systems, systems with either moderate or extreme pluralism, and pre-dominant party systems, parties 'counting' if they have either coalition or blackmail potential. Pre-dominant party systems are those in which parties hold office alone for a considerable period of time. Two-party systems are marked by minimal ideological distance, centripetal competition, and alternation in office. Systems of moderate pluralism also operate in a centripetal manner. They are bipolar, have between three and five parties competing for a position in a coalition government, and have a low degree of ideological polarization. Finally, extreme or polarized pluralism is multi-polar and characterized by a high degree of ideological distance and the presence of anti-system parties at both ends of the party spectrum. The centrifugal forces generated by such a system result in radical bilateral opposition to the centre-placed governing party.

Dahl (1966: 336–45) argues that it is the competitiveness of opposition in both the electoral and parliamentary arenas that is the key to classifying party systems. Dahl (1966: 336) claims that 'parties are strictly competitive ... if they pursue strategies such that both cannot simultaneously belong to a winning coalition' and he posits a sliding scale with competitive strategies at one endpoint and coalescent strategies at the other. A range of cooperative strategies lie between both endpoints. He is therefore able to distinguish between four types of party system: strictly competitive; cooperative-competitive; coalescent-competitive; and strictly coalescent. The classic example of a strictly competitive party system is Britain where the electoral system ensures that parties expect to govern alone and therefore opposition parties adopt competitive strategies. In a cooperative-competitive system, opposition parties aim to maximize their strength but also have an eye on maximizing their influence through coalition negotiations. While coalescent systems are not well defined by Dahl, they imply a situation where parties gradually fuse into one in order to overcome the government of the day.

Despite the dynamism suggested by these arguments, party systems tend to appear more stable than changing. The classic formulation of this is by Lipset and Rokkan (1967) who suggest that centre–periphery, state–church, land–industry and owner–worker cleavages were 'frozen' by extension of the mass franchise. More recently, Mair (1997) has forcefully restated this argument. Nevertheless, the years since Lipset and Rokkan advanced their thesis have seen what would seem to many to be radical change in party systems. One manifestation of this is that new party alternatives have emerged and now participate in government in numerous European countries. Five main sources of change are regularly cited. First, institutional alterations, although rare, can lead to party system change. This can take the form of the creation of new institutions, or the introduction of new electoral systems or thresholds, both of which occurred in Scotland. Second, changes in the social structure can lead to gradual changes in the support for parties. Third, values may change. In an ever more affluent society, Inglehart (1990) suggests that instead of being motivated by material values such as economic security, there has been a shift towards values concerned with the quality of life. Fourth, social and value change has contributed to electoral volatility through the processes of partisan and class dealignment. Finally, the strategy adopted by parties themselves can also contribute to party system change (Wolinetz, 1979).

Smith's (1989) 'core' party system model attempts to combine both stability and change. The core of a system consists of the features of that system that appear most resistant to change. Essentially this means the party or parties that have been in leading positions for a considerable period and the party alignments, particularly in coalition formation, that have emerged (Smith, 1989: 161). Smith (1989: 166) outlines four degrees of change that can take place: temporary fluctuations; restricted change; general change; and transformation. A three-election time span, it is suggested, distinguishes between temporary fluctuations and restricted change. When it comes to transformation, this is viewed as a rare event, but need not mean the establishment of a new party system. Instead, it could be signified by one of the leading parties going 'into a steep and irreversible decline' (Smith, 1989: 167).

Any assessment of a particular party system must therefore consider a number of these features. In particular, the relative size and electoral volatility of the parties, the ideological/policy distance between the parties, and the nature of competition and/or cooperation are vital variables if party systems are to be understood and classified. The remainder of the article seeks to apply this framework to an analysis of the Scottish party system.

The Electoral Strength of the Parties: The End of Labour Hegemony

Prior to devolution, the Labour Party dominated electoral politics in Scotland. The party's strength had become increasingly pronounced in the final third of the twentieth century, particularly in the central belt's industrial, urban areas. This was an impressive electoral achievement for a party that spent most of this time in official opposition at Westminster. Labour's share of the votes in general elections declined with the rise in support for other parties, however its ability to win seats under the first-past-the-post electoral system became even more apparent. In 1966 Labour won 46 seats with 49.9 per cent of the vote; in 1992, the party won 49 seats with only 39 per cent of the vote (Table 1). Key to Labour's success was the party's ability to balance Scottish and British interests. Election Study data, and regular opinion polls conducted in Scotland, point to Labour's successful promotion of working class and national identities (Bennie et al.,

1997; Brown et al., 1999). In essence the party was associated with Scottish aspirations for greater autonomy, and with popular aspects of the British state such as welfare provision and central economic management. The Conservatives, by contrast, were viewed as anti-Scottish and a threat to state-run welfare (Mitchell and Bennie, 1996). The use of the semi-proportional Additional Member System (AMS) for the first elections to the Scottish Parliament in 1999 meant that Labour would not enjoy the same kind of dominance (Table 2). Despite Labour being the most successful party in these elections (winning 53 of the 73 first-past-the-post seats) the new electoral system ensured a result that was much more representative of voter support, depriving Labour of an overall majority (see Denver and MacAllister, 1999).

TABLE 1

UK GENERAL ELECTION RESULTS IN SCOTLAND, 1945–2001

	CON	LAB	LIB	SNP	OTHER
1945	41.1	47.6	5.0	1.2	5.1
1950	44.8	46.2	6.6	0.4	2.0
1951	48.6	47.9	2.7	0.3	0.5
1955	50.1	46.7	1.9	0.5	0.8
1959	47.2	46.7	4.1	0.8	1.2
1964	40.6	48.7	7.6	2.4	0.7
1966	37.7	49.9	6.8	5.0	0.6
1970	38.0	44.5	5.5	11.4	0.6
1974 (F)	32.9	36.6	8.0	21.9	0.6
1974 (O)	24.7	36.3	8.3	30.4	0.3
1979	31.4	41.5	9.0	17.3	0.8
1983	28.4	35.1	24.5	11.8	0.3
1987	24.0	42.4	19.2	14.0	0.3
1992	25.6	39.0	13.1	21.5	0.8
1997	17.5	45.6	13.0	22.1	1.9
2001	15.6	43.9	16.4	20.1	4.0

Sources: Hassan and Lynch, 2001: 349–52; Brown, 2001: 140.

Unlike Labour, Liberal and Liberal Democrat general election performances in Scotland have lagged behind their counterparts in England. Moreover, Liberal (and Liberal Democrat) support in Scotland has always been concentrated: in the rural areas of the Borders, the North East, the Highlands, and the Northern Isles – areas where Liberal policies were seen to protect rural interests. In the 1990s, the Liberal Democrat overall share of the Westminster vote stood at 13 per cent. In the 1999 Scottish Parliament elections, the Scottish Liberal Democrats maintained a similar level of support, rather than making any major breakthrough, finishing fourth in percentage of votes and seats. However, the 1999 elections signalled a new era for the party in Scotland. The new electoral system presented the Liberal Democrats with an opportunity to enter a coalition government, a dramatic turnaround in the party's fortunes, and leading to expectations that the party may perform the role of permanent coalition partner (see Lynch, 2001: 172).

TABLE 2
SCOTTISH PARLIAMENT ELECTION 1999

	Constituencies		Lists		Total Seats
	%	Seats	%	Seats	
Labour	38.8	53	33.6	3	56
SNP	28.7	7	27.3	28	35
Conservative	15.5	0	15.4	18	18
Liberal Democrat	14.2	12	12.4	5	17
Other	2.7	1	11.3	2	3
Total					129

Sources: Denver and MacAllister, 1999: 12; Paterson et al., 2001: 19.

The Scottish National Party (SNP) has experienced distinct peaks and troughs in electoral support. Westminster highlights included the jump from 5.0 to 30 per cent in the eight years between 1966 and October 1974, and the general elections of 1992 and 1997 when the party achieved more than 20 per cent. During these periods the SNP were able to exploit the image of a Scotland that fared badly under the British government (see Brand, Mitchell and Surridge, 1994: 626–9). Nevertheless, the electoral high point for the SNP came in the 1999 Scottish parliamentary elections. The adoption of AMS saw the party break out of the 'third party' status accorded it by some (Levy, 1990: 1–5; Brand, Mitchell and Surridge, 1994: 617) to win a total of 35 seats and become the official opposition to the Labour-Liberal Democrat Executive.

In contrast to the SNP's fluctuating fortunes, the Scottish Conservative and Unionist Party has experienced steady electoral decline since its high of 50.1 per cent of the Scottish vote in the 1955 general election, leaving the party with no MPs in Scotland by 1997. Explanations range from the poor performance of Scotland's economy under Conservatism to the secularization of Scottish Protestantism (Dyer, 2001; Mitchell and Bennie, 1996; Seawright, 1999). Most fundamental was the party's decreasing success in addressing centre–periphery concerns in Scotland. By the time of the Scottish Parliament election, Conservative unpopularity was deeply ingrained. Given the party's opposition to electoral reform, it is paradoxical that the Scottish Conservatives were rescued from parliamentary oblivion by the new electoral system which delivered 18 list MSPs.

Small parties had faced insurmountable difficulties under the single member plurality electoral system used in British general elections. However, 1999 proved a real turning point for these parties (Bennie, 2002). In total, the small parties and independents attracted just over 11 per cent of the regional vote, and 2.7 per cent of the constituency vote. The leader of the Scottish Socialist Party (SSP), Tommy Sheridan, was elected in Glasgow, and Robin Harper of the Greens was successful in the Lothians region. The one independent elected – Dennis Canavan in Falkirk West – was the locally popular sitting Westminster MP who had been rejected by Labour as a candidate for the Scottish election (see Bradbury et al., 2000).

Ideology and Policy Character: Convergence and Divergence

The Scottish Labour Party's ethos has been described as a combination of the labour movement and nineteenth century Scottish Liberal radicalism, including a belief in home rule and land reform (Hassan, 2002: 30). Since devolution, Labour in Scotland has attempted to project the image of a modern, social democratic, and progressive party. Certainly, the image projected by the first Scottish cabinet, which contained young, female, middle class professional politicians, was very different from the old-style Labour class politics (Leicester, 2000: 12). In the early years of devolution, Labour was criticized for confusing policy priorities. For example, it could be argued that the abolition of Section 28/Clause 2a (the legislation that barred local authorities form 'promoting' homosexuality) was a distraction from the main business of government. The first First Minister Donald Dewar, despite his stewardship of devolution, was unadventurous and 'no single innovative policy became attached to his name' (Mitchell et al., 2001: 51). Dewar's successor, Henry McLeish was associated with some clear policy proposals, namely free personal care for the elderly and a generous pay settlement for Scotland's teachers. However, his time in the post was fraught with media criticism of his leadership and scrutiny of his constituency office arrangements as a Westminster MP (see Taylor, 2002: Ch.3). The third First Minster Jack McConnell likes to be associated with a modernizing, pro-autonomy agenda. McConnell (2002a; 2002b) refers to 'we on the left', and advocates egalitarianism, social inclusion and meritocracy. However, he is also keen to 'engage the private sector' in the delivery of public services. Above all else, McConnell appears to be a pragmatist, with a constant emphasis on stability and 'doing what works'. In developing these themes, the current Scottish Labour leadership is entirely compatible with New Labour counterparts south of the border. The Liberal Democrats represent the coming together of two traditions – liberalism and social democracy. In Scotland they are also associated with antinuclear policies and a degree of scepticism about economic liberalism (see Bennie et al., 1997: 92). Another distinctive flavour of the Scottish Liberal Democrats is their defence of rural welfare, an objective that sometimes clashes with environmental themes. Finally, the Scottish Liberal Democrats have been forceful in their promotion of a parliament for Scotland. The 1999 policy programme of the Scottish Liberal Democrats reflected this ethos of liberty, social justice and community. Most prominent were the party's commitments to abolish up-front student tuition fees, and to support free personal care for the elderly, a new pay deal for teachers, and freedom of information legislation. These policy ideas have had a high profile in the legislative agenda of the coalition.

The SNP's central aim is to achieve Scottish independence. Brand (1978: 8–18) traces this to two arguments; a 'spiritual' appeal based on a right of national self-determination, and a pragmatic appeal which suggests that self-government will result in more responsive government. Moreover, Brand (1978: 31) argues that Scottish nationalism is a modernizing creed, which aims to create a prosperous independent Scotland. Over time the party has adopted a centre-left position on socio-economic matters. Finally, through the 1980s the party gradually accepted the pro-European emphasis of its then leader, Gordon Wilson, and adopted a policy of 'independence in Europe' (Levy, 1994: 161). In 1999, the party campaigned on a range of key policies. Most noteworthy was 'Scotland's penny' where the party asked the Scottish electorate to forego a one pence tax reduction offered by Labour at Westminster so that it might invest £690 million in health, education and housing. Other policies included: introducing Public Service Trusts in health and education; promoting small business; and bringing water back under democratic control. If it won power, an independence referendum would be held within the first four-year term of the parliament.

The Conservatives in Scotland were traditionally associated with Unionism (Dyer, 2001; Mitchell, 1990; Seawright, 1999). The values linked with this approach include an affinity with working-class Protestantism, an appeal to symbols of Scottish culture that were also British, and moderate intervention on socio-economic matters such as the provision of affordable housing. Conservative decline in Scotland coincided with a move away from these principles. The party's emerging character, however, is highly reminiscent of the Unionism of the past (Mitchell, 1990, 1996). First, the Conservatives are again appealing to Scottish symbols. In a 1999 speech at the symbolic venue of Hampden Park, Scottish leader David McLetchie proclaimed a 'New Unionism' where 'from now on, in Scotland's first and oldest political party, we will be putting Scotland first ... we are the Tartan Tories, Scotland's other national party' (cited in Taylor, 2002: 192). The party's recent acceptance of devolution is cast as the best way of avoiding independence. Second, the party is adopting a moderate and interventionist approach to socio-economic matters. McLetchie (2002a) has argued for 'first class public services for all', particularly in health and education, while advocating a channelling of resources to volunteer groups to help community projects in deprived areas. More generally, the rhetoric being used is that of compassion for the vulnerable, demonstrated by high profile visits to poorer parts of Glasgow, such as Easterhouse.

The other parties represented in the new parliament promote a more radical set of ideas than the four main parties. The SSP's ideology is Trotskyist. Like its Militant predecessors it criticizes the evils of capitalism, as well as the bureaucratic state centrism of the former Soviet Union, while advocating a democratically planned socialist economy and egalitarianism. However, the tone and strategy of the SSP is very different from that of the hard-line 1980s Militants. It advocates a democratic, 'modern' and socially libertarian socialism; decentralist, high-tech and environmentally responsible. Manifestos have included commitments to: collective ownership of public utilities; progressive taxation; the reintroduction of student grants; free TV licenses and heating vouchers for pensioners; rejection of public-private partnerships (PPP); and a nuclear free Scotland (Sheridan and McCombes, 2000). The party also stands for an independent Scottish Republic. The Scottish Green Party's ecological principles – sustainability, decentralization, and redistribution of wealth – reveal some clear overlaps with the left. Indeed, the party's policy programme rests on a wide range of both environmental and social issues: pollution controls; a basic income scheme; a Scottish community bank to fund community businesses; local currency schemes; the reintroduction of grants for the less well off; and a ban on GM crops.

The existence of the small parties adds to the diversity of party policies on offer to the Scottish electorate. Table 3 sets out a selection of some key policy emphases of the Scottish parties.[1] Although intended to highlight areas of policy overlaps and differences between the parties, such a presentation does however hide a range of ambiguities, particularly on the use of the parliament's tax raising powers. This is often omitted from party discussions of the parliament's broader 'powers', and establishing the precise position of the parties on this subject can be like pinning down a blancmange. Although previously in favour (Lynch, 2002: 89), the Scottish Liberal Democrat (2002: 18) pre-manifesto document merely states that the party does not favour hasty or destabilizing change in Holyrood's powers. By contrast, the SNP are more inclined to refer to 'full financial powers'.

TABLE 3
POLICY EMPHASES OF SCOTTISH PARTIES

Policy Areas	LAB	SNP	CON	LDEM	SSP	SGP
Left–right Issues						
PPP	✓	–	✓	–	–	–
Cut tax	–	–	✓	–	–	–
Business deregulation	–	✓	✓	–	–	–
Maintain public services	✓	✓	✓	✓	✓	✓
Law and order	✓	✓	✓	✓	–	–
State social justice	✓	✓	–	✓	✓	✓
Post-materialism						
Traditional values	–	–	✓	–	–	–
Libertarian values	✓	✓	–	✓	✓	✓
Environment protection	✓	✓	–	✓	✓	✓
Nuclear disarmament	–	✓	–	–	✓	✓
Constitutional Issues						
Scottish Independence Devolution	–	✓	–	–	✓	✓
More powers Holyrood	✓	–	–	✓	✓	–
Keep powers the same	✓	–	✓	✓	–	–
Reduce no. of MSPs	–	–	✓	–	–	–
PR for local govt.	–	✓	–	✓	✓	✓
Use Parliament's tax- raising powers	–	✓	–	✓	✓	✓

Sources: McConnell (2002a, b), www.scottishlabour.org.uk, SNP (2001), www.snp.org, McLetchie (2002a, b), www.scottishtories.org.uk, Scottish Liberal Democrats (2002), www.scotlibdems.org.uk, www.libdems.org.uk, Sheridan and McCombes (2000), www.scottishsocialistparty.org, www.scottishgreens,org.uk

They have been reported as rejecting the use of these powers (Dinwoodie, 2002) as to some this implies an acceptance of the devolution settlement. Elsewhere, however, Swinney (2002) has spoken in favour of using the tax system to help those on low incomes. Other nuances in policy positions include PPPs and business deregulation. While the Liberal Democrats support the development of mutual and non-profit organizations for financing public assets, they do not necessarily reject PPPs outright. Instead, the aim is to ensure greater choice between differing methods of funding in order to achieve best value for the taxpayer (Scottish Liberal Democrats, 2002: 19). Furthermore, while the Conservatives are for business deregulation per se, it is business taxes in particular that the SNP have promised to cut. This notwithstanding, such a presentation does highlight some of the key similarities and differences between the parties. On constitutional issues, for instance, the coalition parties and the Conservatives are broadly in favour of the current settlement, while the

SNP, SSP and Greens argue both for more powers for Holyrood and for eventual Scottish independence. More particularly, it demonstrates that while all parties stress themes such as public services, the Conservatives are the most distinctive party due to their emphasis on tax cuts, deregulation, traditional values and cutting the number of MSPs.[2]

Strategic Dilemmas: Competition and Cooperation

Strategically, the Scottish parties face some interesting dilemmas. In the case of the Labour Party, most fundamentally it has had to learn to live with coalition. Although the party accepted this as an implicit outcome in the years of negotiation in the Constitutional Convention, coalition politics has been difficult for Labour (Hassan, 2002: 39). The party had to publicly give ground to its coalition partners on issues as prominent as tuition fees. Perhaps even more demanding, electoral reform at the level of local government involves extending the principles of coalition politics and the likely end of Labour fiefdoms in West Central Scotland. Under first-past-the-post in 1999, 74 of 79 Glasgow seats went to Labour with only 49.6 per cent of the vote. The Kerley Committee review of local government has recommended proportional representation, and the system is likely to be changed by 2007. This will prove a crucial test for the coalition at Holyrood. Without reform, the Liberal Democrats are not likely to stay on board, and while the Labour leadership is reported to be broadly in favour, sections of the party will be resistant. This issue will test McConnell's reputation for being a modernizer and fixer.

Even more worrying for Labour, the party's core support may not be as loyal as it would hope. For example, Labour's image as a party that protects working class interests declined sharply between 1997 and 1999, and this coincided with a decline in the party's share of working-class support (Paterson et al., 2001: 58 and Ch.3). Blair's New Labour themes are generally perceived as less popular in Scotland, leading to pressure on the Scottish party to demonstrate its independence from Labour at Westminster. Consequently, there have been some signs that Scottish and British Labour are becoming more distinct. In the first post-devolution general election of May 2001, the Westminster manifesto pledged increased involvement of the private sector as a means of improving public services. Scottish Labour, however, avoided such commitments. Unlike the British manifesto, for example, the Scottish document did not promise to use spare capacity in private sector hospitals to treat NHS patients. As Curtice (2002: 69) argues: 'It seems unlikely that such an omission would have occurred if the Prime Minister's remit still ran in such matters in Scotland'. It is clear that, with the SNP, SSP and Greens to the left, and Conservatives to the right, Scottish

Labour operate in a very different context from the British party. Attempts to remain consistent with New Labour while vying with these different electoral competitors may prove a difficult balancing act for Labour in Scotland.

Overall, the position of Labour in Scotland appears to have been weakened by devolution. However, this process should not necessarily be interpreted as decline. Curtice's (2002) analysis of the 2001 general election indicates little evidence of protest voting against the party, despite fears that the voters might have used this election to express discontent. However, Labour still faces the problem of lower levels of support at Holyrood than at Westminster, with support declining in Labour's traditional strongholds. Furthermore, a potential threat to Labour's position at Holyrood exists in the shape of the far-left SSP.

At first sight, Labour's coalition partners, the Liberal Democrats, appear to be enjoying a period of success. They were prominent participants in the Scottish Constitutional Convention (1989–95) and can claim credit for the move away from the first-past-the-post electoral system (although this was a compromise for the party whose preferred system was the Single Transferable Vote). As a member of the Scottish Executive the party is now able to put policy ideas into practice, challenging the argument that a vote for this party is a wasted vote. Unsurprisingly, the Scottish Liberal Democrats attempt to highlight their own policy achievements, in an attempt to persuade voters that they can fulfil their commitments from within a coalition government. In the 2001 general election, for the first time, the party campaigned on its record in office, announcing that it had implemented 185 policy proposals contained in the 1999 manifesto, amounting to more than 70 per cent of its programme (Scottish Liberal Democrats, 1999).

Nevertheless, it has been suggested that the compromises of government may be eroding the party's core beliefs. The issue of higher education tuition fees is noteworthy here. During the 1999 campaign, abolition of the fees was described as 'non-negotiable' by Scottish leader Jim Wallace. In the post-election coalition talks, Labour and the Liberal Democrats did indeed negotiate a compromise which involved an inquiry into student fees and student finance, with the parties free to submit their own proposals (Finnie, 1999: 55). The final policy 'solution' was fees payable after graduation, with an increase in access grants for the less well off. The Liberal Democrats claim credit for the abolition of up-front tuition fees but the policy is hotly debated to this day, critics claiming that the policy is a messy compromise and that the Liberal Democrats abandoned their principles for their place in government.

Following 1999, Mitchell (2000: 27) criticized the Liberal Democrats, referring to them as 'the party in most need of help' in developing a strategy. The party's central problem has been maintaining its identity in the coalition with Labour. There was always a risk, for example, that voters might have difficulty identifying Liberal Democrat policies implemented by Labour Ministers. So far at least, however, the party does not appear to have suffered electorally. At the 2001 general election, its share of the vote increased by nearly three per cent on 1997 and it held all of its ten Westminster seats (Table 1). However, as Curtice (2002: 76) argues the Liberal Democrats have not benefited greatly from the coalition either. Certainly, polls do not suggest that the party is attracting new voters (Figures 1 and 2). A key question for the party is how to expand its vote base and make inroads into new areas across Scotland. While most of the current Liberal Democrat MSPs represent constituencies, in 2003 and beyond the party will look to the regional lists to boost numbers. However, it is difficult to see how the party can expand its electoral base, given the lack of popularity in central Scotland. In 1999 and 2001 the party held only one central constituency – Edinburgh West, and in Glasgow the party had only one MSP elected through the regional list.

The SNP faces a different set of challenges. If it is to be successful in achieving independence, the party must achieve a parliamentary majority. In this it faces a number of problems. Firstly, it must find a balance between its successful populist approach (Brand, 1978: 33; McEwen, 2002: 57) and projecting an image of being a competent government-in-waiting. In this sense, the party's internal democratic structure continues to contribute to divisions which have damaged the party electorally (Levy, 1990: 7–17; Bennie et al., 1997: 78–9). Results from Scottish respondents to the 2001 British Election Study suggest that the party is, to some extent, succeeding in this. In questions tapping perceptions of party competence, a majority thought the SNP was united, moderate, kept its promises and in touch with public opinion. Nevertheless, 53.1 per cent thought that the SNP would not provide strong government.

Secondly, the party has to address the tension between fundamentalist and gradualist approaches to independence. Despite occasional outbursts by fundamentalists (see Neil, 2002), the SNP has largely coalesced around a gradualist strategy (McEwen, 2002: 54–7). Although this might disillusion party activists it is difficult to see what else the SNP can do as support for independence is unstable. Moreover, McCrone and Paterson (2002: 63) note that one third of the SNP's own identifiers do not support their core policy of independence. However, with 66 per cent of respondents to the 2000 Scottish Social Attitudes Survey agreeing that the Scottish Parliament needs more powers, there is clearly scope for the party to develop this theme in the hope that independence will be the eventual result.

FIGURE 1
POLL STANDING OF THE PARTIES AT HOLYROOD CONSTITUENCY VOTE

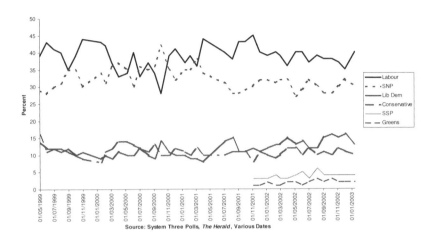

Source: System Three Polls, *The Herald*, Various Dates

FIGURE 2
POLL STANDING OF THE PARTIES HOLYROOD SECOND VOTE

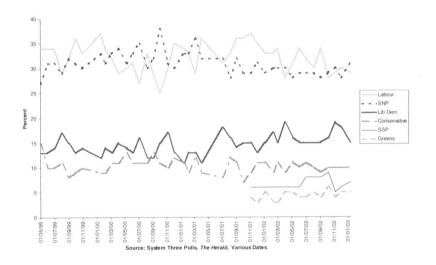

Source: System Three Polls, *The Herald*, Various Dates

The party's third challenge is that it must break into the central belt stronghold of Labour. This is problematic for a number of reasons. The SNP is hampered by Labour's domination of the constituency vote, and, while the SNP can try to outflank Labour on its left wing, particularly in Glasgow it also faces a challenge to its own left from the pro-independence SSP. This threatens the SNP's left-wing working class vote (Bennie et al., 1997; Brown et al., 1999; Paterson et al., 2001). Furthermore, under Swinney there has been a shift to target 'middle Scotland' electoral groups which have hitherto been relatively immune to the SNP message. These include women and career-oriented voters. With attitudes towards independence spread widely, this strategy has potential benefits. However, it risks alienating the party's core working class vote and limiting its progress in the central belt.

Yet another difficulty for the SNP to overcome is its traditional suspicion of working with others. There have been few reports on the party's preferences in forming a coalition but the electoral system makes this a crucial calculation if the party wants to win office.[3] While coalition with Labour can be ruled out, an SNP-SSP-Green coalition is not impossible were each of these parties to dramatically increase their vote at Labour's expense. Most likely, given the Liberal Democrats' commitment to decentralization and democracy, is an SNP-Liberal Democrat coalition (McEwen, 2002: 61).

The SNP faces the sternest test of its history in the Spring 2003 and subsequent Scottish elections. It has to combine its populist independence rhetoric with a gravitas that suggests it is a government in waiting. At the same time it must broaden its appeal to electoral groups beyond its working class male electorate without alienating that core vote. This will be a difficult transition and intra-party conflict over list rankings and independence since 1999 suggests that it is a transition that the party has not yet completed.

As for the Conservatives, a key question is what is driving their apparent return to unionism? The obvious answer is electoral reality. However, as the centre-ground is already overcrowded, the party faces a relatively closed opportunity structure where other parties have set the tenor of debate. Polls consequently show little immediate return for the party. Instead, the strategy seems to be a long-term one predicated upon Labour losing popularity. It is also unclear how deep these changes run. Despite moderating the party's language, the policies remain largely unchanged. In economic policy, for instance, low tax and regulation regimes are argued to be the best way to lift people out of poverty, while law and order policies are justified because of the regressive effects that crime has on the poor (McLetchie, 2002b). The party is also doing a precarious balancing act in its attempt to appear

Scottish. Its support for a reduction in the number of MSPs runs the risk of being seen as anti-Scottish. Moreover, 'apologies' for the record of the Thatcher years (Duncan Smith, 2002: McLetchie, 2002a) can seem grudging. Consequently, the Scottish Conservatives have a long way to go if they are to reverse the electoral decline that began in the 1960s.

Nevertheless, there are signs that the party is beginning to realize that it is unlikely to be able to wield influence alone at Holyrood. For instance, although the party's stance on constitutional matters makes it fundamentally opposed to the SNP, at a 2002 Conference fringe event, education spokesman Brian Monteith raised the prospect of coalition with the nationalists. More realistically, cooperation will take the form of loose issue-based alliances. The Conservatives have already displayed a willingness to cooperate with other parties in parliament over some issues, including tuition fees and fishing industry compensation. Moreover, McLetchie has not ruled out collaborating with any party, including Labour, if it means that Conservative ideas on public service reform can be implemented.

The central challenge for the SSP and Greens is to build support and establish a larger presence in the parliament. In the years following the first Holyrood elections, a number of by-elections suggested that the SSP in particular might improve its position (Bennie, 2002), and in the 2001 general election, the SSP continued to build support, standing in all constituencies and attracting 3.13 per cent of all votes. The party began to make inroads into areas beyond Glasgow and was by far the most prominent of the smaller parties in these elections. Curtice (2002: 76) refers to this as 'the most serious incursion in any of the territories of Great Britain since the rise of the nationalists in Scotland and Wales in 1970'. Future levels of support will depend on the extent to which Labour voters turn to the small parties. Paterson et al. (2001: 138–9) illustrate increasing disillusionment with Labour amongst its core supporters, and argue that the SNP, the SSP and to a lesser extent the Greens all benefit from this. Furthermore, 2002 polls continued to suggest that a significant number of voters were willing to vote for the small parties with their regional list vote (Figure 2). *The Herald*'s System Three polls showed SSP support peaking at 9 per cent in the regional contests in October 2002, a level of support which could return up to seven socialist MSPs. The same polls pointed to the Greens on 4–5 per cent, suggesting the return of three MSPs. Were this scenario realized in an election, a red-green grouping of MSPs could be numerically as strong as the Conservative group at Holyrood. These parties still face enormous difficulties, not least an electoral system with a high *de facto* threshold that makes it hard for small parties to win seats (Curtice and Steed, 2000: 210). However, it is certainly possible that the small parties will gain more seats in future elections, particularly at times when voters are disaffected with the main parties. In this event, the forming of alliances with each other and with sympathetic rebels within other parties could lead to these parties exercising significant influence in the parliament.

Assessing Scotland's Post-Devolution Party System

Two phases are traditionally identified in the development of Scottish electoral behaviour. Between 1945 and 1970 the Scottish party system closely resembled the rest of Britain. However, between 1974 and 1997 Scotland displayed voting patterns that appeared distinctive and required explanation. Kellas (1989: 113), for instance, referred to the 'idiosyncrasies of Scottish political behaviour' which were explained by a complex mix of different economic experiences, and how these were communicated through Scottish political media. Despite the impact of other parties during this period, however, Kellas (1989: 99) offered a picture of relative stability, or 'rigidity' in the British party system, suggesting that the differences between Scotland and other parts of Britain could be exaggerated.

Conversely, Smith's (1989) 'core' party system model would suggest that during this second phase Scotland's party system experienced transformation. Particularly after 1970 the electoral performance of the Scottish Tories declined steeply, thereby rendering the Scottish party virtually non-existent at Westminster and preceding the decline of the party at national level by more than a decade. This would seem to point to a very real difference between Scotland and the rest of the UK. In parallel, this same period saw the rise of the Liberal and SNP vote, notably in previous Conservative strongholds.

In the aftermath of devolution, has Scotland embarked upon a third period of party system change, and, if so, how should this be understood? In short, we would argue that there has been significant party system change in Scotland. While social, value and electoral change all matter, institutional engineering in the short to medium term matters more. The introduction of a form of proportional representation has meant that at Scottish parliamentary level no one party can govern alone, and that new parties have entered the equation. At the most basic level Hassan (2002: 43) refers to this as a move from 'an asymmetrical party system to a more pluralist, multi-party politics'. To establish the dynamics at work between the parties, however, a more sophisticated analysis is necessary. This is provided by application of a Sartorian framework. It is tempting to see the Scottish party system as analogous to the left-hand side of Sartori's (1966, 1976) model of extreme pluralism. A high degree of ideological polarization is evident between the SSP and Greens on the left, the Liberal Democrats, SNP and

Labour in the centre-left, and the Conservatives on the centre-right. Indeed, despite their lack of numbers in the parliament, at times it seems that the radical parties are making the running, thereby pulling the dynamics of party competition to the left. The SNP, for instance, has been forced by Sheridan's anti-nuclear protests to shore up their 'pacifist' image in a variety of ways.

A number of qualifications are however necessary. First, Sartori's framework hinges on the undefined notion of anti-system parties positioned at the ends of the ideological spectrum. However, the concept of anti-system is problematic in a Scottish perspective. Because of its promotion of independence, which would lead to the break-up of the British state, the largest 'anti-system' party is in one sense the SNP. Ideologically, the most radical parties are the far-left SSP and ecological Greens. However, as all three parties are committed to achieving their aims through democratic means, the extent to which they can be described as 'anti-system' is questionable, particularly since the SNP is the official opposition in the Scottish parliament. Secondly, because the Scottish Executive is not a minority administration no radical party is large enough to form an 'irresponsible opposition' and have blackmail potential. Thirdly, while the rhetoric and symbolism of party competition in post-devolution Scotland has appeared more radical as a result of the presence of the SSP and Greens, in practice policies have remained remarkably pragmatic and centrist.

If extreme pluralism is problematic, does moderate pluralism (Sartori, 1966, 1976), with its emphasis on ideological similarities and coalitions, help describe the Scottish party system? Excluding the SSP and Greens, there are four main parties competing for a place in a coalition government. With the movement of the Conservatives towards a more centrist unionist approach, competition between these four parties on the left–right spectrum is centripetal rather than centrifugal. We therefore see a relatively low degree of ideological polarization between these parties. Two qualifications are however necessary. Firstly, ideological distance remains between the SNP and the other three main parties over independence. Secondly, this means that rather than working in a bi-polar manner the Scottish party system is currently tri-polar with the SNP and Conservatives continuing to view each other with suspicion rather than combining to oppose the Labour-Liberal Democrat executive. This notwithstanding, a model of moderate pluralism does seem to capture some of the dynamics of the Scottish party system

A central feature of moderate pluralism is that no one party should be able to govern alone. This forces a number of strategic choices on parties. Dahl's (1966) classification is useful in capturing party system dynamics here. His example of a strictly competitive party system is post-war Britain where the two major parties expect to govern alone. Consequently, both parties can afford to adopt strictly competitive strategies in both the electoral and the parliamentary arenas. Despite increased electoral volatility, the first-past-the-post electoral system ensures that this largely remains the case. However, in the Scottish context the new electoral system forces parties to consider cooperating if they wish to participate in a coalition government. In Dahl's terms this means that Scotland now has a cooperative-competitive party system where parties cannot solely consider competitive strategies. Instead, while maximizing the vote may be crucial, they must also look towards forming an executive which can command a parliamentary majority. Such a consideration may limit competition.

Labour and the Liberal Democrats demonstrate this move towards cooperative strategies. In many respects, these parties are natural allies. They share a history of collaboration – both at Westminster and in Scotland – and there exist some clear philosophical and policy overlaps. In 1999 these included land reform, the abolition of feudal tenure, and more liberal social policy. However, in a strictly competitive party context, the parties' policy *differences* would dominate – tuition fees, PR for local government and the use of Scotland's tax varying powers to name but three. Although there have undoubtedly been tensions between the coalition parties (see Taylor 2002, Ch. 5), it was nevertheless a shared objective of constitutional reform and a desire to make home rule 'work' that laid the ground for collaboration in the parliamentary context. In order to form an executive the parties had to overcome policy disputes and, in this sense, the ability to thrash out a coherent partnership agreement (Finnie, 1999) was a good example of cooperative-competitive politics.

The other parties do not share the same history of cooperation. Neither the SNP nor the Conservatives participated in the Constitutional Convention, and ideologically they appear less than compatible. Webb (2000: 18) goes as far as to describe these parties as 'virtually ideological antipodes'. Nevertheless, the logic of AMS means that all parties are potential coalition partners. Thus, if the SNP or Conservatives are ever to form part of a Scottish executive they must look to opening up lines of communication with other parties. So far, there have been few signs that the Conservatives and SNP are likely to form a coherent opposition bloc (Cowley, 2001: 98–9), thus confirming the tri-polar nature of Scotland's party system in the parliament.

Table 4 summarizes the emerging features of the Scottish party system, with its moderate pluralist tendencies. These categories and labels are far from fixed, but they point to a Scottish party system that has developed beyond the traditional Westminster model. The number of relevant parties is debatable, as the SSP and Greens do not appear strictly 'relevant' in Sartori's terms i.e. they did not have coalition potential following the first

Parliamentary elections. However, these parties do contribute to post-devolution politics in a way that was not possible under Westminster rules, providing a flavour of multi-party politics. The extent of ideological polarization is also open to debate. There has been minimal change in the ideological character of the four main parties, as centripetal forces continue to pull parties to the centre. However, the Scottish system continues to be characterized by tripolarism and the inclusion of the SSP and Greens in this analysis suggests a diversity of ideas and policies that did not exist before 1999. Finally, the Scottish parties are showing signs of moving towards cooperative strategies in the parliamentary arena, a requirement of the new electoral rules that does not apply to Westminster. In the electoral context, the parties in Scotland remain competitive.

TABLE 4
PARTY SYSTEM CHARACTERISTICS

	Westminster Model	Scottish Model
Number of Parties	two/two and a half	four/multi
Ideological Polarization	bipolar/ suppressed pluralism	tripolar/moderate pluralism
Party Relationships		
electoral arena	competitive	competitive
parliamentary arena	competitive	cooperative

Conclusion

In the approach to the second round of Scottish Parliament elections, the Scottish media began to speculate about coalitions which might take shape beyond 2003, the assumption being that the Liberal Democrats would perform the role of 'swing' party. The Liberal Democrats publicly ruled out coalition with the SNP in Autumn 2002, confirming the likelihood of a second-term Labour–Liberal Democrat partnership. In the longer term, a different combination of parties may emerge, perhaps multi-party coalitions. For this to happen, however, the opposition parties must make more effective preparations for cooperative politics. The study of coalition formation (Axelrod, 1970; Riker, 1962) suggests that a 'minimum-winning' logic will prevail, when a combination of parties emerges that is the smallest possible coalition to ensure an overall majority. This assumes that the largest party will woo a party only just big enough to produce a combined majority, in preference to turning to a larger party that would produce a wasted 'surplus' and would mean more of a sharing of power in the eventual coalition. According to this logic, there would be no point to a Labour–SNP coalition. However, ideological compatibility is another key factor in coalition formation. It is difficult to imagine the SNP and Conservatives, for example, finding sufficient common ground to form a partnership agreement.

The creation of a Scottish Parliament therefore necessitates a revision of party system assumptions. This article has been a first attempt to assess the complex set of party dynamics created by a new electoral arena and new electoral system. Webb and Fisher (1999) argue that changes in electoral behaviour have been moving Britain's party system towards a Sartori-like model of moderate pluralism, but that the first-past-the-post electoral system suppresses these changes at the legislative level. The removal of a key institutional constraint in the Scottish context – i.e. electoral reform – has made moderate pluralism more of a political reality in Scotland, with major implications for the parties. In particular, the parties in Scotland have to come to terms with the sharing of power.

NOTES

1. These policy areas are not intended as a definitive placement of the Scottish parties on any spectrum, whether left–right or otherwise, but instead are merely indicative of the policy similarities and differences between the parties during the period 1999–2002.
2. While supporting Duncan Smith's tax cutting strategy at the UK level, the Scottish Conservatives do not presently argue that the Scottish Parliament's tax varying power should be used to cut Scottish taxes. Nevertheless, the party campaigned in 2001 on a tax-cutting ticket. It aimed to abolish the 'Graduate Tax', stop the introduction of road tolls on motorists and reduce business rates by 9 per cent.
3. SNP policy currently rules out coalition with the Conservatives.

REFERENCES

Axelrod, R. (1970) *Conflict of Interest.* Chicago: Markham Publishing.
Bennie, L., J. Brand, and J. Mitchell (1997) *How Scotland Votes: Scottish Parties and Elections,* Manchester: Manchester University Press.
Bennie, L. (2002) 'Exploiting New Electoral Opportunities: The Small Parties in Scotland', in G. Hassan and C. Warhurst (eds) *Tomorrow's Scotland,* pp.98–115. London: Lawrence and Wishart.
Blondel, J. (1968) 'Party Systems and Types of Government in Western Democracies', *Canadian Journal of Political Science* 1 (2): 180–203.
Bradbury, J. et al. (2000) Candidate Selection, Devolution and Modernization', in P. Cowley et al., *British Elections and Parties Review Vol.10,* pp.151–172. London and Portland, OR: Frank Cass.
Brand, J. (1978) *The National Movement in Scotland.* London: Routledge and Kegan Paul.
Brand, J., J. Mitchell, and P. Surridge (1994) 'Social Constituency and Ideological Profile: Scottish Nationalism in the 1990s', *Political Studies* 42 (4): 616–29.
Brown, A. et al. (1999) *The Scottish Electorate: The 1997 General Election and Beyond.*

Basingstoke: Macmillan.

Brown, A. (2001) 'Scotland' in P. Norris (ed.) *Britain Votes 2001*, pp.137–47. Oxford: Oxford University Press.

Cowley, P. (2000) 'Voting in the Scottish Parliament: The First Year', in J. Tonge et al. (eds.) *British Elections and Parties Review 11: The 2001 General Election*, pp.84–103. London and Portland, OR: Frank Cass.

Curtice, J. and M. Steed (2000) 'And Now for the Commons? Lessons From Britain's First Experience with Proportional Representation', in P. Cowley et al., *British Elections and Parties Review Vol.10*, pp.192–215, London and Portland, OR: Frank Cass.

Curtice, J. (2002) 'Did Devolution Make a Difference? The First Post-Devolution UK Election in Scotland', in L. Bennie et al. *British Elections and Parties Review 12: The 2001 General Election*, pp.64–79. London and Portland, OR: Frank Cass.

Dahl, R. A. (1966) *Political Oppositions in Western Democracies*. London: Yale University Press.

Denver, D. and I. MacAllister 'The Scottish Parliament Elections 1999: An Analysis of the Results', *Scottish Affairs* 28: 10–31.

Dinwoodie, R. (2002) 'Majority Back More Holyrood Tax Powers', *The Herald*, 7t October, p.1.

Duncan Smith, I. (2002) 'The Conservative Task is to Make the Scottish Parliament Work', Speech given to Scottish Conservative and Unionist Party Conference, 18t May.

Duverger, M. (1964) *Political Parties: Their Organization and Activity in the Modern State*, 3rd edn. London: Methuen.

Dyer, M. (2001) 'The Evolution of the Centre-Right and the State of Scottish Conservatism', *Political Studies* 49: 30–50.

Finnie, R. (1999) 'The Negotiation Diaries' *Scottish Affairs* 28: 51–6.

Hassan, G. and P. Lynch (2001) *The Almanac of Scottish Politics*. London: Politicos.

Hassan, G. (2002) 'The Paradoxes of Scottish Labour: Devolution, Change and Conservatism', in G. Hassan and C. Warhurst (eds.) *Tomorrow's Scotland*, pp.26–48. London: Lawrence & Wishart).

Inglehart, R. (1990) 'From Class-Based to Value-Based Politics', in P. Mair (ed.) *The West European Party System*, pp.266–82. Oxford: Oxford University Press.

Kellas, J. (1989) *The Scottish Political System*, 4th edn. Cambridge: Cambridge University Press.

Leicester, G. (2000) 'Scotland', in R. Hazell (ed.) *The State and the Nations: The First Year of Devolution in the United Kingdom*, pp.13–36. Thorverton: Imprint Academic.

Levy, R. (1990) *Scottish Nationalism at the Crossroads*. Edinburgh: Scottish Academic Press.

Levy, R. (1994) 'Nationalist Parties in Scotland and Wales', in L. Robins, H. Blackmore and R. Pyper (eds.) *Britain's Changing Party System*, pp.147–65. London: Leicester University Press.

Lipset, S.M. and S. Rokkan (1967) 'Cleavage Structures, Party Systems and Voter Alignments: An Introduction', in S.M. Lipset and S. Rokkan (eds.) *Party Systems and Voter Alignments*. London: Collier-Macmillan.

Lynch, P. (2001) *Scottish Government and Politics: An Introduction*. Edinburgh: Edinburgh University Press.

Lynch, P. (2002) 'Partnership, Pluralism and Party Identity: The Liberal Democrats after Devolution', in G. Hassan and C. Warhurst (eds.) *Tomorrow's Scotland* pp.83–97. London: Lawrence & Wishart.

Mair, P. (1997) *Party System Change: Approaches and Interpretations*. Oxford: Clarendon Press.

McConnell (2002a) Speech to the Fabian Society, June.

McConnell (2002b) Speech to Scottish Centre for Research on Social Justice, 1 July.

McCrone, D. and L. Paterson (2002) 'The Conundrum of Scottish Independence', *Scottish Affairs* 40: 54–75.

McEwen, N. (2002) 'The Scottish National Party After Devolution: Progress and Prospects', in G. Hassan and C. Warhurst (eds.) *Tomorrow's Scotland*, pp.49–65. London: Lawrence & Wishart.

McLetchie, D. (2002a) Speech to the Conservative Christian Fellowship Scotland, 10 May.

McLetchie, D. (2002b) Speech to Conference, 17 May.

Mitchell, J. (1990) *Conservatives and the Union: A Study of Conservative Party Attitudes to*

Scotland. Edinburgh: Edinburgh University Press.

Mitchell, J. (1996) 'Conservatives and the Changing Meaning of Union', *Regional and Federal Studies* 6: 30–44.

Mitchell, J. (2000) 'The Challenge to the Parties: Institutions, Ideas and Strategies', in G. Hassan and C. Warhurst, *The New Scottish Politics: The First Year of the Scottish Parliament and Beyond*, pp.24–30. Norwich: The Stationery Office.

Mitchell, J. (2001) 'The Study of Scottish Politics Post-Devolution: New Evidence, New Analysis and New Methods?', *West European Politics* 24: 216–23.

Mitchell, J. and L. Bennie (1996) 'Thatcherism and the Scottish Question', in C. Rallings et al. (eds.) *British Elections and Parties Yearbook 1995*, pp.90–104, London and Portland, OR: Frank Cass.

Neil, A. (2002) 'SNP Must Go on the Attack in Its War Against Unionists, *Scotland on Sunday*, 25 August, p.17.

Paterson, L. et al. (2001) *New Scotland, New Politics?* Edinburgh: Polygon.

Riker, W. H. (1962) *The Theory of Political Coalitions*. New Haven: Yale University Press.

Sartori, G. (1966) 'European Political Parties: The Case of Polarized Pluralism', in J. LaPalombara and M. Weiner (eds.) *Political Parties and Political Development*, pp.137–76. Princeton: Princeton University Press.

Sartori, G. (1976) *Parties and Party Systems: A Framework for Analysis*. Cambridge: Cambridge University Press.

Scottish Liberal Democrats (1999), www.scotlibdems.org.uk/docs/difference.htm.

Scottish Liberal Democrats (2002) *Choices and Opportunities: Fresh Thinking for Four More Years*. Edinburgh, Scottish Liberal Democrats.

Scottish National Party (2001a) *Manifesto*. Edinburgh: Scottish National Party.

Scottish National Party (2001b) *Heart of the Manifesto*. Edinburgh: Scottish National Party.

Seawright, D. (1999) *An Important Matter of Principle: The Decline of the Scottish Conservative and Unionist Party*. Aldershot: Ashgate.

Sheridan, T. and A. McCombes (2000) *Imagine: A Socialist Vision for the 21st Century*. Edinburgh: Rebel Inc.

Smith, G. (1989) 'Core Persistence: Change and the People's Party', *West European Politics* 12: 157–68.

Swinney, J. (2002) *Address to SNP Conference*, 27 September.

Taylor, B. (2002) *Scotland's Parliament: Triumph and Disaster*. Edinburgh: Edinburgh University Press.

Webb, P. and J. Fisher (1999) 'The Changing British Party System: Two-Party Equilibrium, or the Emergence of Moderate Pluralism?' in D. Broughton and M. Donovan (eds.) *Changing Party Systems in Western Europe*. London: Pinter.

Webb, P. (2000) *The Modern British Party System*, London: Sage.

Wolinetz, S.B. (1979) 'The Transformation of Western European Party Systems Revisited', *West European Politics* 2: 4–27.

TURNOUT

Electoral Turnout:
The New Generation Gap

Martin P. Wattenberg

In the November 2000 US Presidential election I did not vote. Like many of my fellow baby-boomers, I was relatively nonchalant about failing to participate. In my own mind, I felt that I had a pretty good excuse. About a week before the election my father had undergone heart bypass surgery. I had flown across the country on short notice to be there, and the thought of getting an absentee ballot before I left California was not something that crossed my mind. (By the time I arrived back on the East Coast it was too late to request an absentee ballot by mail, but I later realized I could have requested one in person just before I left.) Ironically, I was able to keep a few commitments on election day to do radio interviews on the topic of non-voting by simply emailing the producers that I would be at a different phone number. The fact that I was not voting that day came up a couple times on the air and led to further interesting discussion, but no real embarrassment on my part.

My father, by contrast, took a different view of voting. He had just got out of the hospital a couple of days before the election, and had scarcely been able to walk ten yards outside the house, but nevertheless said on Tuesday morning that he wanted to be driven to the polls. This idea did not sound so wise to me under the circumstances. I proposed an alternative: given that my parents were going to vote for different candidates for governor, I suggested that neither one vote rather than going to the trouble of cancelling each other out. This suggestion met with resistance from both my parents, who reminded me that there were many offices on the ballot besides governor and that they probably would agree on some of them. Yet, they acknowledged that without the use of a wheelchair it would be very difficult for my father to make it from the curb to the high school gym where their community votes. We agreed that I would first go to the polling place and see if there was a wheelchair there. When I returned from my scouting trip I reported that the biggest problem we would be up against was competition for the wheelchair – there were a lot of very elderly people there. But all went well, and as I waited for my parents to punch their ballots it occurred to me that the average age of the people then voting around them was clearly above retirement age. When I mentioned this observation on the way out, my mother replied that elderly people naturally realize they have a lot at stake on election day.

The fact that young people are so much less likely to vote is now so readily apparent that it hardly takes a PhD in political science to notice it when observing activity at a typical polling place. In the summer of 1998, a Chinese delegation observing a primary election in Georgia expressed amazement that so few people had shown up at the polls, and particularly noted that very few young people had cast ballots. Xu Liugen, the leader of the delegation, summarized his observations to the Associated Press as follows: 'I would have some doubts about the representativeness of those who are elected. Why such a low interest? Why don't the young people come to the polls?' (Preston, 1998).

To understand America's current turnout problems, one must answer the questions posed by Xu Liugen. My father's insistence that he really wanted to vote, my casual baby-boomer attitude, and the outright political apathy I frequently see among today's college students are apparently all representative of current generational attitudes towards voting. How, when, and why these generational differences developed are the challenging questions that this article seeks to address.

A Comparative Perspective

The phenomenon of relatively low turnout among young people is one that has drawn attention from political analysts in many countries. Recently, the International Institute for Democracy and Electoral Assistance (IDEA) issued a report showing the problem to be common throughout the democratic world, and described various voter education programmes targeted at young people that countries have adopted to try to combat it (IDEA, 1999). The data presented in the IDEA report are less than ideal for the task, however. They are derived from a hodgepodge of studies that differ widely in terms of the time elapsed since the last election, and some refer to a nation's most important election whereas others do not. Fortunately, the Comparative Study of Electoral Systems project (CSES) now provides an ideal set of comparable national election studies from which generational differences can be assessed.

While America is almost unique in terms of the extent to which those with lower degrees of education do not vote, it does not stand out so dramatically in terms of a generation gap in electoral participation. Table 1 shows that among the advanced industrialized democracies included in the

CSES thus far, Americans under the age of 30 report the second-lowest level of turnout, with only Swiss youth turning out at lower rates. The largest turnout gap between the young and the old is found in Japan, but the United Kingdom, USA and Switzerland are not far behind in this respect. Overall, the problem of getting young people to the polls is fairly common. Leaving aside the Australian case, where compulsory election attendance eliminates any substantial turnout rate differences, people under 30 are at least 10% less likely to vote in 7 out of the 9 cases.

TABLE 1
TURNOUT BY AGE IN ADVANCED INDUSTRIALIZED DEMOCRACIES
IN RECENT YEARS (%)

	18–29	30–44	45–64	65+	Difference between <30 and >65
Japan	55	82	89	92	−37
United Kingdom	55	67	81	87	−32
USA	53	72	80	84	−31
Switzerland	46	56	75	76	−30
New Zealand	76	83	90	94	−18
Norway	73	85	94	90	−17
Germany	86	92	95	97	−11
Spain	85	90	92	93	−8
Netherlands	88	91	92	94	−6
Australia	98	99	99	100	−2

Note: New Zealand data were validated by checking the public records of participation by the respondents.

Sources: Comparative Study of Electoral Systems; 2001 British Election Study; 2000 American National Election Study. Validated New Zealand data provided by Jack Vowles.

It might be thought that young people today, having grown up in an age free of nuclear threats and the Cold War, are satisfied with the way that democracy is working and are therefore less concerned about participating than previous generations. The cross-national data do not support this theory, however. Of the ten countries represented in Table 1, young people report significantly higher rates of satisfaction with how democracy is working compared with senior citizens in just two – New Zealand and the Netherlands. In three other countries there was no significant difference, and in five countries those under 30 expressed a substantially higher rate of dissatisfaction. Given that the relationship between turnout and dissatisfaction with democracy is not that strong, one should not jump to the conclusion that many young people are abstaining from the electoral process because they are alienated. But the theory that young people are not voting because they are satisfied can be ruled out.

Of course, there is nothing in the CSES data to indicate that declining turnout rates in advanced industrial democracies are due to increasing levels of non-voting among young people. The simple cross-sectional differences between young and old shown here could be due to life-cycle and/or generational factors; only the latter would imply that the changing behaviour of young citizens explains overall decline in turnout, and time-series data would be necessary to sort this out. Thus far, such research has been done on Canada (Blais et al., 2001) and Japan (Cox and Campbell, 2001); findings indicate strong generational effects in the decline of turnout in these countries. In the United States, a wealth of comparable data over time exists, making it possible to investigate this question in detail.

The Political Know-Nothing Generation

There is little doubt that life-cycle factors play at least some role in explaining the low turnout rates of young people in the United States. National surveys over the last half-century have consistently found that electoral participation tends to increase with age. Benjamin Highton and Raymond Wolfinger (2001) outline a series of major life changes that young people commonly go through, each of which might make it less likely for them to vote while they sort out their lives. Their analysis of the 1996 Census turnout dataset, however, demonstrates that only a small portion of the age differential in turnout can be accounted for by such lifestyle transitions.

A more general reason that may explain some of the steady rise in turnout rates throughout the life-cycle is what Donald Green and Ron Shachar (2000) call 'consuetude.' They write that 'an act may be said to be subject to consuetude if, other things being equal, merely engaging in the activity today makes it more likely that one will engage in the same activity in the future' (Green and Shachar, 2000: 562). Their analysis of the (American) National Election Study (NES) panel surveys shows that people are more likely to vote if they have voted in the previous election, even after a host of individual factors that typically predict turnout are controlled for. People who vote regularly learn to feel comfortable with the activity, they argue. And given that American ballots are extraordinarily long and complicated by international standards, this familiarity is likely to be of special importance in the United States. Furthermore, because Americans are asked to vote so often, the process of doing so repeatedly eventually leads to what Green and Scharar (2000) describe as an attitude that going to the polls is 'what people like me do on election day'. The story at the outset of this article about my father insisting on voting reflects just such an attitude; obviously young people need time to develop this feeling. The problems of youth turnout in America today, however, go well beyond the normal life-cycle factors. An analyst looking at the various data from 1972, when 18–21-year-olds were first enfranchised, could have reasonably concluded that young people were interested in politics, but many just had not yet got around to clearing the registration hurdles and getting into the habit of voting. Today, the situation is clearly different. A tremendous gap has opened up between the young and the elderly on measures of political interest, media consumption of politics, political knowledge and, of course, turnout.

The high level of political apathy among young people today is unexpected given that their educational achievement levels are so high. Even those who have made it into college are expressing remarkably little concern for politics. A yearly nationwide study of college freshmen recently found that among the class of 2002 only 26% said that 'keeping up with politics' was an important priority for them, compared with 58% among the class of 1970 – their parents' generation (Edwards et al., 2002: 3). If one looks more broadly at all people under the age of 30, the NES data on 'following what's going on in government and public affairs' display a striking decline in political attentiveness among young people since 1964. Table 2 shows that from 1964 to 1976 there was little difference between those under 30 and those over 65 in terms of this measure of general political interest, with young people actually showing a bit more interest in 1968 and 1972. Since 1980, however, the youngest voting-age citizens have consistently expressed the least interest in public affairs by a substantial margin. The 2000 survey findings, in particular, mark a new low in political interest among young people. Only 33% of respondents under 30 said they followed government and public affairs most or some of the time; among senior citizens, the figure was 73%. As expected, campaign interest was also at a new low for young people in 2000 – only 11% said they were very interested in the campaign as opposed to 39% among the elderly.

Why young people today are not interested in public affairs is a difficult question to answer. Since I started asking my students for their opinion on this nearly a decade ago, I have received more possible answers than I ever could have dreamed of. Typically, the first response I get is something to the effect that politics just has not affected their generation the way it did previous generations. Certainly, today's youth have not had any policy touch their lives the way the draft and the Vietnam War affected their parents, or the way Medicare has benefited their grandparents. Mark Gray and I asked a question regarding people's perceptions of this in our post-2000 election survey of four Southern California counties. The question

TABLE 2
GENERAL INTEREST IN PUBLIC AFFAIRS IN THE UNITED STATES BY AGE,
1964–2000

	18–29	30–44	45–64	65+	Difference between < 30 and >65
1964	56	67	64	63	–7
1968	58	60	63	53	+5
1972	65	68	67	62	+3
1976	58	67	70	65	–7
1980	48	56	62	64	–16
1984	50	57	62	64	–14
1988	46	54	58	63	–17
1992	53	60	65	65	–12
1996	45	51	64	64	–19
2000	38	50	60	64	–26

Note: There are four possible response categories to the general political interest question: hardly at all, only now and then, some of the time, and most of the time. These four response categories have been recoded as follows: hardly at all = 0; only now and then = 33; some of the time = 66; most of the time = 100. Cell entries are averages for each age group.

Source: American National Election Studies.

went as follows: 'Some of the issues discussed during the campaigns for the November election directly related to policies affecting people of your generation. Do you think that politicians pay too much attention to these issues, about the right amount or too little?' 62% of respondents under the age of 30 said 'too little', 21% said 'about the right amount', and 9% said 'too much'. The percentages for those 65 and over were 33%, 41%, and 11%, respectively.

However, I believe that the cause of young people's apathy runs much deeper than a sense that the issues are not relevant to them and that the politicians ignore them. Central to any generational hypothesis are changes in socialization experiences. For the last two decades, young people have been socialized in a rapidly changing media environment that has been radically different from that experienced by the past couple of generations. Political scientists were slow to realize the impact of television – as late as 1980 there was surprisingly little literature on this subject. Today, a similar shortcoming is the lack of research concerning how the shift from broadcasting to narrowcasting has dramatically altered how much exposure a young adult has received to politics while growing up. The first major networks – ABC, NBC and CBS – chose to use the term 'broadcasting' in their corporate names because their signal was being sent out to a broad audience. As long as these networks dominated the industry, each would have to deal with general topics that the public as a whole was concerned with, such as politics and government. But with the development of cable TV, market segmentation has taken hold. Sports buffs can watch ESPN all day, music buffs can tune to MTV or VH1, history buffs can go to the History Channel, and so forth. Rather than appealing to a general audience, channels such as ESPN, MTV and C-SPAN focus on a narrow particular interest. Hence, their mission has often been termed 'narrowcasting,' rather than the traditional 'broadcasting.' This is even more true for websites, which require far less in start-up costs than a television channel and hence can be successful with a very small and specific audience.

Because of the narrowcasting revolution, today's youth have grown up in an environment in which public affairs news has not been as readily visible as it has been in the past. It has become particularly difficult to convince members of a generation that has channel-surfed all its life that politics really does matter. Major political events were once shared national experiences. The current generation of young adults is the first to grow up in a media environment in which there are few such shared experiences. When CBS, NBC and ABC dominated the airwaves, their blanket coverage of presidential speeches, political conventions and presidential debates sometimes left little else to watch on TV. As channels have proliferated over the last two decades, though, it has become much easier to avoid exposure to politics altogether by simply grabbing the remote control. Whereas President Nixon got an average rating of 50 for his televised addresses to the nation (meaning that half the population was watching), President Clinton averaged only about 30 in his first term (Kernell, 1997: 132). Political conventions, which once received more television coverage than the summer Olympics, have been relegated to an hour per night, and even this highly condensed coverage gets poor ratings. The presidential debates of 1996 and 2000 drew respectable average ratings of 28, but this was only half the typical level of viewers drawn by debates held between 1960 and 1980. In sum, young people today have never known a time when most citizens paid attention to major political events. This is one of the key reasons why so many of them have yet to get into the habit of following and participating in politics.

Moreover, one key media consumption habit that young people have not developed is reading the daily newspaper. As Teixeira (1992) shows, newspaper reading is particularly predictive of who votes, even after controlling for a host of demographic and attitudinal variables. Table 3 displays by age group percentages of people reading campaign stories in the newspaper since 1960. From 1960 to 1976, there was no consistent difference in this measure between the youngest and oldest citizens. Since 1980, though, those under 30 have been substantially less likely to pick up a newspaper and read about the presidential race. In both 1996 and 2000, senior citizens were more than twice as likely to say they had read campaign articles in newspapers as those under 30.

TABLE 3
% READING NEWSPAPERS ABOUT THE CAMPAIGN BY AGE, 1960–2000

	18–29	30–44	45–64	65+	Difference between <30 and >65
1960	84	80	81	74	+10
1964	75	80	80	77	−2
1968	68	81	76	72	−4
1972	49	59	62	61	−11
1976	68	78	77	70	−2
1980	56	78	76	72	−16
1984	62	77	77	70	−8
1988*	35	47	57	57	−22
1992	35	50	57	60	−25
1996	28	39	52	60	−32
2000	27	35	48	56	−29

Note: *A major change in question format occurred here.

Source: American National Election Studies.

Because of the media environment in which young people have been socialized, they have learned much less about politics than their elders. The current pattern of political knowledge increasing with age has become well known in recent years. But it was not always that way. The 1964 and 2000 National Election Studies each contain a substantial battery of political knowledge questions that enable this point to be clearly demonstrated. Table 4 shows the percentage of correct answers to eight questions in 1964 and nine questions in 2000 by age category. (Because the level of difficulty of the questions differed somewhat, one should only examine the differences within a year and not necessarily infer that political knowledge as a whole has gone down.) In 1964, there was virtually no pattern by age, with those under 30 actually scoring 5% higher on this test than senior citizens. By contrast, in 2000 young people provided the correct answer to only one out of every three questions, whereas people over 65 were correct half the time. Regardless of whether the question concerned identifying current political leaders, information about the presidential candidates, or partisan control of the Congress, the result was the same: young people were less knowledgeable than the elderly.

TABLE 4
A COMPARISON OF AGE AND POLITICAL KNOWLEDGE IN 1964 AND 2000

	1964	*2000*
18–29	66	34
30–44	71	43
45–64	69	51
65+	61	50

Note: Entries are based on the percentage of accurate responses to a series of 8 questions in 1964 and 9 questions in 2000. In 1964, respondents were given credit for knowing that Goldwater was from Arizona, Johnson was from Texas, Goldwater and Johnson were Protestants, Democrats had the majority in Congress both before and after the election, Johnson had supported civil rights legislation, and Goldwater had opposed it. In 2000, respondents were given credit for knowing that Bush was from Texas, Gore was from Tennessee, Republicans had the majority in the House and Senate before the election, Lieberman was Jewish, and for identifying William Rehnquist, Tony Blair, Janet Reno, and Trent Lott.

Source: 1964 and 2000 National Election Studies.

Given that today's youth have not been exposed to politics through the broadcasting of national shared experiences, the label of the 'know-nothing generation' ought to be considered descriptive, not pejorative. It is not their fault. But nevertheless, the consequences are real and important. Thomas Jefferson once said that there has never been, nor ever will be, a people who are politically ignorant and free. If this is indeed the case, write Stephen Bennett and Eric Rademacher (1997: 39), then 'we can legitimately wonder what the future holds if (Generation) Xers remain as uninformed as they are about government and public affairs.' Although this worry may well be an overreaction, important consequences ensue when citizens lack political information. In *What Americans Know About Politics and Why It Matters*, Michael Delli Carpini and Scott Keeter (1996, ch.6) make a strong case for the importance of staying informed about public affairs. Political knowledge, they argue: (a) fosters civic virtues, such as political tolerance; (b) helps citizens to identify what policies would truly benefit them and to incorporate this information into their voting behaviour; and (c) promotes active participation in politics. It is certainly the case that lacking information about politics in comparison with their elders, fewer young Americans are heading to the polls compared with previous generations – a development that has pulled the nationwide turnout rate down substantially in recent years.

The Age–Turnout Relationship over Time and in Different Types of Elections

The standard source for information on the precise relationship between age and turnout in the United States has long been that displayed in Wolfinger and Rosenstone's (1980) classic work based on 1972 data. These data are displayed in Table 5, along with comparable data from the 1996 census survey. There have been several striking changes in the age–turnout pattern. The data for ages 18–60 show a noticeable decline in turnout from 1972 to 1996; importantly, the rate of decline increases as one moves downwards in age. In contrast, it is readily apparent that turnout has actually gone up for ages 66 and above. Political scientists used to write that the frailties of old age led to a decline in turnout after one became eligible for Social Security; now an examination of the census survey data shows that such a decline occurs only after the age of 80. The greater access to medical care provided to today's seniors must surely be given some of the credit for this change. Because senior citizens can perceive personal benefits from government programmes like Medicare it is particularly easy for them to believe that politics does indeed make a difference.

TABLE 5
A COMPARISON OF AGE AND TURNOUT IN PRESIDENTIAL ELECTIONS IN 1972
AND 1996

	1972	*1996*
18–24	49.6	32.4
25–30	58.4	40.3
31–35	62.2	47.1
36–40	65.1	54.1
41–45	68.5	58.5
46–50	70.8	62.6
51–55	71.5	63.2
56–60	71.0	66.9
61–65	70.0	68.7
66–70	69.5	70.9
71–75	65.2	69.4
76–80	61.0	68.1
81+	46.2	56.1

Note: All figures are percentages.

Source: U.S. Census Bureau Studies.

This phenomenon can also be seen in public records of turnout rates by age in primaries and special elections. Table 6 presents data on such elections from a variety of US localities that have posted such information on the Internet. These percentages are based on registered voters only, because the local election officials who compiled the data are strictly interested in who on their registration rolls has turned out. If one were to take into account the lower registration rates of young people, then the generational differences would be even greater. The results just for registered voters, however, are disturbing enough. Young registrants, being more likely to be Independents, rarely participate in primaries. Their single-digit primary participation is dwarfed by margins ranging from 4:1 to 12:1 in the localities shown in Table 6. Young people are thus taking a very small part in the choosing of party nominees. The situation with regard to special elections held to decide referenda questions does not seem to be quite as bad. Nevertheless, it is clear that separating such policy decisions from high-salience elections gives extra weight to the opinions of the elderly, who are much more likely to turn out in such circumstances.

TABLE 6
TURNOUT AMONG REGISTERED VOTERS BY AGE IN SPECIAL ELECTIONS AND
PRIMARIES FOR VARIOUS COUNTIES AND STATES (%)

Pierce County, Washington state 1999 referendum		*Alaska 1999 referendum*		*Johnson County, Kansas 2000 primary*	
18–25	26.3	18–24	22.3	18–24	3.2
26–35	40.2	25–34	27.9	25–39	15.0
36 50	60.4	35–54	45.4	40–59	44.8
51–65	76.8	55–64	56.3	60+	37.0
66+	81.4	65+	61.8	–	–

Brevard County, Florida 1st 1998 primary		*Tri-County, Oregon 1998 primary*		*South Carolina 2000 primary*	
18–29	5.5	18–29	10.0	18–21	8.8
30–39	13.8	30–39	19.0	22–44	11.0
40–49	19.3	40–49	32.9	45–64	23.9
50–59	24.0	50–59	44.2	65+	31.1
60–69	29.7	60–69	58.8	–	–
70–79	30.5	70–79	66.0	–	–
80+	23.6	–	–	–	–

Why Low Youth Turnout Matters

Although many young people seem to think it does not matter if they do not vote, it does. Harold Lasswell wrote many years ago that 'politics is who gets what, when, and how'. As long as young people have low rates of participation in the electoral process, then they should expect to be getting

TABLE 7
YOUNG VS. ELDERLY OPINION ON POLITICAL ISSUES IN THE 1990s

	Under 30	65 and over
Liberal	23	11
Moderate	25	28
Conservative	26	31
DK	27	29
Favour government help to get people jobs	35	19
In-between	19	23
People must get ahead on their own	35	43
DK	11	16
Favour more government spending for things like education and health care	39	21
In-between	22	30
Prefer less domestic spending	23	30
DK	16	19
Favour increased spending for public schools	80	54
Same	17	41
Want decreased school spending	3	6
Favour increased spending to protect the environment	61	41
Same	34	53
Want decreased environmental spending	5	6
Favour equal role for women	67	44
In-between	15	20
Women's place is in the home	14	25
DK	4	12
Never permit abortion	11	14
OK for rape, incest, health	28	34
OK for other reasons	15	14
Abortion should be a matter of personal choice	45	36
DK	1	3

Note: All figures are percentages.

Source: Combined data from the 1992–98 National Election Studies.

relatively little of whatever there is to get from government. Yet, until they start showing up in greater numbers at the polls, there will be little incentive for politicians to focus on programmes that will help them. Politicians are not fools; they know who their customers are. Why should they worry about young non-voters any more than the makers of denture cream worry about people with healthy teeth?

Of course, most everyone can look forward to getting older eventually. Those who were neglected in the 2000 presidential campaign will probably be seriously courted in the campaign of 2040. From this perspective, it could be argued that most people will one day get the chance to be heard in the electoral process and to reap the political benefits. Such a perspective, however, assumes that there are not generational differences in attitudes that can influence the course of public policy. Who gets what does not just involve material goods, but has also been increasingly about basic non-material values in recent years. Ronald Inglehart (1997) has documented a shift from materialist to post-materialist values throughout the advanced industrialized world, which has been largely driven by generational change and replacement.

There are indeed sharp differences between younger and older Americans on both material and non-material issue questions, as displayed in Table 7. In order to provide plenty of cases for analysis, data from the 1992 through 1998 National Election Studies were combined, yielding 1,526 respondents under the age of 30 and 1,252 respondents who were at least 65. As expected, young people are substantially more supportive of government spending that would particularly help them, such as for public schools and jobs programmes. Roughly similar differences in terms of magnitude can also be found for value questions. Young people are more in favour of spending to protect the environment, an equal role for women in society and abortion rights. In terms of general ideological labelling, young people are virtually as likely to say they are liberals as conservatives on the ideological scale, whereas among senior citizens conservatives outnumber liberals by 20%. In sum, if young people had turnout rates equal to those of older people, voting behaviour and public policy would probably be shifted noticeably to the left.

Conclusion

It is not young people's fault that they have not been exposed much to politics while growing up and hence are less informed about politics than previous generations. Their low turnout rates are understandable in light of their unique socialization experience.

American politicians are not really to blame for this inequitable pattern of generational representation, either. They did not consciously try to create a situation that would greatly benefit older people. It is only natural for them to study who has voted in the past and to focus on these people, thereby leaving most young adults out of the picture. But if politicians were to ponder the principles universally valued in any democracy they might be moved to try to address this problem. If official election observers in a third-world country noticed that older people were three times as likely as younger people to vote, they would no doubt call this fact to the attention of local authorities, and suggest that such an imbalance ought to be looked into.

A well-established democracy like the United States ironically has fewer options than a third-world country for dealing with such a problem. In a new democracy, for example, it would be easier to change the electoral system to facilitate the emergence of a party that would particularly appeal to young people. It seems unlikely, however, that there will ever be any serious consideration of changing the single-member district system in the United States. A strong independent candidacy, such as that of Ross Perot in 1992, may emerge from time to time to energize young people a bit, but an enduring viable third party is nowhere on the horizon. Of course, nothing precludes one of the existing two major parties from strongly targeting this large block of unmobilized young adults. Given young people's opinions on policy questions, however, there is little reason to expect the Republicans to do so. And the Democrats, having spent decades building up their image as creators and protectors of Social Security and Medicare programmes, would find it difficult to switch gears and try to make themselves the party of the young.

It would theoretically be easier to make additions to the modern television campaign so that everyone, especially young people, would be more likely to be exposed to the discussion of the issues. In 1992, the presidential candidates were suddenly everywhere on the television dial, appearing on MTV, the Nashville Network, the 'Arsenio Hall Show' and many forums. Voters seemed to like the idea of candidates cutting through the journalistic filters and talking to them on programmes they regularly watched. This election was the only one since 1960 when turnout went up substantially, a pattern that was especially evident among young people. Such broad-based exposure for the candidates needs to be somehow institutionalized for the narrowcasting age.

Although the solution to the new generation gap in voting participation in the United States is going to be difficult to find, the consequences for the present are readily apparent. Major issues that affect young adults are not even making it onto the public agenda, and young people's opinions on the issues are not being faithfully represented through the political process.

REFERENCES

Bennett, Stephen Earl and Eric W. Rademacher (1997) 'The Age of Indifference Revisited: Patterns of Political Interest, Media Exposure, and Knowledge among Generation X', in Stephen C. Craig and Stephen Earl Bennett (eds.), *After the Boom: The Politics of Generation X*. Lanham, MD: Rowman and Littlefield.
Blais, Andre, Elisabeth Gidengil, Neil Nevitte and Richard Nadeau (2001) 'The Evolving Nature of Non-Voting: Evidence From Canada'. Paper prepared for delivery at the annual meeting of the American Political Science Association.

Cox, Karen and John Creighton Campbell (2001) 'Generational Change or Periodic Fluctuation? Age and Political Attitudes in the US and Japan.' Paper prepared for delivery at the Annual Meeting of the American Political Science Association.

Delli Carpini, Michael X. and Scott Keeter (1996) *What Americans Know About Politics and Why it Matters.* New Haven, CT: Yale University Press.

Edwards, George C. III, Martin P. Wattenberg, and Robert L. Lineberry (2002) *Government in America*, 10th edn. New York: Longman.

Green, Donald P. and Ron Shachar (2000) 'Habit Formation and Political Behaviour: Evidence of Consuetude in Voter Behaviour', *British Journal of Political Science* 30: 561–73.

Highton, Benjamin and Raymond E. Wolfinger (2001) 'The First Seven Years of the Political Life-cycle', *American Journal of Political Science* 45: 202–9.

International Institute for Democracy and Electoral Assistance (1999) *Youth Voter Participation: Involving Today's Young in Tomorrow's Democracy.* Stockholm: International IDEA.

Kernell, Samuel (1997) *Going Public: New Strategies of Presidential Leadership*, 3rd edn. Washington, DC: Congressional Quarterly Press.

Preston, June (1998) 'Chinese Observers Slam U.S. Voter Turnout.' *Associated Press*, August 12.

Teixeira, Ruy A. (1992) *The Disappearing American Voter.* Washington, D.C.: The Brookings Institution.

Wolfinger, Raymond E. and Steven J. Rosenstone (1980) *Who Votes?* New Haven: Yale University Press.

Constituency Marginality and Turnout in Britain Revisited

David Denver, Gordon Hands and Iain MacAllister

Almost 30 years ago, two of the present authors published an article which showed that in British general elections from 1959 to 1970 variations in turnout across constituencies were clearly related to marginality (the closeness of the constituency contest) in the preceding election – the closer the previous contest, the higher was the turnout (Denver and Hands, 1974). In a later piece, the analysis was extended to cover the three elections of the 1970s and previous marginality was again found to have a significant effect (Denver and Hands, 1985). Since then, accounts of variations in constituency turnout have included previous marginality as an explanatory variable almost as a matter of course and all have found that it remains a statistically significant predictor of turnout when included in multivariate analyses of constituency-level data (see, for example, Denver and Halfacree, 1992; Denver and Hands, 1997a; Whiteley et al., 2001; McAllister, 2001).

While there is broad agreement that greater marginality is associated with higher turnouts, there is less on how the relationship between marginality and turnout is to be explained. There are two main hypotheses. The first focuses on individual voters and assumes that they have some awareness of how close the electoral contest is likely to be in their constituency. The more marginal the constituency the more likely it is that every vote will count and, therefore, the greater the incentive to go to the polls. In simple rational choice terms, the potential benefits to the voter are greater where there is more chance that the outcome in the constituency concerned will be close.

The second hypothesis focuses on the mobilizing activities of parties. Parties also act rationally by campaigning more strongly in 'key' seats where the outcome of the election is expected to be close. In recent elections, indeed, the parties have almost ignored hopeless and (to a lesser extent) safe seats. On polling day, extensive and intensive get-out-the-vote efforts are mounted in targeted (invariably marginal) seats (see Denver and Hands, 1997b; Denver et al., 2002). On this account, the relationship between turnout and marginality is to be explained by variations in the intensity of party efforts across constituencies. In our original articles, we used constituency campaign expenditure data as a surrogate indicator of campaign activity and showed that there was a positive relationship between spending on the part of the leading contending parties and turnout. In this article, we firstly examine trends in the relationship between marginality, campaign intensity, the socio-economic status of constituencies and turnout over the post-war period as a whole. This raises some important methodological issues, relating in particular to the relationships between the different variables involved, which have not so far been considered in any depth. We explore these issues and suggest that traditional techniques of analysis do not take us very far in disentangling the relationships and, therefore, in understanding and explaining the impact of marginality.

Constituency Marginality, Campaign Spending and Turnout 1951–2001

Both hypotheses referred to above assume that voters and/or parties make some calculation of the likely closeness of the results in different constituencies in a current election. The best guide to this, almost without exception, is the constituency result in the preceding election. Marginality in the previous election is, therefore, the relevant independent variable for our purposes and it is conventionally measured as the percentage majority of the first over the second party subtracted from 100. The closer the score is to 100, therefore, the more marginal the seat.

We begin by showing (Table 1) the simple bivariate correlation coefficients measuring the strength of the association between previous marginality and turnout at relevant elections from 1951 to 2001.[1] The first point to emphasize is that for every election the correlation between marginality and turnout is positive and significant. In every election turnout was significantly higher in more marginal seats and significantly lower in those that were safer for one party or another. Secondly, however, the strength of the relationship has varied a good deal from election to election. In the second of the original articles referred to above we suggested that the relationship tended to strengthen from the 1950s to 1979 and this is confirmed by the current analysis – apart from a dip in 1964 there is a generally upward trend from 1951 to 1979. We confidently expected this trend to continue as parties' and individual voters' understanding of the operation of the first-past-the-post electoral system became more sophisticated but, in fact, the correlation declined sharply in 1983 and fell further to record low levels in 1987 and 1992. There was then some recovery in 1997, before a sharp jump to a new high in 2001.

TABLE 1
BIVARIATE CORRELATION COEFFICIENTS FOR CONSTITUENCY MARGINALITY
AND TURNOUT, 1951–2001

	1951	1959	1964	1966	1970	1974O	1979
	0.276	0.334	0.235	0.459	0.442	0.480	0.511
(N)	(612)	(617)	(618)	(617)	(617)	(623)	(622)

	1983	1987	1992	1997	2001
	0.273	0.161	0.168	0.255	0.690
(N)	(633)	(633)	(634)	(640)	(639)

Notes: All coefficients are statistically significant (p < 0.001). The Speaker's seat is excluded where appropriate. For 1983 and 1997 previous marginality is based on estimates of what the party shares of votes in the preceding election would have been under the new boundaries (see Note 1 for sources).

TABLE 2
SUMMARY OF MULTIPLE REGRESSION ANALYSES: THE IMPACT OF
MARGINALITY ON TURNOUT, CONTROLLING FOR SOCIO-ECONOMIC STATUS
AND REGION, 1959–2001

	R^2	Beta		R^2	Beta
1959	0.611	0.348	1983	0.680	0.360
1964	0.718	0.340	1987	0.646	0.291
1966	0.708	0.425	1992	0.740	0.196
1970	0.727	0.388	1997	0.781	0.252
1974O	0.790	0.358	2001	0.751	0.304
1979	0.743	0.350			

Notes: The R^2 figures show the percentage of variance in turnout explained by the relevant equations. Beta weights are the standardized regression coefficients for the impact of marginality on turnout, controlling for other independent variables in the equations. All regression coefficients are statistically significant (p < 0.001).

Before discussing these patterns further, however, we follow the conventional path of testing whether the association between marginality and turnout remains significant when other factors that might impact upon turnout are taken into account. It is well-established that turnout varies according to the socio-economic character of constituencies (see, for example, Denver, 2003: 32–4) and we therefore incorporated a standard set of five socio-demographic variables that are available for constituencies throughout the period from 1959, and also five dummy variables to take account of region, into a series of multivariate regression equations with turnout as the dependent variable.[2] The results of these analyses are summarized in Table 2.[3]

The standardized regression coefficients from these multivariate analyses, which measure the impact of marginality on turnout after taking account of socio-economic status and region, suggest a somewhat different pattern over time from that indicated by the bivariate correlations reported in Table 1, with less dramatic fluctuations. In particular, when controls for socio-economic status and region are introduced, it appears that there was a gentle decline in the impact of marginality from 1966 until 1983, a sharp fall in 1987 and again in 1992, followed by increases in 1997 and 2001 – though not as marked as the increases in the size of the simple correlations. Perhaps the most important point to note, however, is simply that constituency marginality remains a significant predictor of turnout even when regional and socio-economic variations are taken into account, all the relevant coefficients being statistically significant. We can use the unstandardized regression coefficients (not shown here) to give an indication of the magnitude of the effect of marginality on turnout. Taking 2001 as an example, the unstandardized coefficient for marginality (0.113) implies that, other things being equal, turnout in a constituency with a previous marginality score of 95 would have been 2.8 per cent higher than in a relatively safe one with a previous marginality score of 70. In the 1966 election (unstandardized coefficient for marginality 0.197) the difference would have been 4.9 per cent. We can be confident, then, that constituency marginality has been and remains a significant influence on turnout although, as suggested at the outset, this is not a startlingly new conclusion.

The second hypothesis mentioned above suggests that campaigning by the political parties plays a crucial mediating role in the relationship between marginality and turnout. Parties appreciate the importance of focussing on marginal seats and organize effective campaigns in them. As they campaign to maximize their own votes, the effect will be to raise the overall turnout in the constituencies concerned. To test this hypothesis we need some measure of the strength of party campaigning and in our earlier work we used party campaign spending as a surrogate indicator of campaign strength. Others have subsequently adopted the same strategy (see, for example, Pattie et al., 1995). Campaign expenditure at constituency level has always been closely restricted and we have taken the proportion of the legal maximum spent by a candidate (excluding personal expenses) as a rough indicator of the intensity of the local campaign fought by the candidate's party in the constituency concerned. It is easy to think of objections to this – in some cases spending money (on leaflets and posters, for example) may well be a soft alternative to the hard graft of canvassing and mounting a get-out-the-vote operation. On the other hand, it seems very likely that parties will spend less where they are making only a token campaign effort and more where they are campaigning strongly. Given this, and the fact that the data can be obtained easily – being collected and published officially – and are available for all modern general elections, it seems reasonable to use campaign spending as an indicator of campaign effort.[4] Nonetheless, it could not be claimed that campaign spending per se affects turnout. It is campaign activities such as canvassing, leafletting and the get-out-the-vote operation on polling day that might do. We have measured constituency campaigning of this kind directly and systematically in the last three general elections by means of surveys of election agents.[5] Based on the survey responses, we have devised a series of indexes of campaign intensity which enable us to make a more accurate comparison of the level of campaign activity across parties and constituencies (for details see Denver and Hands, 1997b; Denver et al., 2002). For these three elections, therefore, when analysing the impact of campaigning we present data based on the direct measures of campaign intensity as well as on spending.[6]

In general, we would expect parties to campaign more strongly and spend more in more marginal seats and this expectation is confirmed by the data in Table 3, which shows the simple bivariate correlations between the proportion of the maximum spent in a constituency by a party and the marginality of the constituency in the preceding election for the party concerned. In this case, if the party won the constituency, marginality is measured as 100 minus its percentage majority over the second party; where the party did not win, marginality is defined as the 100 minus the difference between its vote share and that of the winner.

These data show, first of all, that there is nothing new about targeted campaigning (or at least targeted spending). At every election from 1951 each party spent a greater proportion of its allowance in its more marginal seats and a smaller proportion in constituencies that were either safe or relatively poor prospects. In general, the associations are stronger for the Conservatives than for Labour, but strongest of all for the Liberals and their successors. It is not easy to discern any clear trend in the strength of the associations over time, however, although it is worth noting that after reaching a low point in 1987 (0.307) the coefficient for the Conservatives increased fairly steadily thereafter to reach a high of 0.821 in 2001. The figures derived from the direct measure of campaign intensity confirm that Conservative campaign efforts in 2001 were more effectively directed into more marginal seats. In contrast, the coefficient for Labour spending peaked in 1987 and declined after that, falling dramatically to only 0.142, the smallest of the series, in 2001. Initially, this last figure might appear surprising, since it is generally acknowledged that by 2001 Labour had a highly efficient and rigorous local campaigning strategy which involved concentrating resources into target seats. In fact, it is precisely this which

TABLE 3
BIVARIATE CORRELATION COEFFICIENTS FOR CAMPAIGN EXPENDITURE
(INTENSITY) AND MARGINALITY OF SEAT FOR PARTY CONCERNED, 1951–2001

Election	Con	N	Lab	N	Lib	N
1951	0.625	(601)	0.430	(612)	0.600	(104)
1959	0.514	(609)	0.575	(617)	0.556	(91)
1964	0.410	(612)	0.524	(617)	0.358	(196)
1966	0.682	(617)	0.446	(617)	0.561	(277)
1970	0.724	(616)	0.298	(617)	0.680	(246)
1974O	0.717	(622)	0.590	(623)	0.646	(517)
1979	0.699	(622)	0.411	(622)	0.665	(576)
1983	0.377	(633)	0.629	(633)	0.500	(593)
1987	0.307	(632)	0.735	(633)	0.471	(633)
1992	0.461	(634)	0.661	(634)	0.638	(634)
1997	0.417	(640)	0.650	(639)	0.726	(639)
2001	0.821	(639)	0.142	(637)	0.728	(637)
Campaign intensity						
1992	0.441	(634)	0.727	(634)	0.608	(633)
1997	0.392	(640)	0.712	(639)	0.703	(639)
2001	0.783	(639)	0.369	(637)	0.718	(637)

Notes: All coefficients are statistically significant (p < 0.001). 'Lib' refers to the Liberal party from 1951 to 1979, the Alliance in 1983 and 1987 and the Liberal Democrats thereafter. The last three rows are based on the survey-derived indexes of campaign intensity.

helps to explain the weak correlation between spending and marginality in 2001. In seats that the party already held – which included almost all of their target seats – spending was much higher (the mean being 77.0 per cent of the maximum allowed) than in those which they did not hold (a mean of 40.7 per cent). Within both categories, spending was clearly related to marginality (the correlation coefficient is 0.520 in both cases) but the effect when all seats are considered together is to produce a relatively weak overall relationship. Nonetheless, the figures for campaign intensity suggest that Labour's efforts in 2001 were not as well-directed as they had been in 1992 and 1997.

For the moment, however, our main concern is to assess the effect of constituency campaigning on turnout. Since we are interested in the overall level of campaigning rather than the amount undertaken by each party separately, our measure when using campaign expenditure is the total spent by the parties which came first and second in the constituency as a proportion of the combined total allowed for two candidates.[7] Similarly, when using campaign intensity we combine the scores for the top two parties for elections from 1992 to 2001. Table 4 shows bivariate correlations measuring the association between spending by the top two parties (and

campaign intensity) in each constituency and turnout. As with marginality,
all coefficients are positive and significant – the more the main contending
parties spent in constituencies, the higher the turnout. There is no clear trend
in the strength of this relationship from 1951 to October 1974 but there was
a marked decline in 1979 and the relationship remained relatively weak
until 1992. In 1997 and 2001, however, spending and turnout were more
strongly associated than at any other post-war election. The associations
between campaign intensity and turnout in the 1992, 1997 and 2001 are also
positive and significant. As with marginality, campaign spending and
intensity remain significant influences on turnout in all cases when they are
incorporated into multivariate analyses together with the socio-economic
and regional variables described above. We do not reproduce the details
here, but the results suggest that in 2001, for example, net of socio-
economic variables and region, turnout in constituencies in the top quartile
of campaign intensity would have been, on average, 4.3 per cent higher than
in constituencies in the bottom quartile.

The evidence we have presented thus far provides support for both
hypotheses put forward to explain the relationship between marginality and
turnout. On the one hand, marginality itself has been significantly related to
constituency turnout, even when a range of socio-economic and regional
control variables are taken into account, at every election since 1959 for
which we have a reliable measure of previous marginality. This may reflect
the calculations of voters. It should be noted, however, that an attempt to
confirm the relationship between marginality and turnout at the individual
level using data from the 1992 British Election Study found no significant
link once other variables had been taken into account (Johnston and Pattie,
1998). On the other hand, campaign spending and intensity are also

TABLE 4
BIVARIATE CORRELATION COEFFICIENTS FOR CAMPAIGN EXPENDITURE
(INTENSITY) BY TOP TWO PARTIES AND TURNOUT, 1951–2001

Campaign	1951	1955	1959	1964	1966	1970	1974F
spending	0.321	0.442	0.365	0.330	0.415	0.382	0.340
(N)	(613)	(617)	(618)	(618)	(617)	(617)	(621)
Campaign	1974O	1979	1983	1987	1992	1997	2001
spending	0.429	0.298	0.261	0.243	0.277	0.467	0.511
(N)	(622)	(622)	(633)	(633)	(634)	(640)	(639)
Campaign	1992	1997	2001				
intensity	0.376	0.515	0.511				
	(631)	(639)	(636)				

Notes: Since previous marginality is not involved here figures for 1955 and February 1974 are
included in this table. The Speaker's seat is excluded where appropriate. All coefficients are
statistically significant (p < 0.001).

significantly related to turnout, which suggests that party activity has played a role. On the basis of these data it is difficult to know how we could determine which hypothesis is better supported by the evidence. Simply comparing the size of the correlation coefficients, for example, shows that in six elections the association between spending and turnout is stronger than that between marginality and turnout, while the opposite is true in the six other elections. The three variables – marginality, campaign intensity and turnout – are strongly inter-related and it is not clear at this stage how the relationships can be disentangled.

Issues Arising from the Analyses

Two considerations arising from the analysis to this point suggest a way of exploring the data further. The first relates to the association between party spending and the marginality of constituencies for the party concerned (Table 3). It is striking that in the Conservative column every coefficient is clearly larger in elections which the party entered as the Opposition (1951, 1966, 1970, October 1974, 1979 and 2001) than in those which it entered as the incumbent government (1959, 1964, 1983 to 1997). The mean coefficient in the former is 0.711 and for the latter 0.414. With the exception of October 1974 (when the government had only a tiny majority, and had only been in office for 8 months) the same is true of the coefficients for Labour spending – the means are 0.386 when the party was in government and 0.629 when in opposition. This regular pattern might occur simply because incumbent MPs are willing to spend more money, irrespective of the marginality of their seat, in order to retain their position. Since the governing party will have more incumbents this will result in a weakening of the marginality/spending relationship. It is striking, however, that although we have only three cases (1992, 1997 and 2001) where we have direct campaign intensity data exactly the same pattern is repeated. It might be, therefore, that the pattern reflects different campaigning strategies. At least since the 1960s, parties (and voters) have had ample pre-election information about the direction in which the political pendulum is swinging. When there is a clear expectation that one of the parties will gain seats then party efforts are likely to be greater in the marginal seats it is attacking than in the ones it is defending. In 2001, for instance, the parties could assume that the Conservatives would hold on to seats that had survived the 1997 landslide and concentrate efforts into those that Labour had narrowly won. We can try to take account of this possibility by analysing Conservative-held and Labour-held seats separately.

The second consideration reinforces the case for this strategy. This arises from the observation that, with the exception of 1951, the elections which

Labour entered as the governing party all produced clearly stronger associations between marginality and turnout than those at which the Conservatives were defending most seats. The point comes out very clearly in Table 1 – the mean coefficient for the five elections from 1959 called by Labour governments is 0.516; for the six called by Conservative governments it is 0.238. This pattern is less marked when we look at the results of multiple regressions shown in Table 2, but it still holds (the corresponding mean regression coefficients being 0.365 and 0.298 respectively). How is this to be explained?

It appears to be a consequence of the complex inter-relationship that exists between turnout, marginality and socio-economic variables such as class. Imagine how the marginality of a constituency would change as its class composition varied. Simplifying somewhat, a constituency which was heavily middle class would normally be safely Conservative (leaving aside, for the moment, seats in which the Conservatives and Liberal Democrats are in close contention). As the proportion of middle-class residents declines, the constituency would become less strongly Conservative (hence more marginal), but as it declines further it would firstly become a marginal Labour seat and then more and more safely Labour (hence less marginal). Broadly speaking, therefore, one would expect that in Labour seats an increasing middle-class presence would result in increasing marginality while in Conservative seats this would produce decreasing marginality. That this is the case is simple to demonstrate. In every election analysed here the correlation coefficient measuring the association between marginality and percentage professional and managerial workers is strongly negative in seats won by the Conservatives and strongly positive is seats won by Labour.[8]

However, both marginality and the proportion of middle-class residents are positively associated with turnout. When Labour is in power, and therefore holding more seats, there will be more constituencies on the side of the dividing line where an increasing proportion of middle-class voters results in increasing marginality. The effect of marginality and class composition on turnout is, therefore, reinforcing. Conversely, when the Conservatives are the incumbents there will be more constituencies in which increasing middle-classness results in decreasing marginality. Class composition and marginality will influence turnout in the opposite directions and the effect will be to produce weaker associations between marginality and turnout. Again this suggests that it may be advisable to consider Labour-held and Conservative-held seats separately, and that is what we do in the remainder of this article.

Marginality and Turnout in Conservative-held and Labour-held Constituencies

We first examine the trend in the relationship between marginality and turnout over the post-war period in the two categories of constituency. This raises a difficulty in respect of Labour-held seats, however. In our original (1974) analysis, examination of residuals showed that there was a group of seats in which coal miners formed a substantial proportion of the work force and in which turnout was exceptionally high, given their social composition and level of marginality. As is well known, voting – and voting Labour – was an important part of the local culture in mining areas. Coal mining has declined dramatically over the last 20 years, of course, so that a more accurate picture of the trend in the relationship between marginality and turnout in Labour seats might be drawn if these seats are excluded from the analysis and we have done so where appropriate.[9]

In Table 5 we show the bivariate correlations measuring the association between previous marginality and turnout for Conservative-held and Labour-held seats separately. In the light of the preceding discussion of the inter-relationship between class and marginality we would expect the correlation to be higher for Labour-held than for Conservative seats, since the effects of class and marginality will reinforce each another. In fact, in the 1950s and 1960s the coefficients for Conservative-held seats are slightly stronger, but from 1970 the coefficients for Labour-held constituencies indicate a much stronger relationship than in Conservative seats. The pattern over time for Labour seats is very similar to that for all constituencies, with the largest coefficients tending to be found in elections at which Labour was the party defending most seats. As far as Conservative seats are concerned, however, the figures suggest a steady decline in the strength of the relationship between marginality and turnout (which is statistically significant). From 1966 there is a marked decrease until 1992, with only a slight recovery in 1997 and 2001. In both 1992 and 2001 the relationship was not statistically significant.

Table 6 gives summary results of the corresponding multivariate analyses using the same socio-economic and regional control variables as before. Here, in contrast to the situation described by the bivariate correlations, marginality clearly has a greater impact on turnout in Conservative-held than in Labour-held seats in every election except 2001. This is because the cross-cutting effect of socio-economic variables in Conservative seats and their reinforcing effect in Labour seats have been neutralized. When this is done there is no very clear trend in the impact of marginality in either case. In Labour seats over the whole period and in Conservative seats from 1970 fluctuations in the strength of the relationship seem fairly random.

TABLE 5
BIVARIATE CORRELATION COEFFICIENTS FOR CONSTITUENCY MARGINALITY
AND TURNOUT IN CONSERVATIVE-HELD AND LABOUR-HELD SEATS, 1951–2001

	Con Held	(N)	Lab Held	(N)
1951	0.574	(287)	0.335	(283)
1959	0.545	(334)	0.418	(244)
1964	0.375	(353)	0.368	(225)
1966	0.558	(292)	0.519	(283)
1970	0.392	(242)	0.549	(330)
1974O	0.378	(297)	0.544	(269)
1979	0.254	(277)	0.607	(285)
1983	0.224	(359)	0.458	(229)
1987	0.224	(397)	0.267	(179)
1992	0.030*	(377)	0.274	(199)
1997	0.109	(343)	0.446	(241)
2001	0.102*	(165)	0.700	(384)

Notes: Non-significant coefficients are asterisked. All others are statistically significant
($p < 0.001$). 'Mining seats' are excluded.

TABLE 6
SUMMARY OF MULTIPLE REGRESSION ANALYSES: THE IMPACT OF
MARGINALITY ON TURNOUT CONTROLLING FOR SOCIO-ECONOMIC STATUS
AND REGION IN CONSERVATIVE-HELD AND LABOUR-HELD SEATS, 1959–2001

	Conservative-held		Labour-held	
	R^2	Beta	R^2	Beta
1959	0.592	0.726	0.769	0.180
1964	0.689	0.623	0.820	0.100
1966	0.685	0.716	0.779	0.258
1970	0.683	0.359	0.783	0.322
1974O	0.698	0.454	0.852	0.177
1979	0.675	0.361	0.822	0.235
1983	0.542	0.655	0.764	0.255
1987	0.520	0.523	0.761	0.082
1992	0.584	0.360	0.697	0.183
1997	0.576	0.527	0.740	0.182
2001	0.637	0.238	0.740	0.259

Notes: All coefficients are statistically significant ($p < 0.01$). For relevant Ns see Table 5. 'Mining
seats' are excluded.

Next, we look again at the relationship between campaign
spending/campaign intensity and turnout but now separately for seats held
by the Conservatives and Labour. Table 7 reports the relevant bivariate
correlation coefficients. Here the trends for the two parties follow each other
fairly closely. In both cases, the relationship between spending and turnout
tends to weaken from 1970 to 1992 but then strengthens in 1997 and 2001.
In both 1992 and 1997 the relationship is not statistically significant in

TABLE 7
BIVARIATE CORRELATION COEFFICIENTS FOR CAMPAIGN EXPENDITURE
(INTENSITY) BY TOP TWO PARTIES AND TURNOUT IN CONSERVATIVE-HELD
AND LABOUR-HELD SEATS, 1951–2001

	Con Held	(N)	Lab Held	(N)
1951	0.456	(287)	0.336	(283)
1959	0.484	(334)	0.399	(244)
1964	0.222	(353)	0.417	(225)
1966	0.455	(292)	0.432	(283)
1970	0.278	(242)	0.490	(330)
1974O	0.313	(297)	0.419	(269)
1979	0.171	(277)	0.379	(285)
1983	0.148	(358)	0.213	(229)
1987	0.116	(394)	0.078*	(179)
1992	0.008*	(374)	0.099*	(199)
1997	0.090*	(341)	0.277	(241)
2001	0.273	(165)	0.585	(384)
Campaign Intensity				
1992	0.005*	(377)	0.168	(229)
1997	0.105*	(342)	0.362	(272)
2001	0.187	(164)	0.582	(415)

Notes: All coefficients are statistically significant ($p < 0.05$ or better) except those asterisked. 'Mining seats' are excluded from the spending analysis.

Conservative-held seats and the same is true of Labour-held seats in 1987 and 1992. In 2001, on the other hand, the coefficient for Labour seats is the largest of the series. In most elections (8 of the 12) the relationship is stronger in Labour seats. The pattern relating to spending for the last three elections in the series is confirmed by the coefficients for campaign intensity. In both Conservative and Labour seats the correlation strengthened and was statistically significant in 2001.

Following standard procedure, we checked the association between campaign spending (or intensity) and turnout by undertaking a series of multivariate regression analyses with the same control variables as before included in the equations. The results are summarized in Table 8. In both cases spending and campaign intensity remain significant predictors of turnout even when socio-economic and regional controls are taken into account. There is no significant trend in the size of the coefficients but, as with marginality and for the same sorts of reasons, spending and campaign intensity generally appear to have a greater impact in Conservative-held seats than in Labour-held seats after socio-economic differences are taken into account.

These results leave us with a number of puzzles. Perhaps the most obvious is the fact that, whereas bivariate analyses usually indicate that there is a stronger association between turnout and marginality, or campaign spending/campaign intensity in Labour-held than in Conservative-held seats, the opposite is the case when control variables are introduced. This raises significant methodological issues and a brief exploration of these will lead us into the final section of the article.

TABLE 8

SUMMARY OF MULTIPLE REGRESSION ANALYSES: THE IMPACT OF CAMPAIGN SPENDING (INTENSITY) ON TURNOUT CONTROLLING FOR SOCIO-ECONOMIC STATUS AND REGION IN CONSERVATIVE-HELD AND LABOUR-HELD SEATS, 1959–2001

	Conservative-held R^2	Beta	Labour-held R^2	Beta
1959	0.592	0.726	0.769	0.180
1964	0.689	0.623	0.820	0.100
1966	0.685	0.716	0.779	0.258
1970	0.683	0.359	0.783	0.322
1974O	0.698	0.454	0.852	0.177
1979	0.675	0.361	0.822	0.235
1983	0.542	0.655	0.764	0.255
1987	0.520	0.523	0.761	0.082
1992	0.584	0.360	0.697	0.183
1997	0.576	0.527	0.740	0.182
2001	0.637	0.238	0.740	0.259
Campaign intensity				
1992	0.582	0.298	0.716	0.215
1997	0.517	0.339	0.743	0.214
2001	0.626	0.184	0.731	0.229

Notes: 'N's are as in Table 7. All coefficients are statistically significant (p< 0.05 or better). 'Mining seats' are excluded from the spending analysis.

Methodological issues

Clues to explaining the puzzle can be found by examining the R^2 figures (which reveal the overall goodness of fit of the models as indicated by the proportion of variation in turnout which they explain) in Tables 6 and 8. Without exception these are clearly larger in Labour-held seats than in Conservative-held seats. This is due to the fact that in the former the socio-economic and regional variables alone account for much more of the turnout variation than they do in the latter.[10] In other words, turnout variations in Labour-held seats are more predictable on the basis of the socio-economic composition of constituencies than is the case in Conservative-held seats. As a consequence, in Labour seats there is simply less unexplained variation to be accounted for by marginality and campaign spending/intensity and that is why they appear to have a smaller impact in the multivariate analyses.

In addition we have already shown that marginality is strongly related to campaign spending or intensity and also to the socio-economic status of constituencies. To demonstrate the latter more formally, we undertook a series of multivariate regressions with marginality as the dependent variable and the usual socio-economic and regional variables as independent variables. In Labour-held seats the resulting R^2 statistics ranged from 0.541 (1959) to 0.704 (1966) with a mean of 0.630 while in Conservative-held seats the range was from 0.266 (2001) to 0.642 (1959) and the mean 0.496. The fact that marginality in Conservative-held seats is less determined by socio-economic composition than it is in Labour-held seats (especially from February 1974 onwards), and also the unusually small R^2 statistic for 2001, are both likely to be largely due to the increased number of constituencies in which the Liberal Democrats, rather than Labour, are the Conservatives' main contenders. The level of marginality in these constituencies seems likely to be determined to a much smaller extent by the socio-economic characteristics of the constituencies concerned than is the case in Conservative–Labour contests. Nonetheless, marginality levels in both Conservative- and Labour-held seats are clearly related to the socio-economic character of constituencies, even if the relationship is not a straightforward one.

We have, then, three types of variable – marginality, campaign spending or intensity and a cluster relating to socio-economic status and region – which are clearly related to turnout, but are also clearly related to one another. It seems likely, therefore, that multiple regression analysis may confound the effects of marginality and the other variables on turnout. Arguably, the impact of marginality and of campaigning is masked by socio-economic variables and thus underestimated, especially in Labour-held seats in which both marginality and turnout are more strongly dependent upon the socio-economic characteristics of constituencies. This would help to account for the fact that in Table 2 the coefficients measuring the impact of marginality in 1992, 1997 and 2001 are among the smallest of the series (that for 1992 being the smallest of all and that for 1997 the second smallest), since in these elections the proportion of turnout variation explained by the socio-economic and regional variables alone was considerably greater than in any other of the elections included (0.705, 0.722 and 0.712 respectively).

If this line of argument is correct, then it would be helpful to find some way of attempting to disentangle the related effects of socio-economic structure, marginality and campaigning on turnout. We explore a way of doing this in the next section.

Marginality, Campaign Intensity and Turnout in the Elections of 1992, 1997 and 2001: Disentangling the Variables

Despite the fact that the three sorts of variables associated with turnout variations are themselves inter-related, it has been common practice (and one which we ourselves have followed) to assess their relative impact on turnout by means of multiple regression analysis. Johnston and Pattie (1998), for example, claim that in the 1992 election marginality had little effect on turnout, because in the relevant regression equation most of the turnout variation is accounted for by other variables. Similarly, in the 1997 election, they argue that neither marginality nor campaign activity importantly affected turnout, again because most of the variation is explained by socio-economic characteristics (Johnston and Pattie, 2001). We suggest, however, that this is not the correct way to approach the matter – instead we need to take account of the fact that there will be both direct and indirect effects. Turnout may be directly affected by the socio-economic character of a constituency (assuming that some kinds of people are more likely to vote, the more there are of them in a constituency the higher will be the constituency turnout); and it may also be directly affected by the marginality of the constituency. As we have shown, however, the socio-economic character of a constituency will also directly affect its marginality, albeit in a complicated way, and so in conventional multiple regression analysis some of the effect of marginality on turnout may be masked. In turn, marginality may directly affect turnout, in that some people independently realize that they live in a safe or closely contested seat and accordingly make less or more effort to vote; but it will also affect the effort which parties put into the constituency and this, on the mobilization hypothesis, is what affects the turnout level. While marginality has a direct effect on turnout, therefore, there is also likely to be an indirect effect via campaigning which should be taken into consideration.

    We can begin to explore both of these complex relationships by using structural equation modelling (SEM) (see Tabachnik and Fidell, 1996), a technique which, among other things, provides estimates of the direct and indirect effects of a number of independent variables upon a dependent variable. Since our intention here is simply to explore and illustrate this technique, we have simplified the analysis by creating a single 'socio-economic status' (SES) variable for each constituency.[11] This variable was strongly negatively related to turnout, the relevant correlation coefficients being –0.782 (1992), –0.801 (1997) and –0.817 in 2001. In addition, we use the direct measure of campaign intensity rather than spending.

Using SEM the inter-relationships between variables can be modelled in various ways and the first simple model reported here (Figure 1) concerns connections between marginality, SES and turnout. The arrow going from marginality to SES is not intended to indicate a causal connection. Rather, the model is designed to allow for the possibility that some of the direct effect of SES on turnout may actually be an indirect effect of marginality. When this model is applied to Conservative-held and Labour-held seats separately in the 1992, 1997 and 2001 elections, the results in terms of direct and indirect effects are as shown in Table 9. To aid interpretation we have calculated indirect effects as a percentage of direct effects (ignoring signs) and it can be seen that in both types of seat – but especially in Labour-held seats – the estimates of indirect effects are substantial. While the conventional approach using multiple regression analysis may minimize the impact of marginality – because it assumes that socio-economic effects are dominant – this approach may exaggerate the impact of marginality. The truth seems likely to lie somewhere in between, though we have no way of making a more precise estimate.

Our second SEM example – shown in Figure 2 – focuses on the relationship between marginality, campaigning intensity and turnout, while also taking account of SES. Our interest here is more straightforward – we want to compare the direct effect of marginality with its indirect effect via campaigning intensity. The relevant estimates are shown in Table 10. In this case, indirect effects appear relatively small in Conservative-held seats, although still clearly present. In Labour-held seats, however, all of the positive effect of marginality in 1992 and 1997 is mediated through campaigning, although the direct effect is more important in 2001. Speculatively, we might suggest that these results indicate that in traditional Labour marginals (i.e., those held before the landslide of 1997) voters need the spur of local campaigning to get to the polls in greater numbers, whereas in traditional Conservative marginals they are more inclined to do so of their own accord. In terms of the hypotheses mentioned at the outset, the analysis suggests that party mobilization may best explain the relationship between marginality and turnout in traditionally Labour-supporting areas, while in Conservative-dominated areas the suggestion that the relationship is a function of individuals acting rationally may be more appropriate.

Conclusion

As explained above, the use of SEM, and of these models in particular, is intended to be exploratory and suggestive of future lines of research on this

BRITISH ELECTIONS & PARTIES REVIEW

FIGURE 1
SEM MODEL SHOWING EFFECT OF MARTINALITY ON TURNOUT THROUGH SES

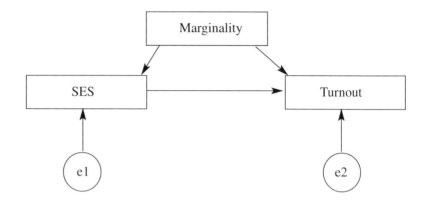

Note: 'e1' and 'e2' denote error terms.

TABLE 9
DIRECT AND INDIRECT (VIA SES) EFFECTS OF MARGINALITY ON TURNOUT,
1992–2001

| | *Conservative-held seats* | | |
	Net effect	*Direct effect*	*Indirect effect*	*Indirect as % of direct*
1992	0.030	0.283	–0.253	89.4
1997	0.112	0.351	–0.239	68.1
2001	0.108	0.203	–0.094	46.3

| | *Labour-held seats* | | |
	Net effect	*Direct effect*	*Indirect effect*	*Indirect as % of direct*
1992	0.221	0.106	0.115	108.5
1997	0.371	0.203	0.168	82.8
2001	0.657	0.345	0.313	90.7

FIGURE 2
SEM MODEL SHOWING EFFECT OF SES, MARGINALITY AND CAMPAIGN
INTENSITY ON TURNOUT

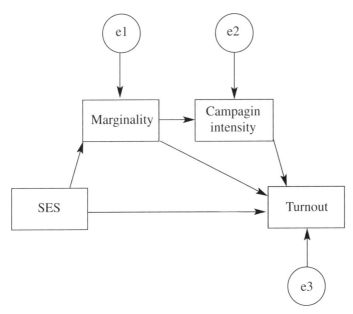

Note: 'e1', 'e2' and 'e3' denote error terms.

TABLE 10
DIRECT AND INDIRECT (VIA CAMPAIGN INTENSITY) EFFECTS OF
MARGINALITY ON TURNOUT

	Net effect	*Direct effect*	*Indirect effect*	*Indirect as % of direct*
		Conservative-held seats		
1992	0.289	0.209	0.080	38.3
1997	0.356	0.241	0.115	47.7
2001	0.203	0.149	0.054	36.2
		Labour-held seats		
	Net effect	*Direct effect*	*Indirect effect*	*Indirect as % of direct*
1992	0.098	–0.102	0.200	196.1
1997	0.191	–0.065	0.256	393.8
2001	0.345	0.235	0.110	46.8

topic rather than to provide an exhaustive and conclusive analysis of the relationship between marginality and turnout in British elections. Nonetheless, the results of the analysis of the first model considered tend to confirm our argument that it is mistaken to dismiss the effect of marginality on turnout on the basis of multiple regression analyses in which the direct effect of marginality is 'washed out' by socio-economic variables. Because marginality and SES are themselves related there are also indirect effects to be taken into account and these can be considerable. The data from the second model provide some support for the view that it is the intensity of campaigning rather than of marginality per se that affects turnout levels, especially in Labour seats. Much of the effect of marginality appears to operate via the decisions of the parties about where to target resources and campaign more strongly. Finally, the models suggest that all of the explanatory variables – SES, marginality and campaign intensity – have some independent direct effects on turnout. That should not come as a surprise since the real world is complicated and rarely conforms perfectly to one among a series of competing hypotheses. Clearly, however, sorting out these complicated relationships, while also taking account of the electoral context and the campaigning strategies of the parties, is a task that has really barely begun and which demands a good deal of thought and further analysis.

ACKNOWLEDGEMENT

We are indebted to Dr D. Berridge of the Centre for Applied Statistics, Lancaster University, for advice and assistance.

NOTES

1. The elections of 1955 and February 1974, which followed major reviews of constituency boundaries, are excluded. There are no estimates available of what the 1951 results would have been in the revised 1955 constituencies and, therefore, no way of calculating the previous marginality of the new seats. 'Hypothetical' 1970 results in the February 1974 constituencies are available (in the British Parliamentary Elections data set held by the ESRC Data Archive), but these appear to have been computed after the event and were certainly not common knowledge beforehand. There were also major boundary reviews preceding the 1983 and 1997 elections, but in these cases estimates of previous results in the new constituencies were published in advance and were extensively used by the media and the parties (BBC/ITN, 1983; Rallings and Thrasher, 1995). In the rest of this article, therefore, analysis involving previous marginality excludes the elections of 1955 and February 1974, but includes 1983 and 1997.

2. The predictor variables are: % of households in owner-occupied accommodation, % professional and managerial, % ethnic minority, % older voters and number of electors per hectare, together with dummy variables for Scotland, Wales, the North, the South and Greater London (the Midlands being the comparator region). The social and demographic

variables are taken from the censuses of 1966, 1971, 1981 and 1991. The definition of % owner-occupiers is consistent throughout (% of households). 'Older voters' was defined in 1966 as those aged 65 and over as a percentage of all aged 15 and above; in 1971 as those aged 65 and over as a percentage of the population; and in 1981 and 1991 as those of pensionable age (60 for women and 65 for men) as a percentage of the population. 'Ethnic minority' voters were defined in 1966 as those born in the New Commonwealth and Pakistan as a percentage of the population. In 1971 this changed to those born in, or having at least one parent born in, the New Commonwealth and Pakistan, while in 1981 it was the percentage which had a head of household born in the New Commonwealth. In 1991 the figures refer to the percentage of the population which was 'non-white'. The percentage of professional and managerial workers in 1966 related to economically active and retired men; in 1971 to economically active and retired persons; in 1981 to the population in households headed by a professional or managerial worker, and in 1991 to the percentage of employees and self-employed people. Electors per hectare was calculated separately for each election.

3. All variables were entered into each equation together.

4. The sources for expenditure figures used in this article are the following House of Commons papers (session in brackets): 210 (1951–52); 141 (1955–56); 173 (1959–60); 220 (1965–65); 162 (1966–67); 305 (1970–71); 69 (1974–75); 478 (1974–75); 374 (1979–80); 130 (1983–84); 426 (1987–88); 603 (1992–93); 260 (1998–99). For the 2001 election data published by the Electoral Commission have been used. We are grateful to Ron Johnston for providing expenditure data for 1951 to 1970 in electronic form.

5. The surveys covered the major parties in every British constituency. They were undertaken with the support of the ESRC research grants (Y304 25 3004 [1992], R000222027 [1997] and R000239396 [2001]). The overall response rates from the three main parties were, respectively, 53.0%, 68.5% and 65.6%.

6. For the purposes of this article we have used the index scores for respondents to estimate scores for non-respondents. The estimates were calculated by predicting the actual index scores for each party in each constituency on the basis of marginality, campaign spending, performance in 1997 and a variety of socio-economic variables and then applying the resulting equations to non-responding constituencies. Analyses using the combined actual and estimated scores produce very similar results to those based on actual scores only.

7. We have repeated the analyses using spending by the top three parties in each constituency which was contested by more than two parties (all since 1983). While this probably gives a better indication of the level of campaigning in close three-way contests, there are relatively few of these. Using the top two figures gives a better estimate in the (many more) cases where only two parties are in serious contention and the third-placed candidate lags far behind. Nonetheless, the results obtained using spending by the top three parties are very similar to those obtained using only the top two.

8. In Conservative-held seats the coefficients vary from – 0.702 in 1959 (N = 353) to –0.510 in 1997 (N = 165). In Labour-held seats the range is from + 0.730 in 1966 (N = 363) to + 0.464 in 1992 (N = 272).

9. More precisely, the seats excluded are those in which, in 1966, coal miners comprised 20 per cent or more of the male labour force (33 seats). For 1951 the 'predecessors' of these seats are the ones excluded and after 1970 their 'successor' constituencies.

10. When constituency turnouts are predicted for each election from 1959 on the basis of the socio-economic and regional variables that we have used throughout, the R2 statistic in Conservative-held seats ranges from 0.370 (1983) to 0.626 (1970) and has a mean for all elections of 0.499. In Labour-held seats the figures range from 0.683 (1992) to 0.842 (October 1974) with a mean of 0.760.

11. This was done by undertaking a factor analysis of nine socio-economic variables and taking the factor scores on the first factor as an index of socio-economic status. The first factor extracted explained 48.7% of the variance (compared with 19.5% for the second) and clearly differentiated poorer, inner city and more working-class constituencies from those

which are more affluent, rural or suburban and more middle class. The variables and their
loadings on the factor are as follows:

% households with no car	+0.878
% aged 18–29	+0.803
persons per hectare	+0.774
% households council tenants	+0.738
% ethnic minority resident	+0.626
% professional and managerial	–0.478
% pensionable age	–0.419
% employed in agriculture	–0.560
% households owner occupiers	–0.845

REFERENCES

BBC/ITN (1983) *Guide to the New Parliamentary Constituencies*, Chichester: Parliamentary
    Research Services.
Denver, D. (2003) *Elections and Voters in Britain*. Basingstoke: Palgrave.
Denver, D. and K. Halfacree (1992) 'Inter-constituency Migration and Turnout at the British
    General Election of 1983', *British Journal of Political Science* 22: 248–54.
Denver, D. and G. Hands (1997a) 'Turnout' in P. Norris and N. Gavin (eds.) *Britain Votes 1997*,
    212–24. Oxford: Oxford University Press.
Denver, D. and G. Hands (1997b) *Modern Constituency Electioneering*. London and Portland,
    OR: Frank Cass.
Denver, D. and G. Hands (1974) 'Marginality and Turnout in British General Elections', *British
    Journal of Political Science* 4: 17–35.
Denver, D. and Hands (1985) 'Marginality and Turnout in General Elections in the 1970s',
    British Journal of Political Science 15: 381–8.
Denver, D., G. Hands J. Fisher and I. MacAllister (2002) 'The Impact of Constituency
    Campaigning in the 2001 General Election', *British Elections and Parties Review* 12:
    80–94.
Johnston, R. and C. Pattie (1998) 'Voter Turnout at the British General Election of 1992:
    Rational Choice, Social Standing or Political Efficacy', *European Journal of Political
    Research* 33: 263–83.
Johnston, R. and C. Pattie (2001) 'Is There a Crisis of Democracy in Great Britain? Turnout at
    General Elections Reconsidered' in K. Dowding, J. Hughes and H. Margetts (eds.)
    Challenges to Democracy, 61–80. London: Palgrave.
McAllister, I. (2001) 'Explaining Turnout in the 2001 British General Election', *Representation*
    38: 256–67.
Pattie, C., R. Johnston and E. Fieldhouse (1995) 'Winning the Local Vote: The Effectiveness of
    Constituency Campaign Spending in Great Britain, 1983–1992', *American Political
    Science Review* 89 (4): 969–83.
Rallings, C. and M. Thrasher (1995) *Media Guide to the New Parliamentary Constituencies*.
    Plymouth: Local Government Chronicle Elections Centre.
Tabachnik, B. and L. Fidell (1996) *Using Multivariate Statistics*, 3rd edn. New York:
    HarperCollins.
Whiteley, P., H. Clarke, D. Sanders and M. Stewart (2001) 'Turnout' in P. Norris (ed.) *Britain
    Votes 2001*, 211–24. Oxford: Oxford University Press.

Turnout in European Parliament Elections: Towards a European-Centred Model

Donley Studlar, Richard S. Flickinger and Stephen Bennett

The Turnout Puzzle in European Parliament Elections

It is now widely recognized that overall turnout in European Parliament (EP) elections has fallen steadily since direct elections began in 1979, reaching its nadir in the fifth election in 1999. Table 1 shows the figures, by country, for each of the five elections since 1979. Declining turnout in EP elections has concerned policymakers as well as scholars since turnout is widely considered a major indicator of institutional legitimacy in democracies (Powell, 1982; Flickinger and Studlar, 1992; Delwit, 2002).

Turnout in EP elections matters for several other reasons as well. It indicates the public's perception of the relevance of the institution, the standing of national governments and political parties, and may help to shape the future of parties' EU policies (Butler and Westlake, 2000). Who votes also matters for who is elected, who holds power in the EP, and the attendant policy consequences (Lord, 2002).

The lowest-ever turnout occurred in 1999 despite a well-documented increase in the EP's power over EU legislation (through procedures introduced in the Single European Act of 1986, the 1992 Maastricht Treaty, and the Amsterdam Treaty of 1997), the conflict with the European Commission that led to the Commissioners' *en masse* resignation in 1998, and the EP's important role in the introduction of the euro and European Central Bank (Perrineau et al., 2002; Hix, 2002). In principle, these developments, especially those occurring since 1994, should have made the 1999 EU elections more salient to the public and, *ceteris paribus*, generated higher turnout.

Many studies of turnout in EP elections have stressed individual characteristics such as socioeconomic traits (class, education, gender, age, income), attitudes (general political interest, party identification, sense of civic responsibility), and political behaviour (organizational membership, discussion of politics). Others have considered institutional factors

TABLE 1
TURNOUT IN EUROPEAN PARLIAMENT ELECTIONS (%)

Country	1979	1984	1989	1994	1999	Mean Turnout
Belgium	91.4	92.2	90.7	90.7	91.0	91.2
Denmark	47.8	52.2	47.4	52.9	50.4	50.1
France	60.7	56.7	48.8	52.7	46.8	53.1
Germany	65.7	56.8	62.3	60.0	45.2	58.0
Britain	32.2	31.8	36.6	36.4	24.0	32.2
Greece	78.6*	77.2	80.1	80.4	75.3	78.3
Ireland	63.6	47.6	68.3	44.0	50.7	54.8
Italy	84.9	83.4	81.4	74.8	70.8	79.1
Luxembourg	88.9	87.0	96.2	88.5	85.8	89.3
Netherlands	58.1	50.6	47.5	35.6	29.9	44.3
Portugal	–	72.4**	51.2	35.5	40.4	49.9
Spain	–	68.9**	54.7	59.1	64.4	61.8
Austria	–	–	–	67.7***	49.0	58.4
Finland	–	–	–	57.6***	30.1	43.9
Sweden	–	–	–	41.6***	38.8	40.2
Overall Mean	67.2	64.7	63.8	55.1	49.9	59.0

*   The first Greek election occurred in 1981.
**   The first elections in Portugal and Spain occurred in 1987
***   The first elections in Austria and Finland occurred in 1995, in Sweden in 1996.

Sources: Smith (1999) and European Parliament web site, www2.europarl.eu.int/election/newep/en/tctp.htm (1999).

(electoral systems, patterns of party competition, forms of government, election cycles). Individual and institutional approaches to explaining turnout are especially important in the conventional explanation of European elections as 'second order': that is, the results are seen as basically derivative of recent national elections and current party standings domestically rather than being based on issues and attitudes relating to the EU per se. Because EP elections do not determine who forms the executive in the EU, the perceived salience of the election is low, and citizens who stay away from the polls may be acting rationally. Because the elections are not perceived as important for European Union policies, their outcome depends primarily on national level partisan concerns, similar to many lower-level elections in these countries. Examining two EP elections – 1989 and 1994 – van der Eijk and Franklin (1996) argue that among the institutional effects are compulsory voting, Sunday voting, proportionality of the party system, and the timing of EP elections within the national election cycle. General political interest is the most important individual level determinant, and political orientation and an appealing party are more important than socio-demographic variables. Overall, the growing body of work on participation in EU elections continues to affirm second-order explanations, directing attention to national level variables rather than European ones (Reif and Schmitt, 1980; Reif, 1997; van der Eijk and Franklin, 1996; Marsh, 1998; Heath et al., 1999).

Despite acceptance of the second-order thesis by many analysts of EU voting, its tenets can be questioned (Perrineau et al., 2002; Curtice and Steed, 2000). The second-order explanation has usually been a static, general one which does less well in explaining variations over time and space. Why has turnout continued to decline even as the EU, and especially the EP, become more significant political actors? Why does turnout vary so much from one country to another?

Explaining Turnout Decline: Franklin's Model

In a series of articles (especially Franklin, 2001b), Mark Franklin has addressed some of the problems in the second-order explanation, especially that of continued turnout decline. This work is a product of his more general comparative approach to turnout, which links individual and institutional approaches to create 'instrumental' explanations (Franklin, 1996, 2002). He argues that resource (individual) characteristics and mobilization (party) factors, when combined with other contextual variables, especially the attributes of specific elections, provide the best explanations of voting turnout across countries. 'Turnout varies much more from country to country than it does between individuals' (Franklin, 1996: 218; see also Franklin, 1999; van der Eijk and Franklin, 1996; Anderson, 1998; cf. Blondel et al., 1998).

In applying this approach to EP elections, Franklin (2001b) emphasizes two particular structural factors which have led to turnout declining over time. The first is the declining share of EU members with compulsory voting, from three of nine countries (Belgium, Luxembourg, Italy) in 1979 to three of 15 in 1999 (Greece was added in 1984, but Italy formally abandoned the practice in 1993).

Second, Franklin (2001b) finds that turnout tends to be relatively high in a country's first EP election, but is followed by a substantial drop at the next one. Turnout in the second election then becomes the norm for subsequent ones. At the first EU elections in 1979, all countries choosing EP members were subject to this first-time boost in turnout. But in 1999, with a reduced share of compulsory voting countries and no member experiencing its first election, there were structural reasons for expecting a low turnout, absent other factors which might raise the salience of the election.

Following other second-order analyses, Franklin (2001b) also employs an electoral cycle measure to try to capture the salience of an EP election, based on national politics. He argues that the closer an EP election occurs before an expected national election, the more salient it becomes for national politics; consequently the EP election then arouses greater interest among the electorate. Electoral interest may also be boosted in these circumstances by the fact that parties have greater incentives to campaign and mobilize their voters than they do when an EP election is further removed in time from the next national election. Thus, turnout may be expected to be higher when the national election cycle is shorter.

Franklin's (2001b) three-variable model provides a parsimonious and robust explanation of why overall turnout in EP elections continues to decline, accounting for more than 80% of the variation in turnout in EP elections among EU member states over these elections. An analysis of the estimated impact of change in each of the three predictors enables Franklin accurately to account for the difference in turnout between the 1979 election and that of 1999 (2001b: 317–18). Because of the low number of cases (only 2–5 elections in each country) Franklin cannot apply his model systematically to turnout variation in individual countries except by an analysis of residuals. Nevertheless, even this helps account for the wide variation in turnout among EU member countries in any given election.

Developing an Alternative Model of European Election Turnout

Franklin provides an impressive addition to the second-order explanation. Yet, as even he acknowledges, it is not the final word:

> We have admittedly made no attempt to apportion responsibility for turnout decline as between the variables investigated in this study and other potential effects on turnout, so there is still the possibility that other influences may have played a part, attenuating the effects we measure in this paper (Franklin, 2001b: 321).

There are, in fact, several problems with Franklin's model which suggest scope for developing an alternative. First, as he recognizes, his model does better retrospectively rather than prospectively in explaining turnout in EP elections. The declining share of countries with compulsory voting will reduce the model's power over time, as none of the current first-wave candidates for EU membership features compulsory voting. Second, it is unclear whether the first EP election boost will occur among the new members. The new democracies of Central and Eastern Europe have had falling turnout in national elections after initially high levels (Institute for Democracy and Electoral Assistance, 2002). Whether the first EP election will have the same effect there that it did among current EU members remains an open question.

Third, as Table 1 attests, turnout after the first EP election has varied considerably among countries without compulsory voting. The election cycle variable alone cannot adequately account for this. Excluding compulsory voting countries and using only the first election and election cycle variables results in a substantial reduction in turnout variance explained for the five EP elections taken together. The adjusted R^2 for this two-variable model falls to .19, compared to .80 for the three-variable one.[1]

It is also doubtful whether the election cycle variable alone is the best way to measure the salience of EP elections. It is a good measure if we assume that national political considerations are what matters in EP elections, as the second-order explanation claims. But can we assume that any longer? For example, Schmitt and Thomassen (2002) recently found that attitudes towards Europe have emerged as a new dimension in the electoral politics of West European countries, which cuts across the traditional left–right cleavage. Studies of recent elections, both national and EP, in one of the most 'eurosceptical' of countries, the United Kingdom, have suggested that the Europe Union may be a developing cleavage (Evans, 1999; Curtice and Steed, 2000). Where and how should we look for indications that EP elections are also about European matters?

Scholars have looked for connections between attitudes towards the EU and turnout in EP elections, but these have been elusive (Schmitt and Mannheimer, 1991; see also Gabel, 2000). One study of the 1999 election finds a positive relationship between European identity and turnout, but it does not consider that several of the countries with high levels of European identity also have compulsory voting (Frognier, 2002). Eurobarometer 52 (2002) data indicate that opinions such as whether the country's membership is a good or bad thing, or whether one's country has benefited from membership, are not statistically related to turnout (data not shown). According to another recent study 'the evidence on the cognitive aspect of the orientations of citizens to the European Union confirms the view that well-structured, well-informed, and supportive attitudes commensurate with the current stage of integration have not in fact developed' (Cautrès and Sinnott, 2002: 12). Abram de Swaan (2002: 11) suggests this is due to the absence of a 'European public space', with the result that 'in every member state opinions take shape within a national framework' – yet another version of the 'second order elections' argument.

But there are alternative measures of the salience of EU effects on member countries, measured at the aggregate level, which may affect turnout. We are particularly interested in economic indicators that tap the areas where EU policies are most developed: agriculture, trade, aid to economically underdeveloped areas within the organization, and monetary union. We have identified a series of indicators of these effects, for example, agricultural workers as a percentage of a country's total work force, trade as a percentage of GNP, status of net contributor to or net beneficiary of the EU budget, and adoption of the euro (see Appendix for details). Our expectations are that those countries with a higher percentage of agricultural workers and GNP in trade will have higher turnout, as will countries which are net budget beneficiaries and participants in EMU. Since the major achievements of the EU are in trade policy, citizens in trade-dependent economies may have greater reason for paying attention to EU matters. From a rational-expectations perspective, one would anticipate that where there is a substantial economic impact, voters may conclude that more is at stake in elections and therefore be more likely to vote. Thus, where the EU's overall impact is large (or perceived to be important from a national perspective), turnout in EP elections should be higher than in countries where these conditions are not present.[2]

Several political factors may also affect turnout: length of membership in the EU, being an original member of the EU, hosting a major EU institution, party competition in European Parliament elections, and European identity within the population. Long-term membership of the EU, along with hosting a major EU institution, creates the possibility of greater EU awareness. We also distinguish the original six members of the EU because there may be special concerns associated with being one of the founding members that do not apply to later members and are not completely captured solely by a 'years of membership' variable. Major EU institutions and their host countries are the Commission (Belgium), Parliament (France, Belgium), Court of Justice (Luxembourg), and Central Bank (Germany). We also examine a retrospective indicator of party competition, namely the number of political parties per country that won seats in the current EP election. When more parties win seats, the opportunity for more meaningful voter choice is likely to encourage turnout (Crepaz, 1990). More parties act to mobilize voters, and some of the 'minor' parties may stress European issues which large national parties avoid.[3] Finally, the general sense of European identity within a population should increase participation in EU elections.

We retain, in a slightly revised form, Franklin's variable on the electoral cycle, by including the amount of time between the European Parliament election and the next national election. The shorter the time between the EP election and the next national election, the greater the incentives for parties to mobilize their supporters, which should lead to higher turnout.

We believe these measures of EU impact provide an opportunity to explain variations among countries and over time, which can serve as a forward-looking complement to Franklin's (2001b) model. We seek a model that works for countries where neither compulsory voting nor the first election phenomenon is present.

TABLE 2
CORRELATIONS OF OBJECTIVE CONDITIONS AND ATTITUDES
TOWARDS THE EU IN THE 1990s

	Host	Orig 6	Trade	AgWork	EuroMem	EuroID	EUGood
EU Host							
Original 6	.676**	–	–	–	–	–	–
GDP Trade	.435*	.289	–	–	–	–	–
AgWorker	–.418*	–.434*	–.319	–	–	–	–
Euro Member	.364	.492	.323	–.077	–	–	–
European ID	.452*	.660**	.274	–.065	.631*	–	–
EU Good	.087	.387*	.485**	.256	.436	.472*	–
EU Benefits	–.023	.070	.436*	.420*	.241	.173	.874**

Notes:
Data are for 1994 and 1999. N =30 except for European ID (27) and Euro Member (15).
Euro membership applied only in 1999 and there were no data on European ID for the three
newest members in 1994.

* significant at .05 level;
** significant at .01 level.

Our data offer some support for this line of reasoning. Although many
Europeans may not have well-formed positions about the EU, they do seem
to be aware of its impact. This is suggested by the existence of a number of
statistically significant correlations between objective conditions and
attitudes in the 1990s (see Table 2). Living in a net beneficiary country (in
terms of the EU budget) is positively associated with the perception that EU
membership benefits one's country. People in countries with higher
proportions of agricultural workers are also more likely to see benefits from
membership. Citizens of countries hosting an EU institution, being one of
the 'original six' members, or having adopted the euro are more likely to
report they identify with Europe than do inhabitants of other countries.
Finally, having a higher portion of GDP in international trade is positively
correlated with seeing EU membership as good and benefiting one's
country. Thus we see some connection between our indicators of salience
and aggregate-level national attitudes.[4]

Comparing Models: Explaining Overall Turnout

We created a series of regression equations to test for the hypothesized
effects of our indicators on EU turnout by adding them to Franklin's model
for all five EP elections combined. None of our economic variables added
to his model's power, nor did hosting a EU institution. However, two non-
economic variables did contribute: being one of the 'original six' member
states (.013 increase in R^2) and hosting an EU institution (.017).

One difficulty with Franklin's model, however, is the very large proportion of explained variance accounted for by compulsory voting (adjusted R^2 of .66 in simple regression for all five elections). As noted previously, the performance of his model declines dramatically when this variable is excluded. Although compulsory voting countries account for a declining share of EU members, the influence of this variable remains dominant because of a widening gap between turnout in compulsory and non-compulsory countries. However, the dominance of this variable may mask the influence of others, especially in explaining turnout variation in those countries where voting is not compulsory. Therefore, we sought an alternative variable, less restrictive than compulsory turnout, to capture the influence of national voting regulations and participation habits. Arguably, the best candidate for this task is turnout in the last national election preceding the EP election. This captures at least some of the second-order effects influencing turnout in EP elections, such as national registration variation, weekend voting, and habitual voting as well as compulsory voting. When this variable is included in a model with Franklin's three, it is significant and increases the model's explanatory power from an adjusted R^2 of .756 to .783.

We then developed a series of regression models employing the last national election variable in concert with the economic and political variables described above (data not shown). Because the first vote variable was no longer significant in the presence of the last national election variable it was dropped. Next, we tested the potency of our other variables, as we had done with Franklin's model. As before, neither the GDP in trade nor the net beneficiary variables were significant. The 'original six' variable was no longer significant. But percentage of agricultural workers (.08 increase in variance explained) and EU host (.07) became significant. When we added these two indicators to those of last national election and election cycle, and regressed them on EP turnout for all five elections, all four variables achieved significance, with an adjusted R^2 of .789 (see Table 3). Since two of the four EU institutional host countries have compulsory voting, this may be distorting our results despite the presence of the last national election factor as a control. Nevertheless, our revised model points to the need to look to a combination of national and EU influences to explain turnout in EP elections.

TABLE 3
TWO MODELS: MULTIPLE REGRESSION OF EP TURNOUT WITH SELECTED
EU AND NATIONAL INFLUENCE INDICATORS
(1979–1999 POOLED DATA)

Variables	Franklin Model b (s.e.b)	Alternative Model b (s.e.b)
(Constant)	54.081***	–66.507***
	(12.095)	
First Vote	8.554*	–
	(2.811)	–
Compulsory Voting	32.254***	–
	(2.692)	–
Election Cycle	–.273**	–.234**
	(.087)	(.082)
Turnout in last national election	–	1.444***
	–	(.141)
EU institution host	–	19.906***
	–	(2.875)
Agricultural workers (%)	–	1.272***
–	(.177)	
Adjusted R2	.756	.789
S.E.E.	9.51	8.84
F statistic	66.119***	60.003***
N=	64	64

*= significant at .05 level; **= significant at .01 level; ***=significant at .001 level.
See Appendix for data sources.

Comparing Model Performance over Time

Part of our critique of Franklin's model hinges on its future viability. One way to explore this is to compare the performance of his model for earlier and more recent EU elections. Thus we ran regressions based on pooled results for the two earliest elections, 1979 and 1984, and compared them with results for the most recent ones, 1994 and 1999 (see Table 4).[5] Both models perform well. However, our alternative model is superior in both time periods. With the exception of the electoral cycle in the first period, all of our variables are significant for both periods while only compulsory voting is significant in Franklin's model. This difference is even greater when Franklin's model is utilized without treating Italy as a case of compulsory voting in the 1994–99 period (which he does).[6] Then the R^2 declines to .597. Compared to the earlier period, the R^2 in our model also declines for the most recent period, but all of its predictors are significant.[7]

TABLE 4
COMPARISON OF FRANKLIN AND ALTERNATIVE MODELS
FOR 1979–84 AND 1994–99

Model Variables	Franklin 1979–84	Alternative 1979–84	Franklin 1994–99	Alternative 1994–99
(Constant)	60.152 (5.749)***	–95.187 (19.933)***	51.388 (3.923)***	–75.080 (19.914)***
First Vote	4.160 (4.170)	– –	14.429 (6.345)	– –
Comp Vote	28.004 (4.483)***	– –	33.791 (4.459)***	– –
Eleccycle	–.316 (.162)	.0184 (.125)	–.302 (.141)	–.365 (.128)**
Last National	– –	1.661 (.208)***	– –	1.561 (.241)***
EU Host	– –	25.184 (3.791)***	– –	16.639 (4.892)**
Agworker	– –	1.410 .206)***	– –	1.833 (.392)***
Adjusted R2	.734	.869	.736	.754
S.E.E.	9.38	6.59	9.91	9.56
F Statistic	20.357***	35.885***	27.923***	23.235***
N=	22	22	30	30

*= significant at .05 level; **= significant at .01 level; ***=significant at .001 level.
See Appendix for data sources.

New variables available for the 1994 and 1999 elections permit the development of a further alternative testing for the influence of EU factors in explaining turnout variation. These are a more refined measure of the EU budget status of each member state, a revised Eurobarometer question tapping people's sense of European identity (see Frognier, 2002), and whether or not a country had adopted the euro as its currency (for 1999 only). We tested the impact of each of these by adding them individually to the model reported in Table 4. Neither the new budget measure nor euro membership provided significant additions to our model. However, the European identity measure did. When this five-variable model was tested with the data for 1994 and 1999 combined, all the variables were significant and the model's adjusted R^2 was .864 (see Table 5).[8]

TABLE 5
MULTIPLE REGRESSION OF EP TURNOUT WITH SELECTED EU AND
NATIONAL INFLUENCE INDICATORS
(1994 AND 1999 POOLED DATA)

Variables	b	s.e.b.
(Constant)	−100.430***	17.536
Turnout in last national election	1.638***	.201
Election cycle	−.348**	.105
EU institution host	12.825**	4.174
Agricultural workers (%)	1.681***	.309
European Identity	.361*	.165
Adjusted R2	.864	–
S.E.E.	7.3774	–
F Statistic	34.132***	–
	N = 27	

*Significant at the .05 level; **Significant at the .01 level; ***Significant at the .001 level.

Although our model includes more variables than Franklin's, it performs substantially better for the two most recent EP elections. It also offers another explanation of why turnout in EP elections continues to decline. One factor is the decline of the agricultural workforce as a proportion of the total workforce (from 10.6% in 1979 to 6.5% in 1999). Second is the uncertain growth of European identity; it actually declined slightly between 1994 and 1999, in tandem with the spread of Euroscepticism (Taggart and Szczerbiak, 2001; McAllister and Studlar, 2000). Since our model shows that when a higher proportion of a country's population is engaged in agriculture or are European identifiers turnout will be higher, the decline of the first and the stagnation of the second do not bode well for turnout. Even more important is the historic trend of our last national election variable. The mean value for it has declined steadily since 1979, from 84.4% to 76.6% for 1999. This is not due simply to the declining portion of EU members with compulsory voting, but to a reduction in turnout for national elections. There is a modest but measurable general decline in the salience of elections, whether national or EP (Flickinger and Studlar, 1992; Franklin et al., 2001). Countries hosting major EU institutions are similar to compulsory voting countries in that they have declined as a proportion of EU members. Thus the turnout boost associated with this effect is limited to fewer countries.[9]

Conclusion

Our alternative model attests to the presence of EU-related influences in the explanation of turnout in EP elections. Moreover, these influences – hosting a European institution, European identity, and the presence of agricultural workers – are theoretically meaningful. The last national election and electoral cycle variables indicate that domestic factors continue to be important for explaining EP turnout. The British case offers an illustration of both. In both 1994 and 1999 Britain was below the European mean for turnout in the last national election (77.8% vs. 79% in 1994, 71.5% vs. 76.6% in 1999). Its electoral cycle was longer than the European mean in both elections and therefore also acted to reduce turnout. But Britain is also below the European mean for size of the agricultural workforce (1.9% vs. 6.5%) and for European identity (38% vs. 55.6%). In terms of our model, this helps explain why British turnout was well below the European mean. It is no longer justifiable to treat European elections as simply second order. True, no government is being selected through this process, and 'rational' voters may find fewer reasons to take part. But European considerations are now among those reasons. As others have suggested (Evans, 1999; Curtice and Steed, 2000), we may be witnessing the 'creeping Europeanization' of elections.

APPENDIX

DESCRIPTION AND SOURCES OF VARIABLES IN THE ANALYSES

Turnout. The percentage of registered voters who voted. Smith (1999) for 1979–94 and the European Parliament, accessed at www2.europarl.eu.int/election/newep/en/tctp.htm for 1999.

Compulsory Vote. The compulsory voting countries are Belgium, Greece and Luxembourg. Italy was classified as compulsory for 1979–89, but not for the past two elections. Italy formally abandoned compulsory voting in 1994 although enforcement of the provisions was always loose (Gray and Caul, 2000; Franklin, 2001b).

Last National. Turnout in the most recent national election, whether parliamentary or presidential (in those cases where presidents are directly elected).

EU Host. Belgium, Luxembourg and France are the countries for the Commission, Court and Parliament, respectively. Germany became Central Bank host before the 1999 election.

Member Long. Calculated as the time from a country's initial year of membership to the election year.

Original Member. Belgium, Netherlands, Luxembourg, France, Germany, Italy.

GDP trade. Exports as a percentage of the country's GDP. Calculated from *The OECD in Figures.*

Agricultural Workers. Share of the country's workforce employed in agriculture. *The OECD in Figures.*

Net Beneficiary. Whether a country gains more from the EU budget than it contributes. Begg and Grimwade (1998).

Budget Contribution. Operational budgetary balance for each member state as % of GDP (1994 and 1999 only). Source: http://europa.eu.int/comm/budget/agenda2000/reports_en.htm.

Euro Member. Whether or not a country has adopted the euro (1999 only).

EU Good. Is European unification a good thing or a bad thing? Calculated from the Eurobarometer cumulative file, Eurobarometers 41, 49 and 51.

Euro ID. Calculated from Eurobarometers 40 (1993) and 50 (1998).

EU Benefits Country. Does your country benefit from being a member of the EU? Calculated from the Eurobarometer cumulative file, Eurobarometers 41, 49 and 51.

Election Cycle. Time in months from the date of the EP election to the next national election. Calculated from data in Institute for Democracy and Electoral Assistance (1998) and Facts on File.

N of parties. The number of political parties in a country winning at least one seat in the European Parliament election of the year. Smith (1999).

ACKNOWLEDGEMENTS

This is a revision of a paper presented at the Conference on Elections, Parties, and Public Opinion, University of Salford, 13–15 September 2002. Earlier versions were presented at meetings of the Southern Political Science Association and the European Union Studies Association.

NOTES

1. We have attempted to replicate Franklin's model, but there are slight differences between our sources in reported turnout, and our election cycle measure is in months whereas Franklin's is in years with decimal fractions for partial years. Our election cycle data also differ from his in that we have actual data for the national elections coming after the 1999 EP election. He had to estimate it. Franklin also treats Italy as a compulsory voting country for all five elections, despite the fact that as of 1994 Italy no longer has compulsory voting (see Gray and Caul, 2000). However, in our replications we have treated Italy as Franklin does whenever the compulsory voting variable is used.
2. This may be true from a costs as well as a benefits perspective, e.g., citizens of large contributor countries may also have this fact as an incentive to turn out. However, we do not test this hypothesis here.
3. Gray and Caul (2000) argue that extreme multi-partyism in national elections diminishes the voter's role in choosing a government and therefore discourages turnout. Franklin (2001a: 211) finds that over a quarter of voters choose different parties in EU elections than in national ones. He argues that this is because their EU votes are unconstrained by tactical consideration of who will form the government. But it can also be argued that citizens may be choosing parties at least partially on the basis of EU issues. Of course, EP elections are not about choosing a government.
4. EU salience, even if perceived, does not equal EP salience. Some indicators may be salient for sub-groups of the population and could affect their turnout levels, but investigating this is beyond the scope of this article.
5. The election of 1989 was omitted to enable comparison of the earliest and latest elections.
6. Franklin (2001b) argues that habits formed by compulsory voting are likely to linger even after it is abolished. But even under compulsory voting turnout in Italy for both EP and national elections was never as high as in Belgium or Luxembourg.
7. Of course we must be wary of instability introduced by a diminished number of cases.
8. We are aware that this may be inflated by the small number of cases.
9. The electoral cycle variable can have different effects for each election, but its impact is bounded by the maximum time that may elapse between elections in each member state. Thus it is unlikely to be useful for explaining trends over several elections.

REFERENCES

Anderson, Christopher (1998) 'Parties, Party Systems and Satisfaction with Democratic Performance in the New Europe', *Political Studies* 46: 572–88.

Bingham, G. Jr. (1982) *Contemporary Democracies: Participation, Stability, and Violence.* Cambridge, MA: Harvard University Press.

Blondel, Jean, Richard Sinnott and Palle Svensson (1998) *People and Parliament in the European Union.* Oxford: Clarendon Press.

Butler, David and Martine Westlake (eds.) *British Politics and European Elections 1999.* New York: St. Martin's Press.

Cautrès, Bruno and Richard Sinnott (2002) 'The 1999 European Parliament Election and the Political Culture of European Integration', in Pascal Perrineau, Gérard Grunberg and Colette Ysmal (eds.) *Europe at the Polls: The European Elections of 1999*, pp.3–21. New York: Palgrave.

Crepaz, Markus M. L. (1990) 'The Impact of Party Polarization and Post-Materialism on Voter Turnout: A Comparative Study of 16 Industrial Democracies', *European Journal of Political Research* 18: 183–205.

Curtice, John and Michael Steed (2000) 'Appendix: An Analysis of the Results', in David Butler and Martine Westlake (eds.) *British Politics and European Elections 1999*, pp.240–56. New York: St. Martin's Press.

Delwit, Pascal (2002) 'Electoral Participation and the European Poll: A Limited Legitimacy' in Pascal Perrineau, Gérard Grunberg and Colette Ysmal (eds.) *Europe at the Polls: The European Elections of 1999*, pp.207–22. New York: Palgrave.

de Swaan, Abram (2002) 'The European Void: The Democratic Deficit as a Cultural Lack', *European Studies Newsletter* 31 (5/6): 11–12.

Evans, Geoffrey (1999) 'Europe: A New Electoral Cleavage?', in Geoffrey Evans and Pippa Norris (eds.) *Critical Elections: British Parties and Voters in Long-Term Perspective*, pp.207–22. London: Sage.

Flickinger, Richard S. and Donley T. Studlar (1992) 'The Disappearing Voters? Exploring Declining Turnout in Western European Elections', *West European Politics* 15 (2): 1–16.

Franklin, Mark N. (2002) 'The Dynamics of Electoral Participation', in Lawrence LeDuc, Richard G. Niemi and Pippa Norris (eds.) *Comparing Democracies 2: New Challenges in the Study of Elections and Voting*, pp.148–68. Thousand Oaks, CA: Sage.

Franklin, Mark N. (2001a) 'European Elections and the European Voter', in Jeremy Richardson (ed.) *European Union: Power and Policy-making*, 2nd edn., pp.201–16. London: Routledge.

Franklin, Mark N. (2001b) 'How Structural Factors Cause Turnout Variations at European Parliament Elections', *European Union Politics* 2: 309–28.

Franklin, Mark N. (1999) 'Electoral Engineering and Cross-National Turnout Differences: What Role for Compulsory Voting?', *British Journal of Political Science* 29: 205–24.

Franklin, Mark N. (1996) 'Electoral Participation', in Lawrence LeDuc, Richard G. Niemi and Pippa Norris (eds.) *Comparing Democracies: Elections and Voting in Global Perspective*, pp.216–35. Thousand Oaks, CA: Sage.

Franklin, Mark, Patrick Lyons and Michael Marsh (2001) 'The Tally of Turnout: How the Changing Character of Elections Drives Voter Turnout Variations in Established Democracies', Paper at Congress of European Consortium for Political Research, Canterbury.

Frognier, Andre-Paul (2002) 'Identity and Electoral Participation: For a European Approach to European Elections', in Pascal Perrineau, Gérard Grunberg, and Colette Ysmal (eds.) *Europe at the Polls: The European Elections of 1999*, pp.43–58. New York: Palgrave.

Gabel, Matthew (2000) 'European Integration, Voters and National Politics', *West European Politics* 23 (4): 52–72.

Gray, Mark and Miki Caul (2000) 'Declining Voter Turnout in Advanced Industrial Democracies, 1950–1997: The Effects of Declining Group Mobilization', *Comparative Political Studies* 33: 1091–122.

Heath, Anthony, Iain McLean, Bridget Taylor and John Curtice (1999) 'Between First and Second Order: A Comparison of Voting Behaviour in European and Local Elections in Britain', *European Journal of Political Research* 35: 389–414.

Hix, Simon (2002) 'Constitutional Agenda-Setting Through Discretion in Rule Interpretation: Why the European Parliament Won at Amsterdam', *British Journal of Political Science* 32: 259–80.

Institute for Democracy and Electoral Assistance (2002) accessed at voter turnout section of website, www.idea.int/vt/ introduction.cfm.

Lord, Christopher (2002) 'The New European Parliament', in Pascal Perrineau, Gérard Grunberg and Colette Ysmal (eds.) *Europe at the Polls: The European Elections of 1999*, pp.223–38. New York: Palgrave.

McAllister, Ian and Donley T. Studlar (2000) 'Conservative Euroscepticism and the Referendum Party in the 1997 British General Election', *Party Politics* 6: 359–71.

Marsh, Michael (1998) 'Testing the Second Order Elections Model after Four European Elections', *British Journal of Political Science* 28: 591–607.

Melich, Anna (2002) Eurobarometer 52.0: European Parliament Elections, the Single European Currency, and Financial Services, October–November 1999 [computer file]. 2nd ICPSR version. Brussels, Belgium: INRA (Europe) [producer],1999. Cologne, Germany: Zentralarchiv fur Empirische Sozialforschung/Ann Arbor, MI: Inter- university Consortium for Political and Social Research [distributors].

Perrineau, Pascal, Gérard Grunberg and Colette Ysmal (eds.) (2002) *Europe at the Polls: The European Elections of 1999*. New York: Palgrave Powell,

Reif, Karlheinz (1997). 'European Elections as Member State Second-Order Elections Revisited', *European Journal of Political Research* 31: 17–43.

Reif, Karlheinz and Hermann Schmitt (1980) 'Nine Second-Order National Elections: A Conceptual Framework for the Analysis of European Election Results', *European Journal of Political Research* 8: 3–44.

Schmitt, Hermann and Renato Mannheimer (1991) 'About Voting and Non-Voting in the European Elections of June 1989', *European Journal of Political Research* 19: 31–54.

Schmitt, Hermann and Jacques Thomassen (2002) 'Dynamic Representation: The Case of European Integration', in Pascal Perrineau, Gérald Grunberg and Colette Ysmal (eds.) *Europe at the Polls: The European Elections of 1999*, pp.22–42. New York: Palgrave.

Smith, Julie (1999) *Europe's Elected Parliament*. Sheffield, UK: Sheffield Academic Press.

Taggart. Paul and Aleks Szczerbiak (2001) 'Crossing Europe: Patterns of Contemporary Party-Based Euroscepticism in EU Member States and the Candidate States of Central and Eastern Europe', Paper presented at American Political Science Association, San Francisco.

van der Eijk, Cees and Mark Franklin (1996) *Choosing Europe? The European Electorate and National Politics in the Face of Union*. Ann Arbor: University of Michigan Press.

Electoral Systems, Party Mobilization and Turnout: Evidence from the European Parliamentary Elections

Jeffrey A. Karp, Shaun Bowler and Susan A. Banducci

Parties, Electoral Systems and Turnout

Voter turnout is higher in countries with proportional representation (PR) systems than in single member plurality (SMP) systems. Depending on the countries and elections analysed, proportional systems are estimated to have a turnout advantage of 7–9% (Lijphart, 1999; Blais and Carty, 1990; Jackman, 1987). This higher level of turnout under PR is one of the more robust findings in the comparative electoral systems literature. But while scholars agree over what impact PR may have, there is much less certainty over the mechanism that produces such higher turnout. The most likely suspect, in terms of mechanism, is that of party competition and an increased level of party campaigning that occurs in multi-party PR systems. In this article we use survey data from a range of European countries to show that party campaign activity is not the mechanism that produces higher levels of turnout. If anything, campaign activity is higher under systems other than list PR. There are, moreover, predictable differences in campaign activity across different electoral systems. We begin by outlining the argument in favour of the view that turnout is a product of party campaigning.

Turnout and Party Mobilization

In principle, parties should expend greater effort on mobilizing voters when the expected benefits of turning out voters will be greatest, relative to the costs, i.e. when extra votes are likely to turn into extra seats for the party (for a review see Cox, 1999). Therefore, competitive elections and electoral formulas that ensure greater proportionality between seats and votes should increase the efforts parties expend on contacting voters. Because voters respond to the cues they receive from parties about the competitiveness of the election, this process leads to higher turnout. As Denver and Hands (1974: 35) argue: 'Higher turnout in marginal seats is rarely the product of a "rational" appreciation of the situation by voters, but results from parties creating greater awareness amongst voters or simply cajoling them into going to the polls.'

More competitive elections and a proportional translation of votes to seats assures that PR systems would encourage greater mobilization efforts. Because every vote counts in PR, parties have an incentive to mobilize everywhere, resulting in more competitive elections (Gosnell, 1930; Tingsten, 1937). Plurality systems, by contrast, typically favour a two-party system where only a relatively small number of seats are marginal (Downs, 1957). In SMP systems, parties have a strong incentive to concentrate their resources on marginal or competitive races and neglect those where the outcome is more certain. In those districts that are non-competitive, voters have less of an incentive to vote and parties have less of an incentive to mobilize (Powell, 1980: 12). The greater competitiveness of elections under PR means that more effort should be expended in trying to get voters out to the polls. And it is this effort that is thought to enhance political participation. With fewer competitive races under SMP and fewer parties, the overall level of party campaign activity is expected to be lower and the incentive to vote is diminished. In short, outside of a very few seats, SMP systems are likely *a priori* to be associated with low levels of campaign effort.

Aside from encouraging a higher level of mobilization effort than under SMP, party contacting may be more effective in PR systems. Not only is there likely to be a bigger payoff in terms of extra votes translating in seats, it may take less effort to convert potential voters to actual voters in PR systems. It has long been suggested that PR systems enhance political efficacy because votes are not wasted (Banducci et al., 1999). Greater stores of efficacy may make it easier for parties in PR systems to persuade potential supporters to vote. Additionally, party supporters may be persuaded to turn out to maximize the party's representation in parliament. Even if the party cannot win a majority, every vote can translate into seats that give useful bargaining power over coalition arrangements. By contrast, in plurality systems, parties that are not in a competitive position may find it difficult to persuade potential supporters to go to the polls since their votes may be perceived as making little difference to the outcome. Parties that have little chance of winning but nevertheless attempt to mobilize support for their cause may do so not primarily to influence the outcome but instead to register a protest with the political establishment. Their potential supporters, however, who are likely to be disillusioned with the political process, may be more difficult to mobilize.

No study has yet directly examined whether voters are more likely to be mobilized in multi-party (PR) systems, and instead most studies have taken a more indirect approach by examining how party systems influence turnout. Although it has been assumed that the number of parties competing for votes leads to an increase in turnout, the empirical evidence is mixed. Blais and Dobrzynska (1998) find, for example, that while increased competitiveness fosters higher turnout, a greater number of parties competing for votes decreases turnout. The overall impact is positive with PR countries having 3% higher turnout (Blais and Dobrzynska, 1998: 251), but the negative aspects via multi-partyism can be quite substantial (Jackman, 1987; Jackman and Miller, 1995; Gray and Caul, 2000; but see Ladner and Milner, 1999 for a counter view).

While these previous studies do not directly examine party mobilization, they nevertheless raise doubts that multi-partyism necessarily promotes greater voter mobilization. Although PR systems may appear to provide strong incentives for party mobilization, it is also quite plausible to think that systems with single member districts, where a personal vote is more likely to be cultivated (Carey and Shugart, 1995; Bowler and Farrell, 1993; Bowler, 1996; Mitchell, 2000; Ames, 1995; Samuels, 1999), will foster greater mobilization and party contact. While often over-stated, the role of the personal vote in helping candidates become elected can prompt campaign efforts at the local level (Cain et al., 1987). The importance of 'home style' is buttressed by evidence that constituents are more likely to have contacted representatives in electoral systems with lower district magnitudes (Curtice and Shively, 2000; Bowler and Farrell, 1993). Citizens are also more likely to correctly name their representative in plurality and mixed systems than in pure PR systems (Klingemann and Wessels, 2001).

Therefore, even after controlling for the effects of marginality, plurality systems such as SMP may still be associated with greater campaign effort by candidates since – in general – where voters can choose individual candidates those candidates have incentives to get out the vote regardless of whether the national party is allocating resources to that particular district. Even if a party adopts a national focus to its campaign, local candidates may still think it worthwhile to canvass support for their own campaign rather than sit back and rely on the national campaign to win the seat for them. Thus, while PR may well be associated with higher levels of turnout, the mechanism that produces the turnout may not be that of party activism. Moreover, the impact of party mobilization may be overstated; it is not at all clear how effective parties are in mobilizing voters.

Party Campaign Strategy and Effectiveness

Assessments about what impact party mobilization has on turnout depend not just on how many citizens are reached by parties but also on who is contacted. There is ample evidence from the US to suggest that the effectiveness of party canvassing is limited because parties tend to contact members of the electorate who are active in politics and thus predisposed to vote (Goldstein and Ridout, 2002; Rosenstone and Hansen, 1993; Huckfeldt and Sprague, 1992). Nevertheless, parties in the US continue to invest heavily in canvassing efforts and most survey-based studies show that reported contact by a party has a positive impact on turnout even when controlling for an individual's likelihood of voting (Kramer, 1970; Caldeira, Clausen and Patterson, 1990; Goldstein and Ridout, 2002; Rosenstone and Hansen, 1983; Wielhouwer and Lockerbie, 1994). After examining the effect of party contacting from 1952 to 1990, Wielhouwer and Lockerbie (1994: 220) conclude that 'contrary to most of the literature heralding the demise of political parties, their effectiveness in mobilizing voters has increased over the last 40 years', especially in presidential election years. Field experiments in the US beginning with Gosnell (1927) have demonstrated that citizens are more likely to vote when they are contacted. Experimental studies that compare the type of contact made indicate that canvassing (personal contact) is more effective than mail and telephone contacting (see Eldersveld, 1956; Miller, Bositis and Baer, 1981; Gerber and Green, 2000). There is also evidence that canvassing tends to increase turnout among occasional voters but not chronic non-voters (Niven, 2001) and that contacts closer to the election tend to be more effective (Niven, 2002).

Evidence from other countries about party canvassing and turnout is less voluminous in comparison. Some of this literature focuses on turnout, but other studies focus on the impact of local campaigning on a party's share of the vote. Evidence based on a field experiment during local elections in the UK suggests that party canvassing can appreciably increase turnout (Bochel and Denver, 1971, 1972), but others emphasize the relative unimportance of party canvassing when compared to television appeals (McAllister, 1985). Whiteley and Seyd (1994) find that local campaigning efforts had more of an influence on the distribution of votes rather than overall turnout. In an aggregate analysis that measures local campaigning effort as the number of volunteers available, Carty and Eagles (1999) find that opposition candidates benefit the most from local canvassing efforts. In New Zealand, a change in 1996 from SMP (also referred to as first-past-the-post or FPP) to PR led to a shift in party strategies. Rather than focusing their contacting efforts entirely on marginal seats, as they had seemed to do in the past, parties focused their efforts somewhat more broadly in the first election held under the new system, in an attempt to capture the nationwide 'list' vote (Denemark, 1998). In another study, Vowles (2002) reports a decline in party mobilization since New Zealand adopted PR, which he finds contributed to a decline in overall turnout.

Because these individual country studies cannot explicitly test institutional effects, the mechanism linking electoral systems to mobilization efforts is more a matter of conjecture than empirical findings. The evidence based on single country studies, while suggestive, does little to tell us about the relative rates of contacting across various political systems. While we know that turnout is higher under PR than under other systems we do not know why that is so. Indeed, in general, we know very little about either the effects of the electoral system on party mobilization efforts or, at the micro-level, about party attempts to mobilize voters across different systems. We can address this question by looking at evidence across a range of countries.

We have two main hypotheses in relation to the argument that it is party competition and/or mobilization that generates higher turnout under PR. For party mobilization efforts to be the mechanism that produces higher turnout, we must see two patterns. First, proportional systems should be associated with generally higher levels of campaign activity and, second, that campaign activity promotes turnout. It is the first of these steps that is especially critical since, as we saw, a plausible argument may be advanced that candidate based systems – typically the less proportional systems – are likely to produce much more active campaigns. If this latter pattern holds then we can have ruled out party campaigning as the mechanism by which PR produces higher turnout.

Data and Methods

To test these hypotheses, we rely on individual level data measuring citizen contact with political parties and activists across a range of different electoral settings. *Eurobarometer 52* provides a useful source for testing these hypotheses. The survey was conducted in October and November 1999 following the European Parliamentary Elections in June of that year and includes questions that measure whether a citizen was canvassed by a political party, received campaign literature or was exposed to campaign advertisements during the European Parliamentary campaign (see Appendix for question wording). We have two sets of questions to address in our empirical work. First, we assess the impact of electoral system upon party campaigns and party contact with voters. Second, we assess the impact of party contact upon the decision to turn out.

The main independent variables of interest are those relating to electoral system effects. The classification of electoral systems is the subject of a considerable literature within political science (for a comprehensive review see Farrell, 2001; see also Lijphart, 1999; Carey and Shugart, 1995; Bowler, 1996; Bowler and Farrell, 1993; Blais and Dobrzynska, 1998). Here we wish to focus on the (hypothesized) virtues of pure proportional representation and so focus on relatively broad categorizations. If party competition is the main mechanism at work that produces higher turnout, closed list PR should result in higher levels of campaign activity. Britain, France, Germany, Greece, Netherlands, Portugal and Spain are coded as closed list based on a description of their electoral systems for Euro-elections.[1] It is, of course, possible to argue that given the 'second order' nature of European elections the crucial incentives facing party organization are those associated with national electoral systems. In some models, therefore, we include a measure of national electoral systems. In this case, Britain, France, Ireland and Italy are classified as candidate based, districted systems while the remaining countries are classified as closed list PR.[2]

While our main hypothesis of interest is that electoral systems will be associated with certain kinds of campaign activity, party campaigns do not exist in isolation but are often subject to contextual factors and it is important to take these into account. For example, exposure to campaign advertisements will depend on campaign regulations within a given country. Using the information in Bowler et al. (2003) allowed us to identify those countries which actually allow paid TV advertisements for political campaigns (Austria, Germany, Italy and Sweden). Whether or not the country was a new democracy or not could also shape overall levels of campaign activity. Here expectations are contradictory: relatively new democracies could see more energized campaigns and parties and therefore generally higher levels of activity independent of electoral system or, alternatively, they could see lower levels as party systems develop to become organizations of mobilization. Either way, the age of the democratic experience could shape turnout levels and produce a different level of campaign activity. Greece, Portugal, Spain and East Germany are counted as new democracies for this purpose. Of potentially more consequence is the number of parties in a particular system: more parties should produce more campaign activity, everything else being equal. Of more significance still is the level of polarization among these parties over the EU. If parties within the party system are in disagreement over questions concerning the European Union, then campaigns are likely to be much more heated and active than if there is general agreement. Overall levels of campaign activity should, then, be higher when there are high levels of polarization in the party system (see e.g. Zaller, 1992). To measure polarization we rely on data collected by Marks and Steenbergen on party positions towards European integration. We take the maximum distance between any two parties on a 7-point scale. Finally we included a battery of standard demographic controls for party contact including age, education, gender, ideology and level of media use and attention.

In addressing turnout, the dependent variable is whether or not the individual voted (specifically vote recall) which we model, in line with previous work, as a function of electoral and party system attributes plus a series of demographic attributes. Over and above these kinds of concerns we include three other sets of variables of interest. First, whether or not voting is compulsory.[3] Second, whether or not there was a concurrent national election likely to produce higher turnout. Third, measures of general assessments of economic circumstances as well as assessments of the EU and its importance to the respondent. As part of this we also include a measure for border regions – the areas most affected by EU membership and hence likely to be interested in EU elections. In this model, however, the main independent variables concern party contact – the dependent variables in the first set of models. Party contact should increase levels of turnout.

In both the model of party contact and the turnout model we have included batteries of variables intended to capture confounding effects. Some of these variables are of more inherent interest than others. The impact of polarization, for example, is of more interest than demographic controls. Here we simply consider them as control variables: factors that may shape turnout independent of factors associated with party campaign efforts. Because the dependent variables are dichotomous we use logistic regression to estimate the models. To ease the interpretation of these results, we consider the substantive importance by reporting the probabilities for our main variables of interest in the following figures. The results for the complete models are reported in Tables 1 and 2.

Results

Figure 1 shows the relative distributions of campaign activity across the 15 member states of the EU. As can be seen, there is substantial variation in the levels and kinds of campaign activities conducted. The figure for the Republic of Ireland seems especially striking. The EP elections in Ireland were concurrent with national elections and so we would expect to see high levels of campaign activity, but the figure for canvassing is so high that there could be possibility of error in the data. Since Ireland is one of our 'candidate based' electoral systems this could bias results in our favour. For this reason we ran models both excluding and including Ireland as a dummy variable to take into account possible errors. Our results do not change and are robust to a wide range of different specifications. Overall, campaign activity is significantly lower in countries that employ a closed list electoral system for European Parliamentary elections (see Table 1). These effects hold regardless of whether we include a dummy variable representing

FIGURE 1
CAMPAIGN ACTIVITY BY COUNTRY
(% who report being exposed to …)

Canvass

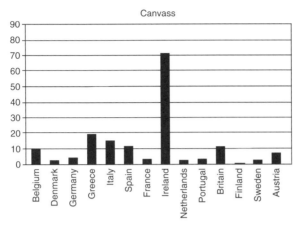

Leaflets

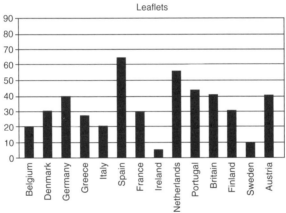

Advertisements

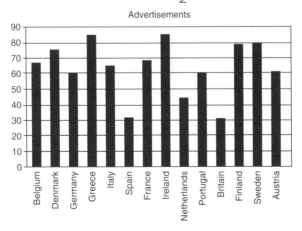

TABLE 1
PREDICTING CAMPAIGN ACTIVITY

	(Model 1) Canvass	(Model 2) Canvass	(Model 3) Leaflet	(Model 4) Leaflet	(Model 5) Ads	(Model 6) Ads	(Model 7) All
Age	0.006 (0.35)	-0.001 (0.05)	0.017 (1.44)	0.011 (0.89)	-0.004 (0.32)	-0.006 (0.51)	0.003 (0.37)
Education	0.018 (0.75)	0.009 (0.40)	0.076*** (4.70)	0.065*** (4.00)	0.084*** (5.16)	0.080*** (4.92)	0.042*** (3.96)
Student	-0.271*** (3.70)	-0.271*** (3.74)	-0.271*** (5.72)	-0.260*** (5.50)	-0.202*** (4.24)	-0.199*** (4.17)	-0.145*** (4.66)
Sex	-0.038 (1.23)	-0.049 (1.62)	-0.020 (0.96)	-0.028 (1.31)	-0.029 (1.34)	-0.031 (1.46)	-0.017 (1.23)
Left	-0.014 (0.33)	0.003 (0.07)	0.102*** (3.48)	0.119*** (4.07)	0.085*** (2.88)	0.091*** (3.09)	0.050*** (2.61)
Right	0.191*** (4.16)	0.197*** (4.36)	0.094*** (2.81)	0.102*** (3.08)	0.074** (2.21)	0.077** (2.31)	0.056*** (2.71)
Party numbers	-0.096*** (8.90)	-0.037*** (4.10)	-0.033*** (5.04)	-0.012* (1.96)	-0.021*** (3.21)	-0.012* (1.96)	-0.028*** (6.07)
New democracy	0.670*** (12.12)	0.542*** (9.90)	0.076** (2.03)	-0.036 (0.98)	0.185*** (4.96)	0.149*** (4.07)	0.141*** (5.44)
Media use	0.012** (2.01)	-0.003 (0.43)	0.032*** (7.53)	0.018*** (4.41)	0.049*** (11.57)	0.044*** (10.71)	0.023*** (8.09)
Paid TV ads allowed	0.198*** (4.44)	0.267*** (6.02)	-0.117*** (4.10)	-0.098*** (3.50)	-0.257*** (9.12)	-0.247*** (8.78)	-0.087*** (4.75)
Polarization	-0.029 (1.07)	-0.214*** (8.70)	0.249*** (14.32)	0.156*** (9.77)	0.406*** (23.18)	0.374*** (22.94)	0.198*** (16.33)
Ireland	1.131*** (12.63)	1.830*** (27.12)	0.542*** (7.58)	0.981*** (15.16)	0.958*** (14.17)	1.114*** (18.47)	0.511*** (12.58)
EP closed list	-0.397*** (7.92)	-0.222*** (5.02)	-0.556*** (19.72)	-0.474*** (17.22)	-0.410*** (14.60)	-0.382*** (13.88)	-0.331*** (16.46)
NP Candidate system	0.722*** (12.32)		0.478*** (14.42)		0.167*** (5.10)		0.267*** (11.61)
Concurrent election	0.658*** (8.05)	0.095 (1.49)	0.192*** (3.98)	-0.063 (1.42)	0.066 (1.37)	-0.028 (0.64)	0.164*** (4.73)
Constant	-1.149*** (6.44)	-0.265 (1.58)	-1.078*** (8.85)	-0.456*** (4.01)	-2.111*** (17.15)	-1.903*** (16.37)	-0.825*** (9.84)
Observations	15728	15728	15728	15728	15728	15728	15728

Absolute value of z statistics in parentheses; *P<.10; **P<.05; ***P<.01

TABLE 2
PREDICTING TURNOUT AS A FUNCTION OF CAMPAIGN ACTIVITY

	(Model 1)	(Model 2)
Age	0.205***	0.206***
	(15.95)	(16.03)
Education	0.048***	0.049***
	(2.84)	(2.87)
Student	-0.617***	-0.618***
	(12.47)	(12.47)
Sex	-0.028	-0.027
	(1.24)	(1.18)
Left	0.172***	0.168***
	(5.53)	(5.41)
Right	0.202***	0.202***
	(5.73)	(5.75)
Party numbers	0.094***	0.094***
	(12.58)	(12.51)
Compulsory voting	1.035***	1.092***
	(21.41)	(21.38)
Concurrent election	0.318***	0.352***
	(7.22)	(7.81)
Media usage	0.038***	0.040***
	(8.67)	(9.13)
Polarization	0.202***	0.231***
	(12.13)	(12.38)
Canvass	0.342***	0.317***
	(7.96)	(7.28)
Leaflet	0.195***	0.183***
	(7.31)	(6.79)
Ads	0.288***	0.287***
	(10.74)	(10.70)
Paid	0.167***	0.159***
	(4.65)	(4.42)
EU important	-0.036***	-0.033***
	(2.92)	(2.67)
EU a Good Thing	0.396***	0.399***
	(15.46)	(15.57)
EU a Bad Thing	-0.159***	-0.160***
	(4.26)	(4.27)
Sociotropic	-0.032*	-0.029
	(1.76)	(1.60)
Pocketbook	0.008	0.004
	(0.35)	(0.20)
Border area	-0.026	-0.015
	(0.63)	(0.38)
EP closed list	0.422***	0.442***
	(11.51)	(11.91)
NP Candidate system		0.113***
		(3.46)
Constant	-3.356***	-3.582***
	(22.82)	(22.25)
Observations	14984	14984

Absolute value of z statistics in parentheses
*P<.10; **P<.05; ***P<.01

whether the national electoral system is candidate based. They also hold regardless of whether we consider each type of campaign activity individually (models 1–6) or cumulatively (model 7). While the multi-partyism associated with PR systems is expected to contribute to higher levels of party contact, we see that it is negatively associated with all forms of party activity. As expected, in all but one model, polarization of the party system appears to generate more activity. Those on the right side of the ideological spectrum are also more likely to be mobilized while students are less likely to be exposed to the campaign.

FIGURE 2
PROBABILITY OF EXPOSURE TO PARTY CAMPAIGN ACTIVITY
BY ELECTORAL SYSTEM

EP Electoral System

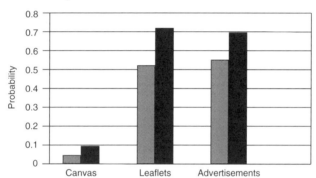

National Electoral System

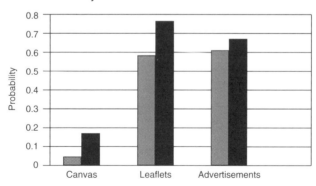

Source: Eurobarometer 52; October, November 1999

Figure 2 shows the probabilities of being exposed to the campaign through party canvassing, leaflets and advertisements. These probabilities are derived from Table 1 and represent the likelihood of campaign exposure for closed list and candidate-based electoral systems, holding all other variables constant at their mean values. As is evident from the figure, citizens are more likely to be exposed to leaflets and advertisements. Yet in candidate-based systems, the odds of being contacted increase substantially. To be specific, in a candidate-based system, a citizen has a 20% greater chance of receiving a leaflet or seeing an advertisement than a citizen who is in a closed list PR system. The difference is greatest for canvassing, where voters under a candidate-based system are twice as likely to be contacted as those under a closed list system (albeit at a still relatively low level of probability).

To consider the impact that these campaign efforts might have on turnout we can note several patterns. First we do see from Table 2 that campaign activity has a positive impact on a citizen's likelihood of voting. Parties, then, can and do make a difference to the overall rate of voting. To estimate the size of the difference we report probabilities in Figure 3 that show the likelihood of voting when a citizen reports being exposed to various types of campaign activity. As Figure 3 shows, personal visits are the most effective means of mobilizing voters. Those who are canvassed have a probability of voting of .73, while those who are not have a probability of voting of .60, all other things being equal. Other forms of campaign activity produce similar, albeit smaller, effects. Nevertheless, when one considers the greater proportion of citizens reached by advertisements and leaflets (see Figure 1), these activities can effectively produce higher rates of overall turnout.

Second, we also see the basic pattern that we noted at the outset to this article: list PR is associated with generally higher levels of turnout than candidate-based systems. Even after controlling for such other institutional factors as concurrent elections and compulsory voting, both of which increase the odds that citizens will vote in the European elections, list-based systems still produce higher turnout. Specifically, citizens in list PR systems have a probability of voting of .70 compared to citizens who reside in systems without a list system who have a probability of voting of .54. As with the models on campaign activity these results are robust to a wide range of different definitions of electoral systems. PR systems are thus associated with both higher turnout and lower levels of campaign activity than systems that are district based. Thus while list-based systems produce higher turnout, the mechanism at work does not appear to be one of party mobilization.

FIGURE 3
INFLUENCE OF EXPOSURE TO CAMPAIGN ACTIVITY ON PROBABILITY
OF VOTING

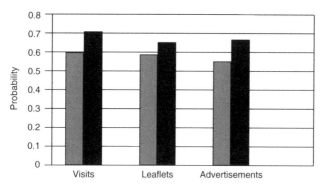

Source: Eurobarometer 52; October, November 1999

☒ Not contracted

■ Contracted

Conclusion

Advocates of PR have long argued that voters are more likely to be mobilized in proportional systems because there are more parties competing for votes. This has led to the assumption that there is greater mobilization under PR because of the increased competition in multi-party systems. The empirical evidence, however, indicates that this is not necessarily the case. While polarized party systems appear to contribute to greater campaign activity, a larger number of parties seem to produce the opposite result. Closed list (PR) systems have lower levels of campaign activity than candidate-based systems. While our analysis has been confined to European Parliamentary elections, we believe the findings may also extend to national elections. Using national election survey data, we examined whether citizens were more likely to report being contacted by a political party in seven countries representing PR and SMP systems (Karp, Banducci and Bowler, 2002). The results were generally consistent with the findings presented here. Citizens in SMP systems (all candidate-based) systems were far more likely to be contacted by a political party in a national election campaign than in closed list PR systems.

These findings lead us to conclude that candidate-based systems may have advantages that stimulate greater mobilization even though overall turnout may be lower than in PR systems. One possible explanation for this result is that candidates are more likely to be touch with their supporters when they have an incentive to cultivate a personal vote. Such a pattern presents a puzzle for our understanding of turnout since, plainly, the higher levels of turnout under PR cannot be associated with higher levels of party campaigning under PR. We must, then, look elsewhere for an explanation of turnout under PR.

APPENDIX:
QUESTION WORDING

'At the European election last June parties and candidates campaigned for votes. For each of the following please tell me whether their campaign came to your attention in that way or not?'

[possible answers: Yes, No, DK]

Party workers called to your home to ask for votes

Elections leaflets put in your letterbox or given to you on the street or in shopping centers etc

Advertising on behalf of the candidates or parties

NOTES

1. Descriptions of electoral systems were accessed at www3.europarl.eu.int/election/law/en/maps_en.htm.
2. In alternative models, we considered finer-grained distinctions between national electoral systems that distinguished between closed and open list PR as well as mixed systems and constructed a four-fold classification of electoral systems. See e.g. Bowler and Farrell 1993 for a similar categorization of electoral systems and campaign activity among MEPs. Results from these models are available on request.
3. We follow the categorization used by IDEA. The source for the data was accessed at www.idea.int/vt/analysis/Compulsory_Voting.cfm#compulsory and allowed us to categorize Belgium and Luxembourg as strongly enforcing compulsory voting and Austria and Greece as weakly enforcing.

REFERENCES

Ames, Barry (1995) 'Electoral Rules, Constituency Pressures, and Pork Barrel: Bases of Voting in the Brazilian Congress', *The Journal of Politics* 57: 324–43.
Banducci, Susan A., Todd Donovan and Jeffrey A. Karp (1999) 'Proportional Representation and Attitudes about Politics: Evidence from New Zealand', *Electoral Studies* 18: 533–55.
Banducci, Susan A. and Jeffrey A. Karp (2001) 'Mobilizing American Voters: A Reassessment'. Paper prepared for presentation at the Annual Conference of the American Political Science Association. San Francisco, 30 August–2 September.
Blais, André and Agnieszka Dobrzynska (1998) 'Turnout in Electoral Democracies', *European Journal of Political Research* 33 (2): 239–61.
Blais, André and R.K. Carty (1990) 'Does Proportional Representation Foster Voter Turnout', *European Journal of Political Research* 18 (2): 167–81.

Bochel, John M. and David D. Denver (1971) 'Canvassing, Turnout and Party Support: An Experiment', *British Journal of Political Science* 1: 257–69.

Bochel, John M. and David D. Denver (1972) 'The Impact of the Campaign on the Results of Local Government Elections', *British Journal of Political Science* 2:239–43.

Bowler Shaun (1996) 'Reasoning Voters, Voter Behaviour and Institutions' in David Farrell, David Broughton, David Denver and Justin Fisher (eds.) *British Elections and Parties Yearbook 1996.* London and Portland, OR: Frank Cass.

Bowler Shaun, Elisabeth Carter and David M. Farrell (2003) 'Changing Party Access to Politics' in Bruce Cain, Russ Dalton and Susan Scarrow (eds.) *New Forms of Democracy? The Reform and Transformation of Democratic Institutions.* Oxford: Oxford University Press.

Bowler, Shaun and David M. Farrell (1993) 'Legislator Shirking and Voter Monitoring: Impacts of European Parliament Electoral Systems upon Legislator-Voter Relationship', *Journal of Common Market Studies* 31:45–69.

Bowler, Shaun, David Farrell and Ian McAllister (1996) 'Constituency Campaigning in Parliamentary Systems with Preferential Voting: Is There a Paradox', *Electoral Studies* 14: 461–76.

Cain, Bruce, John Ferejohn and Morris Fiorina (1987) *The Personal Vote: Constituency Service and Electoral Independence.* Cambridge, MA: Harvard University Press.

Caldeira, Gregory A., Aage R. Clausen and Samuel C. Patterson (1990) 'Partisan Mobilization and Electoral Participation', *Electoral Studies* 9: 191–204.

Carey, John and Matthew S. Shugart (1995) 'Incentive to Cultivate a Personal Vote: A Rank Ordering of Electoral Systems', *Electoral Studies* 14: 417–39.

Carty, R.K. and Eagles M. (1999) 'Do Local Campaigns Matter? Campaign Spending, the Local Canvass and Party Support in Canada', *Electoral Studies* 18: 69–87

Cox, Gary (1999) 'Electoral Rules and the Calculus of Mobilization', *Legislative Studies Quarterly* 3: 387–419.

Curtice, John and Phil Shively (2000) 'Who Represents Us Best? One Member or Many', Working Paper No.79, Centre for Research into Elections and Social Trends.

Denemark, David (1998) 'Campaign Activities and Marginality: The Transition to MMP Campaigns' in Jack Vowles, Peter Aimer, Susan Banducci and Jeffrey Karp (eds.) *Voter's Victory? New Zealand's First Election Under Proportional Representation.* Auckland: Auckland University Press.

Denver, David and Gordon Hands (1974) 'Marginality and Turnout in British General Elections', *British Journal of Political Science* 4: 17–35.

Downs, Anthony (1957) *An Economic Theory of Democracy.* New York: Harper & Row.

Eldversveld, Samual J. (1956) 'Experimental Propaganda Techniques and Voting Behavior', *American Political Science Review* 50: 154–65.

Farrell, David M. (1996) 'Campaign Strategies and Tactics', in Lawrence LeDuc, Richard G. Niemi and Pippa Norris (eds.) *Comparing Democracies: Elections and Voting in Global Perspective.* Oxford University Press.

Farrell, David M. (2001) *Electoral Systems: A Comparative Introduction.* London and New York: Palgrave.

Gerber, Alan S. and Donald P. Green (2000) 'The Effects of Canvassing, Telephone Calls, and Direct Mail on Voter Turnout: A Field Experiment' *American Political Science Review* 94: 653–63.

Glaser, William A. (1965) 'Television and Voting Turnout', *Public Opinion Quarterly* 29: 71–86.

Goldstein, Kenneth M. and Travis N. Ridout (2002) 'The Politics of Participation: Mobilization and Turnout over Time', *Political Behavior* 24: 3–29.

Gosnell, Harold F. (1927) *Getting-Out-the-Vote: An Experiment in the Stimulation of Voting.* Chicago: University of Chicago Press.

Gosnell, Harold F. (1930) *Why Europe Votes.* Chicago: University of Chicago Press.

Gray, Mark and Miki Caul (2000) 'Declining Voter Turnout in Advanced Industrial Democracies, 1950–1997: The Effects of Declining Group Mobilization', *Comparative Political Studies* 33 (9): 1091–122.

Huckfeldt, Robert and John Sprague (1992) 'Political Parties and Electoral Mobilization: Political Structure, Social Structure, and the Party Canvass', *American Political Science Review* 86: 70–86.

Jackman, Robert W. (1987) 'Political Institutions and Voter Turnout in the Industrial Democracies', *American Political Science Review* 81 (2): 405–23.

Jackman, Robert W. and Ross A. Miller (1995) 'Voter Turnout in the Industrial Democracies During the 1980s', *Comparative Political Studies* 27 (4): 467–92.

Karp, Jeffrey A., Susan A. Banducci and Shaun Bowler (2002) 'Getting out the Vote: Party Mobilization in Comparative Perspective'. Paper presented at the Annual Conference of the American Political Science Association. Boston, 29 August –1 September.

Klingemann, Hans-Dieter and Bernhard Wessels (2001) 'The Political Consequences of Germany's Mixed-Member System: Personalization at the Grass Roots?' in Matthew S. Shugart and Martin P. Wattenberg (eds.) *Mixed Member Electoral Systems: The Best of Both Worlds?* Oxford: Oxford University Press.

Kramer, Gerald H. (1970) 'The Effects of Precinct-Level Canvassing on Voting Behavior', *Public Opinion Quarterly* 34: 560–72.

Ladner, Andrea and Henry Milner (1999) 'Do Voters Turn out More under Proportional then Majoritarian Systems? The Evidence from Swiss Communal Elections', *Electoral Studies* 18 (2): 235–50.

Lijphart, Arend (1999) *Patterns of Democracy: Government Forms and Performance in Thirty-Six Countries.* New Haven: Yale University Press.

Marks, Gary and Marco Steenbergen. nd. 'Party Dataset' electronic datafile. Center for European Studies: University of North Carolina.

McAllister, Ian (1985) 'Campaign Activities and Electoral Outcomes in Britain 1979 and 1983', *Public Opinion Quarterly* 49: 489–503.

Miller, Roy E., David A. Bositis and Denise L. Baer (1981) 'Stimulating Voter Turnout in a Primary: Field Experiment with Precinct Committeemen', *International Political Science Review* 2: 445–60.

Niven, David (2001) 'The Limits of Mobilization: Turnout Evidence from State House Primaries', *Political Behavior* 23: 335–50.

Niven, David (2002) 'The Mobilization Calendar – The Time-Dependent Effects of Personal Contact on Turnout', *American Politics Research* 30: 307–22.

Plutzer, Eric (2002) 'Becoming a Habitual Voter: Inertia, Resources, and Growth in Young Adulthood', *American Political Science Review* 96: 41–56.

Powell, G.B. Jr. (1980) Voting Turnout in Thirty Democracies: Partisan, Legal, and Socio-Economic Influences', in R. Rose (ed.), *Electoral Participation: A Comparative Analysis.* Beverly Hills, CA: Sage.

Powell, G.B. Jr. (1986) 'American Voter Turnout in Comparative Perspective' *American Political Science Review* 80 (1): 17–43.

Rohrschneider, Robert (2002) 'Mobilizing versus Chasing: How Do Parties Target Voters in Election Campaigns?' *Electoral Studies* 21: 367–82.

Rosenstone, Steven J. and John Mark Hansen (1993) *Mobilization, Participation, and Democracy in America.* Macmillan.

Samuels, D. (1999) Incentives to Cultivate a Party Vote in Candidate Centric Electoral Systems: Evidence from Brazil', *Comparative Political Studies* 32: 487–518.

Vowles, Jack (1995) 'The Politics of Electoral Reform in New Zealand', *International Political Science Review* 16: 95–115.

Vowles, Jack (2002) 'Offsetting the PR Effect? Party Mobilization and Turnout Decline in New Zealand, 1996–1999', *Party Politics* 8: 587–605.

Whiteley, Paul F. and Patrick Seyd (1994) 'Local Party Campaigning and Electoral Mobilization in Britain', *Journal of Politics* 56: 242–52.

Wielhouwer, Peter W. and Brad Lockerbie (1994) 'Party Contacting and Political Participation, 1952–90', *American Journal of Political Science* 38: 211–29.

Zaller, John (1992) *The Nature and Origins of Mass Opinion.* Cambridge University Press.

2001 GENERAL ELECTION

Who Blairs Wins?
Leadership and Voting in the 2001 Election

Robert Andersen and Geoffrey Evans

It is well known that political parties market their leaders to mass appeal. Physical makeovers such as new styles of dress and hair, and carefully planned speeches designed to make leaders appear as though they can relate to voters are now common practices of party strategists (see McGinniss, 1969; Wattenberg, 1991). The growing emphasis on leaders rather than parties is also evident in the vast number of countries that now have leaders' debates during election campaigns (Smith, 1981). But are voters really that concerned with the image of leaders? There is certainly no consensus on the matter. Some US research suggests that leader effects do matter (Rosenberg et al., 1986). Other research is more sceptical, however. For example, Bartels (2002: 66–7) argues that 'most important relationships between vote choice and comparative evaluations of the candidates' personal qualities should be seen as misleading or spurious.' Nevertheless, there is also evidence that even in a parliamentary system like Britain's where the party is elected, not the Prime Minister, the appraisals of leaders can matter (Mughan, 2000; Bean and Mughan, 1989; Crewe, 1984: 203–4).

There has been no shortage of commentary on the role of leadership in the 2001 British election. It was widely thought that the Conservative Party suffered because of William Hague's leadership. Hague was attacked by 'friends as well as enemies' (Norton, 2002: 90) for his apparent uncertainty, lack of clarity, and general lack of personal appeal (see Butler and Kavanagh, 2002) during his leadership of the Conservative Party, and this allegedly resulted in a lack of support from voters. As Simon Walters argues, 'There is little question that [Hague's] inability to convince people he was a credible alternative Prime Minister to Tony Blair was the single biggest reason for his failure to mount a stronger election challenge' (2001: 202). In comparison, Blair was generally agreed to be favourably perceived by most voters, which in turn, contributed to the success of the Labour Party (see, for example, King, 2002; Butler and Kavanagh, 2002; Norton, 2002; Seymour-Ure, 2002).

Not all agree, however, that the differences in appraisals of Hague and Blair were important for the result of the 2001 election. For example, with respect to Hague's apparent unpopularity, Bartle (2002: 192) writes: 'To be sure, voters thought that Tony Blair would make a better prime minister than William Hague, but these evaluations are almost entirely predictable on the basis of voter predispositions, policy preferences and evaluations of party competence. William Hague was not the Conservative Party's problem. Quite the reverse: the Conservative Party was William Hague's.'

The identification of 'leadership effects' is not at all straightforward (see King, 2002). The presence of differential popularity of leaders at the aggregate level is not in itself sufficient to infer an association with vote choice. Instead, popularity must be linked with vote at the individual level. The separation of party image from leader image is also necessary if one is to identify their distinct impact. Moreover, it is important to control for a range of other influences, both long-term and short-term, that condition voting. Even with such controls, the inference of any causal impact is open to question, as Bartle and Crewe (2002; see also King and Crewe, 1994; Worcestor and Mortimore, 1999: 129) have observed. Nonetheless, it is still possible to provide evidence that assesses rigorously whether there is an association between perceptions of leaders and voting that *might* indicate a causal connection. In such an exercise, data quality – in particular the availability of appropriate indicators – and model specification are of paramount importance.

This article contributes to the debate over leadership effects in the 2001 British election through a systematic analysis of the British Election Panel Study 1997–2001 (BEPS). BEPS data allow for the control of long-term orientations – past vote and stable values (Heath et al., 1994; Evans et al., 1996) – as well as a range of more typical short-term 'influences', such as economic expectations and retrospective appraisals (i.e. Sanders et al., 2001; Alvarez et al., 2000; Evans, 1999) and attitudes towards politically salient issues. In particular, we are interested in such issues as the Euro, which was an issue that the Conservatives sought to make more prominent in 2001 (Lansley, 2002) with some success (Evans, 2002). Since there is evidence that they are intertwined with views of leaders (Bartle, 2002; Worcestor and Mortimore, 1999), we also control for the effects of party images.

Finally, despite the sceptical assertions of many commentators – Bartle (2002: 201), for example, claims that: 'The outcome of the 2001 general election was not determined by Britain's social structure. Voters are no longer, if they were ever, chained to parties by virtue of their social location.' – we also include social structural variables. While it is true that social changes generally have a gradual character and the four years from 1997 to 2001 are not likely to exhibit any substantial change – unlike, for example, the marked changes in the class structure over the longer period from 1964 which clearly did provide important long-term influences on changes in party strategy and voting behaviour (Evans et al., 1999; Andersen and Heath, 2002) – social structural effects are less open to doubt about their exogeneity than are many of the subjective perceptions currently favoured as independent variables in political science models of voting.

Data and Methods

Data are from the 1997–2001 British Election Panel Study (BEPS). The baseline sample for BEPS 1997–2001 was the 1997 British Election Study (BES), totalling 3615 respondents. In total there were eight waves: three telephone and five face-to-face interviews. Since our interest is in long and short-term political influences, we utilize information from all five years of the study. Aside from vote in 2001 (which was asked in the final telephone interview immediately following the 2001 election) the questions of interest to this study were asked face-to-face, so we restrict our analysis to these waves, which were asked in each of the years of the study, and the 2001 telephone survey. We also employ data only from those respondents who reside in England, omitting residents of Scotland and Wales because of the more complex structures of party competition in the two countries (i.e., the existence of nationalist parties). This leaves a final analytical sample of 1471 observations.

Statistical Methods

The statistical analysis employs multinomial logit models and binary logit models of vote. The dependent variable, vote in 2001, is divided into three categories for the multinomial logit models: Labour, Liberal Democrat and Conservative. Those who voted for smaller parties or who did not vote are excluded from the analysis. We report the overall fit of various multinomial logit models in an analysis of deviance table. We refit the model in order to allow for different contrasts in the dependent variable, reporting the coefficients from the Labour/Liberal Democrat, Labour/Conservative, and Conservative/Liberal Democrat contrasts. Since each dependent variable contrast has different significant effects, the final models are from separate binary logit models for each of the dependent variable contrasts from the multinomial logit models. Details regarding the explanatory variables are given below.

Socio-Demographics

Our analysis controls for *age* (operationalized by both linear and squared terms in order to account for the possibility of curvilinear effects); *gender;*

education, operationalized as a set of four dummy regressors coded (1) degree, (2) some post secondary education, (3) A-level, (4) O-level/CSE, and 'other' (the reference category); and *social class*. Our measure of social class is a modification of the Goldthorpe class-schema, operationalized as a set of three dummy regressors: (1) salariat; (2) self-employed; (3) routine non-manual. The working class is coded as the reference category.

Long-term Influences

We employ three measures of possible long-term political influence: left/right values, liberal/authoritarian values, and vote in 1997.

Left/right values and *liberal/authoritarian values* are measured using adaptations of the well-established additive scales developed by the CREST research team which have been regularly employed in the British Election Studies and British Election Panel Studies (Heath et al., 1994). Each of these scales includes six Likert-items measured on five-point scales (see Appendix A). These scales were developed to tap enduring values (i.e., each of the items are expected to yield fairly stable responses over time). In order to further ensure that we are truly tapping 'enduring' values, and to compensate for possible measurement errors, each of the items is averaged over five waves of the BEPS before being included in the scale.

Past vote is operationalized by asking respondents which party they voted for in the 1997 election. In order to prevent recall bias, we utilize the panel element of the data, employing a question asked immediately following the 1997 election.

Political Influences

Political influences are assessed by respondents' perceptions of the three major parties and evaluations of the leaders of those parties.

The three *party image* variables are additive scales including three 3-point items asking respondents whether the party keeps its promises, whether it is divided or united, and whether the party is capable of strong government. Each of these items is coded so that positive responses were scored 1, negative responses were coded –1, and neutral or 'don't know' responses were coded as 0. The items were then added together to create scales ranging from –3 to +3.

Leader evaluations were tapped with five-point Likert items asking respondents about each of the leader's abilities as Prime Minister. For Tony Blair this meant asking how well a job he was doing as Prime Minister. For Hague and Kennedy this meant asking respondents how well they thought each of them would do as Prime Minister.

Election Issues and Economic Perceptions

Election issues and economic perceptions are grouped together because they constitute similar types of influences on an election. That is, they can both be seen as types of evaluations of party platforms.

Following the established literature on economic perceptions (i.e. Fiorina, 1981; Kinder and Kiewiet, 1981), we include four measures: (1) *retrospective egocentric perceptions*; (2) *retrospective sociotropic perceptions*; (3) *prospective egocentric perceptions*; (4) *prospective sociotropic perceptions*. Sociotropic perceptions were measured by a question asking respondents how well they thought the British economy was performing or would perform. The egocentric perception items asked respondents how they felt their own personal household income had been affected in the past year, or would be affected in the coming year. Each of these is measured by four-point scales coded so that high values indicate positive perceptions (i.e., the perception that the economic situation was/would be better).

We also include measures of opinions of three issues of importance in the 2001 election campaign: (1) support for cuts to waiting lists for National Health Service (NHS); (2) support for policy cutting school classroom sizes (CUTCLASS); and (3) that the respondent would vote 'yes' in a referendum to adopt the Euro (EURO). These questions were coded as three-point scales.

Results

Table 1 displays the means of the leader evaluations for Blair, Hague and Kennedy, and image scores for each of the three parties. We can see that in the pre-election survey Blair was indeed well ahead of Hague with respect perceptions of the job he was doing as Prime Minister, with Kennedy's appraisal sitting between the two. The pattern for party images is similar in terms of the relative positions of the party leaders. Now, however, Labour and the Liberal Democrats receive very similar appraisals, with perceptions of the Conservatives falling last with distinctively negative appraisals. The large differences in appraisal suggest that there was indeed room for leader images to play a role in the 2001 election.

We now turn to the multinomial logit models. Table 2 presents an analysis of deviance of several nested models. As the table indicates, the models were fitted in a sequence that reflects the likely position of different blocks of variables in a causal chain leading to vote. If we contrast nested models, we can test how adding groups of new variables to the model improves the fit. The differences in deviance between these models provide

TABLE 1
DESCRIPTIVE STATISTICS FOR PARTY IMAGE AND LEADER
EVALUATION VARIABLES

	Mean	Std. Deviation
Party images		
Labour Party	.73	2.0
Conservative Party	–.85	2.1
Liberal Democrats	.78	1.5
Leader evaluations		
Tony Blair	2.5	1.1
William Hague	1.7	1.2
Charles Kennedy	2.2	1.1

Note: High scores represent positive images or evaluations.

a likelihood ratio test which is distributed as chi-square with degrees of freedom equal to the number of new predictors added to the model (see Fox, 1997: Ch.15).

It is clear from Table 2 that, before considering enduring values and former vote, social position was still an important determinant of vote in 2001. Similarly, other long-term factors, such as values and 1997 vote also have a very strong impact on 2001 vote. Still, even when we control for these long-term factors, the model fits significantly better when political factors, such as party images and leader evaluations, are added (see the contrast between models 2–7). Finally, adding respondents' perceptions of the economy and position on election issues also improves the model, though much less so than do the factors discussed previously. As we shall see when we examine the coefficients from these models, many of the variables have differing effects – in terms of direction, magnitude and statistical significance – depending on which party voting contrast is examined.

Labour *versus* Conservative Voting

We now turn to a detailed examination of the individual models, starting with the contrast between the Labour and Conservative vote. Model 1 indicates that social class is the primary variable responsible for the impact of the social structural variables uncovered in the analysis of deviance. In other words, the usual pattern of class voting, with the working class proportionately more likely to favour Labour and the middle classes more likely to favour the Conservatives, was still strong in 2001. As other variables later in the causal chain – e.g., enduring values and previous vote – are added to the model, social class loses its statistical significance, but

TABLE 2
ANALYSIS OF DEVIANCE FOR THE MULTINOMIAL LOGIT MODELS FIT TO VOTE

(a) Deviance and degrees of freedom for each model

Model		Deviance	df
0	Constant only	2371	1469
1	Constant, Demographics	2185	1447
2	Constant, Demographics, Enduring Influences	1187	1435
3	Constant, Demographics, Enduring Influences, Party Images	905	1429
4	Constant, Demographics, Enduring influences, Leader Images	946	1429
5	Constant, Demographics, Enduring Influences, Party Images, Leader Images	847	1423
6	Constant, Demographics, Enduring Influences, Party Images, Leader Images, Issues and Economic Perceptions	796	1409

(b) Likelihood ratio tests for various effects

Models Contrasted	Source	Likelihood-ratio Chi-square test	df	p-value
0–1	Demographics	186	22	<<.001
1–2	Enduring Influences	997	12	<<.001
2–5	Party and Leader Images	340	12	<<.001
2–3	Party Images	282	6	<<.001
2–4	Leader Images	242	6	<<.001
5-6	Issues and Economic Perceptions	51	14	<.001

Number of cases used in each model is 1471

the general pattern remains. That much of the class effect is consumed by values and past vote should not be surprising since these factors are themselves influenced by social position.

We can see from Model 2 that past vote and enduring values affect vote in predictable ways. The finding that those who voted Labour before were more likely than others to vote Labour in 2001 is obvious. Also not surprising, given the ideological similarity of the two parties (see Bara and Budge 2001), those who switched from the Liberal Democrats were far more likely to vote for the Labour Party rather than the Conservative Party in 2001.

Model 2 also shows that right-wing and authoritarian voters are more likely to vote for the Conservatives over Labour. Moreover, although liberal/authoritarian values decrease in importance (and are no longer statistically significant) once Political influences are added to the model, left/right values continue to be a strong predictor of Labour versus Conservative vote even after including party and leader images, issue preferences and economic perceptions (see Model 6).

TABLE 3
COEFFICIENTS (STANDARD ERRORS IN PARENTHESES) FOR THE
LABOUR/CONSERVATIVE CONTRAST FROM SELECTED MULTINOMIAL LOGIT
MODELS (SEE TABLE 2)

	Model 1	Model 2	Model 5	Model 6
Intercept	3.074 (.821)***	11.19 (1.96)***	6.294 (2.77)*	2.547 (3.41)
Socio-demographics				
Age	-.116 (.084)	-.060 (.031)*	-.127 (.054)*	-.121 (.071)
Age2	.0004 (.0003)	.0011 (.0005)*	.0009 (.0007)	.0008 (.0008)
Gender (male)	.391 (.160)*	.385 (.277)	.381 (.425)	.393 (.484)
Education				
Degree	-.093 (.295)	-.233 (.527)	-.210 (.742)	-.445 (.885)
Some post secondary	-.173 (.262)	.006 (.452)	-.332 (.652)	-.651 (.759)
A-level	-.486 (.291)	-.806 (.504)	-1.269 (.690)	-1.408 (.768)
O-level	-.257 (.204)	-.433 (.357)	-.430 (.557)	-.712 (.616)
None	0	0	0	0
Social Class				
Salariat	-1.023 (.213)***	-.306 (.352)	-.311 (.518)	-.309 (.547)
Self-employed	-1.77 (.278)***	-1.001 (.478)*	-1.211 (.737)	-1.174 (.809)
Routine non-manual	-.668 (.227)**	-.254 (.397)	-.686 (.591)	-.874 (.648)
Working class	0	0	0	0
Long-term influences				
(a) Enduring values				
Left/right values	–	-.310 (.049)***	-.290 (.073)***	-.292 (.085)***
Liberal/auth. values	–	-.219 (.057)***	-.103 (.084)	-.031 (.092)
(b) Vote in 1997				
Labour	–	4.129 (.335)***	3.569 (.499)***	3.675 (.557)***
Conservative		0	0	0
Liberal Democrat	–	2.041 (.401)***	1.870 (.572)**	1.703 (.633)**
Other	–	.721 (.522)	1.104 (.919)	1.502 (.936)
Didn't vote	–	1.440 (.372)***	.936 (.543)	1.147 (.622)
Political influences				
(a) Party images				
Labour Party image	–	–	.499 (.124)***	.402 (.143)**
Cons. Party image	–	–	-.476 (.107)***	-.476 (.118)***
LD Party image	–	–	-.046 (.136)	.104 (.158)
(b) Leader evaluations				
Evaluation of Blair	–	–	1.012 (.235)***	.965 (.285)***
Evaluation of Hague	–	–	-.668 (.175)***	-.734 (.201)***
Evaluation of Kennedy	–	–	.371 (.179)*	.275 (.200)
Issues and economic perceptions				
Retro. sociotropic	–	–	–	.351 (.281)
Prosp. sociotropic	–	–	–	.993 (.316)**
Retro. egocentric	–	–	–	.110 (.247)
Prosp. egocentric	–	–	–	.046 (.343)
NHS spending	–	–	–	-.479 (.681)
Education spending	–	–	–	-.206 (.447)
Euro	–	–	–	.552 (.254)*

* p<.05; ** p<.01; *** p<.001

Model 5 includes political influences such as party images and leader evaluations. Since we are presently concerned with the Labour/ Conservative vote contrast, of particular interest are evaluations of these two parties and their leaders. As one would expect, positive opinions of the Labour Party and the Conservative Party are associated with higher probability of voting for the respective parties. The finding is in the same general direction for evaluations of the party leaders – i.e., a high opinion of Blair's performance as Prime Minister is related to a higher propensity to vote Labour, and a high opinion of Hague is related to a higher likelihood of voting Conservative. Where our results differ from some other suggestions, however, is in the magnitude of the strength of the effects of the two leaders' evaluations. We find very little difference between the impact of Hague and the impact of Blair. In other words, vote choices were made according to appraisals of the ability of both leaders. This finding remains virtually unchanged even after adding issues and economic perceptions to the model.

In Model 6 we include the opinions of election issues and perceptions of economic conditions. For the Labour/Conservative vote contrast, only two of the seven measures included in the model are important: prospective sociotropic economic perceptions and opinions about the Euro. Believing that the economy would improve in the next year was significantly related to a higher likelihood of voting Labour rather than Conservative, thus suggesting that the Labour Party was being rewarded for good economic management. Respondents who said they would vote for the Euro if a referendum on the issue were called, were more likely than others to vote Labour. Interestingly, the impact of perceptions of how the economy fared in the previous year was small and statistically insignificant. While the fact that improved NHS and educational services had minimal effects reflects that there was little variation in opinions on these issues.

Labour versus Liberal Democrats

We now turn to an assessment of the factors associated with Labour versus Liberal Democrat vote. The coefficients listed in Table 4 are from the same multinomial logit models displayed in Table 2. Starting with Model 1, perhaps the most striking finding is that social class has very little impact on the Labour versus Liberal Democrat vote – the effects are much smaller than for the Labour/Conservative contrast and except for the difference between the self-employed and working class (the latter are more likely to vote Labour) fail to reach statistical significance. As we can see from Model 2 there is also virtually no impact of either left/right or libertarian/authoritarian values. In other words, in 2001, voting behaviour accurately reflected the convergence between the Labour Party and the Liberal Democrats in terms of left/right policies.

TABLE 4
COEFFICIENTS (STANDARD ERRORS IN PARENTHESES) FOR THE
LABOUR/LIBERAL DEMOCRAT CONTRAST FROM SELECTED MULTINOMIAL
LOGIT MODELS (SEE TABLE 2)

	Model 1	Model 2	Model 5	Model 6
Intercept	419 (.885)**	.142 (1.41)	–1.018 (1.74)	–4.008 (2.09)
Socio-demographics				
Age	–.053 (.034)	–.107 (.044)*	–.121 (.051)*	–.087 (.054)
Age2	.0004 (.0003)	.0010 (.0004)*	.0011 (.0004)*	.0007 (.0005)
Gender (male)	.165 (.172)	.289 (.228)	.140 (.257)	.118 (.272)
Education				
Degree	–.742 (.319)*	–.387 (.444)	–.343 (.501)	–.312 (.543)
Some post secondary	–.772 (.285)**	–.006 (.452)	–.257 (.422)	–.372 (.457)
A-level	–.177 (.340)	–.318 (.370)	.081 (.510)	–.072 (.527)
O-level	–.075 (.236)	–.077 (.311)	.174 (.355)	.239 (.373)
None	0	0	0	0
Social Class				
Salariat	–.232 (.240)	.137 (.323)	.053 (.367)	.098 (.384)
Self-employed	–.648 (.327)*	–.267 (.431)	–.054 (.507)	.133 (.324)
Routine non-manual	–.200 (.250)	–.208 (.325)	–.478 (.376)	–.577 (.398)
Working class	0	0	0	0
Long-term influences				
(a) Enduring values				
Left/right values	–	–.027 (.043)	.035 (.049)	.045 (.053)
Liberal/auth. values	–	–.036 (.042)	.056 (.048)	.076 (.052)
(b) Vote in 1997				
Labour	–	3.437 (.279)***	3.446 (.313)***	3.519 (.328)***
Conservative	–	1.14 (.346)**	1.328 (.395)***	1.375 (.422)**
Liberal Democrat	–	0	0	0
Other	–	1.201 (.504)*	1.340 (.598)*	1.239 (.598)*
Didn't vote	–	2.020 (.390)***	1.931 (.445)***	1.883 (.469)***
Political influences				
(a)Party images				
Labour Party image	–	–	.396 (.081)***	.353 (.085)***
Cons. party image	–	–	–.075 (.081)	–.073 (.084)
LD party image	–	–	–.359 (.098)***	–.348 (.104)***
(b) Leader evaluations				
Evaluation of Blair	–	–	.562 (.173)**	.507 (.180)**
Evaluation of Hague	–	–	–.007 (.132)	.025 (.138)
Evaluation of Kennedy	–	–	–.302 (.138)*	–.318 (.143)*
Issues and economic perceptions				
Retro. sociotropic	–	–	–	.086 (.176)
Prosp. sociotropic	–	–	–	.562 (.187)**
Retro. egocentric	–	–	–	.415 (.156)**
Prosp. egocentric	–	–	–	.051 (.186)
NHS spending	–	–	–	–.281 (.422)
Education spending	–	–	–	–.047 (.304)
Euro	–	–	–	.078 (.150)

* $p<.05$; ** $p<.01$; *** $p<.001$

Previous vote also affected the vote in 2001 in the expected manner: Those who were Labour supporters in 1997 were most likely to be Labour rather than Liberal Democrat supporters in 2001. Labour's continued success is also reflected in the fact that those who switched from parties other than Labour or the Liberal Democrats were far more likely to vote Labour rather than Liberal Democrat in 2001.

Model 5 adds political influences. Not surprisingly, perceptions of the Conservatives and their leader William Hague are irrelevant for the choice between Labour and Liberal Democrats. However, there is a very strong positive impact for perceptions of the Labour Party and of Tony Blair. Perceptions of the Liberal Democrats, and of their leader Charles Kennedy, also mattered. In fact, perceptions of the Liberal Democrats were as important as perceptions of Labour, but evaluations of Kennedy were slightly less important for vote than perceptions of Blair. These party and leader effects persist even after economic perceptions and election issues are added in Model 6.

In Model 6 we see that as with the Labour/Conservative vote contrast, perceptions of the state of the economy in the past year mattered little but future expectations of the economy were positively associated with Labour voting. Unlike with the Conservative/Labour contrast, however, how respondents' perceived their own economic situation during the past year is significantly associated with vote – i.e. the better their personal economic situation, the more likely they were to vote Labour. None of the specific election issues affected the choice between these two parties, again reflecting the similarity in party policies.

Conservative versus Liberal Democrat Voting

Table 5 displays the coefficients for the Conservative versus Liberal Democrat vote contrast. For Model 1, we see that the coefficients for social class are statistically significant, and are almost the same as those for the Labour/ Conservative contrast. As in the case of the Labour/Conservative contrast, these class effects remain but diminish and lose statistical significance after values and previous vote are added in Model 2. These findings confirm that the class profile of Liberal Democrat voters is similar to the class profile of Labour voters.

In Model 2 we again see a similarity in Liberal Democrat voters and Labour voters in the effects of left/right and liberal/authoritarian values. The more right-wing and authoritarian the respondents were, the more likely they were to vote for the Conservative Party. As in the case for the Labour/Conservative contrast, the impact of left/right values is still present even after party and leader images are added to the model while the impact of liberal/authoritarian values becomes negligible. Once again we also see

TABLE 5
COEFFICIENTS (STANDARD ERRORS IN PARENTHESES) FOR THE
CONSERVATIVE/LIBERAL DEMOCRAT CONTRAST FROM SELECTED
MULTINOMIAL LOGIT MODELS (SEE TABLE 2)

	Model 1	Model 2	Model 5	Model 6
Intercept	−.578 (.919)	−11.41 (1.96)***	−4.932 (2.511)*	−5.777 (2.85)*
Socio-demographics				
Age	.006 (.036)	.043 (.057)	−.022 (.070)	−.004 (.074)
Age2	.0001 (.0003)	−.0003 (.0005)	.0003 (.0007)	.0001 (.0007)
Gender (male)	−.114 (.185)	−.067 (.275)	−.003 (.356)	.008 (.369)
Education				
Degree	−.593 (.327)	−.032 (.522)	−.183 (.663)	.167 (.698)
Some post secondary	−.484 (.286)	−.781 (.417)	−.925 (.526)	−.606 (.561)
A-level	.298 (.348)	.461 (.502)	713 (.679)	.988 (.720)
O-level	.311 (.256)	.112 (.363)	−.194 (.492)	−.078 (.511)
None	0	0	0	0
Social Class				
Salariat	.681 (.255)**	.397 (.367)	.689 (.470)	.544 (.487)
Self-employed	1.084 (.322)***	.357 (.440)	.703 (.626)	.788 (.642)
Routine non-manual	.463 (.279)	.332 (.398)	.828 (.528)	.999 (.542)
Working class	0	0	0	0
Long-term influences				
(a) Enduring values				
Left/right values	–	.308 (.051)***	.267 (.065)***	.277 (.069)***
Liberal/auth. values	–	.187 (.055)***	.083 (.071)	.070 (.075)
(b) Vote in 1997				
Labour	–	1.195 (.415)**	.810 (.557)	.956 (.575)
Conservative	–	3.175 (.338)***	2.533 (.414)***	2.542 (.422)***
Liberal Democrat	–	0	0	0
Other	–	2.042 (.487)***	1.507 (.634)*	1.590 (.656)*
Didn't vote	–	2.141 (.434)***	1.863 (.567)**	2.016 (.595)***
Political influences				
(a) Party images				
Labour Party image	–	–	−.173 (.099)	−.159 (.107)
Cons. party image	–	–	.496 (.095)***	.482 (.096)***
LD party image	–	–	−.473 (.137)***	−.514 (.142)***
(b) Leader evaluations				
Evaluation of Blair	–	–	−.280 (.165)	−.264 (.173)
Evaluation of Hague	–	–	.344 (.148)*	.341 (.157)*
Evaluation of Kennedy	–	–	−.740 (.173)***	−.694 (.180)***
Issues and economic perceptions				
Retro. sociotropic	–	–	–	−.166 (.206)
Prosp. Sociotropic	–	–	–	.314 (.228)
Retro. Egocentric	–	–	–	.063 (.199)
Prosp. Egocentric	–	–	–	.479 (.256)
NHS spending	–	–	–	.468 (.530)
Education spending	–	–	–	−.412 (.375)
Euro	–	–	–	−.419 (.202)*

* $p<.05$; ** $p<.01$; *** $p<.001$

from Model 2 that voting for a party in 1997 is strongly related to voting for that party again in 2001. As in the case of the Labour/Liberal Democrat contrast, the Liberal Democrats benefited least from those who switched from 1997.

Our findings with respect to the importance of leaders and party images are again confirmed in Model 5. Positive appraisals of the Conservative Party and Hague, and of the Liberal Democrats and Kennedy, are positively related to vote for the respective parties. In Model 6 we again see that this finding is robust – after including issues and economic perceptions the coefficients change very little.

Given that both of these parties were in opposition for the previous four years, it is not surprising that the impact of assessments of the economic situation are statistically insignificant – neither party could be blamed or rewarded for the state of the economy. Finally, as in the case of the Labour/Conservative contrast, the salience of the Euro issue is evident in that those who would vote to adopt the Euro if a referendum were held are significantly less likely to vote Conservative rather than Liberal Democrat.

Assessing Relative Importance

The analysis so far has assessed the impact of various factors for each of the party contrasts separately. To get a better handle on the relative importance of the various influences of vote across the different vote contrasts, we turn to Table 6. Table 6 displays the coefficients and model fit for separate binary logit models fit to each of the dependent variable contrasts in the original multinomial logit models. These models include only effects that were statistically significant in the final multinomial logit models (Model 6).

For each of the party contrasts, the relevant party images have similar impacts on vote. However, the pattern is less consistent for leader images. As one might expect considering the media exposure given to Blair relative to the media exposure given to Kennedy, evaluations of Blair were far more important than evaluations of Kennedy when it comes to the Labour/Liberal Democrat contrast. On the other hand, Kennedy's appraisal is somewhat more important (although the difference is not statistically significant) than evaluations of Hague with respect to the Conservative/Liberal Democrat contrast. Finally, and perhaps most interesting, the influence of leader evaluations on the choice between Labour and Conservative is very strong and, more importantly, there is very little difference between the influence of appraisals of Blair and appraisals of Hague.

It is also of interest to compare the relative importance of blocks of variables. We do so using the measure of relative importance proposed by Silber et al. (1995), and implemented using the *relimp* package for the statistical computing programme *R*. This measure is a generalization of

TABLE 6
FINAL BINOMIAL LOGIT MODELS (STANDARD ERRORS IN PARENTHESES) FOR
VOTE (INCLUDE ONLY STATISTICALLY SIGNIFICANT EFFECTS FROM MODEL 6)

| | Dependent variable contrast | | |
	Labour/Cons.	Labour/LD	Cons./LD
Intercept	−.280 (1.32)	−4.791 (.691)***	−3.260 (1.04)**
Long-term influences			
(a) Enduring values			
Left/right values	−.237 (.067)***	–	.226 (.058)**
(b) Vote in 1997			
Labour	3.643 (.480)***	3.460 (.289)***	.660 (.497)
Conservative	0	1.456 (.381)***	2.601 (.376)***
Liberal Democrat	1.777 (.554)**	0	0
Other	1.644 (.839)	1.348 (.531)*	1.546 (.560)***
Didn't vote	1.386 (.521)**	1.925 (.403)***	1.927 (.545)**
Political influences			
(a) Party images			
Labour	.468 (.112)***	.359 (.076)***	–
Conservative	−.413 (.097)***	–	.470 (.085)***
Liberal Democrat	–	−.302 (.092)**	−.490 (.124)***
(b) Leader evaluations			
Blair	.845 (.222)***	.576 (.160)***	–
Hague	−.727 (.165)***	–	.447 (.135)**
Kennedy	–	−.322 (.128)*	−.646 (.156)***
Issues and economic perceptions			
Prosp. sociotropic	1.155 (.244)***	.661 (.148)***	–
Retro. egocentric	–	.380 (.129)**	–
Euro	.598 (.207)**	–	−.594 (.172)***
Model fit			
Chi-square	853.80***	420.65***	468.58***
df	11	10	10
N	782	723	583

* *p*<.05; ** *p*<.01; *** *p*<.001

standardized variables to non-quantitative regressors or sets of regressors. The measure compares the overall contribution to the dependent variable of two *sets* of variables through the log of the standard deviation ratio between the two sets.

The relative importance of various sets of variables in the final models is displayed in Table 7. The first column of the table displays the ratio considered. The next three columns display the log of the standard deviation ratio for the groups of variables for the models. Positive values indicate that the numerator is of more importance; negative numbers indicate that the denominator is of more importance. Three general points can be made.

First, party images and leader evaluations were far more important than issues and economic perceptions in determining vote (all of the ratios are positive and statistically significant). Secondly, there is no significant difference in the relative importance of all party images grouped together compared to all leader evaluations grouped together. Thirdly, for any particular vote contrast, there is no evidence that one party's image and/or leader evaluations mattered more than another's. Most interesting is that there is no difference whatsoever in terms of the importance of evaluations of the Conservative Party and Hague and evaluations of the Labour Party and Blair.

TABLE 7
RELATIVE IMPORTANCE (MEASURED BY THE LOG OF THE STANDARD DEVIATION RATIO) OF SETS OF VARIABLES IN THE FINAL BINOMIAL LOGIT MODELS FIT TO VOTE (SEE TABLE 6)

| | Dependent variable contrast | | |
	Labour/Cons.	Labour/LD	Cons./LD
Party Images and Leader Evaluations/Issues	.842 (.208)***	.524 (.212)*	1.434 (.310)***
Party Images/Leader Evaluations	.015 (.298)	.207 (.356)	.257 (.283)
Political influences by party			
Labour + Blair/Cons. + Hague	.029 (.184)	–	–
Labour + Blair/L.D. + Kennedy	–	.359 (.217)	–
Cons. + Hague/L.D. + Kennedy	–	–	.151 (.158)
Leader evaluations/All other influences			
Blair + Hague/all other	−1.020 (.221)***	–	–
Blair + Kennedy/all other	–	−1.231 (.262)***	–
Hague + Kennedy/all other	–	–	−.987 (.242)***

* $p<.05$; ** $p<.01$; *** $p<.001$
Standard errors are in parentheses.

Discussion and Conclusions

This article set out to test the importance of leader appraisals on voting in the 2001 British election. To ensure that we did not uncover spurious relationships, our analysis controlled for other factors commonly used to predict vote. We can draw the following conclusions.

Contrary to the findings of Bartle (2002, also Bartle and Crewe, 2002) our results indicate that appraisal of leaders were indeed substantially associated with vote in the 2001 election. Moreover, appraisals of Tony

Blair and William Hague had very similar effects with respect to Conservative/Labour voting. We also showed that these effects were more important than party images, and they persist even after controlling for long-term values, past vote, party record and respondents' position on election issues. Moreover, these effects were found using only simple, single-item measures of leadership evaluations.

Simply put, Blair's popularity helped Labour win the election and Hague's unpopularity contributed to the misfortunes of the Conservatives. It is also important to note, however, that the evaluations of Charles Kennedy had differential effects depending on the party contrast examined. For example, Kennedy's perceived ability to be Prime Minister was less significant than evaluations of Tony Blair for Labour/Liberal Democrat voting but more significant than evaluations of Hague for Conservative/Liberal Democratic voting. This last point indicates that, contrary to the emphasis on Hague's global negative impact stressed by many journalistic commentators, Blair's impact was actually a little more broad-ranging in its effect.

Some more general conclusions about the 2001 election can also be made. First, we found that aside from party images and leader images, short-term electoral change from 1997–2001 was also strongly influenced by voters' long-term value orientations. This finding thus suggests the importance of retaining these measures in models of voting behaviour in Britain. Given that voters' stable values were able to partially predict relatively short-term vote switching, this suggests that shifts in party platform are important factors in accounting for what sorts of voter characteristics will predict changes in vote.

Secondly, it was clear that voters saw the Liberal Democrats and Labour as very similar. The two parties were not only similar in terms of platforms, but also in terms of party and leader image scores given by the BEPS respondents. The difference in public support at the polls between the two parties is perhaps largely related to long-term party attachments and the fact that Labour benefited from a reasonably strong economic situation. Although our findings do not address it directly, it is also likely that the Liberal Democrats received less support simply because they were not seen as likely winners of the election. For example, regarding the 1997 election, Worcestor and Mortimore (1999: 136) found evidence that 'more than a quarter of those intending to vote Labour said they would have been more likely to vote Liberal Democrat if they thought the party could win.'

Thirdly, in terms of campaign related issues and economic perceptions there were some findings that confirm previous research. For example, consistent with Evans' (2002) previous analysis, the Euro was the only current issue to weigh in the vote switching calculus. Moreover, we found that *sociotropic* economic expectations had a significant impact on vote, but not *personal* economic expectations, contrary to the model proposed by David Sanders and his colleagues (Sanders et al., 2001). That is, those who felt the economy in general would do better in the next year were more likely to vote for the incumbent Labour Party.

Some considerations must be kept in mind when making causal inferences from these data. Our analysis represents only a weak test of causal impact since we estimate covariation at one point in time while controlling for past vote. It is entirely possible that evaluations of leaders are strongly conditioned by previous partisanship. Given that partisan change can precede and impact on changes in leadership perceptions through processes of cognitive consistency (Abelson 1968) and framing (Campbell et al., 1960), more demanding tests that model the dynamic relations between party support and subjective perceptions over time (see Evans 1999; Evans and Andersen 2002) are likely to lead to a revised and more conservative interpretation.

Of course, leader images are not the only variables typically employed in models of voting behaviour that might be 'contaminated' by prior influences – economic perceptions, party images, and even positions on elections issues could possibly be strongly influenced by previous partisanship (see Evans and Andersen, 2002 for an elaboration of this argument with respect to economic perceptions). Only socio-demographic factors such as age, sex, religion, education and social class are exempted from this concern. Thus our analyses indicate that although they are only *indirect* influences on vote, in that they are removed once subjective perceptions are included in the models, social-structural influences, in particular social class, continue to be important for electoral outcomes in Britain. Clearly there remains a structural basis for vote in Britain that is not vulnerable to criticisms concerning the effects of framing or cognitive consistency in the way that perceptions of leaders or the economy, for example, clearly are.

To conclude, even in a comprehensively specified model that contains indicators of long-standing partisanship and political values, we find robust leadership effects. Taken at face value these results confirm journalistic commonsense rather than some of the more sceptical interpretations taken by survey analysts. All of the main party leaders would appear to have played their role, for good or ill, in the relative electoral fates of their parties. Whether this strong interpretation survives further research into the endogeneity of the public's perceptions of their merits and demerits remains to be seen.

REFERENCES

Abelson, R. (1968) *Theories of Cognitive Consistency: A Sourcebook.* Chicago: Rand McNally.
Alvarez, R.M., J. Nagler and S. Bowler (2000) 'Issues, Economics, and the Dynamics of
Multiparty Elections: The British 1987 General Election', *American Political Science
Review* 94 (1): 131–49.
Andersen, R. and A. Heath (2002) 'Class Matters: The Persisting Effects of Contextual Social
Class on Individual Voting Behaviour in Britain, 1964–97,' *European Sociological Review*
18 (2): 125–38.
Bara, J. and I. Budge, (2001) 'Party Policy and Ideology: Still New Labour?' in P. Norris (ed.)
Britain Votes 2001, special issue of *Parliamentary Affairs,* 54, pp.590–606.
Bartels, L. (2002) 'The Impact of Candidate Traits in American Presidential Elections', in A.
King (ed.) *Leaders' Personalities and the Outcomes of Democratic Elections,* pp.44–69.
Bartle, J. (2002) 'Why Labour Won – Again', in A. King (ed.), *Britain at the Polls 2001.*
Chatham, NJ: Chatham House, pp.164–206.
Bartle, J. and I. Crewe (2002) 'The Impact of Party Leaders in Britain: Strong Assumptions,
Weak Evidence', in A. King (ed.) *Leaders' Personalities and the Outcomes of Democratic
Elections,* pp.70–95.
Bean, C. and A. Mughan (1989) 'Leadership Effects in Parliamentary Elections in Australia and
Britain,' *American Political Science Review* 83: 1165–79.
British Election Panel Survey, 1997–2001. Centre for Research into Elections and Social Trends.
ESRC Data Archive, Colchester, UK.
Butler, D. and D. Kavanagh (2002) *The British General Election of 2001.* New York: Palgrave.
Campbell, A., P. Converse, W. Miller, and D. Stokes (1960) *The American Voter.* New York:
Wiley & Sons.
Crewe, I. (1984) 'The Electorate: Partisan Dealignment Ten Years On', in H. Berrington (ed.)
Change in British Politics. London: Frank Cass.
Crewe, I. and A. King (1994) 'Did Major Win? Did Kinnock Lose? Leadership Effects in the
1992 Election', in *Labour's Last Chance? The 1992 Election and Beyond* (eds.) A. Heath, R.
Jowell and J. Curtice with B. Taylor. Aldershot: Dartmouth.
Evans, G. (1999) 'Economics and Politics Revisited: Explaining the Decline in Conservative
Support, 1992–95', *Political Studies* 47: 139–51.
Evans, G. and R. Andersen (2001) 'Endogenizing the Economy: Political Preferences and
Economic Perceptions across the Electoral Cycle', *CREST Working Paper Series,* No.88,
accessed at www.crest.ox.ac.uk/papers.htm.
Evans, G., A. Heath and M. Lalljee (1996) 'Measuring Left–Right and Libertarian–Authoritarian
Values in the British Electorate', *British Journal of Sociology* 47 (1), 93–112.
Evans, G., A. Heath and C. Payne (1999) 'Class: Labour as a Catch-All Party?' in G. Evans and
P. Norris (eds.) *Critical Elections.* London: Sage.
Fiorina, M. (1981) *Retrospective Voting in American National Elections.* New Haven: Yale
University Press.
Fox, J. (1997) *Applied Regression Analysis, Linear Models, and Related Methods.* London: Sage.
Heath, A., R. Jowell and J. Curtice (2001) *The Rise of New Labour: Party Policies and Voter
Choices.* Oxford: Oxford University Press.
Heath, A., G. Evans and J. Martin (1994) 'The Measurement of Core Beliefs and Values: The
Development of Balanced Socialist/Laissez-faire and Libertarian/authoritarian scales',
British Journal of Political Science 24 (1): 115–32.
Kinder, D., and D.R. Kiewiet (1981) 'Sociotropic Politics: The American Case,' *British Journal
of Political Science* 11 (1): 129–61.
King, A. (ed.) (2002) *Leaders' Personalities and the Outcomes of Democratic Elections.* Oxford:
Oxford University Press.
Lansley, A. (2002) 'Conservative Strategy', in J. Bartle, S. Atkinson and R. Mortimore (eds.),
Political Communications: The General Election Campaign of 2001. London and Portland,
OR: Frank Cass.
McGinniss, J. (1969) *The Selling of the President 1968.* New York: Trident Press.

Mughan, A. (2000) *Media and the Presidentialization of Parliamentary Elections*. New York: Palgrave.

Norton, P. (2002) 'The Conservative Party: Is There Anyone Out There?' in A. King (ed.) *Britain at the Polls, 2001*. London: Chatham House.

Sanders, D. (1999) 'The Impact of Left-Right Ideology,' in G. Evans and P. Norris (eds.) *Critical Elections: British Parties and Voters in Long-Term Perspective*. London: Sage.

Rosenberg, S., L. Bohan, P. McCafferty, and K. Harris (1986) 'The Image and the Vote: The Effect of Candidate Presentation on Voter Preference,' *American Journal of Political Science* 30: 108–27.

Sanders, D., H. Clarke, M. Stewart and P. Whitely (2001) 'The Economy and Voting,' in P. Norris (ed.) *Britain Votes 2001*. Oxford: Oxford University Press.

Seymour-Ure, C. (2002) 'New Labour and the Media,' in A. King (ed.) *Britain at the Polls, 2001*. London: Chatham House.

Silber, J. H., Rosenbaum, P.R. and Ross, R.N. (1995) 'Comparing the Contributions of Groups of Predictors: Which Outcomes Vary with Hospital Rather than Patient Characteristics?' *Journal of the American Statistical Association* 90, 7–18.

Smith, A. (1981) 'Mass Communications', in D. Butler, H. Penniman and A. Ranney (eds.), *Democracy at the Polls*. Washington, D.C.: American Enterprise Institute.

Walters, S. (2001) *Tory Wars: The Conservatives in Crisis*. London: Politico's.

Wattenberg, M. (1991) *The Rise of Candidate-Centered Politics: Presidential Elections of the 1980s*. Cambridge, Mass.: Harvard University Press.

Wlezien, C., M. Franklin and D. Twiggs (1997) 'Economic Perceptions and Vote Choice: Disentangling the Endogeneity', *Political Behavior* 19: 7–17.

Worcestor, R. and R. Mortimore (1999) *Explaining Labour's Landslide*. London: Politico's.

Do Canvassing and Campaigning Work? Evidence from the 2001 General Election in England

Ron Johnston and Charles Pattie

From the 1960s on, British election campaigns became increasingly dominated by the mass media, notably television. Parties sold their policies to the electorate, and presented their major candidates (especially those for Prime Minister) through that medium, using both the formal mechanisms provided – the party election broadcasts (Pattie and Johnston, 2002) and staged question-and-answer sessions – and opportunities for other coverage, notably in news programmes. As this form of campaigning grew, so increasingly campaigns became 'nationalized', with each party's candidates in the individual constituencies riding on the coattails of the national campaign – their prospects were progressively more tied to the fate of their party as a whole. The nature of their campaigning also changed: as TV audiences grew and other leisure activities became more popular, audiences for political meetings dwindled, and local campaigns became predominantly activities designed to turn out the vote – to ensure that a party's known (or believed) supporters either applied for and used a postal vote or actually went to their designated polling station on election day – and less about convincing the electorate to vote for one party rather than another.

This change in the nature of election campaigning was reflected in analyses of the results. Leading psephologists – notably David Butler and the co-authors of the Nuffield election studies – decided that the local campaigns were irrelevant to the election outcome. Their evidence for this was largely indirect, and not based on detailed analyses of local campaigns and their impact: indeed, there were very few such studies by political scientists, with most of the classics (such as Benny et al., 1956, Brown, 1958, and Holt and Turner, 1968) conducted before the TV-dominated campaigns came to the fore. Butler's analyses of election results had indicated a *uniform swing* in the shift of support between the two main parties (Conservative and Labour) across the entire country (see Butler and Stokes, 1969, 1974), which provided strong circumstantial grounds for concluding that local campaigns had no influence on the outcome: the degree of support for a party was determined by its performance (and that of its leaders) in the national media spotlight, and the whole country moved in the same direction as a consequence. This assumption rapidly gained the status of received wisdom about UK general elections. Local campaigns were dismissed as irrelevant exercises, useful for maintaining local activist interest but little more. The uniform swing was a statistical artefact only, however, and the inferences drawn over-simplified the situation, for two main reasons. First, there was always constituency-to-constituency variation around the national mean figure; the standard deviations were not large at some elections, but nevertheless showed that whatever the national trend some constituencies moved further and some less – which might reflect greater success for the local campaigns in some constituencies relative to others.[1] Secondly, even if the swing were the same everywhere this would not indicate a similar shift in every constituency. As Berrington (1964) had argued early on, and Johnston (1983) later demonstrated, a 2% swing away from Labour in a constituency where it had 70% of the votes at the first contest would involve a much smaller haemorrhage of support than would be the case where its support was only 20%. (It would lose less than 3% of its votes in the first case, but 10% in the second.)

Although these arguments were recognized, the 'received wisdom' became the 'accepted truth' – a situation that prevailed for some time despite an increasing volume of evidence to the contrary. Three groups of researchers studied the local campaigns in different ways – and all reached the same conclusion: local campaigns matter, and the more that a party campaigns in a constituency, relative to its opponents, the better its performance there. One group concentrated their analyses on the reported amount spent by each party on its local campaign in each constituency: there is a legal restriction on that amount, and although parties – specifically candidates and their agents – employed a variety of procedures to circumvent the regulations to some extent,[2] nevertheless in general terms it is apparent that the more intensively a party campaigns in a constituency, the more they also report spending on that campaign. Thus, using the amount spent as a surrogate for the intensity of the local campaign, a range of studies – using a number of statistical methodologies – has shown that campaign intensity and campaign outcomes are linked (see, for example, Johnston, 1987; Pattie, Johnston and Fieldhouse, 1995; Pattie and Johnston, 1996).

The second group of scholars has deployed data gained from surveys of candidates' agents conducted after each of the last three general elections (1992, 1997, 2001). Information was obtained on a range of campaign intensity measures – such as the number of canvassers employed, the number of leaflets printed and distributed, etc. – from which indices of campaign intensity were derived. Regressions of these indices against electoral performance show once again that campaign intensity and outcome are related: the more intense a party's local campaign, relative to its opponents', the better the party does (e.g., Denver and Hands, 1997; and also Denver et al. in this volume). Finally, the third group has used data gathered from surveys of party members to see whether there is a relationship between the amount of reported membership activity and a party's electoral performance at constituency level, with the same results: the more that members of a local party are involved in mobilizing voters in a constituency, the more votes their candidate is likely to get (see Whiteley and Seyd, 1994).

Together, these three bodies of work – along with others which combine variables from the different approaches (e.g., Pattie et al., 1994; Johnston and Pattie, 1997, 1998) – provide strong evidence that challenges the old 'received wisdom' regarding the efficacy of local campaigns. To some extent, this evidence is producing a positive response with changed attitudes to the campaigns' importance, but questions and doubts still remain. Some reflect the aggregate nature of all three approaches: each, in some way, regresses election outcome against party activity and interprets the results as evidence that campaigning matters. Such approaches cannot identify cause-and-effect, however; they show that where parties campaign more they get more votes, but there is no direct evidence that the one produces the other. Indeed, such evidence would be very difficult to obtain – as indicated by comparable research seeking to establish the impact of television coverage on political attitudes (Norris et al., 1999).

It is possible to take the argument forward by combining aggregate and individual level data, however, in ways not previously possible. This is undertaken here with material on the 2001 UK general election. Having reviewed the arguments for the efficacy of local campaigning, the first set of empirical analyses reported here presents the findings from aggregate data analysis that continues the pattern identified at previous elections. The second set builds on these in an original way, using survey data that have not heretofore been collected in a form that allows direct testing of campaign impact. These, too, are consistent with the arguments about local campaign efficacy and provide powerful additional evidence in support of the case developed over the last two decades.

The Role of the Constituency Campaign

Parties are involved in two inter-related functions during election campaigns: convincing people that their policies and personnel are the best on offer; and ensuring that the people who are so convinced actually record a vote for them. As already noted, increasingly the former function is undertaken through the national mass media: the role of the local campaign is not to persuade, but rather to mobilize – to identify those likely to vote for the party and then encourage them to put that likelihood into action at the polling booth or on a postal voting ballot paper.

The mobilization function has traditionally involved party workers visiting members of the electorate at their homes, and inquiring whether they were likely to support the party's candidate at the forthcoming election – an activity accompanied by various publicity campaigns with posters displayed and, especially, leaflets distributed. This information is recorded on a 'marked-up' version of the electoral roll, distinguishing between, for example, definite supporters, possible supporters and those who would not vote for the party/candidate. That roll is then used on election day to inform the party's canvassers. Party activists are placed at the polling stations and ask each voter their name (not how they voted). This information is relayed back to the party's office, and used to check how many of the known (assumed) supporters have voted. As the day proceeds, the local organizers then have a list of those who have not yet voted, who could be targeted in last-minute efforts to persuade them to go the polling station and vote.

This goal remains the central function of the local campaign during the final few weeks before an election. So, in general, do the means of getting the needed information, though they have been enhanced in recent years. Developments in information technology are enabling better storage of records (including from previous elections) and targeting of particular groups of voters, aided by computerized electoral rolls. And an increasing proportion of the contact with voters is being made by telephone – not only from within the constituency by local activists but also by paid staff working in national and regional call centres. To some extent these latter changes are being forced on the parties by the problems of finding activists able and willing to give their time for the canvassing work. But activists are still needed for some parts of the procedure – especially on polling day.

Much campaigning and canvassing effort is dependent on labour power, therefore, either paid or voluntary. Resources are needed too: offices must be obtained and furnished, supplies (such as computerized electoral rolls) must be bought, and so on. And posters and leaflets must be printed, to provide the electorate with information about the candidates seeking their support. Spending is thus a necessary but not a sufficient part of the campaign. At the 2001 election for both Labour and Conservative parties 82% of their reported expenditure in the constituencies was on printing; for the Liberal Democrats it was 92%. This provides the basic materials distributed by canvassers to ensure that voters know (a) that an election is being held in their constituency, and (b) who the party's candidate is.

Such local canvassing is a key part of any party's general election campaign, therefore. And it is becoming increasingly important, despite the nationalization of the overall contest between parties. Many members of the electorate are believed to be increasingly reluctant to go out and vote (although data on a clear trend are difficult to obtain: see Johnston and Pattie, 2001): turnout is falling, for a variety of reasons, some apparently related to long-term attitudes to partisan politics and others to the nature of the current contest. Thus parties need local workers to mobilize turnout, to ensure that their known supporters vote – either in the traditional method at the polling booth on election day or, increasingly given recent changes in the law, through applying for a postal vote beforehand. Pollsters have estimated that about 30% of the electorate comprises the Labour Party's core vote (i.e., people who in normal circumstances are unlikely to vote other than Labour – assuming that they vote at all), with another 30% comprising the Conservative core vote (Worcester and Mortimore, 2001: 9). But they have to be encouraged to cast a ballot at any particular election – especially those among Labour's core, who are less likely to vote out of civic duty (see, for example: Johnston and Pattie, 2001) than Conservative core supporters are.

Of course, in a first-past-the-post electoral system, the need to mobilize a party's supporters is greater in some constituencies than others. In those where a party has little chance of victory the incentive to recruit workers, raise funds and then conduct a canvass is slight: the effort is unlikely to bear valuable fruit. The situation is somewhat similar in constituencies where victory is almost certain. Here, it may be easier to recruit workers (there are likely to be more party members than in the hopeless seats) and to raise funds, but again the effort may bring little reward since victory is virtually assured. The resources are best concentrated in the marginal seats, which the party could either win or lose, and so every vote counts.

In sum, then, local campaigns are predominantly mobilization exercises in which parties identify their likely supporters and seek to ensure that they turn out. (All converts are welcome, of course, but the parties recognize that this is only a marginal concern for these campaigns.) Workers are recruited to perform these tasks, and money is raised to spend on the needed resources – especially the printing of leaflets and other materials designed to promote the party's local image and candidate. Some of this activity will be undertaken everywhere: all candidates want to perform well. But the greatest pressure for intense campaigns is (or should be – see below) in constituencies where the entire election could be won or lost – in the marginals where mobilizing as much potential support as possible is crucial.

Modelling the Relationships

If the goal of a party's local campaign is to mobilize as many of its potential votes as possible, which might otherwise be abstentions, if not votes for another party, then any attempt to model this statistically should focus on the extent to which a campaign's intensity – as indexed by the amount reportedly spent on it – succeeds. A method of doing that was proposed in 1994 (Johnston and Pattie, 1995), and is applied in modified form here.

Take the local campaigns run by the Labour Party. The goal is to increase its share of the vote relative to the result at the previous election. If there is a uniform shift in support across all constituencies between elections, and the proportion of abstainers remains constant, then there should be a perfect relationship between the ratio of Labour to non-Labour votes at one election and the next.

$$L_2/NL_2 = f (L_1/NL_1) \qquad (1)$$

where

L/NL is the ratio of votes for Labour to votes for other parties; and
the subscripts 1 and 2 refer to the first and second elections respectively.

This can be evaluated using linear regression, whereby

$$L_2/ NL_2 = a + b(L_1/NL_1) \qquad (2)$$

where
a is a constant indicating the size of the inter-election shift;
b is 1.0;
and the correlation coefficient (r) is 1.0.

The Labour Party's goal is to reduce that correlation coefficient, increasing the value of L_2/NL_2 by the intensity of its campaign in some constituencies. The other parties will aim at reducing the value of L_2/NL_2, giving a model of the form

$$L_2/NL_2 = f (L_1/NL_1, LS_2, OS_2) \qquad (3)$$

where

LS_2 is spending by Labour during the second election campaign; and
OS_2 is spending by the other parties during the second election campaign.

In regression terms, this would appear as

$$L_2/ NL_2 = a + b_1(L_1/NL_1) + b_2LS_2 - b_3 OS_2 \qquad (4)$$

We evaluate that model in the next section, using data for the 2001 general election in England. (Scotland and Wales are excluded because they have four-party systems compared to England's three-party system. Their inclusion would introduce variations in the potential size of OS_2 across constituencies.)

Party Rationality

One potential difficulty with these models is that if each party acts both rationally and to the greatest efficacy, then in any one constituency the parties should be campaigning at the same intensity, thereby cancelling out each other's attempts to increase their vote shares. Given the earlier discussion of the importance of winning marginal seats, then the parties should campaign most in such places, and least in the seats which either they expect to win easily – based on their past performance there – or where they have little hope of victory.

Figures 1A–1C show that such targeting of campaigns characterized each of England's three political parties in 2001, though the form of the relationship between expenditure (as a percentage of the maximum allowed in each constituency) and marginality varied.[3] Marginality was measured thus: (a) in constituencies that the party won in 1997, the percentage points distance between that party's share of the votes cast in 1997 and the second-placed party's share; and (b) in constituencies that the party lost in 1997, the distance between its share and that of the winning candidate. In the graphs, negative marginality values refer to constituencies that the party lost in 1997, and positive values to constituencies that they won.

All three parties spent least in the constituencies where they lost badly in 1997, with the amount spent increasing the smaller the gap between them and the winning party. Their maximum expenditure was in the marginal constituencies – both those where they had a chance of winning (a margin of –20 or less) and which they held by small margins (between 0 and 20). But the Conservative Party also spent close to the limits in safe seats which it stood little chance of losing: with Labour, the larger its margin of victory in 1997 the smaller its expenditure on the subsequent campaign. The Conservatives spent to the limit defending everything they held: Labour were less concerned to conduct intensive campaigns in their safer seats – of which they had many more than the Conservatives. The Liberal Democrats had very few safe seats, so there was no significant fall in expenditure to the right-hand edge of the graph.

FIGURE 1A
CONSERVATIVE SPENDING AT THE 2001 GENERAL ELECTION (AS A
PERCENTAGE OF THE ALLOWED MAXIMUM) BY MAJORITY AT THE 1997
ELECTION IN ENGLAND

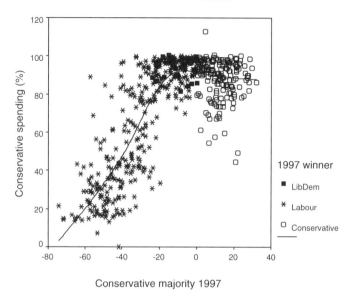

Conservative majority 1997

Note: A positive margin indicates a Conservative-held seat. The best-fit line is a lowest moving average.

Figures 1A–1C suggest that each of the parties was rational in targeting its constituency campaigns on the marginal constituencies, although there was considerable scatter about the best-fit lines. So did their spending largely counter that of their opponents? Figure 2A, which compares Labour and Conservative spending across all constituencies, suggests not: indeed quite the opposite – the correlation between the two variables across all 521 constituencies was only 0.04.[4] But those parties were unlikely to counter each other's spending in a number of constituencies because the main competitor was from the Liberal Democrats. So Figure 2B looks at the 391 constituencies where the Conservatives and Labour occupied first and second places in 1997: again there is virtually no relationship (r=0.18). And even when we look just at the most marginal seats (those where the margin of victory between those two parties was less than 10 percentage points in 1997), the values for the 95 constituencies were widely scattered (see Figure 2C: r = 0.22). Restricting the analysis yet further to the most marginal seats (where victory was achieved by less than 5 percentage points in 1997) brings no improvement: an r value across the 36 constituencies of only 0.07.

FIGURE 1B
LABOUR SPENDING AT THE 2001 GENERAL ELECITON (AS A PERCENTAGE OF
THE ALLOWED MAXIMUM) BY MAJORITY AT THE 1997 ELECTION IN ENGLAND

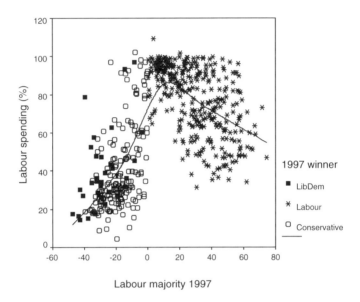

Labour majority 1997

Note: A positive margin indicates a Labour-held seat. The best-fit line is a lowest moving average.

Although each of the parties on average spent more in marginal than in safe/hopeless constituencies, therefore, there was no matching of campaign intensity in each constituency. So were the variations in spending reflected in the election outcome? To answer this we return to model (4) above.

Spending and Votes in England at the 2001 General Election

The Aggregate-Level Pattern

To evaluate model (4) we regressed each party's vote total in 2001 divided by the vote total obtained by its two competitors against:

- the same ratio in 1997;
- that party's spending (as a percentage of the allowed maximum, giving a range of values from 0 to 100); and
- its opponents' total spending (a range from 0 to 200).

FIGURE 1C

LIBERAL DEMOCRAT SPENDING AT THE 2001 GENERAL ELECTION (AS A
PERCENTAGE OF THE ALLOWED MAXIMUM) BY MAJORITY AT THE
1997 ELECTION IN ENGLAND

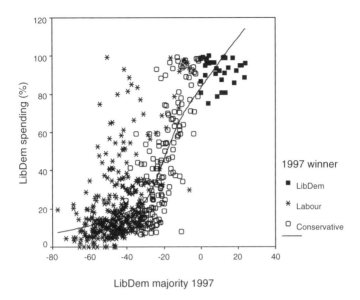

LibDem majority 1997

Note: A positive margin indicates a Liberal Democrat-held seat. The best-fit line is a lowest moving average.

In each case we used a stepwise procedure: at the first step the only independent variable was the ratio for 1997; at the second, the two spending variables were introduced.

The results for all 521 constituencies are reported in Table 1. They show, not surprisingly, that in each case the main influence on the election outcome in 2001 was the 1997 outcome: each party's share of the vote total relative to that of its opponents was fairly consistent across the two contests. But they also show that the two spending variables were significant in every case, and had the expected signs. The more that each party spent the better its performance relative to its opponents', but the more that its opponents spent, the poorer its own performance. Labour and Liberal Democrat spending was more effective than their opponents' – the positive b_1 coefficients are larger than the negative b_2 coefficients. But for the Conservatives, their opponents' campaigning had a greater impact than did their own.

FIGURE 2A
LABOUR AND CONSERVATIVE SPENDING (AS A PERCENTAGE OF THE
ALLOWED CONSTITUENCY MAXIMUM) AT THE 2001 GENERAL ELECTION
IN ENGLAND

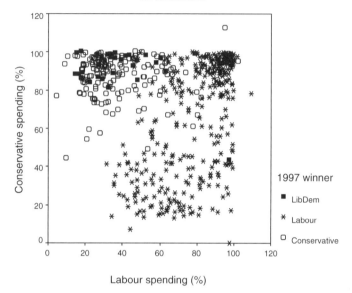

Labour spending (%)

TABLE 1
CAMPAIGN SPENDING AND ELECTION RESULTS IN ENGLAND:
2001 GENERAL ELECTION

	a	$b1$	$b2$	$b3$	R^2
All constituencies					
Conservative	0.002	**1.049**			0.918
	0.005	**1.006**	**0.049**	**−0.067**	0.922
Labour	0.100	**0.802**			0.934
	0.199	**0.740**	**0.158**	**−0.118**	0.939
Liberal Democrat	0.021	**0.997**			0.840
	0.060	**0.805**	**0.182**	**−0.037**	0.858
Marginal constituencies: Labour–Conservative contests					
Conservative	−0.229	**1.395**			0.700
	−0.050	**1.098**	**0.019**	**−0.013**	0.744
Labour	0.012	**1.002**			0.588
	−0.018	**0.779**	**0.024**	−0.002	0.658

Notes: Significant regression coefficients at the 0.10 level are shown in bold. The column
headings relate to the coefficients in model (4).

FIGURE 2B
LABOUR AND CONSERVATIVE SPENDING (AS A PERCENTAGE OF THE
ALLOWED CONSTITUENCY MAXIMUM) AT THE 2001 GENERAL ELECTION IN
ENGLAND: LABOUR/CONSERVATIVE CONTESTS

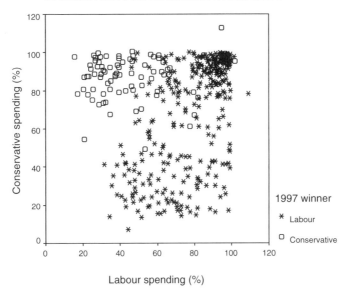

Labour spending (%)

Note: Data relates to constituencies where Labour and Conservative occupied the first two places in 1997.

The differences in the size of the regression coefficients for the spending variables reflect differences already noted between the parties – especially Labour and the Conservatives – in mobilizing their core supporters. In general, the Conservative core voters are more likely to turn out irrespective of the intensity of the local campaign than is the case with Labour voters – hence the smaller coefficients for the Conservatives: with fewer potential voters to be turned out, the less the impact of the campaign spending. Labour core supporters are more reluctant to go to the ballot box, so the effect of the campaign is greater. The Liberal Democrat core is small, and many of its voters have been encouraged to support its candidates for tactical considerations in marginal constituencies – hence Whiteley and Seyd's (2002) conclusion regarding the crucial importance of campaign intensity for the party at the constituency level.

Across all constituencies, therefore, campaign intensity as measured by party spending was related to the outcome. The correlation coefficients in Table 1 indicate that these relationships were significant, but also suggest

FIGURE 2C
LABOUR AND CONSERVATIVE SPENDING (AS A PERCENTAGE OF THE
ALLOWED CONSTITUENCY MAXIMUM) AT THE 2001 GENERAL ELECTION IN
ENGLAND: LABOUR/CONSERVATIVE MARGINALS

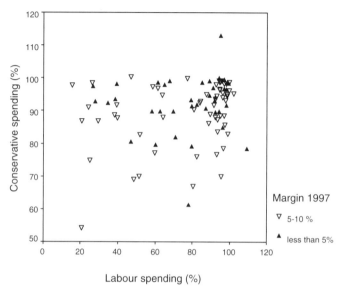

Labour spending (%)

Note: Data relate to constituencies where Labour and Conservative occupied the first two places in 1997 and the margin between the two was less than ten percentage points.

that they were relatively minor. Continuity in the pattern of votes across constituencies has characterized English election results for almost a century, however. Ever since the Conservative and Labour parties came to dominate the electoral scene in the late 1920s each has performed well in the same places at virtually every election: the relative relief on the 'topographic' map of Labour support has remained virtually constant, therefore, although the absolute relief has changed as Labour's national standing has waxed and waned. Very high correlations for the first step in the regression analyses are therefore not surprising. What is important for these analyses is that the spending variables account for some of the residual variation – for the deviations from the general pattern of change (the ups and downs of the relief map). This is especially so in the case of the Liberal Democrats, who gain much less public attention between elections and rely more than their opponents on effective local campaigns at election time to improve their visibility – and hence their performance.

Campaigning is linked to (and presumably influences) results, therefore, but does it influence them where it really matters – in the marginal constituencies where, in effect, elections are won and lost? To answer this, the second block in Table 1 reports on regressions run only for the 95 constituencies where the Conservative and Labour candidates occupied the first two places in 1997 and the margin of victory then was less than ten percentage points. In these, there was greater variation in the pattern of vote share between the two elections – as shown by the much smaller correlation coefficients. And spending also mattered – to a greater relative extent – in accounting for the residual variation in the 2001 results. For the Conservatives, the more that they spent the better their performance, which was countered by the negative effect of their opponents' spending – though the larger coefficient in the former case indicates that, contrary to the finding for all seats, Conservative spending was the more efficacious; intense Conservative campaigns in marginal constituencies really ensure that the core supporters turn out, it seems. For Labour, only its own spending had a significant (and quite substantial) impact on the outcome; the amount spent by the Conservatives and the Liberal Democrats did not cut into Labour's lead over its opponents in these marginal seats.[5]

Prior to the 2001 election, there was a great deal of speculation that turnout would be much lower than ever before, and Labour politicians in particular were concerned that an increase in abstentions could damage their prospects, especially in marginal seats. (The stated reason for this fear was that too many Labour supporters would abstain because they thought a Labour victory certain; some commentators, however, believed that many traditional Labour supporters would abstain because of their alienation from New Labour.) The overall predictions were right, and turnout fell by some 13 percentage points – though less in the marginal seats where the parties campaigned most. And Labour's focused campaigns on the marginal seats clearly helped: the more that it spent, the greater its share of the votes relative to the Conservatives, and (along with Liberal Democrat spending) the smaller the Conservative share relative to the two other parties. Labour spending paid off. (It paid off, too, in the non-marginal seats: wherever Labour campaigned intensively, it improved its vote share relative to 1997.) As a consequence, turnout fell by less the greater the expenditure by all three parties.[6]

The Individual-Level Pattern

To test whether the patterns that come through at the aggregate level (and have done in analyses of all general elections since 1950: Johnston, 1987) also appear at the individual level, we use data from the 2001 British Election Study (BES). Unlike its predecessor, this had the advantage for studies of local campaigns that it included a substantial before-and-after design. A sample of voters was questioned 2–3 months before the election (in March 2001), and as many respondents as possible were re-interviewed soon after the election on 7 June.

In the pre-election survey, respondents were asked whether they had decided how to vote when the election was held and, if not, which party they were leaning towards. These questions identify each party's potential supporters, plus the strength of that potential. After the election, they were asked which party – if any – they voted for. They were also asked whether they were called on at their home by a canvasser from any party, whether any party telephoned them during the campaign, whether any party contacted them on election day to see if they had voted, and whether they had seen any of the parties' election broadcasts (PEBs). Together, these variables identify the degree to which voters were subject to canvassing during the campaign, and also whether they had been exposed to one aspect of the national campaign (the PEBs), all of which may have influenced their final voting decision. In addition, we were able to add data on the amount spent on the local campaign in each respondent's constituency as an index of campaign intensity there and exposure to party mobilization strategies.

As expected, the parties campaigned most intensively in those constituencies where votes mattered most to them. In Table 2, we have divided the respondents providing information to both pre- and the post-election surveys according to their constituency electoral situation, into six types:

Marginals (margin of victory in 1997 less than 5 percentage points):
1. Conservative and Labour parties in first and second places, 1997
2. Conservative and Liberal Democrat parties in first and second places, 1997

Winnables (margin of victory in 1997 5–10 percentage points):
3. Conservative and Labour parties in first and second places, 1997
4. Conservative and Liberal Democrat parties in first and second places, 1997

Safe (margin of victory in 1997 10–19 percentage points):
5. All constituencies

Ultra-safe (margin of victory in 1997 20 or more percentage points):
6. All constituencies

(Note that there were too few respondents to allow separate study of the small number of constituencies where Labour and the Liberal Democrats occupied the first two places in 1997.) Each of the parties canvassed support much more in the marginal seats where it was involved than in those where it was not (with some exceptions relating to the Liberal Democrats), and each spent much more on local campaigns in the marginals. But there was, not surprisingly, no relationship between constituency marginality and whether a respondent had seen any of a party's PEBs.

TABLE 2
CONSTITUENCY CAMPAIGNING BY MARGINALITY:
SURVEY RESPONDENTS CONTACTED BY THE PARTIES (%)

	Seat Type					
	Marginals		Winnables		Safe	Ultra-Safe
	C:L	C:LD	C:L	C:LD		
Canvassed by Labour	10.2	8.3	10.7	1.2	6.5	8.0
Phoned by Labour	8.5	2.1	5.3	0.0	3.3	1.4
Election day by Labour	5.1	0.0	2.9	0.0	2.3	1.2
Saw Labour PEB	31.6	45.8	35.9	37.3	38.0	39.2
Canvassed by Conservatives	9.0	25.0	11.2	10.8	9.8	3.7
Phoned by Conservatives	5.1	2.1	2.9	3.6	4.2	0.8
Election day by Conservatives	2.8	2.1	0.5	1.2	1.7	0.3
Saw Conservatives PEB	28.8	43.8	34.0	32.5	36.5	35.1
Canvassed by LibDem	4.5	18.8	3.9	13.3	7.8	2.1
Phoned by LibDem	1.1	0.0	1.0	2.4	0.8	0.3
Election day by LibDem	1.1	0.0	0.0	8.4	1.0	0.3
Saw LibDem PEB	26.6	43.8	29.1	28.9	32.5	31.0
Mean Labour spending	70.8	25.0	73.8	52.7	57.6	66.9
Mean Conservative spending	89.6	97.4	93.5	88.9	88.3	47.9
Mean LibDem spending	35.6	86.1	24.4	91.4	45.0	18.0
N	177	48	206	83	779	1772

Note: C:L – constituencies where the Conservative and Labour parties occupied first and second places in 1997; C:LD – constituencies where the Conservative and Liberal Democrat parties occupied first and second places in 1997.

Each party's potential voters were exposed to its canvassing and PEBs during the campaign period, therefore. If our models tested at the aggregate level are valid representations of what happens, those who were so exposed should have been more likely to cast their vote for the party concerned than those who were not. Table 3 suggests that this was the case among the 1341 respondents who indicated that they were potential Labour voters in the pre-election survey, of whom 70.5% said that they intended to vote Labour and the remainder were leaning towards Labour. Of these, the first column shows that, for example, 8.9% were canvassed by Labour during the campaign and 42.1% had seen a Labour PEB. Of the 689 who actually voted Labour on 7 June, a larger percentage had intended to do so from the outset (79.1%: i.e. Labour was better at mobilizing the firm intentions than it was the 'leaners'), had been canvassed by Labour (either on the doorstep or by phone: 14.2% and 4.8% respectively, compared to 8.9% and 2.9% among all 'Labour intenders'), had been contacted by Labour on election day (5.1% rather than 2.8%), and had seen at least one of the party's PEBs (60.4% rather than 42.1%).

TABLE 3
THE CAMPAIGN AND POTENTIAL LABOUR VOTERS, 2001:
THOSE WHO INDICATED IN A PRE-ELECTION SURVEY THAT THEY WERE
LIKELY TO VOTE LABOUR (%)

	All	Voted Labour	Voted LibDem	Abstained
Intended to vote Labour	70.5	79.1	52.4	56.7
Canvassed by Labour	8.9	14.2	6.1	6.7
Phoned by Labour	2.9	4.8	1.2	1.5
Election day by Labour	2.8	5.1	1.2	1.0
Saw Labour PEB	42.1	60.4	61.0	40.2
Canvassed by Conservatives	5.6	8.6	6.1	4.1
Phoned by Conservatives	1.6	2.2	1.2	2.1
Election day by Conservatives	0.6	0.7	0.0	1.0
Saw Conservatives PEB	35.8	51.2	46.3	35.1
Canvassed by LibDem	3.8	5.4	4.9	4.1
Phoned by LibDem	0.3	0.4	0.0	0.0
Election day by LibDem	0.9	1.2	3.7	0.5
Saw LibDem PEB	33.0	47.6	59.8	25.8
Mean Labour spending	67.0	69.3	54.3	66.5
Mean Conservative spending	61.4	60.2	73.5	61.1
Mean LibDem spending	25.4	24.2	44.8	25.4
N	1341	689	82	194

Of those who voted Liberal Democrat despite having initially indicated that they were likely to vote Labour, on the other hand, many fewer had been canvassed or contacted by Labour and many more had been contacted by the Liberal Democrats, especially on election day, than was the case among all potential Labour voters: many more, too, had seen a Liberal Democrat PEB. The clear implication is that the voters targeted by the Liberal Democrats were more likely to switch their allegiance, especially if they were not also contacted by Labour.

Very few potential Labour voters eventually voted for the Conservative Party, so it is not possible to derive similar data for that group. But almost 15% of those who either intended to vote Labour or were leaning in that direction eventually abstained, with that percentage being much greater among the latter category of potential Labour voters. There was much less contact between any of the parties and these respondents during the campaign period (though as many had seen Labour and Conservative PEBs), suggesting that abstention was much more likely among those potential supporters who were not contacted by the party in efforts to convert that potential into actual votes.

Similar patterns to those shown in Table 3 characterize potential voters for each of the other two parties (they are not shown here). Thus we have considerable circumstantial evidence that potential voters who were contacted by a party during the campaign were much more likely to vote for it. To test that conclusion more formally, we employed logistic regression, looking in turn at each party's potential supporters. We hypothesized that realizing that potential would be a function of three sets of variables:

$$Vp = f (FIp, CApp, Spp) \tag{5}$$

where

$Vp = 1$ if the respondent voted for party p, 0 otherwise;
$FIp = $ the firmness of the respondent's intention to vote for party p, as expressed in the pre-election survey;
$CApp = $ the amount of canvassing and other activity the respondent was exposed to from the parties involved; and
$Spp = $ the amount of campaign spending by the parties.

In regression terms, in analyses for the Labour Party – involving only those who indicated in the pre-election survey that they were either intending to vote Labour or leaning towards Labour – this was operationalized as:

$$V_L = a + b_1(I_L) + b_2(S_L) + b_3(C_L) + b_4(P_L) + b_5(ED_L) + b_6(L_{PEB}) \tag{6}$$

where

$V_L = $ voted Labour (coded 1; 0 otherwise)
$I_L = $ coded 1 if they intended to vote Labour: 0 if they were only leaning towards it;
$S_L = $ spending by Labour in the respondent's constituency

C_L = respondent was canvassed at home by Labour (coded 1; 0 otherwise)

P_L = respondent was phoned by Labour (coded 1; 0 otherwise)

ED_L = respondent was contacted by Labour on election day (coded 1; 0 otherwise)

L_{PEB} = respondent saw at least one of Labour's PEBs (coded 1; 0 otherwise)

For those who were potential Labour voters at the start of the campaign, but actually voted Liberal Democrat, the equation was:

$$V_{LD} = a + b_1(I_L) + b_2(S_L) + b_3(C_L) + b_4(P_L) + b_5(ED_L) + b_6(L_{PEB}) - b_7(S_{LD}) - b_8(C_{LD}) - b_9(P_{LD}) - b_{10}(ED_{LD}) - b_{11}(LD_{PEB}) \tag{7}$$

where the variables are as in equation (6), with the subscript LD referring to the Liberal Democrat Party.

Finally, for those who were intending to vote Labour but actually abstained, the regression was:

$$V_A = a - b_1(I_L) - b_2(S_L) - b_3(C_L) - b_4(P_L) - b_5(ED_L) - b_6(L_{PEB}) \tag{8}$$

where

V_A = the respondent abstained (coded 1; 0 otherwise)

Similar regression equations were derived for the other parties.

Table 4 gives the results of these regressions for those respondents who indicated in the pre-election survey that they either intended to vote Labour or were leaning towards that party. All three regressions have significant coefficients for the firmness of that vote intention, with the expected signs: those who intended to vote Labour were much more likely to do so than those who were only leaning towards the party, and much less likely either to vote Liberal Democrat or to abstain. The most committed to Labour when the campaign began were most likely to vote for it on election day.

But did the campaign also have an influence? In general terms, the answer is yes – given the significant relationships with spending. The more intensive the Labour campaign, as indexed by the amount spent in the constituency (most of which went on printing leaflets and posters), the greater the likelihood that respondents would vote Labour – and not vote Liberal Democrat: countering that, the more that the Liberal Democrats spent, the greater the likelihood that they converted some potential Labour

TABLE 4
LOCAL CAMPAIGNING AND VOTING OUTCOME:
LABOUR POTENTIAL VOTERS AT START OF THE 2001 CAMPAIGN –
LOGISTIC REGRESSIONS

	Labour	LibDem	Abstain
Intended to vote Labour	**0.80**	**–0.84**	**–0.70**
Labour spending	**0.005**	**–0.011**	–0.000
LibDem spending		**0.020**	
Canvassed by Labour	**1.24**	–0.29	–0.19
Phoned by Labour	**1.08**	–0.97	–0.43
Election day by Labour	**2.17**	–0.48	–0.96
Saw Labour PEB	**1.62**	0.01	–0.01
Canvassed by LibDem		–0.61	
Phoned by LibDem		–5.63	
Election day by LibDem		**1.34**	
Saw LibDem PEB		**1.35**	
Correctly classified (%)			
Total	72.3	94.0	85.5
Dependent variable	67.1	6.1	0.0
Nagelkerke R^2	0.28	0.19	0.03

Note: Significant regression coefficients at the 0.10 level are shown in bold.

voters to their cause. And contact with the voters paid off too: those canvassed or phoned by Labour, as well as those contacted on polling day, were more likely to vote Labour than those who were not: and those contacted on polling day by the Liberal Democrats were more likely to switch their support (though this did not apply also to canvassing). Contact with Labour did not apparently stem the flow to the Liberal Democrats, however: all of the coefficients for specific Labour campaign activity are insignificant in the second equation. And the party election broadcasts were also influential: those who saw a Labour PEB were more likely to vote Labour than those who did not: those who saw a Liberal Democrat PEB were more likely to switch support to that party.

More intensive campaigns, however measured, did not influence the proportion who abstained, however. The more committed were more likely to turn out on election day, but understanding why some abstained – far from an easy task, as many are finding (Whiteley et al., 2001; Worcester and Mortimore, 2001; Johnston and Pattie, 2003) – is not advanced by looking at the intensity of local campaigns.

Tables 5 and 6 report similar analyses for those respondents who indicated support for the Conservatives and Liberal Democrats respectively in the pre-election survey. In general terms, they confirm the results of the Labour analyses – though the measure of goodness-of-fit employed (Nagelkerke's R^2) indicates that the models fitted better for pro-Labour respondents. Among those inclined to vote Conservative at the start of the campaign (Table 5), the more intensive the Conservative campaign and the greater the level of campaign contact with the party, the greater the probability of a Conservative vote at the election (although election day contact with the party was insignificant, again suggesting that Conservative core voters do not need much last-minute encouragement to turn out on polling day). Those canvassed by the Liberal Democrats were the most likely to change their voting intention. Again, apart from the fact that Conservative 'leaners' were less likely to turn out than those firmly intending to vote for the party, there was little explanation for the pattern of abstentions. The same was true for those favouring the Liberal Democrats but who eventually abstained (Table 6): furthermore, contact with the Liberal Democrats during the campaign had no significant effect on the final outcome – the small number of committed Liberal Democrat supporters did not need to be canvassed in order to ensure that they voted!

TABLE 5
LOCAL CAMPAIGNING AND VOTING OUTCOME:
CONSERVATIVE POTENTIAL VOTERS AT START OF THE 2001 CAMPAIGN –
LOGISTIC REGRESSIONS

	Conservative	LibDem	Abstain
Intended to vote Conservative	**0.51**	**–0.69**	**–0.50**
Conservative spending	**0.006**	–0.001	–0.002
LibDem spending		0.004	
Canvassed by Conservatives	**0.69**	**–1.57**	0.48
Phoned by Conservatives	**1.63**	**–6.68**	–5.67
Election day by Conservatives	–0.06	–5.95	0.84
Saw Conservatives PEB	**1.25**	0.81	0.04
Canvassed by LibDem		**1.21**	
Phoned by LibDem		**2.16**	
Election day by LibDem		1.54	
Saw LibDem PEB		0.14	
Correctly classified (%)			
Total	68.0	94.7	85.6
Dependent variable	59.0	4.9	0.0
Nagelkerke R^2	0.18	0.12	0.04

Note: Significant regression coefficients at the 0.10 level are shown in bold.

TABLE 6
LOCAL CAMPAIGNING AND VOTING OUTCOME:
LIBERAL DEMOCRAT POTENTIAL VOTERS AT START OF THE 2001 CAMPAIGN –
LOGISTIC REGRESSIONS

	LibDem	Abstain
Intended to vote LibDem	**0.78**	**–0.37**
LibDem spending	**0.008**	–0.002
Canvassed by LibDem	0.52	0.56
Phoned by LibDem	1.22	0.74
Election day by LibDem	–1.27	0.92
Saw LibDem PEB	**1.60**	–0.12
Correctly classified (%)		
Total	71.8	86.6
Dependent variable	63.2	0.0
Nagelkerke R^2	0.27	0.02

Note: Significant regression coefficients at the 0.10 level are shown in bold.

Finally, Table 7 reports analyses of respondents who were undecided at the time of the pre-election survey – i.e., were not even leaning towards one of the parties. Here again, the goodness-of-fit measures are small, but there are nevertheless clear indicators that the campaign had an impact on converting those 'waverers' into voters for one of the three parties. (But there was no success in trying to account for those who abstained; the equation is not given here.) Thus the more that each of the parties spent on their constituency campaigns, the more likely they were to attract votes from the undecided: in addition the more that the Conservatives and Liberal Democrats spent, the less successful were Labour, and similarly intensive Labour campaigns reduced the probability of a Conservative vote. In general terms, intensive local campaigns helped to win over the undecided. In addition, each party's PEBs were influential: if respondents saw one or more of these (which may, of course, be a self-selective process), they were more likely to vote for the party which produced them. But canvassing their support did not help: the undecideds were to some extent influenced by the intensity of the local campaigns (as indexed by the relationships with the spending variables), but their decisions on which party to support were not (with one exception: Labour contact on polling day) apparently influenced by personal contacts (most of which are designed not to convert but rather just to identify support and then make sure it is expressed on a voting slip).

TABLE 7
LOCAL CAMPAIGNING AND VOTING OUTCOME:
UNDECIDED VOTERS AT START OF THE 2001 CAMPAIGN
– LOGISTIC REGRESSIONS

	Labour	*Conservative*	*LibDem*
Labour spending	**0.007**	**–0.005**	–0.003
Conservative spending	**–0.006**	**0.014**	0.000
LibDem spending	**–0.011**	–0.006	**0.016**
Canvassed by Labour	0.41		
Phoned by Labour	0.49		
Election day by Labour	**1.43**		
Saw Labour PEB	**0.96**		
Canvassed by Conservatives		0.51	
Phoned by Conservatives		0.47	
Election day by Conservatives		0.77	
Saw Conservatives PEB		**0.80**	
Canvassed by LibDem			0.50
Phoned by LibDem			0.44
Election day by LibDem			0.02
Saw LibDem PEB			**1.06**
Correctly classified (%)			
Total	82.4	87.3	87.9
Dependent variable	2.7	0.0	2.6
Nagelkerke R^2	0.11	0.08	0.11

Note: Significant regression coefficients at the 0.10 level are shown in bold.

Conclusions

The challengers to the 'conventional wisdom' regarding the irrelevance of constituency campaigning at UK general elections have more than sustained their case through analyses at the aggregate level: a party's performance in a constituency is linked to how intensively both it and its opponents campaign there. These arguments have been sustained by the analyses reported here for the most recent general election in England.

There is always the possibility of an ecological fallacy being committed with such data – of assuming that the aggregate pattern applies to the individual. In this context, the assumption is that the more people are exposed to parties' attempts to get them to turn out and vote, the more likely they are to do so. To be sure that is not the case, individual-level analyses are needed. The 2001 BES provided an excellent opportunity for this, not only because it collected data on whether people were contacted by the parties during the campaign period, but also on how they intended to vote before the campaign started – thus allowing tests for whether those exposed to a party's canvassing and campaigning were more likely to follow through on their original intention. The results have confirmed the ecological scale findings: people's intentions to vote in a certain way are more likely to be fulfilled if they are contacted by their chosen party and that party also campaigns intensively in the constituency; they are less likely to be fulfilled if their original intention was fairly weak and another party campaigned hard for their support.

Voters make choices when they go to the polling booth. For some, that choice is readily made, as they always vote for the same party. For many others, the outcome is not so predetermined: they want to be convinced, and that calls for information. Some may be interested enough in politics and the election outcome to seek out relevant information, but many will not bother, and instead rely on the information that reaches them – directly or indirectly – from the parties competing for their support. Information is key (as Downs, 1957, argued), but it is costly to accumulate: those without the necessary resources (money, time and inclination) may take the least-cost route, and make their choice on the basis of what is provided free-of-charge, or virtually so. And so, for those who are making up their minds how to vote during the campaign, information – campaigning materials – matters.

But even when they have information and know who they support, are they necessarily convinced that it is worthwhile taking the time and effort to visit a polling station and vote? Again, for some it is – they think it important to vote, not only for the personal benefits that might accrue if their chosen party gets into power but also because they think it important that they exercise their democratic duty. Others may be less civic-minded – lazier, perhaps, but also less convinced either that their vote will make a difference or that it matters much which party wins the election. They need to be mobilized, to be convinced their vote is needed – which again means they need information, they need the party to call on them (in some way or another, directly or indirectly) and assure them. Party constituency campaigns are thus necessary to galvanize that portion of the electorate which is less than fully convinced that going to the polling booth is important. Information is needed to turn out the vote.

The value of that information has been clearly demonstrated here for the most recent general election in England. At the ecological level we have demonstrated – yet again – that where the parties campaign hardest, they tend to perform best: at the individual level, we have shown (for the first time) that parties perform best with those voters exposed to such campaign information and other techniques and resources. Of course, we have not established a causal link at the individual level – that being canvassed by a party 'made' people go out and vote for it: actually identifying such links may be extremely difficult, if not impossible. But we have produced sufficient evidence to ensure that claims of the irrelevance of local campaigns can now readily be rebutted: local activity matters!

ACKNOWLEDGEMENTS

The 2001 BES was conducted at the University of Essex, directed by David Sanders, Paul Whiteley, Harold Clarke and Marianne Stewart. We are grateful to them for their work on this, not least the early release of the data. The spending data by constituency were released by the Electoral Commission (see Electoral Commission, 2002).

NOTES

1. For instance, the average swing from Labour to Conservative between 1955 and 1959 (excluding seats uncontested by one or other of the parties in at least one of the elections) was 0.9%, with a standard deviation of 2.3%. But the swing in some seats was much greater. At one extreme, in Glasgow Cathcart, the swing from Conservative to Labour was 13.4%; at the other, in Anglesey, the swing from Labour to Conservative was 7.6%

2. A range of different strategies are used to get around the spending limits, many of them outlined in the journalist Michael Crick's evidence to the 1998 Neil Committee inquiry into the funding of political parties. For instance, a local party might pay for casual help in cash, with no receipts. There is then no auditable record of the transaction. Mass mailings might be sent out using normal stamps, rather than a franking machine: again, this makes it hard to obtain an auditable record of expenditure. Alternatively, printing materials might be bought in two or three tranches, with only one tranche declared in the expenditure accounts. Telephone canvassing, meanwhile, is on the increase, but is potentially hard to audit, especially when calls are made from activists' own homes on private telephones (even more so when the calls themselves are made from outwith the constituency).

3. The constituency spending limits for the 2001 election were: £5,483 plus 6.2 pence for each registered elector in a county constituency, or plus 4.6 pence per elector in a borough constituency. The actual limit for a given seat therefore depended both on whether it was designated as county or borough (crudely, rural or urban), and how many voters lived there. But in the average constituency, the spending limit for 2001 was £9,182, and over 80% of constituencies had limits within ±£1000 of this.

4. We excluded two constituencies from all of the analyses: Tatton, where there was no Labour or Liberal Democrat candidate in 1997; and West Bromwich West, where the Speaker stood for re-election unopposed by candidates of the main parties in 1997.

5. If we model the ratio of Conservative to Labour voting only in those Con–Lab marginals (i.e. exclude the Liberal Democrats), we find that Labour spending has a significant negative impact on the ratio (the more that Labour spent, the better its performance in 2001 relative to that in 1997), but that the relationship with Conservative spending is insignificant – comparable findings to those for previous elections (Johnston and Pattie, 1997).

6. Across all constituencies, the regression of turnout in 2001 (Y) against turnout in 1997 (X1) and total spending by the three parties (X_2) was $-15.73 + 1.018(X_1) + 0.117(X_2)$, with an R^2 of 0.86.

REFERENCES

Benny, M., A.P. Gray and R. Pear (1956), *How People Vote: A Study of Electoral Behaviour in Greenwich*. London: Routledge & Kegan Paul.

Berrington, H. (1964) 'The General Election of 1964', *Journal of the Royal Statistical Society, Series A* 128: 17–66.

Brown, J. (1958) 'Local Party Efficiency as a Factor in the Outcome of British Elections', *Political Studies* 6: 174–8.

Butler, D. E. and D. Stokes (1969) *Political Change in Britain*. London: Macmillan.

Butler, D. E. and D. Stokes (1974) *Electoral Change in Britain*. London: Macmillan, 2nd edition.

Denver, D. T. and G. Hands (1997) *Modern Constituency Electioneering: The 1992 General Election*. London and Portland, OR: Frank Cass.

Downs, A. (1957) *An Economic Theory of Democracy*. New York: Harper Collins.

Electoral Commission (2002) *Election 2001 Campaign Spending*. London: The Electoral Commission, accessed on www.electoralcommission.org.uk.

Holt, A.T. and J.E. Turner (1968) *Political Parties in Action*. New York: The Free Press.

Johnston, R.J. (1983) 'Spatial Continuity and Individual Variability', *Electoral Studies* 2: 53–68.

Johnston, R.J. (1987) *Money and Votes*. London: Croom Helm.

Johnston, R.J. and C.J. Pattie (1995) 'The Impact of Spending on Party Constituency Campaigns at recent British General Elections', *Party Politics* 1: 261–74.

Johnston, R.J. and C.J. Pattie (1997) 'Where's the Difference? Decomposing the Impact of Local Election Campaigns in Great Britain', *Electoral Studies* 16: 165–74.

Johnston, R.J. and C.J. Pattie (1998) 'Campaigning and Advertising: An Evaluation of the Components of Constituency Activism at Recent British General Elections', *British Journal of Political Science* 28: 677–86.

Johnston, R.J. and C.J. Pattie (2001) 'Is There a Crisis of Democracy in Great Britain? Turnout at General Elections Reconsidered', in K. Dowding, J. Hughes and H. Margetts (eds.) *Challenges to Democracy: Ideas, Involvement and Institutions*. London: Palgrave, pp.61–80.

Johnston, R.J. and C.J. Pattie (2003) 'The Growing Problem of Electoral Turnout: Voters and Non-Voters at the British 2001 General Election', *Representation* 40:

Norris, P., J. Curtice, D. Sanders, M. Scammell and H. Semetko (1999) *On Message: Communicating the Campaign*. London: Sage.

Pattie, C.J. and R.J. Johnston (1996) 'The Value of Making an Extra Effort: Campaign Spending and Electoral Outcomes in Recent British General Elections – a Decomposition Approach', *Environment and Planning A* 28: 2081–90.

Pattie, C.J. and R.J. Johnston (2002) 'Assessing the Television Campaign: the Impact of Party Election Broadcasting on Voters' Opinions at the 1997 British General Election', *Political Communications* 19: 333–58.

Pattie, C.J., R.J. Johnston and E.A. Fieldhouse (1995) 'Winning the Local Vote: the Effectiveness of Constituency Campaign Spending in Great Britain, 1983–1992', *American Political Science Review* 89: 969–86.

Pattie, C.J., P. Whiteley, R.J. Johnston and P. Seyd (1994) 'Measuring Local Political Effects: Labour Party Constituency Campaigning at the 1987 General Election', *Political Studies* 42: 469–79.

Whiteley, P., H. Clarke, M. Stewart and D. Sanders (2001) 'Turnout', in P. Norris (ed.) *Britain Votes 2001*. Oxford: Oxford University Press, pp.211–24.

Whiteley, P. and P. Seyd (1994) 'Local Party Campaigning and Electoral Mobilisation in Britain', *Journal of Politics* 56: 242–52.

Whiteley, P. and P. Seyd (2002) *High Intensity Participation: The Dynamics of Party Activism in Britain*. Michigan: University of Michigan Press.

Worcester, R. and R. Mortimore (2001) *Explaining Labour's Second Landslide*. London: Politico's.

Reference Section

The reference section in this year's *Review* follows the same pattern as last year. It contains a chronology of major events in 2002; details of parliamentary by-elections during the current parliament; a comprehensive record of published public opinion polls in 2002; and the summary results of the 2002 local elections.

I am grateful to colleagues in the LGC Elections Centre at the University of Plymouth for their contributions. Paul Lambe compiled the chronology, Dawn Cole gathered the opinion poll data, and Michael Thrasher and Lawrence Ware were responsible for maintaining the files from which the local election results are drawn.

Collin Rallings

1. Chronology of Events 2002

JANUARY

1.   Euro cash was introduced in 12 European countries. EU leaders expressed the hope that its introduction would strengthen economic and political cooperation across the eurozone, and lead to a higher external value of the currency.

5.   The Prime Minister Tony Blair, on a six-day Anglo-American peace initiative to India and Pakistan, announced that the UK was ready to take a leading role in the fight against terrorism and make Britain a force for good in the wider world.

Shadow defence secretary Bernard Jenkin accused the Prime Minister of attempting to deflect attention from the government's domestic difficulties.

7.   Chancellor Gordon Brown's daughter, Jennifer Jane, born seven weeks prematurely, died aged ten days in the Edinburgh Royal Infirmary's specialist neo-natal unit.

8.   Dr George Carey, the 103rd Archbishop of Canterbury, announced his intention to retire before the end of the year.

Daffyd Wigley, former leader of Plaid Cymru, announced that he was to retire from politics and not stand at the 2003 Welsh Assembly elections.

Stephen Byers, the Transport Secretary, rejected criticism over having taken a holiday abroad at a time when transport policy dominated the political agenda and in the midst of a national rail crisis. Mr Byers said that he recognized that there was never a good time for a Cabinet minister to take a break.

11.   Pat Cox, a Liberal Democrat Member of the European Parliament from the Republic of Ireland, won the election to become the President of the European Parliament.

14. Michael Young, Lord Young of Dartington, died aged 86. He was the author of the 1945 Labour election manifesto, progenitor of the Open University, founder of the Consumers' Association and a committed egalitarian.

20. The arrival of 34 more Taleban and Al-Qaeda suspects at the Guantanamo Bay prison camp, shackled and blindfolded, added to international concern about conditions at the camp. The US government announced that representatives of the International Committee of the Red Cross had full access to all prisoners.

21. Sinn Fein's four MPs, Gerry Adams (Belfast West), Martin McGuiness (Mid-Ulster), Pat Doherty (West Tyrone) and Michelle Gildernew (Fermanagh and South Tyrone), took up residence at Westminster. Allowances and office expenses for the four MPs, who refuse to take the oath of allegiance to the Queen and to take their seats in the debating chamber, are expected to total over £400,000.

22. In a debate in Parliament on public services, the shadow health secretary Dr Liam Fox said that the government's whole approach 'smacked of utter incompetence in education, transport, health, law and order and most other public services'. In reply, Alan Milburn, Secretary of State for Health, said Dr Fox's speech was 'claptrap' and as someone trained as a doctor 'he should know a case of selective amnesia when he sees it'.

   Dublin's Special Criminal Court found Colm Murphy guilty of plotting to cause the Omagh bombing of Saturday 15 August 1998 which killed 29 people and injured hundreds.

   The UK regained its international status as a foot-and-mouth free country. The decision by the Paris based office of the International Animal Health Organisation allowed the resumption of meat exports. Government figures set the cost of the disease to the taxpayer at almost £1.5 billion.

25. Iain Duncan Smith, the Conservative Party leader, accused the government of lying and NHS executives of a culture of deceit over the alleged neglect of 94-year-old Rose Addis at a north London hospital. The case provided the backdrop to a bitter political row over public services and was said by the Conservative Party to exemplify the appalling state of the NHS under Labour.

29.   Calls by opposition MPs for a Commons Inquiry into the Labour Party's relations with the collapsed US energy trader Enron and its accountants Andersens, were dismissed by the Prime Minister's official spokesman as, 'overheated nonsense'. Downing Street denied suggestions that Enron's sponsorship of the Labour Party had smoothed the way for the takeover of Wessex Water and the lifting of the ban on the building of gas-fired power stations.

Margaret Beckett, Secretary of State for Environment, Food and Rural Affairs in a statement to the House on the report of the independent policy commission on the future of farming and food chaired by Sir Donald Curry, said the report 'delivered a clear vision of sustainable, competitive and diverse farming'. The report recommended a shift in emphasis from the subsidy of crop production to that of conserving the countryside, an increase in organic farming, and qualification for subsidies to be linked to proven use of environmentally friendly farming methods.

David Blunkett, the Home Secretary, announced proposals for a wide-ranging reform of the police service in England and Wales.

In his first State of the Union address President George Bush said, 'The United States will not permit the world's most dangerous regimes to threaten us with the world's most destructive weapons', and identified Iraq, North Korea and Iran as 'an axis of evil'.

31.   The House of Commons Transport Committee report, 'Passenger Rail Franchising and the Future of Railway Infrastructure', criticized the Prime Minister Tony Blair for not having given the railways greater priority when he first took office in 1997. The report also claimed that 'just about all the players in the industry have contributed to the chaos that the railways are now in'.

FEBRUARY

3.   The Prime Minister Tony Blair, at the Labour Party's spring conference in Cardiff, announced that the struggle over reform of public services was one of 'reformers versus wreckers', a comment that provoked fury from those leaders of public sector unions opposed to greater private sector involvement in the public services.

4.   Home Secretary David Blunkett announced plans to reform the prison system that included more open prisons, or hostels, and the possibility that those convicted of non-violent crimes could be allowed to go out to work and to return to custody each evening and at weekends.

5.   An inquiry by a House of Lords all-party select committee cleared the pilots of an RAF Chinook helicopter that crashed on the Mull of Kintyre in 1994 killing all 29 people on board.

       Estelle Morris, the Secretary of State for Education, in a statement to the House on the Chief Inspector of Schools' annual report said it 'showed that the quality of education is getting better'.

6.   In a break with tradition, on what in the past has been a private day spent at Windsor, the Queen marked the 50th anniversary of her accession to the throne with a stay at Sandringham and opened a Macmillan cancer relief unit at the Queen Elizabeth hospital in nearby King's Lynn.

       The government defeated the biggest backbench rebellion of this parliament by 405 votes to 87. An amendment to the Education Bill put forward by the former Health Secretary Frank Dobson required faith schools to take at least one quarter of their pupils from other religious backgrounds or none. Forty-five Labour MPs defied the party whip.

7.   Plans to reduce the number of MPs representing the Scottish constituencies from 72 to 59 were revealed in a Boundary Commission report. The planned changes, required by the Scotland Act of 1998, which contained an agreement to end Scotland's over-representation at Westminster, will be the first reduction in the number of MPs since Irish independence in 1922.

       David Blunkett, the Home Secretary, unveiled proposals set out in a nationality, immigration and asylum white paper subtitled 'Secure Borders, Safe Haven'. The proposals included the introduction of English language tests, exams on knowledge about British society and its institutions, an oath of allegiance, a Green-Card system for workers from overseas, and tougher sentencing of people traffickers.

9. Princess Margaret, aged 71, the younger sister of the Queen died at 6.30 a.m. in the King Edward VII Hospital in London.

10. Greg Dyke, the director general of the BBC, speaking on BBC One's Breakfast with Frost denied claims that the corporation is 'dumbing down' its political and current affairs coverage.

12. At the trial of Slobodan Milosevic, the first former head of state to be charged with genocide, crimes against humanity and war crimes, the chief prosecutor, Carla Del Ponte, said that the case would be a powerful demonstration that no one is above the law.

    Downing Street dismissed claims of wrong doing in a 'cash for favours' row centred upon a donation made to the Labour Party during the 2001 general election campaign by Lakshmi Mittal and a subsequent letter written by the Prime Minister to the Romanian Prime Minister in support of the purchase of that country's nationalized steel company, Sidex, by a firm owned by Mr Mittal. Plaid Cymru, which first raised the issue, claimed that Sidex was in competition with British firms such as Corus that recently had to cut 6,000 jobs.

    Estelle Morris, the Education Secretary outlined a government green paper on education for the 14–19 age group which planned for more flexible and work-related subject options to encourage more young people to remain in education and vocational training.

    Jane Davidson, the minister of education in the Welsh Assembly announced the reintroduction of grants for students from low-income families in Wales.

13. Keith Vaz, the Leicester East MP and former Europe Minister was suspended from the House of Commons for a period of one month.

    MSPs passed the Protection of Wild Mammals (Scotland) Bill and made Scotland the first part of the United Kingdom to ban mounted hunting with hounds.

    The appointment of Philip Mawer, secretary general of the Church of England synod, as Parliamentary Commissioner for Standards was confirmed by a vote in the House. Mr Mawer replaced Elizabeth Filkin.

14. Huw Irranca-Davies held the seat for the Labour Party at the Ogmore by-election, albeit with a much reduced majority compared to that at the 2001 general election. The by-election saw a swing of 8% to Plaid Cymru, and a constituency campaign battle fought against the backdrop of steel industry job cuts and the row over the Prime Minister's letter of support for a foreign steel magnate.

22. A census of local authority councillors in England and Wales carried out by the Improvement and Development Agency reported that councillors were unrepresentative of the wider community as a whole, being predominantly male, white and retired.

26. Ken Livingstone, the Mayor of London, announced plans to introduce congestion charges in an eight-square-mile tranche of central London.

28. Spike Milligan, hailed as a comic genius and regarded as a major influence on British comedy, died at the age of 83.

MARCH

1. The Hammond report of the inquiry into the Hinduja passport affair, the row that prompted the resignation of the former Northern Ireland Secretary Peter Mandelson, cleared Mr Mandelson of any improper behaviour.

4. Pentagon officials announced that nine American soldiers were killed in an assault on Al-Qaeda and Taliban forces in the Paktia province of Afghanistan, the highest American casualties in combat since the war began.

5. President Bush announced the imposition of tariffs on steel imports to the US, in a move to safeguard jobs in the country's steel industry.

Richard Balfe, Labour's longest serving Euro MP joined the Conservatives. Mr Balfe is the first elected Labour politician to cross the floor since Reg Prentice defected to the Conservatives in 1977.

The Electoral Commission revealed details of annual grants to be made to political parties to fund policy development. The grants, for those parties with one or more seats at Westminster and calculated in proportion to each party's share of the electorate, are the first regular financial support for political parties from the public coffers, with the exception of so-called Short Money which helps fund opposition parties' research work in the Commons. Sinn Fein does not qualify as their MPs refuse to take their seats in the debating chamber.

11. The Liberal Democrat leader Charles Kennedy revealed plans to meet the leader of the TUC John Monks to offer cooperation with the unions and to promote public services. In a speech at the party's spring conference Mr Kennedy said, 'I am certainly willing to have a dialogue with the trade unions and I am not so sure you can say the same for the Labour Party any more'. However, Tom Watson, Labour MP for West Bromwich East, alluding to the Liberal Democrat conference decision to legalize cannabis said, 'If Charles Kennedy thinks that trade unions will vote Liberal Democrat he must be smoking wacky baccy'.

The Home Secretary set out new stop-and-search guidelines designed to help restore confidence in the way the police deal with ethnic minorities.

13. President Robert Mugabe won a fifth term in office. Mr Mugabe, leader of the Zanu-PF Party became Prime Minister after Zimbabwe achieved independence from Britain in 1980 and has ruled ever since.

14. The towns of Preston, Stirling, Newport, Lisburn and Newry were given city status as part of the celebrations to mark the Queen's Golden Jubilee.

16. Former Conservative MP Sir Marcus Fox died at the age of 74. MP for Shipley in West Yorkshire from 1970 to 1997 and chairman of the backbench 1922 Committee, he had been swept aside in the 1997 Labour electoral landslide. Made vice-chairman of the party by Mrs Thatcher in 1975 and thenceforth responsible for candidate selection and the implementation of a policy to broaden the party's social base, he was nicknamed the 'Shipley Strangler'.

21. Just days after Scotland's First Minister Jack McConnell had urged train drivers to end a campaign of industrial action and accept a 3%

pay rise, members of the Scottish Parliament voted in favour of plans to increase their annual salary by 13.5%, a rise of almost £6,000.

22. Baroness Thatcher's office announced that the 76-year-old former Prime Minister had been ordered to make no more public speeches on health grounds. The announcement came at the end of a week in which Lady Thatcher had stirred political controversy by urging a fundamental renegotiation of Britain's terms of EU membership. Iain Duncan Smith sent his party's best wishes for a speedy recovery.

24. In a dramatic policy U-turn Stephen Byers announced the decision that £300 million in taxpayers' money would be used to bail out Railtrack's shareholders.

26. John Monks announced his decision to stand down as leader of the Trades Union Congress.

30. In an emergency session of the UN Security Council a US-backed resolution called for the withdrawal of Israeli troops from Palestinian cities and for both parties to move immediately to a meaningful cease-fire.

The Queen Mother died at the age of 101 with her daughter Queen Elizabeth II at her bedside. In a statement from Chequers the Prime Minister Tony Blair said the whole nation joined with the Queen and the Royal Family in mourning.

APRIL

8. The widely criticized voucher scheme for payments to asylum seekers was replaced by cash payment.

9. At the funeral service of the Queen Mother in Westminster Abbey the Archbishop of Canterbury paid tribute to her gifts of 'strength, dignity and laughter'. The Queen Mother was laid to rest alongside her husband in St George's chapel Windsor, and the ashes of her daughter Princess Margaret interred at the same time in the Royal Vault.

10. The Prime Minister Tony Blair told a meeting of the Parliamentary Labour Party that the fullest possible consensus would be sought before any military offensive is launched against Iraq. The veteran peace campaigner Alice Mahon, Labour MP for Halifax, said 'MPs were seeking a specific reassurance that the US and Britain would not act alone without going through the UN'.

11. A leaked tape of remarks made by the Conservative spokesman on health, Dr Liam Fox, at a fringe meeting at the party's spring conference revealed that he wanted to break public support for the NHS and to introduce new income sources for health, including insurance and self-pay.

A High Court upheld the decision by Harrow Borough's returning officer that 60 nominations for the May 2002 local elections submitted by Liberal Democrat candidates were invalid under the Political Parties, Elections and Referendum Act, 2000. The nominees had declared as 'Liberal Democrat Focus Team' candidates and not, as the new law required, as 'Liberal Democrat'. The law was introduced following pressure from the Liberal Democrats after Adrian Sanders, the party's official candidate, had narrowly lost at the 1994 Euro elections when a so-called 'Literal Democrat' candidate contested and polled 10,000 votes in the Devon and Plymouth East constituency.

16. Following the Labour Party's damaging entanglements with several business donors over the past months, the Deputy Prime Minister John Prescott came out in favour of state funding of political parties as the only way to make the political system 'properly accountable'.

The government was defeated in the Lords on a series of measures in the Police Reform Bill, including rejection by 205 votes to 131 of plans to give the Home Office greater say in the running of police forces. The introduction of the Bill into the Lords by the Home Secretary deprived him of the ability to use the Parliament Act to impose the will of the Commons should the peers reject the clauses a second time.

17. The Wanless Report, an independent review by Derek Wanless, and the first ever evidence-based assessment of the long-term resource requirements of the NHS concluded that the UK would need to devote more resources to health care and that this must be matched

by reform to ensure that those resources are used effectively.

In his sixth Budget, delayed from its usual March date due to his bereavement leave, the Chancellor of the Exchequer Gordon Brown announced the first increase in direct taxation since taking office. The announcement of a 1p in the pound increase in National Insurance contributions, intended to pay for the biggest ever increase in UK health service funding, dominated the Budget and eclipsed measures announced on education, transport and crime.

18.   After 29 years in exile the former Afghan king Zahia Shah returned to Kabul.

        Terje Roed-Larsen, a UN envoy described the devastation left by Israeli forces in the West Bank refugee camp of Jenin as 'horrific beyond belief'.

21.   In a record low turnout of France's 40 million electorate at the first round of the presidential election, Jean-Marie Le Pen, the far-right National Front politician, won enough support to eliminate the Socialist Prime Minister Lionel Jospin and to go through to contest against the incumbent President Jacques Chirac in the second and final round of the election.

24.   Sinn Fein's President Gerry Adams announced his decision not to appear before the US congressional hearing on the IRA's alleged links with Marxist guerrillas in Columbia. US congressman, Harry Hide, chairman of the House of Representatives international relations committee, said 'the hearing would have given Mr Adams an opportunity to explain what two IRA explosives experts and Sinn Fein's Cuban representative were doing with a group which poses a direct threat to US national interests'.

29.   In a unanimous verdict, seven judges at the European Court of Human Rights in Strasbourg ruled that the refusal by British courts to permit Diane Pretty's husband to assist her to commit suicide did not contravene her human rights.

30.   The Queen addressed the joint Houses of the Commons and the Lords in Westminster Hall to launch the official celebrations of her golden jubilee. Her Majesty vowed to continue 'serving the people of this great nation' and paid tribute to the 'mother of all

parliaments' which had played an essential part in guiding the kingdom through the changing times of the past 50 years.

MAY

2.   Forty of the 174 councils contested in the English local elections changed hands in what was a day of mixed fortunes for the parties. The Labour Party suffered modest net losses of 8 councils. In what was Iain Duncan Smith's first electoral test as leader, the Conservative Party made net gains of 9 councils. The Liberal Democrats made net gains of 2 councils. They took the former Labour stronghold of Norwich, but lost Richmond-on-Thames to the Conservatives and effective control of Sheffield to Labour. The far-right BNP picked up 3 seats on Burnley council. In Hartlepool, one of seven contests for a directly elected executive mayor, the electorate returned Stuart Drummond, a.k.a. H'Angus the Monkey, the local football team's mascot. Parts of England, in a number of pilot studies, were able for the first time to vote by mobile phone or internet.

   The Israeli army ended its siege of Yasser Arafat's headquarters in Ramallah.

3.   Wendy Alexander, the Enterprise, Transport and Lifelong Learning Minister, and the Labour MSP for Paisley North, resigned from the Scottish Cabinet.

   Barbara Castle, former Labour Cabinet minister and MP for Blackburn, 1945–79, died at the age of 91. She had been brought into Harold Wilson's government as Minister for Overseas Development 1964–65, and, as Minister of Transport 1965–69, introduced the breathalyser and traffic wardens. Secretary of State for Social Services in the Wilson government of 1974–76, she resigned her Blackburn seat in 1979 to become a member of the European Parliament.

5.   Ann Winterton, the Conservative MP for Congleton and shadow agriculture spokeswoman, was sacked by party leader Iain Duncan Smith for having told an allegedly racist joke at a Congleton Rugby Club Dinner.

Jacques Chirac was re-elected as President of France by the largest ever margin. He polled over 82% of the vote.

6. Pim Fortuyn, the Dutch right-wing politician who had campaigned on an anti-immigration ticket was shot dead just nine days before the Dutch general election.

7. After months of speculation, select committee hearings, leaks and counter leaks the draft Communications Bill was published jointly by the Trade and Industry Secretary, Patricia Hewitt, and the Culture, Media and Sport Secretary, Tessa Jowell. The draft Bill, a comprehensive reform of the legal framework of communications in response to the technological and market changes in modern media, established Ofcom as a single government regulator for broadcasting and telecom industries.

Stephen Byers, the Transport Secretary, made a Commons statement in answer to allegations that he had misled MPs over the much-disputed circumstances of the resignation of Martin Sixsmith, the department's communications director. The row centred on reports that Mr Sixsmith had warned the controversial special adviser to the Transport Secretary, Jo Moore, not to announce bad news on the day of Princess Margaret's funeral. It had been announced that Ms Moore, who had earlier caused a furore when she had suggested that 11 September was a good day to 'bury bad news', and Mr Sixsmith had agreed to resign. However, Mr Sixsmith had said the first he had heard of his 'resignation' was on the radio.

9. Deputy Prime Minister John Prescott announced proposals for elected English regional assemblies as set out in the White Paper, 'Your Region: Your Choice'.

The Bank of England Monetary Policy Committee decided to hold the interest rate at its 38 year low of 4% for the sixth month in a row.

10. A train crash at Potters Bar station claimed the lives of seven people.

12. In what President Bush heralded as the beginning of a new era in relations between the two countries, Russian and US negotiators announced an agreement to reduce their operational nuclear stockpiles by about two-thirds over the next ten years.

15.   The Register of Lord's Interests was published for the first time. Fifty peers failed to comply with the new rules that require them to list all relevant financial interests in the public register.

17.   Following a series of 'cash for favours scandals', the Electoral Commission recommended to Parliament that all political donations should be capped at £10,000 and that there should be a reduction in the amount that parties are allowed to spend on general election campaigning.

The former Prime Minister of Northern Ireland, James Chichester-Clark, later Lord Moyola, died aged 79.

19.   Bertie Ahern's centre-right Fianna Fail party won the Irish Republic general election. However, it failed narrowly to get the required number of seats necessary for an overall majority to enable it to form the country's first one-party government in 25 years. Sinn Fein increased its representation in the Dail from one to five.

East Timor became the world's newest nation.

28.   Stephen Byers, the Transport Secretary, resigned from the government.

29.   In a cabinet and ministerial reshuffle, the Prime Minister made Alistair Darling the new Secretary for Transport, and passed responsibility for local government and the regions over to John Prescott at the Office of the Deputy Prime Minister. Andrew Smith replaced Mr Darling as the Secretary for Works and Pensions, and Paul Boateng was promoted to Chief Secretary at the Treasury. Mr Boateng became Britain's first black Cabinet minister, and David Lammy, appointed a junior health minister, the youngest minister. The former head of the Number 10 policy unit, David Miliband, less than a year after being parachuted into the safe Labour seat of South Shields, became school standards minister.

JUNE

1.   Speaking at a graduation ceremony at West Point military academy, President Bush, in a repudiation of the cold war policy of deterrence and containment, explained his new thinking on foreign policy. The President warned that the US must take 'pre-emptive action' against potential enemies.

5. The environmental group Friends of the Earth reminded the Deputy Prime Minister of the following statement he had made at a Royal Geographical Society reception in 1997. 'I will have failed if in five years time there are not more people using public transport and fewer journeys by car. It is a tall order, but I urge you to hold me to it'. He had, so they did.

10. In Zimbabwe some 2,900 white farmers, whose land had been selected for seizure under the government's so-called fast-track land reform programme, were legally obliged to cease working the land or face imprisonment.

16. In what is the first time a single party has held an outright majority in the National Assembly during the Fifth Republic, President Jacques Chirac's centre-right party won a resounding victory over the left in the second round of the French general elections. The National Front party failed to win a single seat.

24. Pierre Werner, a former Luxembourg Prime Minister, died aged 88. Werner enjoyed the dubious distinction of being regarded as the 'father of the euro', and had first called for the introduction of a common European currency in 1960.

25. The G8 summit met at the remote Canadian resort of Kananaskis. Protesters had gathered in Calgary but were denied access to the resort in a move to prevent a repeat of the violent clashes at the previous summit in Genoa.

Alan Milburn, the Secretary of Health presented the draft Mental Health Bill to Parliament. The controversial bill amends the law relating to the compulsory care and treatment of mentally disordered persons.

26. As sterling's continued fall against the euro heightened City speculation that joining the single currency was a realistic prospect, Gordon Brown told the City's annual Mansion House dinner, 'If the tests are met then I believe we should join. If the tests are not we should not'. The Chancellor dismissed any notions that the decision to call a referendum would be driven by political considerations.

27. Alistair Darling, the Transport Secretary, announced a rescue package for Railtrack, placed into administration in October 2001

by his predecessor Stephen Byers. Network Rail, a public interest company, would pay Railtrack £500 million, including £300 million provided by the government, to take over Railtrack's £7.1 billion debt and thereby enable Railtrack's shares to be re-listed on the stock exchange.

Government plans to speed up extradition to and from the UK were published. The consultation paper, which set out the draft clauses of the proposed bill, also gave effect to the controversial European arrest warrant.

JULY

1. Andrew Smith, Secretary of State for Work and Pensions apologized to the Commons for statistical errors in government figures that had overestimated the level of pension contributions made last year. At a time of crisis in the pensions industry, with dwindling share values, falling annuities and longer life expectation, the Conservatives accused the government of being 'hopelessly optimistic' about its pension policy.

5. Talks in Vienna between the United Nations and Iraq over the proposed reintroduction of weapons inspectors into the country broke down without agreement.

6. The Afghan vice president, Haji Abdul Qadir was assassinated.

9. In the wake of a series of Wall Street scandals that have undermined confidence in US accounting standards, President Bush said that 'America's greatest economic need is higher ethical standards enforced by strict laws and upheld by responsible leaders'.

11. Alan Pickering issued his report following a Department of Works and Pensions review of how Britain saves for its old age. The report's key proposals plan to remove compulsion for pension schemes to provide for survivors' benefits, and to abolish the right to index-linked pension income. Julie Mellor, chair of the Equal Opportunities Commission, warned that the proposals 'would only make things worse for the many women who have not been able to build up an adequate independent retirement income'.

15. Gordon Brown revealed his much-awaited spending review in a Commons statement. The three-year spending programme increased spending on public services, especially education and was the last review before the next general election.

   Islamic militant Ahmed Sheik was sentenced to death for the murder of Canadian journalist Daniel Pearl.

16. As part of a drive to become more candid and more accountable, the Prime Minister, the first incumbent prime minister to do so since 1937, appeared before a Commons select committee.

17. The government's criminal justice white paper, Justice for All, was unveiled by the Home Secretary David Blunkett. The wide ranging reforms included plans to allow previous acquittals, as well as previous convictions, to be admissible as evidence in court and caused concerns about civil liberties and potential miscarriages of justice.

   The Spanish military, with the consent of the UN security council and NATO, liberated Perejil Island a previously uninhabited island that had been invaded by a detachment of Moroccan soldiers on 11 July. The rock, 200 yards from the Moroccan coast and the size of a football pitch had been overlooked when Spain had relinquished the bulk of her North African colonial possessions in 1956.

21. President Bush told US forces to be ready for pre-emptive action against Iraq.

22. The Anderson report criticized the government's handling of the foot-and-mouth crisis. Secretary of State for the Environment, Food and Rural Affairs, Margaret Beckett, told the Commons that the government was 'determined to learn the lessons'.

23. In a reshuffle of his shadow cabinet, Iain Duncan-Smith, the Conservative Party leader, replaced David Davis with Theresa May as chairman of the party. May, who became the first chair*woman* in the party's history, was replaced at transport by Tim Collins, former shadow minister for the Cabinet Office and Deputy Chairman of the party. Gillian Shephard replaced Mr Collins as Deputy Chairman.

The Archbishop of Wales, Rowan Williams was confirmed as the new head of the Church of England. He is the 104th successor to the throne of St Augustine.

24. Stock markets across the globe crashed and the FTSE 100 index closed at a new six-year low.

In the final Prime Minister's question time before the summer recess Tony Blair indicated that the House of Commons would be properly consulted on whether British forces should be involved in any military action against Iraq but declined to promise MPs a vote.

25. The Prime Minister Tony Blair warned the IRA that if it did not abandon all paramilitary activity Sinn Fein risked being expelled from Northern Ireland's power sharing executive.

30. Gerhard Schroder, the Chancellor of Germany, and Jacques Chirac, the President of France, announced they could not support an attack on Iraq without a United Nations mandate.

AUGUST

4. The Turkish government passed legislative reforms that abolished capital punishment, lifted restrictions on the use of the Kurdish language and removed constraints upon free speech.

5. The Father of the House, Linlithgow MP Tam Dalyell, demanded that Parliament be recalled so that MPs could debate a military attack on Iraq. David Winnick, Labour MP for Walsall North, branded him an appeaser and claimed that most of the Labour benches would support an invasion.

16. Jack McConnell, Scotland's First Minister, conceded in an interview that the first two years of the parliament had been a disappointment to the people of Scotland and that disaffection could in part be explained by the escalation in costs of the Holyrood parliament building from its initial £40 million to £300 million.

21. General Musharraf, Pakistan's military ruler amended the country's constitution. The President granted himself the authority to dissolve parliament and the power to appoint top posts in the military.

23. Pakistan accused India of air strikes against a military post in disputed Kashmir and claimed that the attacks were an attempt to undermine the peace visit of the US Deputy Secretary of State Richard Armitage.

Speaking in Edinburgh the Foreign Secretary Jack Straw called for a written European constitution to 'reconnect European voters with the institutions that act in their name'. The shadow foreign secretary, Michael Ancram, warned of the government moving towards a super-state with full political integration among its members, while the Liberal Democrat foreign affairs spokesman, Menzies Campbell, welcomed the 'government's conversion' to a constitution for Europe.

26. Batasuna, the political wing of the Basque separatist movement Eta, was outlawed by the Spanish government.

The World Summit on Sustainable Development opened in Johannesburg.

29. Northern Ireland security minister, Jane Kennedy, praised attempts by police to keep rival factions apart after what was the latest night in a summer of continued sectarian violence in east and north Belfast.

SEPTEMBER

4. Labour MEPs elected pro-euro veteran Gary Titley as their leader after the resignation of Simon Murphy a week earlier.

5. Henry McLeish, MSP for Central Fife, and former Scottish First Minister, announced that he would not stand at next year's Scottish parliamentary elections.

9. The TUC conference opened in Blackpool. Union leaders approved a general council statement issued prior to the conference that criticized the US and ruled out unilateral action except with explicit UN authority. Bill Hayes, the general secretary of the Communication Workers Union claimed that, by its opposition to an attack on Iraq, and its campaigns against privatization and in support of an increase in the minimum wage, the TUC rather than the government reflected public opinion.

11. Britain remembered and paid tribute to the victims of the September 11, 2001 terrorist attacks in America.

It was confirmed that Parliament would be recalled from its summer recess to discuss the crisis over Iraq. The Prime Minister's decision followed mounting pressure from MPs and from the leaders of the Conservative and Liberal Democrat parties to allow a debate on possible military action against Iraq.

15. The Social Democrats won the Swedish general election. The Prime Minister, Goeran Perrson, said it demonstrated that the centre-left was still a powerful European electoral force despite recent gains for the right across the continent.

16. An ICM poll revealed that only one in five chief executives favoured an early adoption of the euro.

20. In a speech at the party's annual conference in Llandudno, Ieuan Wyn Jones, leader of Plaid Cymru, accused Labour of running the Welsh Assembly like a county council, and called for the same tax-varying and law-making powers as the Scottish Parliament. The party announced that if successful at the 2003 Welsh Assembly elections, it would ban sweets and crisps from schools.

21. David Trimble narrowly avoided being toppled from the leadership of the Ulster Unionist Party at a meeting of the Ulster Unionist Council. In a major policy change the province's First Minister issued an ultimatum that unless the IRA not only disarm but also disband within three months the UUP would resign from the power sharing Stormont Assembly. In what was seen as a victory for the anti-Agreement hardliners led by Trimble's leadership rival, Jeffrey Donaldson, MP for Lagan Valley, the UUP also announced its withdrawal from North-South cross-border bodies that involved Sinn Fein ministers.

In protest against the proposed ban on hunting with hounds and other rural issues such as low incomes and poor services, over 400,000 people descended on central London for the Liberty and Livelihood march organized by the Countryside Alliance.

Against a backdrop of four million unemployed, the German Chancellor Gerhard Schroder and his Social Democratic party in alliance with the Green party narrowly defeated the conservative candidate Edmund Stoiber, who led an alliance between the Christian Democratic Union and the Christian Social Union, at the German general election.

24. Tension between India and Pakistan was increased when 30 worshippers were massacred by Islamic extremists at a Hindu temple in the Indian state of Gujarat.

In an address to a fringe meeting at the Liberal Democrat conference in Brighton, Sam Younger, the Chairman of the Electoral Commission said that he felt it would be inconceivable that any euro referendum result would not be broken down by nation and region.

26. Lord Archer was transferred from open prison to the harsher regime of Lincoln jail. Home release, a privilege given to category D prisoners near the end of their sentence, in part to enable felons to re-establish links with the local community, had been taken rather too literally when it was discovered that the disgraced peer had spent his day's home release at a party given by former Conservative minister Gillian Shephard.

28. At the Scottish National Party conference in Inverness, the SNP leader John Swinney in a keynote address said that the party had 'evolved and proved itself ready to govern', and would 'fight the Holyrood parliamentary elections next year with independence firmly on the agenda'.

30. On the first day of the Labour Party conference in Blackpool, Gordon Brown robustly defended the government's programme to harness private capital for the modernization of British public services.

OCTOBER

4. As one million troops faced each other along the disputed Kashmir border international concern was raised when both India and Pakistan conducted ballistic missile tests.

Burford Yates, former director of accounting at WorldCom, pleaded guilty to conspiracy to commit securities fraud.

9. The EU Commission formally recommended that ten more countries should join the EU in 2004. Of 13 applicants Cyprus, Czech Republic, Estonia, Hungary, Latvia, Lithuania, Malta, Poland, Slovakia and Slovenia were successful, whilst Bulgaria, Romania and Turkey would not yet be admitted.

10. In a speech on the final day of the Conservative Party conference at Bournemouth the party's leader, Iain Duncan Smith, said 'those who do not know me yet will come to understand this: do not underestimate the determination of the quiet man'.

Following four weeks of polling marred by militant violence, the political landscape of Kashmir was radically changed when the National Conference party suffered a crushing defeat at the state elections.

Despite pressure from the Institute of Directors for a cut, the Bank of England left interest rates unchanged for the eleventh month in a row at the 38-year low of 4%.

12. A terrorist bomb that exploded in the beach resort of Kuta on the Indonesian island of Bali killed at least 187 people and left more than 300 injured.

14. Direct rule from Westminster was re-imposed when the Northern Ireland Secretary, John Reid, suspended the power sharing Northern Ireland Assembly, following the discovery of an alleged IRA spy ring at the Northern Ireland Office and the consequent threatened walkout by Unionist ministers unless Sinn Fein was expelled.

Rhodri Morgan, First Minister of the Welsh Assembly said the assembly 'still had a long way to go to convince the voters of its value'.

15. Despite a decline in turnout Saddam Hussein recorded a personal best election performance when he secured 100% of the vote in the one-man-race Iraqi Presidential election.

16.   In Holland the Prime Minister resigned and the country's government collapsed. Mr Balkenende told parliament that the 12-week-old coalition was unworkable.

In the wake of an A-level marking 'fiasco', Iain Duncan Smith said in Parliament that 'faith in A-levels had been shaken to the core' and that 'no one knows whether they are worth the paper they are written on'. Tony Blair called the comments 'a gross insult to students who had just taken the exam'.

17.   Independent and minor party candidates were elected mayor in Bedford, Mansfield and Stoke-on-Trent. The only major party success at the four executive mayoral elections was Labour's Jules Pipe in Hackney.

19.   The Republic of Ireland voted in favour of the Nice Treaty. Its rejection would have halted plans for enlargement of the European Union into central and eastern Europe.

21.   The Tobacco Advertising and Promotions Bill received an unopposed third reading in the House of Commons.

23.   Estelle Morris, the Secretary of State for Education resigned.

24.   In what was Tony Blair's second reshuffle within five months, Peter Hain, the Minister for Europe joined the Cabinet as the new Secretary of State for Wales. Mr Hain retained his job as the government representative on the Laeken convention on the future of Europe. Charles Clarke, the party chairman was appointed Secretary of State for Education, and John Reid the Northern Ireland Secretary took over the role of party chairman.

26.   The lives of more than 150 hostages and captors were lost when the Moscow theatre siege was ended by Russian special forces.

27.   Luiz Inacio Lula da Silva, leader of the Workers Party was elected president of Brazil. In accordance with Brazilian law all six presidential candidates and each of the 18,880 candidates standing in congressional and state elections had been given free 'air-time' on Brazilian television in a month long election campaign.

29.   The City of London (Ward Elections) Bill received an unopposed third reading in the Lords. The legislation reformed the voting arrangements in the City of London and increased the voting rights for businesses.

30.   On a free vote MPs approved a series of proposals to change Commons procedures. They included starting the main business of the chamber at 11.30 am on Tuesday, Wednesday and Thursday, ending late nights, and allowing legislation to be carried over from one parliamentary session to another for a period of 12 months.

31.   Senior doctors in England and Wales rejected the government's proposed new contract aimed at reducing NHS waiting lists.

      Iain Duncan Smith stated categorically that he would not quit as leader of the Conservative Party.

NOVEMBER

1.   The trial of the royal butler Paul Burrell was halted following an intervention by the Queen. Burrell had been accused of stealing more than £6 million of property belonging to the late Diana, Princess of Wales.

4.   David Shayler the former MI5 officer was convicted of charges under the Official Secrets Act.

      Following a week of speculation about a challenge to Iain Duncan Smith's leadership of the Conservative Party, John Bercow, shadow cabinet works and pensions minister, resigned because he could not support a three-line-whip imposed by IDS to block proposals by the government to allow gay and unmarried couples to adopt children. In what was seen by commentators as an open revolt against Iain Duncan Smith's leadership, Michael Portillo, Kenneth Clarke and eight senior Conservative MPs defied the party whip and voted with the government, and a further 35 Conservative MPs were absent from the division lobbies. In what was a free vote for Labour, 344 MPs to 145 voted to uphold the proposals which had come before the Commons because of their rejection by the Lords.

5.   The Republican Party gained control of the Senate and increased its narrow majority in the House of Representatives at the US mid-term elections.

6.   The Federal Reserve cut US interest rates by a higher-than-expected half point to its lowest level in 40 years in an attempt to maintain a faltering recovery.

      Commenting on the leadership crisis in the Conservative Party Lady Thatcher said, 'The Tory Party will last... I don't know about Iain Duncan Smith because we all die...but the party doesn't.'

7.   The Home Office issued a national terror alert that Al-Qaeda could unleash a 'dirty bomb' or poison gas attack on Britain.

      Only 187 of 18,087 people whose vote was counted in the Gibraltar Referendum agreed with the principle of co-sovereignty with Spain.

11.   In reaction to the publication of the Bain Report, Andy Gilchrist, secretary general of the Fire Brigades Union said that the report had effectively wrecked ongoing pay talks.

12.   Dr Frank Luntz, an American academic and one of the Republican Party's most influential pollsters, offered the following advice to Tony Blair on how to win public support for the war against Iraq, 'Don't mention the American President.'

14.   Hu Jintao was confirmed as the new General Secretary of the Communist Party, China's fourth national leader since 1949.

18.   The Prince of Wales was named as Beer Drinker of the Year for his efforts to save rural pubs. The title was bestowed by the all-party Parliamentary Beer Group. Previous winners include the former Chancellor of the Exchequer Kenneth Clarke.

19.   The oil tanker Prestige split in two and sank off the coast of northern Spain.

20.   The US government formally requested the use of British forces in any conflict with Iraq.

22.   Firemen began an eight-day strike after the Fire Brigades Union refused to accept new working practices tied to a 16% pay deal.

      The far-right BNP won a surprise seat in a Blackburn council by-election. Mill Hill, a predominantly white working-class suburb deemed a community regeneration zone in need of extra government help to improve the quality of life, was the fourth seat won by the party in East Lancashire.

24. The People's Party, led by Wolfgang Schussel, won a landslide victory at the Austrian general elections. The far-right extremist Freedom Party, led by Jorg Haider and hitherto a governing partner in the coalition, took barely 10% of the vote.

25. In a lecture to Oxford University's Law Society David Pannick QC called for an end to the immunity that puts the Queen as Head of State above the law.

Law Lords ruled that it was incompatible with human rights law for a politician to have the final say on how long a murderer should serve before being considered for parole and thereby stripped the Home Secretary of his power to set minimum sentences. Lord Steyn had earlier described the Home Secretary's power as a 'striking anomaly in our legal system'.

26. Richard Simpson, the Deputy Justice Minister in Scotland responsible for the fire service, resigned after allegations that he had described striking firemen as 'fascist bastards'.

27. In his sixth pre-Budget report the Chancellor of the Exchequer Gordon Brown blamed the world's worst economic slowdown for almost 30 years for upsetting his calculations made only eight months previously. Mr Brown announced to the Commons an increase in borrowing to £20 billion and revised predictions of annual growth from 2–2.5% down to 1.6%.

28. Official figures revealed that waiting times had increased since the Scottish Executive had taken over the running of the NHS in Scotland in 1999 despite Labour MSPs' election pledge to reduce them.

DECEMBER

1. England lost the Ashes series.

2. The Home Secretary announced that the Sangatte Red Cross centre near Calais would be closed and set out the terms of a deal struck

with the French interior minister Nicholas Sarkozy whereby Britain would accept 1,200 refugees.

A planned eight-day strike by firemen was called off.

4. As the Prime Minister told the House of Commons that there was a crisis in higher education funding and that additional money could only come from the student, the parent or the taxpayer, thousands of students protested in London against the imposition of top-up fees, and demanded an end to all university fees and the return of grants.

    Despite international pressure not to do so Gerhard Schroder announced cuts in the German defence budget and raised fears that Britain and its European partners would be forced to contribute more to ongoing collaborative defence projects.

    Alistair Darling, the Transport Secretary, announced a rescue package of £1.9 billion in legal indemnities to companies bidding for contracts in the part-privatization of the London Underground. The indemnities cover the costs recoverable by the companies if a challenge by Ken Livingstone in the European Courts were to be successful.

5. The European Central Bank cut half a point from its key interest rate in an attempt to revive stuttering economic growth across the continent.

9. President Bush named John Snow as the 73rd Treasury Secretary. Mr Snow replaced Paul O'Neill, the first member of Bush's cabinet to be sacked.

    Lord Tebbit accused Lord Heseltine of being a 'serial Conservative assassin' after the former Cabinet minister said that 'the Tories did not stand a ghost's chance of winning the next election as long as Duncan Smith remained as leader'.

10. Jimmy Carter, the former US President, in his acceptance speech for the Nobel Peace Prize warned the Bush administration that unilateral action against Iraq could have catastrophic consequences and urged Washington to abandon pre-emptive action in favour of working through the United Nations.

In what was the first ever public personal statement made by a prime minister's wife, Cherie Blair apologized and admitted that mistakes had been made in the imbroglio over the purchase of two flats in Bristol.

12. The North Korean government announced that it would restart a nuclear power plant suspected by the US of having in the past supplied weapons-grade plutonium for the manufacture of nuclear warheads.

Gordon Brown announced the resignation of Sir Howard Davies, head of the UK financial services watchdog, who left to become director of the London School of Economics.

13. Regent House approved the appointment of Professor Alison Richard as Cambridge University's vice-chancellor. Ms Richard became the first female chief executive in the university's 800-year history.

16. Pro-hunt supporters clashed with police in Parliament Square as MPs debated the Hunting Bill. A Conservative Party bid to block the bill was defeated by 365 votes to 164. The bill outlawing stag hunting and hare coursing but allowing fox hunting in some areas was given a second reading by 368 votes to 155. Anti-hunt Labour MPs had voted for the bill at its second reading to ensure that they would get the chance to amend it and impose an outright ban when it came before MPs again.

The Deputy Prime Minister John Prescott said he agreed with the Bain report's conclusion on the firefighter's pay claim that legislative changes were needed to modernize the service and warned the Fire Brigades Union that it could not hide from reform.

18. In his first public speech since taking office the Archbishop of Canterbury launched a crusade to put morality back at the heart of society and public life.

19. Following Washington's appraisal of Iraq's weapons declaration the US Secretary of State Colin Powell said that 'Iraq had failed to give a serious account of its weapons arsenal, holding back evidence of its nuclear programme, and its stocks of biological and chemical weapons'.

29.   A furious row erupted over England's decision to compete against
        Zimbabwe in Harare at the cricket World Cup. Despite continued
        insistence that it was not the government's place to tell the
        International Cricket Council or the England and Wales Cricket
        Board what to do, the Prime Minister Tony Blair said the team
        should not take part in the match in Robert Mugabe's famine-
        stricken country.

31.   People working in education, health and community services
        accounted for almost half of those named in the New Year's
        Honours List.

2. Parliamentary By-elections 2002

There was just one by-election in 2002. It was held in Ogmore following the death of Sir Ray Powell on 8 December 2001.

1. OGMORE 14 February 2002 (Death of Sir Ray Powell)

Result

Candidate	Description	Votes
I.H. Irranca-Davies	Labour	9,578
B.W. Hancock	Plaid Cymru	3,827
Mrs V.K. Watkins	Liberal Democrat	1,608
G.ap O. Bebb	Conservative	1,377
C. Herriot	Socialist Labour	1,152
J.H. Spink	Green	250
J.J. Hurford	Socialist Alliance	205
L.D. Edwards	Official Monster Raving Loony	187
C. Beany	New Millennium Bean	122
D.O. Braid	Independent	100

Labour hold: Majority 5,751

Turnout and Major Party Vote Shares (%)

	By-election	General election	Change
Turnout	35.9	58.2	−22.3
Conservative	7.5	11.1	−3.6
Labour	52.0	62.0	−10.0
Liberal Democrat	8.7	12.8	−4.1
Plaid Cymru	20.8	14.0	+6.8

TABLE 2.1 *Summary of By-election Results in 2001 parliament*

	\% Change in share of vote since 2001					
	Con	Lab	LDem	SNP/PC	% Turnout	Change
Ipswich	−2.1	−7.9	+7.2	–	40.2	−16.8
Ogmore	−3.6	−10.0	−4.1	+6.8	35.9	−22.3

3. Public Opinion Polls 2002

TABLE 3.1 *Voting Intentions in Major Polls 2002 (%)*

Fieldwork	Company	Sample size	Con	Lib Lab	Dem	Other
January						
18–20	ICM	1003	30	45	19	6
24–28	MORI	1995	27	51	16	6
February						
15–17	ICM	1003	30	47	18	5
21–26	MORI	1965	28	51	16	5
March						
7–8	YouGov	2043	31	42	20	7
15–17	ICM	1001	34	43	17	6
21–26	MORI	1915	28	47	19	6
April						
18–19	ICM	1004	32	45	17	6
18–22	MORI	1912	27	50	16	7
20–21	ICM	1000	29	45	18	8
May						
17–19	ICM	1003	34	42	19	5
23–24	YouGov	2001	32	40	21	7
23–28	MORI	1899	30	46	17	7
June						
20–24	MORI	1890	29	48	17	6
21–23	ICM	1002	32	42	20	6
21–23	YouGov	1801	35	38	20	7
21–24	NOP	1010	31	41	19	9
July						
18–22	MORI	1781	27	48	18	7
24–26	YouGov	1807	34	38	22	6
26–27	ICM	1002	33	42	20	5
August						
21–23	YouGov	2918	33	40	20	7
23–25	ICM	1003	32	41	21	6
September						
20–22	ICM	1000	34	39	20	7
25–27	YouGov	1997	32	40	22	6
27–30	NOP	1010	28	41	21	10
October						
2–3	ICM	1012	27	42	23	8
18–20	ICM	1001	32	43	20	5
23–25	YouGov	2055	31	40	22	7
28–29	YouGov	1870	31	40	21	8
November						
6–7	ICM	1008	29	43	21	7
15–17	ICM	1000	29	41	22	8
14–19	MORI	1928	30	42	21	7
20–22	YouGov	2054	30	39	23	8

TABLE 3.1 (continued) *Voting Intentions in Major Polls 2002 (%)*

Fieldwork	Company	Sample size	Con	Lab	Lib Dem	Other
December						
5–6	YouGov	1477	31	38	23	8
13–15	ICM	1000	27	41	23	9
12–17	MORI	1843	33	37	24	6

Notes: The figures shown for voting intention are the 'headline' figures published by the polling companies concerned. ICM weight their results to produce adjusted figures. MORI, on the other hand, publishes unadjusted figures calculated in the traditional way. YouGov is an internet pollster using three methods of sampling – passive, active and combination.

TABLE 3.2 *Monthly Averages for Voting Intentions 2002 (%)*

	Con	Lab	Lib Dem		Con	Lab	Lib Dem
Jan	29	48	18	Jul	31	43	20
Feb	29	49	17	Aug	33	41	21
Mar	31	44	19	Sep	31	40	21
Apr	29	47	17	Oct	30	41	22
May	32	43	19	Nov	30	41	22
Jun	32	42	19	Dec	30	39	23

Note: These are the simple means of the figures given in table 4.1.

TABLE 3.3 *Voting Intentions in Scotland 2002 (%)*

	UK Parliament				Scottish Parliament			
	Con	Lab	LDem	SNP	Con	Lab	LDem	SNP
Jan	15	46	12	23	10	39	12	32
Feb	12	47	13	24	9	40	13	31
Mar	13	46	12	24	10	39	13	32
Apr	14	41	15	26	12	36	15	32
May	14	47	14	21	12	40	13	27
Jun	13	49	13	21	10	40	14	29
Jul	15	46	11	23	12	37	12	32
Aug	13	49	10	21	10	39	12	30
Sept	14	46	13	23	11	38	15	28
Oct	11	47	15	21	10	38	16	28
Nov	13	45	16	22	12	37	15	30
Dec	12	43	15	25	11	35	16	32

Note: Rows do not total 100 because 'others' are not shown. The figures shown for the Scottish Parliament are for constituency (not list) voting intention.

Source: System Three Scotland polls, published monthly in The Herald (Glasgow).

TABLE 3.4 *Ratings of Party Leaders 2002 (%)*

	Duncan Smith			Blair			Kennedy		
	Pos	Neg	Net	Pos	Neg	Net	Pos	Neg	Net
Jan	25	33	−8	51	39	+12	53	16	+37
Feb	27	30	−3	46	46	0	46	16	+30
Mar	23	31	−8	42	50	−8	46	15	+31
Apr	26	27	−1	46	46	0	47	14	+33
May	26	35	−9	39	50	−11	41	19	+22
Jun	24	33	−9	46	47	−1	44	16	+28
Jul	22	35	−13	42	50	−8	46	17	+29
			Satisfaction ratings were not asked in August						
Sep	22	39	−17	42	49	−7	43	17	+26
Oct	18	44	−26	41	59	−18	45	19	+26
Nov	22	49	−27	40	51	−11	47	19	+28
Dec	19	49	−30	38	54	−16	43	20	+23

Notes: The figures are based on responses to the questions 'Are you satisfied or dissatisfied with the way Mr Blair is doing his job as Prime Minister?'; 'Are you satisfied or dissatisfied with the way Mr Duncan Smith/Mr Kennedy is doing his job as Leader of the Conservative/Liberal Democratic party?' The difference between 100 and the sum of positive and negative responses is the percentage of respondents who replied 'Don't know'.

Source: MORI.

TABLE 3.5 *Satisfaction/Dissatisfaction with Government 2002 (%)*

	Satisfied	Dissatisfied	Don't know	Satisfied − dissatisfied
Jan	43	45	12	−2
Feb	37	53	10	−16
Mar	33	57	10	−24
Apr	41	47	13	−6
May	33	57	10	−24
Jun	36	52	11	−16
Jul	34	54	11	−22
	Satisfaction ratings were not asked in August			
Sep	37	52	11	−15
Oct	35	55	10	−20
Nov	32	56	12	−24
Dec	32	58	11	−26

Notes: These are answers to the question 'Are you satisfied or dissatisfied with the way the government is running the country?'

Source: MORI.

TABLE 3.6 *Prospective Economic Evaluations 2002 (%)*

	Improve	Stay the same	Get worse	Don't know	Net
Jan	17	42	37	4	−20
Feb	18	38	39	4	−21
Mar	18	38	39	5	−21
Apr	24	41	29	6	−5
May	15	44	37	4	−22
Jun	15	47	32	6	−17
Jul	15	38	42	5	−27
	This question was not asked in August				
Sep	14	42	37	6	−23
Oct	15	40	39	5	−23
Nov	11	41	43	5	−32
Dec	10	36	50	4	−40

Notes: These data derive from answers to the question 'Do you think that the general economic condition of the country will improve, stay the same or get worse over the next 12 months?'

Source: MORI Economic Optimism Index.

TABLE 3.7 *The Current Six Most Important Issues Facing Britain 2002 (%)*

	Crime	Defence	Education	NHS	Nuclear weapons	Race
Jan	23	13	32	66	2	16
Feb	28	11	28	72	1	18
Mar	37	18	30	58	3	15
Apr	29	19	28	66	2	13
May	34	13	32	50	3	39
Jun	31	13	29	54	2	32
Jul	31	10	37	55	2	22
	This question not asked in August					
Sep	28	34	31	41	9	21
Oct	28	35	32	45	8	18
Nov	30	40	29	42	10	18
Dec	23	35	29	38	7	23

Notes: These data derive from answers to the questions 'What would you say is the most important issue facing Britain today?' and 'What do you see as other important issues facing Britain today?'

Source: MORI Political Monitor.

TABLE 3.8 *Attitudes to a Referendum on the European Single Currency 2002 (%)*

	Vote to join	Vote not to join	Don't know
Jan (early)	31	56	12
Jan	30	53	17
Feb	33	52	15
Mar	30	54	16
Apr	28	59	14
May	29	56	15
Jun	25	58	17
Jul	27	56	16
Aug	28	59	14
Sep	28	58	14
Oct	30	58	12
Nov	28	55	17
Dec	26	58	16

Notes: These data derive from answers to the question 'If there were to be a referendum, would you vote to join the European Single Currency (the Euro) or would you vote not to join?'

Source: ICM Single Currency Trends.

4. Local Elections 2002

On 2 May 2002 there were elections in 174 local authorities across England (there were none in Scotland or Wales). They covered all 32 London boroughs and 36 metropolitan boroughs, together with 18 unitary authorities and 88 shire district authorities. In the London boroughs and in 6 unitary and 46 district authorities all seats were at stake following boundary changes.

2002 also saw the first mayoral elections outside London. Seven contests were held in May and a further 4 in October.

A summary of the different types of local authority in Britain and a guide to election cycles is as follows.

England

1. *Counties* (34)
All members are elected every four years. Elections were held in 2001 (on the same day as the general election) and the next round of elections is due in 2005.

2. *Metropolitan Boroughs* (36)
One third of members are elected annually except in those years when there are county elections. Next elections are due in 2003.

3. *Shire Districts with 'annual' elections* (88)
Approximately one third of members are elected annually except in those years when there are county elections. Next elections are due in 2003.

4. *Shire Districts with 'all in' elections* (150)
All members are elected every four years mid-way between county elections. There were elections in 1999 and the next round will be in 2003.

5. *London Boroughs* (32)
All members are elected in a four-year cycle. Next elections are due in 2006.

6. *Unitary Authorities* (46)
The election cycle varies across authorities.

7. *Greater London*
A Mayor and Greater London Assembly were elected for the first time in May 2000. Next elections are due in 2004.

Scotland
Unitary Councils (32)
All members were elected in 1999 (on the same day as the Scottish Parliament elections). A four-year cycle has now been reinstated and the next round will be in 2003.

Wales
Unitary Authorities (22)
All members were elected in 1999 (on the same day as the Welsh National Assembly elections). The next round of elections has been put back to 2004 to avoid clashing with the 2003 Assembly contests.

Colin Rallings and Michael Thrasher have supplied the data presented in the following tables. Full details of the 2002 results, including individual ward results and commentary, can be found in their *Local Elections Handbook 2002* (Local Government Chronicle Elections Centre, University of Plymouth), obtainable from LGC Communications, Greater London House, Hampstead Road, London NW1 7EJ.

TABLE 4.1 *Local Election Results 2002 (England)*

	Candidates	Seats won	Gains/ losses	% Share of vote
London Boroughs (32)				
Turnout 33.1%				
Con	1,769	655	+105	34.2
Lab	1,858	865	−126	34.1
Lib Dem	1,478	307	+14	20.6
Other	988	34	+7	11.1
Metropolitan Boroughs (36)				
Turnout 31.4%				
Con	777	133	+27	26.2
Lab	836	528	−38	43.1
Lib Dem	706	153	+2	23.3
Other	559	24	+9	7.4
Unitary Authorities (18)				
Turnout 30.2%				
Con	442	115		29.7
Lab	514	232		34.9
Lib Dem	443	146		27.2
Other	227	34		8.2
Shire Districts (88)				
Turnout 35.5%				
Con	2,507	1,108		41.2
Lab	2,135	775		28.8
Lib Dem	1,809	657		24.4
Other	768	148		5.4

Note: Boundary changes make precise calculations for gains and losses impossible.

TABLE 4.2 *Summary of 2002 Local Election Results (all authorities)*

	Candidates	Seats won	Gains/ losses	% Share of vote
Turnout 32.8%				
Con	5,495	2,011	+248	32.2
Lab	5,343	2,400	−278	35.2
Lib Dem	4,436	1,263	+49	23.7
Other	2,542	240	+9	8.9

Note: The figures for gains and losses are estimates since boundary changes make precise calculations impossible.

TABLE 4.3 *Monthly Party Vote Shares in Local Government By-elections 2002 (%)*

	Con	Lab	Lib Dem	Others	Number of wards
Jan	36.3	38.9	15.7	9.1	6
Feb	36.6	25.7	24.9	12.8	8
Mar	42.3	31.2	19.6	6.9	8
Apr	28.9	26.4	22.0	22.7	10
May	27.1	32.1	32.1	8.7	18
Jun	35.6	23.4	29.1	11.9	19
Jul	31.4	33.7	28.1	6.8	14
Aug	30.3	23.1	38.6	8.0	4
Sep	41.4	26.8	24.8	7.0	7
Oct	25.9	31.5	25.7	16.9	10
Nov	28.2	26.3	35.8	7.7	18
Dec	23.5	26.8	37.7	12.0	9

Note: These figures relate to the results of local government by-elections in wards and electoral divisions contested by all three major parties.

TABLE 4.4 *Quarterly Party Vote Shares in Local Government By-elections 2002 (%)*

	Con	Lab	Lib Dem	Others	Number of wards
Q1	38.6	30.9	20.7	9.8	22
Q2	31.2	27.3	29.3	12.2	47
Q3	34.8	29.8	28.4	7.0	25
Q4	26.6	28.0	33.1	12.3	37

Note: These figures relate to the results of local government by-elections in wards and electoral divisions contested by all three major parties.

TABLE 4.5 *Seats Won and Lost in Local Government By-elections 2002*

	Con	Lab	Lib Dem	Others
Held	59	56	23	14
Lost	31	26	12	22
Gained	24	13	40	14
Net	−7	−13	+28	−8

TABLE 4.6 *Mayoral Elections 2002*

	Elected	Party	% of 1st vote	% turnout
May 2002				
Doncaster MBC	Martin Winter	Lab	37	27
Hartlepool UA	Stuart Drummond	Ind	29	29
Lewisham LBC	Steve Bullock	Lab	45	25
Middlesbrough MBC	Ray Mallon	Ind	63	42
Newham LBC	Robin Wales	Lab	51	26
North Tyneside MBC	Chris Morgan	Con	36	42
Watford BC	Dorothy Thornhill	LD	49	36
October 2002				
Bedford BC	Francis Branston	Ind	35	25
Hackney LBC	Jules Pipe	Lab	42	25
Mansfield BC	Tony Egginton	Ind	30	19
Stoke on Trent UA	Mike Wolfe	Ind	21	24